*Porn Gold*

ff

# PORN GOLD

*Inside the Pornography Business*

David Hebditch
and Nick Anning

*faber and faber*
LONDON · BOSTON

First published in 1988
by Faber and Faber Limited
3 Queen Square London WC1N 3AU

Photoset by Parker Typesetting Service Leicester
Printed in Great Britain by
Mackays of Chatham Kent



*British Library Cataloguing in Publication Data*

Hebditch, David
Porn gold.
1. Pornography—Economic aspects
I. Title II. Anning, Nick
338.4'7364174 HV6727
ISBN 0-571-14683-X

*Contents*


| | | |
|---|---|---|
| | List of Illustrations | *page* vii |
| | Introduction | ix |
| 1 | The Curious Lech: Pornware in the 1980s | 1 |
| 2 | Real Boom States: the Porn Barons | 33 |
| 3 | The Monkey Inside Yourself: the Foot-Soldiers of Porn | 83 |
| 4 | One-Handed Magazines: Pornography in Print | 119 |
| 5 | The Secret Pages: Men's Magazines in Scandinavia | 161 |
| 6 | Out of the Porn Ghetto: Hard-Core Hollywood | 188 |
| 7 | Hooks to Hang Dreams On: the Video Revolution | 227 |
| 8 | The Collectors: Inside the Child Porn Rings | 265 |
| 9 | Bizarre and Inexplicable Rites: The Law | 314 |
| 10 | The Wide Blue Yonder: Pornography Tomorrow | 354 |
| | Notes and References | 375 |
| | Index | 395 |

# *List of Illustrations*

1. Swedish photographer and publisher of *Private*, Berth Milton
2. The Color Climax Corporation in Copenhagen
3. Hans Moser and Teresa Orlovski in the studio
4. Beate Uhse with her son Uli Rotermund
5. The headquarters of Beate Uhse's porn empire
6. One of Beate Uhse's porn shops at Frankfurt International Airport
7. Georg and Peter Schmitt of ZBF Vertrieb
8. Pornographic video cassettes in ZBF's warehouse
9. Publicity shot of Brigitte, Swedish model
10. Paula Meadows, porn video actress
11. Viper, porn video star
12. Bill Margold, veteran porn actor, scriptwriter, director and critic, on set
13. Bengt Lénberg, editor of Swedish men's magazines
14. Jan Sjölin, reporter on *FiB Aktuellt*
15. Arja Utriainen, editor-in-chief of the Finnish hard-core magazine, *Jallu*

16. The 'Pussycat' cinema in Los Angeles
17. David F. Friedman, Hollywood producer
18. Pussycat Theatres' top dozen porn feature films
19. Henri Pachard, film and video director
20. Jack O'Malley with child-porn dealer, Roland Scherer
21. Manit Thamaree, child pornographer
22. Tuli Tulalanba, US Customs investigator, displays child-sex magazine
23. Willy Strauss, Danish child-pornographer
24. A 'Private Organization' advertisement.

# *Introduction*

When we started to research this book, we knew next to nothing about pornography. Of course, we knew a 'dirty magazine' when we saw one, but certainly couldn't have told you who had published it or how it had been distributed. We had seen the occasional video with explicit sex scenes: we are, after all, investigative writers and it's in the nature of our work to meet all kinds of people with different interests . . .

We soon found out that everyone, in their own way, is interested in sex. That may be no great feat of journalism, but what really fascinated us were the initial reactions from friends, colleagues and family. Writing a dirty book, are you? they would ask pointedly. We became so intrigued by the implications of this cliché that we drew up a league table of the questions and remarks which came up most often. Over the months we became expert at second-guessing people's first responses.

*The top ten reaction chart*

1 Pornography? How revolting! I can't imagine serious writers doing a book on a subject like that.

2 Pornography? How interesting! Are you writing a dirty book?
3 Bet you had a great time reading all those sexy books!
4 The research must be more interesting than writing it up!
5 Do you get to screw the models?
6 It's all run by crooks – isn't it dangerous?
7 Are you going to name names?
8 How will you get people in the business to talk to you?
9 Who needs *another* book on pornography?
10 Er . . . What's pornography like? Do you have to actually *look* at any of it?

We soon realized that the first reaction was the most revealing. It told us more about the questioner than they might be prepared to admit. All the top ten responses are very 'English': they reflect a parochial view of the porn business instilled by the British press and television. Their perspective on the subject is conditioned by an outlook which is at least two decades behind the times.

Much of the tabloid press – and most of the 'quality' newspapers, for that matter – is still living in an era of underworld villains operating in seedy Soho dives offering Cellophane-wrapped black-and-white postcard pictures of local vice-girls at exorbitant prices to dirty old men in raincoats. Porn pedlars turn out blue films in grimy hotel bedrooms: flickering images featuring governesses spanking naughty vicars or tattooed sailors – still wearing their little black socks – meting out similar punishment to disobedient schoolgirls in gymslips. Rickety projectors crank out this smut in smoky club rooms, private parties and stag evenings.

But this imagery no longer fits the reality. As far as the international trade in pornography is concerned, Britain is a quaint backwater with repressive laws and puritan attitudes. As one famous pornographer remarked to us: 'It is well known that Englishmen don't have erections.'

Let's answer the questions first. We've tried to be objective: our views on the subject of pornography itself are of no more value than anybody else's. We found the pornography *trade* a complex and challenging subject, though there were times when we were revolted by the more extreme material, especially that depicting sex with children. As for enjoying research on the products, we are the living refutation of the illusion that pornography is addictive: boring is a more appropriate adjective. Perhaps it was a reflection on us that at no time did we get any offers of sexual favours from anyone in the trade. It is no reflection on anyone in the trade that we would in any case have 'made our excuses and left'.

We had to go out of England to find most of the information we needed. In our travels we met some fascinating characters. It was certainly more interesting to talk to them than to spend endless hours in front of a word processor. Making sense of what they told us and retelling their colourful stories were the rewards.

None of the research for this book involved 'undercover' investigation or any form of deception. We approached members of the pornography industry directly, and explained what we were trying to do. Only two declined to be interviewed; we had more trouble fixing interviews with the Los Angeles Police Department.

Almost every name included in this book is real. The few exceptions have been clearly indicated. Undercover names employed by law enforcement officers have been changed for obvious reasons, but not their real names. We were never threatened by anyone: quite the opposite, we were shown many courtesies.

If there is another comprehensive book on the pornography trade, we didn't find it. There were many informative sources in the form of magazine and newspaper articles and the occasional television programme and these have been acknowledged. Our aim throughout was to persuade people *in the trade* to give their account of the way the business functions.

In answer to the last question in the chart, we offer the words of an American judge who said, when asked to define pornography, 'I don't know what it is, but I recognize it when I see it.'

A number of people with strong opinions for and against censorship tried to influence the direction this book should take on that issue. We have deliberately avoided involving ourselves as authors in the debate about the morality of pornography and for that reason have not quoted campaigners from either side.

We are investigative writers, not sexologists, sociologists, criminologists or psychologists. We had no interest in explaining why people buy pornography or in making judgements about the morality of doing so.

We have not written an encyclopaedia of every film, video, book, and magazine; nor did we try to include the name of every company and individual who turned a hand to the making of pornography in the last twenty years. What we have tried to do is answer the most common questions which occurred to us and to acquaintances who managed to overcome their initial reservations about the project. These questions included:

- Where is pornography made and by whom?
- Are pornographers all criminals?
- Do pornographers seduce people into appearing in porn productions through the use of drugs, blackmail or physical coercion?
- Are pornographers sex-crazy?
- Isn't pornography an underground business?
- Does pornography cause an increase in sex crime?
- Is pornography addictive?
- Does mainstream adult porn lead on to 'stronger' things like sadism and child pornography?
- Is porn consumed only by 'dirty old men'?
- Is all pornography perverted?
- Is pornography obtrusive?

- Does pornography degrade women?
- Can pornography be stopped by legislation?
- Do pornographers exploit sex for profit and become rich as a result?

Our rough starting point is the year 1967, with the first stirrings of liberalization in Sweden and Denmark. A few of the leading figures in the industry merited being traced back before that date.

Our aim throughout has been to identify and portray the personalities and reveal the profits made in the worldwide business of pornography.

There are many people we want to thank for their kind and friendly help.

Associated with the pornography business: Bill Margold, Dave Friedman, John Weston, Ron Sullivan, 'Viper', Al Bloom, Dave Patrick, Jim Holliday and Jared Rutter in the USA; Kent Wisell, Jan Sjölin, Bengt Lénberg, Viggo Berggren, Brigitte, and Carl Delvert in Sweden; Rupert James, Torben Dhalvad, Willy Strauss, Peter Müller and Ejgl Hall in Denmark; Heikki Mattinen, Arja Utriainen and Juhani Salomaa in Finland; Gerd Wasmund, Hans Moser, Teresa Orlovski, Peter Schmitt, Beate Uhse and Uli Rotermund in Germany; Berth Milton in Spain; Alberto Ferro (last known whereabouts, Rome); Tuppy Owens, Paula Meadows, Frank Russell, Roger Hawse, Mike Freeman and 'Erik von Goethe' in England; John Lark in Australia. The support of those not wanting to be named was no less appreciated.

Many people not in the pornography trade but with knowledge of it also helped: Tom Winker and 'Tuli' Tulalamba in Bangkok; Vinnie McGuire in New York, John Sullivan, Robert Cockrell, Ray Martinez and Rob Showers in Washington DC; Jack O'Malley in Chicago, Kelly Wilson and Bill Dworin in Los Angeles; Berl Kutchinsky in Copenhagen; Karen Leander in Stockholm; Ian Donaldson and Falcon Stuart in London; John Forbes, then in Germany but now in Washington DC; Renus Rijk, Hans Heesters and René Craemer in the Netherlands.

We had help and support from numerous colleagues and would like particularly to thank: Mark Nykanen, Henk Ruyssenaars, Malcolm Andrews, Uli Gross, Andreas Orth, Roger Bendisch, Colin Harding, Paul Lashmar, Tanja and Harrij Costa, Willie Schatz, Michael Siegert, Sue and Phil Dorn, Barry Watts, Richard Haywood, Heikki Auvinen, Alex Tepielow (and his laser printer) and especially Celina Bledowska and Pat Fitzgerald for additional research.

Our agents Carole Blake and Julian Friedmann, with their colleague Conrad Williams, were enthusiastic from the conception of the project right through to the delivery of the final manuscript.

Patricia Gregory was indispensable: as researcher, financial manager, travel agent, chauffeuse, nurse and chef. If it had not been for her constant, enthusiastic and understanding support, the book would not have been completed.

# 1

# *The Curious Lech: Pornware in the 1980s*

The global offensive by the 'moral crusaders' against pornography has failed. Although pro-censorship activists may still win occasional skirmishes on the flanks, the spread of hard-core pornography throughout Western Europe, Scandinavia, the Americas and Australasia is rarely hindered by force of law.

Since the liberalization process began in the 1960s not a single country has banned mainstream pornography where it was previously allowed. The few new laws that have been enacted concentrate on redrawing the boundaries of permissiveness to exclude such minority material as child pornography while leaving depictions of adult sexual activity untouched. Following recent legal changes in Spain, Italy and Greece, the British Isles remain the last bastion of pervasive sexual censorship in Europe. But illegality does not imply abstinence and it is estimated that there are well over a million porn video cassettes in circulation in the UK.

Furthermore, any continuing public debate regarding censorship has become irrelevant. Advances in the technology of publishing and broadcasting have already begun to make the enforcement of restrictive laws impossible.

The pornography industry today is characterized by its disregard for national borders. A single issue of a hard-core magazine may include photographs taken in England, France and Sweden, be 'laid out' in Germany, printed in Spain and distributed in multilingual editions throughout fifteen countries between Norway and the Canary Islands, Portugal and Greece. Spanish and Portuguese language editions may be shipped on to South America, those with English text to Australia and New Zealand. Feature-length video productions made in California are universally available. None of this activity need be illegal.

Pornography is a free market for all its participants: performers, photographers and film-makers, producers, printers, editors, distributors and retailers. Where restrictive practices are applied, they are little different from those in conventional publishing: distributors sign exclusive deals with producers, for example.

Although newcomers with sufficient capital can still get started in the business, few become as properous as the dozen or so key figures who dominate the industry worldwide and probably control more than 50 per cent of the trade by value. These porn barons are American, Swedish, Danish, Dutch, German – their nationality is of little relevance to those in the business or to its clientele. Most are colourful veterans who started in an earlier era of backstreet printing presses, cross-border smuggling runs and occasional brushes with officers of the law. The ones who survived are the determined entrepreneurs whose marketing and management skills demonstrate the flair much lauded by many political leaders of the 1980s.

Though the inside of a courtroom might be familiar ground to some porn barons, others remain unscathed after two decades. Certainly, the idea that control of the world pornography industry lies in the hands of the Mafia is a myth. Legalization soon puts paid to extortionate profits and, thereby, the unwelcome attention of organized crime.

Any remaining interest in the porn trade by the American branch of the Mafia, La Cosa Nostra, says more about American society than it does about the publication of sexually explicit material: there is certainly no Mafia involvement in the European pornography business at large.

Today's porn baron or baroness has little motivation to break the law. Indeed, legislation which defines the permissible scope of his or her activities is generally welcomed: within the rules of the game there are glittering prizes for the successful players. Cheating would yield minuscule rewards and threaten the Mercedes 500, the company Cessna, the villa in Marbella and all the other accoutrements of a jet-setting lifestyle.

Neither can it be claimed that pornography stimulates sex crime. In countries like Sweden, Denmark, West Germany and Holland, where pornography has been openly available for many years, there are no official statistics which reveal a correlation between the arrival of pornography and an increase in serious sexual offences. Indeed, in some cases there has been a decline but criminologists are reluctant to claim this as being any more than coincidental.

In no more than twenty years, the porn barons have transformed their trade from a seedy and illicit cottage industry to a stable and well-refined, mass-production business employing the latest know-how and yielding billions in sales revenues. Government trade statistics rarely include a separate classification for sexually explicit material, so it is impossible to state firm figures about the scale of such a multifaceted trade. It is unlikely, however, that worldwide revenues are less than $5 billion annually and they could exceed $10 billion. These rewards are unavoidably shared by many companies which are household names: Sony, Kodak, Panasonic, Fuji, Ericsson, TDK, Canon, as well as post offices, shipping companies and airlines. Governments benefit from taxes, one church even benefits from tithes.

Buying pornography is neither obligatory nor compulsive. Although sales soar in the period immediately following decriminalization, they soon subside to a stable level which reflects underlying demand – a phenomenon which contradicts theories of addiction. The trade has been able to grow because as each national market has 'normalized' another has opened up. But apart from Britain and Ireland, there are few uptapped markets where disposable incomes are high enough to sustain an attractive level of growth. The porn barons hope that such expansion might instead result from a redirection of their commodity to the relatively new market of couples and women: Australia's main distributor records that 30 per cent of his customers are female.

Pornography has existed throughout history as art, education or entertainment. Consumer demand made its commercialization inevitable. Only in the 1970s and 1980s has it become industrialized – but there was one earlier pioneer.

When Metropolitan Police detectives raided the house at 20 Bloomfield Terrace in the Pimlico district of central London they were not disappointed. A less-than-thorough search was needed to find a huge stock of pornographic photographs. It took days for Detective Inspector Harnett and Detective Constables Marshall and Chamberlaine to make a detailed inventory: the 130,248 prints had been made from more than 5,000 negatives.

'Anti-smut' pressure groups had been calling for a clampdown on London's pornography producers. Harnett had acted on information received from a bookshop manager who was willing to trade the name of his supplier to protect his own livelihood. In order to identify other members of the ring, Harnett had put the house under surveillance. Henry Hayler was recognized in polite society as a sculptor, but his underworld contacts knew him better as a top pornographer who was also a good enough businessman to equip his sales agents with illustrated catalogues and itineraries which took them all over Europe.

Hayler's was reputed to be a family business and the detectives' examination of the evidence confirmed that

Hayler, his wife and two sons worked on both sides of the camera. A studio was found to the rear of 20 Bloomfield Terrace. Judging by the furnishings of his substantial residence, Hayler had been engaged in the profitable enterprise for many years.

His survival against the undue attentions of the moral campaigners and the police had clearly been based on good information and equally good planning: someone had tipped off the pornographer about Harnett's impending raid and the house was deserted. The Hayler family had escaped across the English Channel and were last heard of living in the comparative safety of Berlin.[1]

Though it never came to a prosecution the Hayler case contained all the melodramatic ingredients which feed the popular misconception of the pornography business: pressure from a moralist citizens' group for action by the police, the execution of magistrates' search warrants by police teams probing major producers and dealers, the discovery of hoards of illegal merchandise and the flight of the villain to foreign parts.

Yet Henry Hayler's London home in a highly respectable district of the capital city was raided on 30 March 1874, in the midst of the supposedly staid Victorian era. To an unprecedented degree, Hayler had discovered a ready market for mass-produced erotica – in this case forbidden photographs of female nudity and sexual intercourse. He made a very comfortable living for his product did not sell cheaply. What is more, there was a well-established chain of distributors – often reputable booksellers – who were only too happy to take the risks involved in retailing Hayler's products from under the counter. The chain of distribution did not stop at the Channel ports and Hayler's photographs were in demand throughout Europe and North America.

But there is another side to the Hayler story which also anticipates the porn industry of the late twentieth century.

Hayler's was a family concern involving his wife and two sons. He used the very latest in reprographic technology which would give him a high quality end-product. He understood and catered for customer demand in a variety of media (prints and slides) and it was no lucrative hobby or sideline – the number of man-hours invested in producing the bulk of his stock was considerable. He distributed his photographs internationally and, selling to known retailers, made enough money to be able to afford two houses in central London and tickets for his one-way journey to Berlin. In many respects, Henry Hayler of Pimlico in London was a porn baron a century before his time.

Hayler manufactured and sold pornography. He was not supplying 'erotica' to the occasional discerning but eccentric aristocratic collector. Indeed, the fact that he reproduced titillating pictures in large quantities for a broad range of customers was the main reason why he had been targeted by the Society for the Suppression of Vice.

Although frequently used as a term of abuse for anything contrary to personal taste, the word 'pornography' is given (somewhat) more precise meanings. A typical dictionary definition reads:

> **pornography** *n.* **1.** writings, pictures, films, etc., designed to stimulate sexual excitement. **2.** the production of such material [C19: from Greek *pornographos* writing of harlots, from *pornè* a harlot + *graphein* to write].[2]

However, it does not seem to be quite as simple as that. As Walter Kendrick, author of *The Secret Museum*, observed: 'The term "pornographer" – "whore-painter" or "whore-writer" – is an ambiguous one, since it fails to specify on which end of the brush or pen the whore is to be found.' He also went on to observe that, although the explicit depiction of human sexual activity has existed for millennia, the use of the word 'pornography' to describe it dates only from Victorian times.[3]

A more down-to-earth definition has been proposed by

the Danish criminologist Berl Kutchinsky: 'In everyday life, the word *pornography* . . . has acquired a clear meaning, understood by producers, sellers and buyers, as well as by those who are repelled by or indifferent to the material in question. In everyday usage, *pornography* means a product verbally or visually portraying sexual anatomy and behaviour with the main purpose of eliciting sexual arousal.'[4] It should be added that education and entertainment are important subsidiary roles, if only by default.

Perhaps being able to recognize pornography is far more important than being able to define it precisely. Throughout this book the term 'pornography' is used in a very specific sense well understood by the established sex-publishing industry and the late twentieth-century market it occupies. 'Mainstream pornography' categorizes more than 90 per cent of the world production of still photographs and video/film sequences of heterosexual acts of intercourse where penile erection and penetration are the central feature.[5]

Today, however, mainstream pornography also features – as a matter of routine – lesbianism, group sex, anal intercourse, oral–genital contact and visible ejaculation (known in the trade as the 'cum shot'). Indeed, these activities have become essential ingredients and the modern pornographer departs from them at his or her peril. As the bestselling novelist and porn critic, Robert H. Rimmer, reported: '[A producer named Lowell] Pickett tried to eliminate the external cum shots in which an ejaculating male suddenly withdraws his member from whatever female orifice it happens to be in and has his orgasm outside the woman's body, preferably spraying her in the face. But a lot of people stopped showing his films because, while they were sometimes funnier and more developed dramatically, they violated basic pornographic convention.'[6] All modern pornography has become stylized to a high degree.

The word 'obscene' is avoided except in quotations, or where it has a specific legal meaning. Again, Berl Kutchinsky provides an insight:

The word *obscene* may continue to be useful in a legal context since it does refer to the juridically relevant aspect of pornography, that is, to the fact that something is unacceptable in public because of the offence it may cause to people who are unexpectedly or unwillingly exposed to it. The term also applies to matters other than pornography and is not necessarily limited to legal context: there are obscene words, gestures, drawings and telephone calls. In each case it is the offensive aspect, not the arousal, that is in focus – and often is intended as a means of provocation.'[7]

This study concentrates on the bulk trade in sexually explicit – or 'hard-core' – pornography and excludes 'soft-core' material ranging from so-called 'glamour' and 'naturist' portrayals of semi-nude or nude adults, through pictures of genitals, to simulated or suggested acts of intercourse. As Kutchinsky notes: 'The distinction [between "hard core" and "soft core"] refers to the degree of explicitness of the sexual portrayals, not to the proportion of pornographic and non-sexual material in the film or publication. Typically, the "softening" of pornography results either from a restrictive public policy that forbids hard-core pornography, or from the producer's desire to reach an audience larger than that patronizing porn shops or adult cinemas.'[8] Well-known magazines such as *Playboy*, *Hustler*, *Screw* and *Club International*, or videos such as the *Electric Blue* series which, while purporting to be explicit, draw the line at publishing pictures of sexual acts, are therefore of passing interest only.

Incidentally covered is the relatively small market sector which caters for minority or 'bizarre' sexual tastes – this is the term used in the trade – which range from sadism and masochism (S & M), bondage, bestiality and fetishism to a fascination with human excretory functions. The boundary line between the mainstream and bizarre is rarely well defined and some pornographers may deliberately step over it in order to add seasoning to what might otherwise be considered bland fare. For example, the opening scene of the American hard-core film *Tangerine*[9] depicts a party at which actress Cece Malone (now known as Jennifer West) masturbates a dog.[10] This scene has no relevance to the story-line and was cut for legal reasons in the American edition of the film.

In the case of this 'bizarre' market, one major exception has been made for reasons of justifiable public concern. Non-mainstream pornography which depicts children committing overt sexual acts with other children, adults or animals is considered in some detail.

The media employed in the production, distribution and retailing of pornography have gone through a number of quite distinct, but partly overlapping, phases. Indeed, it is no accident that the history of pornography parallels precisely the history of publishing and broadcast media.

The explicit depiction of sexual activity through painting and drawing has been by far the lengthiest epoch in the history of pornography. From cave paintings pre-dating the last Ice Age, through the erotic art of the Orient to the paintings of Rembrandt and Picasso, sexual acts have been a common preoccupation of the artist.

Primitive pornography may have had to limit itself to crude ceramics and clay objects, but the ancient cultures of South America, Africa, Asia and the South Pacific all addressed themselves to such time-honoured themes as masturbation, fellatio, bestiality and copulation in most conceivable positions. Both heterosexual and homosexual activity featured strongly on Greek ceramics four and five hundred years before the birth of Christ.[11]

The predilections of the Roman Empire were frozen in time when Pompeii was engulfed by the eruption of Mount Vesuvius in AD 79. When the city was rediscovered in the eighteenth and nineteenth centuries the changes in social attitudes which had taken place over the intervening years caused a stunned reaction: 'The coarse paintings which decorate this place evidently indicate that it was intended for the most shameful debaucheries,' reported one of the archaeologists.[12]

A more sober analysis of the Pompeiians' public celebration of human sexuality – the erotic frescoes and sculptures were not just in brothels – and the later reactions of middle-class Victorian archaeologists was made by Walter Kendrick: 'In April 1748, the first intact fresco was discovered, in what proved to be an ancient dining room . . . From very early in the excavations, objects were being unearthed that presented a special problem to the authorities. Already in 1758, for example, rumours circulated that "lascivious" frescoes had been found; not long thereafter, a particularly outrageous artefact turned up – a small marble statue, highly naturalistic in style, representing a satyr in sexual congress with an apparently undaunted goat.' Even then, commercial interests soon identified a market and an opportunity for financial gain was not allowed to pass by: 'No doubt the procedure was already in operation, as it remained two centuries later, that a gentleman with appropriate demeanour (and ready cash for the custodian) would be admitted to the locked chamber where controversial items lurked; women, children, and the poor of both sexes and all ages were excluded.'[13]

Such was the horror at the Pompeii findings that anything which could be removed was carried off and the reproductions of what remained were locked up. Access was restricted to scholars and gentlemen whose education and maturity apparently made them immune to moral corruption.

Erotic art declined in the West with the rise and spread of Christianity. This contrasted with eastern religions like Hinduism where philosophical principles encouraged the depiction of the god Siva in sexual congress with her *shakti*. Not all eastern religions are based on similar outlooks and in Buddhism, for example, the male is pre-eminent. It is the female in the Hindu faith. The erotic carved friezes at the Hindu temples of Khajuraho and Konarak (ninth to thirteenth centuries) have been described as the 'ultimate oneness of the spiritual and the carnal'.[14] Famous as they are, these sculptures come closer to being religious art than pornography – there were certainly no commercial connotations – but erotic tastes in India varied as much as culinary tastes with sexual acts being depicted in richly detailed Mogul miniatures, the oil paintings of Tamil Nadu, the pen and brush drawings of Bengal, and the delicate watercolours of Rajput. Although 'bizarre' practices were occasionally shown, the Indian speciality well into the nineteenth century was the variety of positions for heterosexual intercourse, the guidebooks to which were published in the West as *Kama Sutra* and *Ananga Ranga*.

The Chinese made representations of sexual acts on painted scrolls and by woodblock prints (mostly in the Han Dynasty of *c.* 206 BC to AD 24) although ceramics and carved ivory were also used. Poetry from that time and later suggests that pornography played an important part in sex education. This was also true in Japan, where the Taiho Code of AD 701 required that all physicians study illustrated sex manuals – a far cry from twentieth-century Britain where the illustration of an erect penis in birth control booklets is still forbidden. The Japanese scenes were both graphic and imaginative; a scroll from the 1640s shows a man engaged in sexual intercourse with a woman while fending off another man who is trying to initiate anal sex with him. Bondage and sadism (directed against women) appeared in early twentieth-century Japanese art and remains to the present day, often with distinctly anti-Western racist overtones.[15]

The pornography of Japan flourished until the arrival of the traders and Christian missionaries from the West. In an irrational hangover from that period, it is still illegal to show pubic hair in photographs and drawings, regardless of the explicitness of the sexual activity.

In eighteenth-century France, many artists turned to painting and drawing pornographic scenes (and copper engravings for books) which covered everything from the predictable to the exotic. Louis Binet's illustration for *Le Paysan Perverti* by Restif de la Bretonne showed a three-way lesbian coupling. In more modern times, pornography painted or drawn is dubbed 'erotic art', as though that excuses any motivation and commercial intent on the part of the artist. Among the more well-known artists who have produced erotic works are Picasso (extensively), Munch, Grosz, Chagall, Masson, Dubuffet, Dali, Ernst and Rivers.[16]

An early sign of the eagerness of pornographers to exploit new publishing media emerged in the seventeenth century only a few decades after the First Folio edition of Shakespeare's plays. Berl Kutchinsky assessed the significance of this development in these terms:

> The beginnings of the pre-legalization period of pornography can be traced rather precisely to the decade of the 1650s, when three pornographic classics were published: *La Puttana Errante*, *L'Ecole des Filles*, and *Satya*. These books were soon translated into all the major languages and became the models of all later pornographic books (and, indeed, of twentieth-century pornographic photographs and films). One finds in them lesbianism, sodomy, seduction, multiple copulation, flagellation, and sadism – as well as total amorality, a disregard for artistic merit, an absence of affection or other emotions, flimsy plots, stereotyped characterizations, monotonous repetitiousness, and a constant exaggeration of sexual interest, energy and potency.[17]

*L'Ecole des Filles (The Girls' School)* could even pass for the title of a 1980s low-budget video production. Its distribution was effective enough for it to reach London, where Samuel Pepys got hold of a copy in 1655: 'Thence homeward by coach and stopped at Martins my bookseller, where I saw the French book which I did think to have had for my wife to translate, called *L'Escholle des Filles*; but when I came to look into it, it is the most bawdy, lewd book that ever I saw, rather worse than *Puttana Errante* – so that I was ashamed of reading it.' Obviously, Martins carried a stock of such material. Pepys's curiosity overcame his reservations and he bought the book some weeks later. He clearly hid it away until his guests had left, judging from this account couched in coy Spanish and French synonyms:

> We sang till almost night, and drank my good store of wine; and then they parted and I to my chamber, where I did read through *L'Escholle des Filles;* a lewd book, but what doth me no wrong to read for imagination's sake (but it did hazer my prick para stand all the while, and una vez to decharger); and after I had done it, I burned it, that it might not be among my books to my shame . . .[18]

Whatever Pepys thought of the literary and social merits of *The Girls' School*, it seems to have had the effect for which it was intended.

The eighteenth and nineteenth centuries saw the fullest exploitation of the novel form for the purpose of erotic arousal. *The Lustful Turk* was typical of the genre and confirms all Kutchinsky's worst fears about the quality of such material; certainly nothing had improved since *L'Ecole des Filles*. *The Lustful Turk* was first published in 1828 and is a novel based on a series of letters written by the heroine, Emily Barlow, to her friend Sylvia Carey.

Emily and her companion Eliza Gibbs are travelling by ship to India to join her parents when they are captured by 'Moorish pirates'. This may sound like the Middle Eastern politics of a much later period but, in this case, the 'Moorish pirates' were Turks. Emily eventually ends up in the arms of the Dey of Algiers, to whom she loses her virginity. The breathless style is typical of the whole book:

> I quickly felt his finger again introducing the head of that terrible engine I had before felt, and which now felt like a

pillar of ivory entering me . . . My petitions, supplications and tears were of no use. I was on the altar, and, butcher-like, he was determined to complete the sacrifice; indeed, my cries seemed only to excite him to the finishing of my ruin, and sucking my lips and breasts with fury, he unrelentingly rooted up all obstacles my virginity offered, tearing and cutting me to pieces, until the whole of his terrible shaft was buried within me. I could bear the dreadful torment no longer, but uttering a piercing shriek sunk insensible in the arms of my cruel ravisher.[19]

In support of the male fantasy and in a turn-about that would have Women Against Rape up in arms Emily soon falls in love with the Dey, as do her companions in the harem:

Never, oh never shall I forget the delicious transports that followed the stiff insertion; and then, ah me!, by what thrilling degrees did he, by his luxurious movements, fiery kisses, and strange touches of his hand to the most crimson parts of my body, reduce me to a voluptuous state of insensibility. I blush to say so powerfully did his ravishing instrument stir up nature within me, that by mere instinct I returned him kiss for kiss, responsively meeting his fierce thrusts, until the fury of the pleasure and ravishment became so overpowering that, unable to support the excitement I so luxuriously felt, I fainted in his arms with pleasure.[20]

Today, a reprint of *The Lustful Turk* is available in high street book shops throughout Britain and America.

Fifty years later, all pretence at literature (and the need for the women to faint) had disappeared and the material had deteriorated to the level of *The Romance of Lust*, published during the 1870s:

The Count had fucked the Egerton while we were engaged above the divine Frankland. Our first pose was suggested by the Egerton, who had been as yet less

> fucked than any. She had been also greatly taken with the glories of the Frankland's superb body, and especially struck with her extraordinary clitoris, and had taken the curious lech of wishing to have it in her bottomhole while riding St George on my big prick. We all laughed at her odd choice, but agreed at once, especially the Frankland, whose greatest lech was to fuck very fair young women with her long and capable clitoris. A fairer creature than the lovely Egerton could not be found. The Frankland admitted that in her inmost heart she had longed thus to have the Egerton from the moment she had first seen her, and her delight and surprise at finding the dear Egerton had equally desired to possess her, fired her fierce lust with increased desire, I lay down, the Egerton straddled over, and feeling the delight of my huge prick when completely imbedded, she spent profusely with only two rebounds. Then sinking on my belly she presented her lovely arse to the lascivious embraces of the salacious Frankland. The Count next took the Benson in cunt while I blocked the rear aperture, and the Frankland once more enculed the Egerton, who dildoed herself in cunt at the same time; all of us running two courses. We then rose, purified and refreshed.[21]

But not for very long: *The Romance of Lust* continues in the same vein for 600 pages in four volumes. Its preoccupation with sexual activity to the exclusion of all other facets of human social behaviour is rivalled only by the porn video output of Los Angeles in the 1980s.

The circulation of such books in Victorian times was limited by the high cost of the end-product and illiteracy among the population at large. So, for many years, the reading of pornographic books was a surreptitious pastime for the aristocrats and wealthy of the world. The primitive illustrations possible in such books (wood engravings and lithographs) merely had the effect of increasing the price. Even by the late 1800s, printing technology had failed to achieve mass circulation at a price the poorer classes could afford. According to Kendrick:

> The young person was shielded from the corrupting influence of Ashbee's bibliographies by their limited circulation and, especially, high price. The same defences engirdled most of the books Ashbee listed. *The Mysteries of Verbena House* (1882), for example, was published in an edition of only 150 copies at the incredible price of four guineas, despite its mere 143 pages and four colored lithographs – 'obscene and of vile execution', according to Ashbee.
>
> At about that time, the average yearly income of a lower-middle-class English family was estimated at £110; if the absurd idea of buying *Verbena House* had ever occurred to such a family's breadwinner, it would have consumed two weeks' wages. In the United States, salaries were generally higher, though even in New York – then as now among the most expensive American cities – an estimate of 1883 placed the highest average wage of skilled artisans at eighteen dollars per week. A lewd Manhattan plumber would have to work a week and a half for *Verbena House*.[22]

A modern-day skilled craftsman would have to work less than an hour to raise the cover price of a hard-core photographic magazine.

Pornography in the form of the written word still exists in the late twentieth century, but primarily in the niche markets of bondage, S & M and child pornography. A 1986 example is *Lolita Slavinder (Lolita Slaves)* published in Denmark where photographs of children engaged in sexual acts are illegal. However, *Lolita Slavinder* – subtitled 'a book about sexual use and abuse' – is totally explicit textually and contains hard-core drawings, including 'cum shots', involving a girl described as being ten years old. The book is legal and is prominently displayed in the window of a bookshop near the city centre in Copenhagen.[23]

The inclusion of graphically explicit sex scenes has now become commonplace in conventional fiction, as has the use of explicit language. Indeed, much of what caused criminal prosecutions of books such as *Lady Chatterley's Lover* and *Fanny Hill: The Memoirs of a Woman of Pleasure* in the 1960s (only the latter of which books could ever be construed as pornographic by today's standards) has now become routine fare in many bestselling books written by women and aimed at a female readership. *Destiny* by Sally Beauman[24] is reputed to average a sexual coupling every fourteen pages.

The printed Victorian word never really achieved volume production. Photography had all the benefits the porn trade needed. It made few demands on the quality of the viewer's imagination. It could be appreciated by an illiterate, needed no translation prior to international distribution, required few artistic skills in its production and the end-product could be manufactured in bulk for a mass market. The very first successful photograph was probably produced by J. N. Niepce in 1822. The technology was further significantly advanced in 1839 by Daguerre in France and Fox Talbot in England. In 1851 Scott Archer's collodion (wet-plate) process reduced exposure times from ten seconds to one hundredth of a second. A major milestone was the development of the gelatine dry plate by R. L. Maddox in 1871.[25] By this time, Henry Hayler and his family were in business.

Colin Harding is an authority on nineteenth-century photography: 'Hayler was probably using the wet-plate process. Although Maddox's dry-plate process was announced in 1871, the plates were not available in reliable quantities until 1878. He probably made copies on to albumen paper (which had to be sensitized before use) by contact printing from the negatives. This was done by exposure to sunlight. Everything depended on the weather! In bright sunlight an exposure could take two hours. The prints were then fixed and washed. He could have been producing postcard-sized prints, stereo prints, stereo positives or magic lantern slides. Most companies had printing frames set up on their rooftops for this job.'[26] Given the lengthy nature of this printing process – especially during the Holmesian London fogs of the time – Henry Hayler's stock of 130,248 prints was a prodigious inventory representing many man-years of effort. Such an operation could only survive until printing technology enabled photographic prints to be reproduced in quantity. In the meantime, other developments jostled for the attention of wider audiences: the curtain was going up on the motion picture.

It is rumoured that one of the very first uses to which film was put was the depiction of the naked human form and sexual acts. 'The first stag movies were actually made in 1896,'[27] claims Robert Rimmer. This development did not occur in Europe and the United States alone and in the course of time pornographic films were produced in Japan, Cuba and South America.[28]

These black-and-white hard-core melodramas were shot on 16 mm film and were almost exclusively silent. 'Best of the earliest stags was *A Free Ride* aka *Grass Sandwich, circa* 1915, but perhaps as late as the 1920s,' claims Hollywood critic Jim Holliday:

> Best known in the 1920s was *The Casting Couch*. The hottest of the 1930s are *The Modern Magician* and *The Aviator*, which features an inspired lead female. The best post-World War II stag was also the hottest. Known as *The Nun, The Nun's Story* or *The None's Story*, this classic features an unbelievable portrait of sexual intensity by the unknown female . . . In 1951, an allegedly underaged Juanita Slusher made a two-reeler in a motel near Nashville, Tennessee . . . . She became known to the world as Candy Barr and *Smart Aleck* was to become the best-known stag of all time. She had breasts that Traci Lords would be proud of and some enthusiasm for humping, but not for performing oral sex. Her female friend provides that . . . Best French stags of the

> post-World War II era are *The Woman in the Portrait* and *Family Spirit*. Colour came in the early 1960s, but didn't get good until the end of the decade. Overseas, the best British films were black and white – *Pussy Galore, First Edition, End of Term* and *100% Lust*.[29]

The stag movie business remained underground until the late 1960s. Even then, after a decade of skirting around the ultimate hard-core material with 'naturist' films like *Garden of Eden* (1957) (and those made by Harrison Marks in England), and soft-core 'sexploitation' movies such as *Adventures of Lucky Pierre* by David Friedman, Russ Meyer's *Immortal Mr Teas* (both 1959) and Sweden's *I Am Curious – Yellow* (1967), the big sexual act did not reach the big cinema screen internationally until the 1972 release of the notorious *Deep Throat*. Feature films including clear depiction of sexual intercourse and oral sex were being made for limited distribution as early as 1970, and industry critics rated Gerard Damiano's 1972 *The Devil in Miss Jones* as a much better film, but none of these brought the issue to public attention and debate as much as *Deep Throat*.

*Deep Throat* was produced and directed in Florida by Gerard Damiano and starred Linda Lovelace and Harry Reems. It was made for around $25,000 but grossed $96,000 in its first week of showing at Sam Lake's World Theater on Broadway.[30] Today it is reputed to have grossed over $100 million and is still available on video in many parts of the world.[31]

The *Deep Throat* story-line concerned the predicament of a woman whose clitoris was, by a quirk of fantasy, located at the back of her throat. The production presaged the style and explicitness of the whole X-rated film and video genre. By the end of that decade, the industry was producing at least two hard-core feature films each week. In 1987 some two hundred cinemas throughout the United States specialized in showing this output. That figure was down from a peak of over nine hundred in the late 1970s, when it was estimated that they had a clientele of three million customers a week. At a ticket price of at least $5, that represented an annual gross revenue approaching $750 million.

The cinema was not the first medium to bring pornography to the mass market. Credit for that must go to the Scandinavian hard-core magazines which began publication in and around 1967. What made it all possible was the advent of photo-litho colour-printing techniques which radically reduced the overhead cost of magazine publishing, while at the same time dramatically improving print and picture quality. One of the earliest and most successful exponents of this development was Berth Milton in Sweden, but he was closely followed by the Theander brothers in Denmark (see Chapter 2, 'The Porn Barons'). This process, together with the cinema release of 35mm feature films, in the new social and legal climates engendered in the late 1960s, brought hard-core pornography within the reach of mass markets for the first time. In the ensuing two decades, a staggering total of at least 250,000,000 copies of hard-core pornographic magazines must have been published in Europe alone.[32] That represents more than one copy for every other member of the population of greater Europe, including Scandinavia. But there was more to come.

The video revolution was anticipated to some degree by 8mm porn films – sometimes called 'loops'. These were available from the late 1960s for use on home projectors and in the automatic, coin-operated peep-show booths installed in clubs and sex shops. Such loops were typically ten minutes in length, a running time suitable for the technology of the peep-show projectors which could only accommodate small reels. It also suited the perceived physiological response of the average human male.

Unlike the black-and-white 16mm commercial stock on which the original stag movies were shot, this new phase was based on domestic 8mm and 'Super-8' colour film and many loops included sound. The biggest producers for many years were the Theander brothers. They started production in 1969 and by the time the technology became obsolete ten years later, they had produced eight million such prints.[33]

The most recent change in technology, and one speedily adopted by the porn industry, is the video cassette. Once it became clear in the late 1970s that versatile video technology could be packaged into an affordable unit for domestic use (the video cassette recorder, VCR or video tape recorder, VTR) the porn barons moved in. They did this first by transferring existing film productions (single features or two, three or four 8mm loops strung together) to tape using an expensive system called a 'flying spot scanner' and, eventually, by shooting pornware directly on to recording tape.

Although the mass reproduction of video cassettes is presently quite expensive to establish in terms of set-up capital, the price of the in-store product continues to drop rapidly. In most countries of the Western world it is possible to rent a wide range of videos from neighbourhood video stores or 'video libraries', but this form of retailing is beginning to be undermined by the distribution of material which will sell for less than $15 (under £10). The porn industry is about to follow this pattern.

A further characteristic of video is that it makes possible the production of complete programmes and the reproduction of the product on a cottage industry basis. Domestic video cameras can be bought for less than £1,000 (they can also be rented), as can simple editing suites. Production can be achieved by linking two domestic VCRs. This latter technique is most often used to 'bootleg' video tapes where the material is still illegal for sale through open channels.

An example of the accessibility of the technology comes from West Germany where there is a minor craze for *Hausfrauenpornos* (housewife pornos). These are technically crude videos made of sexual encounters between volunteer amateur couples. The sequence is shot virtually without camera movement and minimal editing is performed; the product is in 'real time' and lasts as long as the encounter.

A similar phenomenon exists in the United States for people who want to make and swap their own sex videos. Robert Rimmer describes how it works:

> Susan's Video Exchange . . . offers you the opportunity to see how others are doing it – without committing yourself, if you prefer. If you send Susan's an original videotape of you and your companion making love, they will exchange it – at no cost – for a sixty- to ninety-minute tape containing up to four other couples' tapes . . . *and* they will return your original tape to you. If you are just curious, however, Susan's will send you their tapes for $55 each, and offer you a continuing service as a nonparticipating voyeur . . . Susan's Video Exchange provides a 'safe', yet pleasantly dangerous and sexually provocative, exposure for thousands of young 'experimenters'.[34]

Producers such as Rodox (Denmark) and Video Teresa Orlovski (VTO, West Germany) have exploited the technology to the full by installing devices such as graphics and special effects computers, as well as the very best in editing and production systems. It should be expected that this exploitation of new technology will continue. Mike Hunter in West Germany boasts of being the first to publish porn on video disc. But in this case he was too early; the lack of agreed international standards and the non-availability of a capability to record seems to have stemmed the domestic growth of video-disc players.

The versatility of video in the market place has not gone unnoticed by the porn barons. Video cassettes can be sold or rented for home use. They can be used for public showing in small 'porn kinos', but mostly they play in peep-shows which have been modernized to use a television set and a multi-channel selector which enables the viewer to look at any one of up to twenty programmes being 'broadcast' simultaneously. Equipment is already available which will increase this cable capacity to 200 channels. (By contrast, viewers of films in peep-shows could see one 8mm reel only, unless the viewing booth was fitted with two or more projectors.)

Such has been the success of video that it now totally dominates the US market in a way that magazines have never been able to do. The producers of the moving image have managed to circumvent the law and achieve, if not nationwide distribution, then at least distribution to all the major urban centres. Indeed, they were so early to exploit the medium that US retailers were initially dependent on hard-core sex material for more than 50 per cent of their revenues. The video revolution had arrived.

Regardless of the medium employed, pornography follows a well-understood and thoroughly choreographed schema. It has been said that there are only five jokes in the world – the rest are variations on these. The same also seems to be true of the graphic tales of sexual encounters portrayed in most commercially available pornography. These baseline plots can be identified so often that they are worth outlining here.

First, 'The Lonely Housewife'. In the opening sequence, a woman is on her own, working about the house or relaxing. She might be doing something to suggest that she is bored or, more probably, feeling sexy. A stranger arrives at the door. He will be a delivery boy, a plumber, the postman, a charity collector or perhaps a house decorator. Quite often the only variations are in the casting of this role. The woman will give him an early sign of her desire for sex by offering a drink, taking a bath, changing into 'something more comfortable' or, less subtly, standing over him in a short skirt while he wields a wrench. Variations on this approach will be aimed at shortening the establishing time or adding another sexual dimension and/or partner. For example, the male visitor might surprise the woman while she masturbates or – if the budget permits – while she is having an encounter with another woman. This reinforces the fantasy that the only problems the woman has can easily be solved by the male. A further variant occurs when the 'husband' arrives home and discovers his wife and the visitor in the throes of making love. This being pornography he doesn't object, of course, but joins in. The newcomer might well be another woman, perhaps even the maid.

British porn actress Paula Meadows remembers this story-line being used in the very first X-rated film she saw: 'It was the old, old story of "the postman knocks". The housewife's in there and the next thing you know, she's had him in and there they are on the bed. He's still got his hat on and screwing away!' This production was directed by Lasse Braun, one of the pioneers in the medium, who has a reputation for getting eccentricities into his work: 'But we don't know whether it's her fantasy or whatever. The little touch that he put in was the window cleaner who peers inside and – gasp! – suddenly he comes all over the window! There's this splat on the window and it all drips down. I thought that was lovely – I remembered that bit! So it's all the same thing really, it's just the way you shoot it!'[35]

'The Casual Encounter', or 'Boy Meets Girl'. One persuades the other to return to their apartment (either is acceptable to the fantasy) and sexual activity ensues. The original encounter can take place in a park, on a train, in a shop, or in a café or bar. Because no sexual activity occurs until the performers arrive at the house or apartment, this scenario provides many opportunities for location shots in public places. In the case of the bar and café encounters, the participants will normally be seen in the opening scenes, sitting at outside tables.

Many of Berth Milton's sets in *Private* magazine follow this plot, but with two key differences: the location will be as recognizable as possible (Gibraltar, for example) and the sex scene will take place at the location itself in the open air.

In the case of Milton's Gibraltar set, he was particularly proud of the fact that the coast of North Africa could be seen in the background while the models were engaged in sexual intercourse among the fortifications on the top of the Rock.[36]

Henry Spencer Ashbee, the nineteenth-century English bibliographer of erotic writings under the supposedly witty pseudonym of 'Pisanus Fraxi' found the matter of locations to be of some concern. In a review of *The Pearl* published in 1879 or 1880, he warns that:

> The scenes follow fast upon each other as cruel and as crapulous as any to be found in *Justine* or *La Philosophie dans le Boudoir*, and, it must be owned, far more pernicious, for the enormities in those works are generally enacted in unfrequented forests, in imaginary châteaux, in unknown convents, or in impossible caverns, whereas in the tales before us [i.e. in *The Pearl*] they are brought close home to us, and occur in Belgravian drawing rooms, the chambers of our Inns of Court, or in the back parlours of our London shopkeepers.[37]

Ashbee's alarm at the notion of more-or-less everyday settings for pornographic encounters prompts speculation on his possible reaction to Germany's *Hausfrauenporno* and Susan's Video Exchange in the United States.

'The Casting Couch.' This is a classic plot, the title of which was actually used for a famous American stag movie. To some degree, the purpose here is to reverse the 'Lonely Housewife' scenario. Of course, the idea of the 'househusband' does not suit the male sex fantasy, so the masculine lead will play the part of a working professional, the big boss, someone important with a position of power to exploit. He will be a company executive, a lawyer, a teacher, a bank manager or, of course, a movie producer. The excuse for getting into the sexual activity is that the woman is in desperate need of something that she can only pay for through sex.

This story-line was deftly inverted by Teresa Orlovski who in real life runs Verlag Teresa Orlovski (VTO) in Hanover, West Germany, with her husband Hans Moser. In a video called *The Woman Who Loved Men*, she plays the boss of a sex business 'interviewing' young men for jobs. Of course, they have to prove their sexual competence.[38]

'The Party.' This is still one of the most common scenarios because, like 'The Lonely Housewife', it involves the minimum of cost and effort in finding a suitable location. The establishing shots show the arrivals and the group sitting around a table drinking. They may be looking at some pornography. The group then engages in foreplay, invariably fellatio and cunnilingus. The pairings may be evenly matched between sexes, but it only requires two men to engage with one woman to make a lesbian encounter possible. The swapping of partners will be frequent. The party may start with as few as two people, but three, four or five is more common. It is, of course, easy justification for an orgy scene. Indeed, the story-line is sometimes extended in film or video so that the original intention is that of an orgy – the guests may arrive in fancy dress, for example. In a French film called *Love Hotel*, the whole production is based on non-stop 'partying' among a relatively big cast of about twenty people.[39]

'Doctors and Nurses.' The scenes here take place in a doctor's or dentist's surgery, a hospital or perhaps a convenient sex clinic. With the exception of the 'dentist' variation these scenarios provide the ideal opportunity to introduce beds and a plausible reason for at least one of the parties to undress. The appeal of the dentist's chair lies in the opportunity presented by an anaesthetized patient. The popular 'sex clinic' scenario, apart from providing the best of reasons for showing some 'therapeutic' sex, also enables the director to bring in sex toys, especially dildos, and perhaps a little bizarre sex through the administration of an enema. In all variations, the nurse is ready and willing to turn the doctor/patient duo into a loving threesome.

Rape is not a common theme in the story-lines of pornography and, indeed, may occur less often than in conventional books, films and television. A major directory of 'adult films' listed 138 dominant themes, one of which was rape. Under that heading, there are twenty-one titles out of more than a thousand full-length films and videos so analysed (2 per cent).[40]

Even the slightest variations from prototype porn plots are considered to be innovations. The X-rated film industry in Los Angeles makes life easier for itself by 'borrowing' plots from conventional movies. This is hardly a creative process as scriptwriter and actor Bill Margold readily admits:

> Basically, imitation breeds contempt. One day, Viper [a porn actress and Margold's girlfriend] sat down and wrote an X-rated version of *Gremlins* called *Don't Get Them Wet!* It's the same gremlin motif but here, obviously, the way to get them wet is to do certain things and, of course, you don't feed them meat after midnight! If these gremlins suck dick, they're obviously going to multiply. Which they do.
>
> Right now we just finished a movie called *Let's Talk Dirty* which is nothing more than a rip-off from the mainstream *Some Kind of Wonderful* which is about a guy who thinks he's really in love with this beautiful girl and winds up falling in love with a tomboy.
>
> You have to give the audience something to identify with, they are desperately in need of a hook to hang their dreams on. The problem is that we're putting so much stuff out that it all looks the same and they may not continue to go back.
>
> We're drowning in our own sexual quicksand because there's a lack of imagination.[41]

If anything, the stereotyping of the sex scenes – regardless of the plot – is even more formalized than in Victorian books like *The Romance of Lust*. Bengt Lénberg is an experienced editor of Swedish men's magazines which include hard-core photosets: 'Porn is a very mechanical thing. But there is a formula to pornography. The first photo has to show them with their clothes on. Then there's some sucking: cock-sucking is a very big thing everywhere. There is something about it – she holds your life in her hands, she's in charge and could always bite you. Then you have fucking in at least three different positions – missionary, from behind and with the girl on top. The last pic is always of the man coming on the girl. The photographers know this, so you can always be sure the right shots are included in what they submit.'[42]

But the formula seems to be dictated by the demands of the market place. Lénberg is certainly not happy with the constraints it places on him as an editor:

> The problem is one of stereotyping. Sometimes only the colour of the girl's hair seems to change. You can't abandon the formula, it's very frustrating. The buyers know what they want.
>
> We monitor customer needs, talk to people. Our readers phone a lot and we always take the calls. I even talk to friends in the pub. If a computer engineer tells me he liked the blonde, then I'm sure ten other computer engineers also liked her.
>
> The setting becomes more important when you are working with less attractive models. What do readers feel towards the girl involved? They imagine they are fucking her.[43]

In almost all hard-core sex magazines there is a little text which helps in the development of the story-line: 'We generally have text to go with the pictures,' Lénberg explains. 'Some guys jerk off to the text, some to the pictures, some to both. A couple of years ago we tried publishing without the text, but readers complained and we had to bring it back. Of course, it's pure fiction. We always quarrel in the office about who has to write it. The guy who gets the job is the one who doesn't protest enough. One thing is certain – you don't write porno on a Monday morning! We try to vary the story-line. Sometimes it's short, sometimes long – the layout determines the length.'[44]

The importance of feedback from consumers is underlined by Rupert James, the English editor of a series of porn magazines published in Denmark. 'We get responses from readers that say they are, if not proportionately interested in the text, they are interested,' James confirmed. 'I mean they are more interested in the pictures, naturally – these are picture magazines – but the male masturbation syndrome is a funny thing. These are not called "one-handed magazines" for nothing! I would think on the mag side, that theory still carries a little weight, but I would say there is much more fantasy in the stories from a completely different angle. One can see a progression from the early days where films were shot in black and white from one angle which gave the complete sort of voyeur concept. If you can't move the camera, the person watching is in the same position. It's like looking through a keyhole. There's a great deal of piquancy about that kind of thing.' James continued:[45]

> But photographers have gradually become aware of people's desire for higher quality, for variation, different camera angles, facial close-ups, all that sort of thing. What one might call a normal development with regard to quality has come along with the films. The style of mags has more or less stayed the same, but the quality has improved tremendously. I would say that pornography as far as this company is concerned has moved out of the area of what was regarded as porn and moved into the area of leisure and entertainment. That is, it's much more acceptable at home.
>
> Our productions are beginning to look more and more like *Dallas* or *Dynasty* . . . I don't know how good this is at one level. If you take our magazine stories ten years ago, they were usually shot under fairly humble circumstances, normal flats, whatever, people sitting around

having a drink, talking about something and then getting into some sort of action. Whereas now everybody arrives in Cadillacs and Rolls-Royces at a big house in the country.

So there's a double-edged fantasy in it now. There's not only the sexual fantasy, there's also this escape into the world of the wealthy. I think it's a little perverse, myself, because there's an underlying implication that unless you're rich, and have a big car, you can't fuck. I don't think our readers identify with that side of it – it's something that I see, that's come as a development without anybody in the company actually discussing it. It's just happened that way.[46]

Unsolicited feedback might leave too much to chance. The well-managed *Private* magazine decided to employ a time-honoured technique to obtain more comparable views of reader demands. Kent Wisell was the magazine's marketing manager at the time: 'In *Private* No. 62 we included a questionnaire for people to tell us what they wanted to see: if they wanted some humour, or girls with lots of pubic hair or shaved or whatever. We had lots of replies! And the thing is that the men who replied, they wanted to see mainly lesbians, a big percentage there. But if I talk to some girlfriends of mine, they want to see men. There are lots of girls who want to read porno magazines and they say, no, I don't like to see two girls together, I like to see a man. He doesn't have to be good-looking, just that it's some normal, not stupid story. Not just a man knocking at the door and saying he's arrived to repair the TV.'[47]

But it is unlikely that *Private*'s survey reflected the tastes of the American consumer. After all, pornography is now a worldwide business, and interests do vary from market to market. Actor and writer Bill Margold observes that different strictures might apply in the US:

America is obsessed with the blow job. We are not an enlightened nation and therefore Americans can go home to get laid, but they can't go home to get blown. So we do it for them.

The cum shot in the face is the stock-in-trade of orgasm. It's the ejaculation into a woman's waiting face that gets the audience off more than anything else. They sit there avidly and watch.

And they want the requisite number of orgasms per movie – usually six. That makes them real happy. I have been in audiences where you can hear them counting, as if in unison, they're toking up what they're getting: one, two . . . and if there isn't one: 'What happened to that cum shot? The guy never got off! Boo, boo!' They gotta see it, because it is fulfilling.

We do understand that it is formula video and must have those five or six heterosexual scenes, hopefully one or two of them three-way. It should have your lesbian scene. As I tell [people], the ideal way to watch my movies is to watch them over a period of a week. If you get off seven times, I've given you the perfect form of entertainment; I've given you seven orgasms.

But with most of these things, you'll fall asleep half-way through! At least sixty, sometimes seventy minutes are sex. You need a threadbare story-line, then you bang your brains out.[48]

So, it seems, the anonymous Victorian author of *The Romance of Lust* might in another incarnation have made a good living writing porn video scripts in present-day America. This continuity confirms the geographical and historical prevalence of pornography particularly in the affluent countries of the developed world.

What makes the late twentieth century different from other eras and their pictorial erotica is not simply the removal of the shackles of law. The decriminalization of the sale of graphically explicit sexual material, combined with new publishing technologies in the context of more liberal social attitudes – in most of the Western world – has given rise to a multi-billion-dollar industry. Regardless of the style and quality of the material, nameless multitudes pay millions to see their sexual fantasies incarnate.

Consequently, there are many who profit as the producers and distributors of the industry. They have emerged from a business milieu which is anarchic, often ephemeral, touched by illegality and given shape by an intuitive flair for showmanship. They present themselves as corporate warlords who have marked out their territories and mustered their forces. They are the porn barons.

# 2

## *Real Boom States: the Porn Barons*

From the top dozen business people who control more than 50 per cent of the world pornography business we have chosen to profile six of them in detail. One is an American whose empire stretches around the world and reputedly includes associates who are made members of the Mafia. Another is a Swedish lone ranger who pioneered high-quality colour porn magazines. The third is a dour Dane who was the first to apply modern management techniques to the production of a diversified range of porn products. We then portray a family in Germany who run the world's biggest porn 'cash-and-carry' distribution network. A husband and wife team who are setting new standards for porn quality are seen by other barons as upstarts.

Together, these biographies provide an insight to the way in which the porn industry has developed since the 1960s. But for one key character the case history begins long before then.

The story of Luftwaffe Hauptmann Uhse's second profession begins to take shape only hours after Adolf Hitler committed suicide in his bunker beneath Berlin on the afternoon of 30 April 1945. Above ground, the Red Army's heavy artillery was pounding the last defences in the crumbling capital of the Third Reich. Soviet troops were in the eastern suburbs.

At 7.35 on the evening of that same day, as recorded in the aircraft's log, Hauptmann Uhse's twin-engined Siebel 104 transport plane touched down on a remote airstrip at Leck, in Schleswig-Holstein. A mechanic, a two-year-old boy and his nurse accompanied Hauptmann that day. The plane had made a hazardous trip 250 miles north-west from Berlin to the only part of Germany not yet in the hands of the Allied forces. Leaving from Berlin's Gatow airport had been perilous enough – it was about to be taken by Soviet advance units. Once airborne they could have been shot down at any time, though the weather closed in during the afternoon and offered the vulnerable Siebel some protection from marauding fighters.

In those last few days before Germany's final surrender Schleswig-Holstein was the logical place for the refugees to head. There was still just an outside possibility that Admiral Dönitz's ill-fated attempt to set up a new government in the town of Flensburg might stave off the worst consequences of imminent defeat. But the immediate future on that blustery spring evening in 1945 was one of overcrowding, deprivation and the desperate urge to survive.

The twenty-five-year-old pilot's flying days were over for a considerable time to come. She and her two-year-old son Klaus settled into the area where she had put the Siebel 104 down, and Flensburg became and remained home not just for her, but also for the highly successful business she would build up over the next forty years.

Today Beate Uhse is a household name in West Germany. She is no stranger to controversy and has never shunned publicity. The slight figure of this sixty-eight-year-old grandmother is still as brimful of energy as in those years just after 1945 when her fortunes were at their lowest ebb.

Then, she was a war widow with 200 Reichsmarks to her

name. Her husband Hans-Jürgen Uhse, the man who had taught her to fly, whom she had married at the age of eighteen and whose baby son she had brought with her on her flight from Berlin, was killed on a night-fighter mission towards the end of the war. Her parents had died at the hands of the Russians during the Red Army's remorseless advance into East Prussia, where Beate had been born and raised.

The West German town of Flensburg is close by the border with Denmark – easier to reach by car than by train. A sign at the railway station exit reads 'Danish Border – Turn Left'. The street address of Beate Uhse's business in Flensburg commemorates the man who built Western Europe's first movable-type printing press, Johannes Gutenberg. Visitors to Flensburg who ask for directions to Gutenbergstrasse may get several suggestions, but reactions to requests for the Uhse organization are immediate: 'Ach so, die Uhse? Warum haben Sie nicht gesagt? Die kennen ja *alle* . . .' ('Ah, you want the Uhse place? Why didn't you say? *Everybody* knows *her*.')

Unlike Johannes Gutenberg, who died a pauper, Beate Uhse's business has made her rich and successful. Gutenbergstrasse may be part of an industrial estate, but the headquarters of Beate Uhse Aktiengesellschaft testifies to her success. Set in spacious grounds with flower borders and lawn on one side and ample car-parking space alongside, the Uhse building is more like a combination of a modern theatre and an art gallery than an office. From humble beginnings as a one-person birth control advisory service the Uhse corporation has grown to the point where it now employs 550 people across the Federal Republic and has a turnover of DM90 million (£30 million) per year.

In 1945, after eight years in the Luftwaffe, first as a test pilot, then later as a delivery pilot taking new planes to front-line squadrons, Beate Uhse was finally grounded in the village of Braderup, about thirty miles west of Flensburg. She recalled:

> There were a great many refugees there, women alone, with and without children. A village of 300 people was trying to cope with thousands. And when the war finally ended the men began to turn up, men who had survived the war and had gradually been released from prisoner-of-war camps. In those first days there was enormous joy, then after six weeks – tears and misery because they were having a baby. In Germany at that time there was no bread and butter, no cooking pots, no flannels and towels – nothing; and no contraceptives. So they were stuck there. They had lost their homes, the man had no job, he'd been a soldier for five years, and now there was a baby on the way. It was a total catastrophe.[1]

Not only were contraceptives unavailable, but Nazi ideologues had actively discouraged any sex education about the use of any form of birth control during the years they were in power. Beate Uhse remembered something she had once been told by her mother, who had been one of the first five women in Germany to qualify as doctors. It concerned the calculation of women's 'fertility days' in the menstrual cycle according to a method pioneered by a Swiss specialist, Klaus Ogino – primarily known today as the 'rhythm method'. She managed to locate a copy of his book in a local library and began to work with a doctor in Braderup teaching the women there the Ogino method.

The response amazed her: 'Soon I thought, if it's of interest to women in Braderup, it will be of interest to women in Husum and Bochum.' She drew up a broadsheet outlining the Ogino method, persuaded a local printer with gifts of black-market butter to print several thousand copies and began to sell them for two Reichsmarks in the old, discredited currency.

Not only did she sell the brochures, but the currency reform introduced by the new postwar administration went in her favour, and she began to receive payment in the new, more valuable Deutschmarks. She was soon selling thousands of copies of the leaflet and began making a living from what she still calls 'my second profession'. She then moved to Flensburg, operating from rented rooms at the house of a local pastor. Before long, she was remarried to a local businessman, Ernst-Walter Rotermund, with whom she had two more sons, Dirk and Uli. Her contraceptive advisory service began to expand its horizons.

'People would write to me and ask "Do you remember that book we used to be able to get years ago – Chesser's *Love Without Fear*, or Van De Velde's *Complete Marriage*? Why don't you republish those?"' It was not too long before manufacturers of condoms, as well as newly emergent publishers, were approaching her to market their products for them. From a front-room cottage industry, Beate Uhse-Rotermund's business became fully fledged, to the extent that in 1951 she could set up a mail order house with four female staff in Flensburg, sending contraceptives, sex aids and educational literature to thousands of customers throughout West Germany.

The nature of her business gained her notoriety as a pioneer of sexual frankness in a country with strict laws against obscenity. It was considered legal to sell contraceptives, but any promotion of 'sex aids' which claimed to improve performance or stimulate pleasure was considered to be obscene. In those early days it was also considered unacceptable to sell contraceptives to unmarried men or women. Beate Uhse regularly attracted the attention of the law, though she always defended herself vigorously and was never once found guilty of any offence.

Even without the legal complications she had to steer a narrow path. One of her most successful instruction manuals depicting 120 positions for sexual intercourse had to be illustrated using photographs of coupling naked wooden dolls to avoid prosecution. It sold 800,000 copies, but back-up copies of the galleys were sent to Hamburg in case the Flensburg authorities decided to confiscate it.

Not that Beate was averse to pushing the limits of the law

in 'softer' areas. She recalls one instance from the 1950s when she was hauled before the court in Flensburg by an officious local attorney for publishing a pack of twelve post-card photographs portraying naked young women playing beach-ball at the well-known North Sea nudist island resort of Sylt. Nude pictures were legal in Germany only so long as the subjects did not smile at the camera or give any other hint that they were inciting the viewer sexually. Showing such outrageous behaviour would be considered *unzüchtig* (obscene).

In court, the judge weighed the merits and demerits of each individual picture presented in evidence – only some of these were considered illegal by the prosecution. After two and a half hours of careful deliberation, and still unable to see the distinction, he declared that he had had enough. As far as the judge was concerned all the pictures were the same and he was dismissing the charges against the accused.

By 1953 the mail order house in Flensburg had taken on a further ten employees and was achieving sales of over DM370,000 a year. The business prospered in line with Germany's postwar *Wirtschaftswunder* economic recovery and by the end of the 1950s well over half a million names were on Beate Uhse's customer file index and annual turnover had grown to DM3.4 million.

In 1962 Uhse took another bold step and opened the pompously named Sex Institute for Marital Hygiene in Flensburg. It was the world's first true sex shop, offering a full range of Uhse products and it pointed the way for a further dramatic expansion of the business. Within a decade not one of Germany's major cities was without its 'Beate Uhse Shop'. The considerable income these generated gave Frau Beate the funds to pay for new company premises to be built on the Gutenbergstrasse site. These were duly opened in 1969 by the mayor of Flensburg with the proud civic homily that 'People can work here with pleasure and love for the business of love and pleasure.'

It had not escaped the notice of Flensburgers that Beate Uhse was a major local employer and a top customer of the Deutsche Bundespost. She in turn claims that the taxes she paid built the new Flensburg Town Hall.

The next breakthrough came when West Germany legalized pornography in 1975. Because the new law specified that hard-core pornware could only be sold through licensed sex shops and not by mail order, the high street side of Uhse's empire was well poised to exploit the new situation. Beate had been selling soft-core 'girlie magazines' for a long time and had seen the development towards eventual decriminalization of fully explicit material taking place just to the north in Copenhagen, over the previous seven years. Stocking hard-core pornography was merely a rational extension of her expanding sex empire, so magazines and films quickly began to appear in her shops.

That same year, she also foresaw a large demand for cinemas where customers unable to view pornography at home could watch the latest sex features. From the start, Beate Uhse's 'Blue Movie' theatres were conceived as comfortable and intimate establishments where clients could relax in deeply upholstered seats with a drink from the bar. Certainly, 8mm film loops of the type being made by the Theander brothers in Copenhagen would be out of place in such plush surroundings and only full-length colour features shot on 35mm film were shown. In those early post-legalization years the availability of such material was erratic and what could be found often failed to satisfy Beate's high standards for everything her company traded in.

The response was typically aggressive. She set up a subsidiary company, Beate Uhse Film Distribution, with her youngest son, Uli, in charge, to make original hard-core features or fund other companies to produce them. The new venture was successful enough for the company to be able to justify separating distribution from production. This side of the business was transferred to an independent

Swiss company called Filminvest AG run by Edouardo Stoeckli and based in Zurich. Stoeckli immediately closed a deal with an established porn film director, Alan Vydra, a Czech émigré who had worked on porn feature films in Paris. They would shoot co-productions using international porn stars, but they also negotiated distribution deals through the trade in the United States and Holland. Beate Uhse Film Distribution now owns the rights to over 120 hard-core films and holds more than half the German market against more than a dozen competitors.

By 1979 Beate was poised to take over one of her main domestic business competitors. In buying the fourteen retail outlets of the Dr Müller sex-shop chain, the Uhse organization also acquired three of the highest-profile stores in the world selling hard-core materials: the three Dr Müller shops prominently sited to serve weary travellers in the departure lounges of Frankfurt's huge and prestigious international airport.

All three sons had by now joined their mother working in the family business and everyone prospered into the 1980s. In 1981 there were heated exchanges across the boardroom table which resulted in the Uhse empire being split up the following year. Dirk Rotermund and Klaus Uhse took over the mail-order operation and all magazine and book publishing. Uli stayed loyal to his mother and together they became the sole shareholders in an overall holding company, Beate Uhse AG, which retained control of the shops and the film and video sides of the enterprise.

The break-up certainly didn't result from any financial difficulties and Beate and Uli were left with thirty sex shops, fourteen cinemas (with forty-five screens attracting fifteen million patrons a year, this was the largest porn movie chain in Europe), and the film distribution company with offices in Düsseldorf, Munich and Dreieich near Frankfurt Airport.[2]

Beate Uhse's mail-order operation is obliged to concentrate on erotic lingerie, soft-core books, magazines and videos, contraceptives, vibrators and other sex aids as well as various 'toys' which range from male and female pin-up playing cards, through 'sex trivia' quizzes to penis-shaped candles and ginseng oil. Telephone orders are accepted, along with requests via the *Bildschirmtext* national computer database network. Customers can pay using American Express, Diners Club, Eurocard or Visa credit cards. Everything is sold with a 100 per cent money-back, no-questions-asked warranty.

The headquarters complex in Flensburg remains the heart of Beate Uhse's enterprise. The impressive building has been extended over the years. It houses a staff of over 150 – many of them women – who work in purchasing, warehousing and distribution, store and cinema décor, legal affairs (two full-time lawyers), accounting and personnel departments. As in most German companies, training, career development and staff relations are taken very seriously and some employees have been working for Beate for more than twenty-five years. The photographs of key personnel – especially Beate herself – appear in the Beate Uhse mail-order catalogues along with a signed explanation of what their job is and how they can help the company's many customers. The company even sponsors a women's handball team which competes in the national *Bundesliga*.

At the time of the 1982 split, Beate's part of the company had capital stock of $6.4 million and gross sales of $24 million. The dissection of the company was not terminal and by 1987 turnover had leaped to DM90 million (about £30 million or $55 million) – more than enough porn gold to place Beate Uhse and her supporting trio of sons among the leading figures in the world pornography trade. At sixty-eight years of age Beate Uhse is no longer grounded. She still flies the company's Cessna and Piper light aircraft. The venerable head of the forty-year dynasty is still very firmly in control of her empire, one of the few porn baronesses in a world traditionally dominated by men.

Beate Uhse is not well-known outside West Germany. If there is one outstanding international pioneer of the modern era of pornographic magazines, it is Berth Milton. Since the mid-1960s he has been a determined one-man, single-product campaign for the recognition of the role of pornography in human sexuality, for its legalization in the statute books, for its acceptance in society and, perhaps above all, for its buyers to have quality in content and style.

The Daralana region is the geographical and emotional heart of Sweden. Local people do not sustain traditional dress, architecture, music and folk-lore merely for the region's many tourists. Berth Milton was born in 1927 in this area at Dala-Järna, some twenty miles south-west of Lake Siljan.

An aunt gave him his first camera when he was six years old and he demonstrated a precocious faculty for persuading women to shed their clothes when he took a girl called Carol and his Baby Brownie into the nearby countryside: 'I was nine years old and Carol was twelve. It came out just natural; she wanted to show herself off.'[3] This idyllic incident – *Cider with Rosie* and a box camera – not only presaged an adult philosophy of what Milton has dubbed 'erotography' but also started him out on the road to what would become the single bestselling hard-core sex magazine in the world.

'Milton' was already a famous name in Sweden. For forty years, young Berth's father operated Milton's Tivoli, the country's biggest travelling fairground. Though leading a life that many youngsters dream of running away to, Berth was well aware of the penalties: 'I was going to school in seven different cities,' he recalled. 'Although I was physically the same strength, I could not be in the football team or the hockey team because I was always moving about. I also realized very quickly that any friends I made I was going to lose after a month or so.' That childhood instilled self-sufficiency to a degree where even his most ardent admirers and employees remark on Milton's inability to delegate and his apparent distrust of even close and loyal colleagues. It might also explain his hostility to people who leave his company.

By the 1960s Milton was making a mark in what might be called another branch of show business as a car salesman for Volkswagen. 'I reached the top in Sweden,' Milton boasts. 'I made more money than the managing director of the company. I was selling a hell of a lot of cars. They had a work study engineer trail me to see how I could I sell so many in one month. I know that when they teach salesmen to sell cars they still use the "Milton Method".' His success in such a traditionally tough selling job was a major factor in Milton's ability to turn his erotic *idée fixe* into a fortune. It also provided the seed capital he needed to get started as a publisher of pornography.

In the middle of the 1960s, the decriminalization of pornography in Sweden was not yet complete. Milton decided to start at the retail end of the business and opened a bookshop in Stockholm. The most explicit material available was typified by the magazines of Curth Hson-Nilson. These contained photographs which, although daring for the time, would pass muster for the breakfast table in many of today's tabloid newspapers. Milton supplemented this with more explicit under-the-counter prints and slides of his own making.[4] Milton's move into magazine publishing in 1966 came about with inevitable logic.

'When I saw all the rubbish published and sold for a tremendous amount of money, I said: I can do better than that,' Milton remembers. 'Everybody was printing thirty-six black-and-white pictures in thirty-six pages. *I* started with a well-designed layout, with text and with colour. That was the reason I started the magazine.'[5]

Already a skilled photographer, Milton's first step was to find models prepared to pose for the *risqué* material he needed. 'It was more difficult at that time than now. A girl showing herself off in the nude, spreading her legs, that was a big thing.' Finding a printer was less of a problem because 'everyone thought they'd become multi-millionaires by printing such pictures'. Milton's biggest risk was gambling on the customer's willingness to pay extra for the quality he was so proud of. 'That was the big thing – that it should be in full colour. At that time *no* magazine in black and white sold more than five thousand copies. *I* had to sell more than ten thousand copies to get my money back. So we printed ten thousand.' This unprecedented inventory was rivalled only by his stock of self-confidence. 'I was a good salesman! I said, all right, if I print the best sex magazine in the world, in full colour, I can sell it; and what we sell on top of that will be profit.'[6]

This was long before the well-oiled networks of distributors and retailers in today's porn world. So:

> I sold it myself. For example, I saw a man wheeling his little kiosk out at three o'clock in the afternoon because the evening papers were due. I went up to him because he had some black-and-white Danish magazines. I said, you can buy this one instead – *Private* No 1! 'How much do I pay for it?' he asked. I said eight crowns. 'All right, eight crowns – but what do I have to pay you?' Eight crowns. 'Jesus Christ,' he said, 'what am I supposed to sell it for?' Sixteen crowns. 'Oh, come on, forget it!' So I said, all right, I'll give you three magazines. When you've sold them, give me a ring. The next day he called and said 'Mr Milton, I sold the magazines, could you come over with another five?'
>
> So I went over with another five. The next day, he called again, and said 'Could you come over with another five?' Then I said to him 'Listen to me, I'm not going to deliver five magazines. Take two hundred, pay for them cash, and when *Private* No. 2 is out, if you have any left I'll take them back and give you No. 2 for them.' Before the end of the month, he had sold a thousand. A thousand! He made more money out of *Private* than he did from the rest of the kiosk! Then, of course, I realized the

potential of the magazine. So then came No. 2 and No. 3 and No. 4 . . .[7]

But Milton wanted to do more than set new standards with the latest colour litho techniques. He also wanted the photo-sets to show the detail of sexual acts. Considering his increasing notoriety, the Swede had few skirmishes with the law. He wanted to make money from publishing the new *Private* but did not relish being harassed by the police as he did it. Before going to press, he slipped the photographs for the first issue into an envelope and climbed into his car: 'I went up to the Ministry of Justice to find out what I could publish. "You tell me," I said. "If I steal a bicycle, you can tell me that's against the law. Look at this picture and tell me if I can publish it." And they said "Oh, we don't know! You publish it, then we'll see what happens." "Jesus Christ!" I said, "I am asking *you* – you are the Ministry of Justice, you should be able to tell me." I showed them all the possibilities from so-and-so to so-and-so and they couldn't tell me!'

Berth Milton proceeded cautiously. Initially, the magazine concentrated on photographs of solitary naked women. The first sign of the direction in which he was moving came the following year in 1967: 'It must have been *Private* No. 6 or 7. He used men, you couldn't see their dicks, but you could see they were fucking,' recalls Kent Wisell, Milton's former sales manager. 'People started talking about it and soon after that they changed the law.'[8] Once the constitutional change had taken effect, Milton was free to make the breakthrough. It came with *Private* No. 8. 'Now they could say what was legal and what was illegal,' says Milton. 'Those fuck shots, *my* pictures, were on the desk of the Minister of Justice.'[9]

Milton had been in the right place, at the right time and with the right motivation. Since the early days of the so-called swinging sixties, it had been clear that Sweden's 'Signpost Society' was likely to be the first to make hard-core pornography legal. His determination to take the quality of pornography up-market was just what was needed to place a glossy finish on the sheen of respectability applied by the change in the law. The circulation of *Private* soon exceeded 40,000 copies an issue. The reputation of the magazine spread and by the end of the 1960s, a curious world was clamouring for copies.

For a long time, Milton would take all the cash that came in via mail order and stow it in an old suitcase under his bed. One evening, he retrieved the case, sat down, and heaped the money into multi-coloured piles according to denomination. He carefully counted each stack of bills and noted the total on a piece of paper. Later, in the small hours of the following day, he rubbed his eyes and stared at the figure at the bottom of the paper: he had been sleeping on top of £300,000![10] In 1970 he fathered twin daughters.

Throughout the next decade, Milton worked hard to expand his business. Although *Private* stayed in the same format as the very first issue – slightly larger than A5 – the number of pages increased. He took on more staff to help with production, but few suffered Milton's impatience with the task of managing people he considered less competent than himself. One of the exceptions was a Yugoslavian-born photographer called Joachim 'Jo' Wallach who is today one of Europe's most prolific freelance suppliers of hard and soft pornographic material. Milton and Wallach worked well together for a number of years and many people in the business consider that some of the best issues of *Private* resulted from that partnership.

But the magazine was essentially a one-man operation. Milton would appear in its pages with camera rampant, three naked women draped about his expensive double-breasted suit or leaning against his Rolls-Royce. He even developed a 'philosophy', after the precedent set by Hugh Hefner in *Playboy*. In editorials under the nicely ambiguous headline, 'Moral?', he would espouse views that were as strongly anti-violence as they were pro sex and 'eroto-graphy'.

One of the earliest and perhaps most effective examples

appeared in *Private* No. 8 (1967) when Milton published a set of four photographs. Three of these showed graphic acts of violence, including the bullet-riddled head of 1930s bank robber Clyde Barrow, the Mayor of Saigon shooting a suspected Viet Cong soldier and South Vietnamese special forces showing off the decapitated heads of captured enemy. The fourth depicts a couple engaged in sexual intercourse, the penetration clearly visible. Milton's editorial was as uncompromising as the photographs:

> With the approval of the censoring authorities in question, abnormal and horrible acts of violence have been shown in the greater part of our civilization – distributed via newspapers, magazines, film and television.
>
> Murders and throat-cuttings are obviously matters within the limits of decency.
>
> Why is it then, that in so many parts of the world realism in love-making and sexual intercourse between human beings are not allowed to be shown?
>
> There is only *one* picture in this spread showing *normal* human behaviour. Without violence, without bestiality, without hatred, without revenge. It is not a proof of the Swedish 'sin', just normal good sense and honesty.[11]

Predictably, many newspapers reproduced the picture set. Perhaps with equal predictability, all of them censored the same photograph. Milton had made his point.

It is unlikely, however, that Milton's increasing band of devotees were buying *Private* for the editorials. Post-legalization, the competition was hotting up, especially from magazines like *Color Climax*, which the Theander brothers started publishing at about the same time from their base in Copenhagen. To some degree, the 'story-line' of the photosets was becoming predictable. A group of people would be seen sitting around a coffee table drinking. That would be followed by a little foreplay, culminating in a variety of sexual activities. That became the prototype. Milton recognizes the problem: 'You can put one girl together with two guys, you can put two girls together with one guy and improvise and so on. But there must be a limit.'[12]

There were two elements to his alternative solution; more outdoor shooting – especially in exotic locations, and the use of new and unfamiliar models. Milton has shot sets in Thailand, Southern Germany (at Schloss Reichenstein, on which Disneyland's fairy castle is based), English stately homes, France (on top of the Arc de Triomphe), Gibraltar, Moorish castles in Spain, Sweden (at one of the royal family's country residences), San Francisco, Las Vegas and the Grand Canyon. Milton claims he has enough ideas for the next ten years: 'look at *Private* no. 73, for example. There we have a black girl, a white horse and a Spanish gentleman. Or we have the safari set where we went up into the mountains and had two Mexican guys making love to a beautiful Swedish blonde. All those things, you know, new ideas.'

Finding the locations is one thing, but Milton also seems perfectly able to persuade the owners to provide access: 'Well, everybody is interested in sex! So it's not that difficult to get permission. Of course, they have to be open-minded. I tell them we are going to do this and that and they are quite happy to have a look, to see what we are doing.'

Like most publishers of sex magazines, Milton runs an advertisement in each issue inviting women to apply to be models. This does attract replies, but needs to be supplemented by talent scouts who are usually photographers themselves. Most female models come from England, Germany and Sweden, occasionally from France, Italy and Spain. Many American women also volunteer, but the cost of transporting them to Spain – or Milton and his entourage to the United States – is usually too high. He is not enthusiastic about employing professional models: 'I don't like professional models. You can see the same girl in six or seven different magazines. She's called Anna, she's called Greta, she's called Annette, she's called whatever. We like to have the enthusiasts. The people who like *Private* and would like to appear in nothing but that. We have lots and lots of models who pose for *Private* and nothing but that.'

Former associates of Milton confirm his claim that many people often volunteer for the experience rather than the money. Milton himself supplied an example: 'I got a letter from a woman in Germany saying that she read *Private* with her husband and she would like to appear in the magazine with him. I was just taking off for Germany in a couple of days, so I said I would go and see her. Her husband was running a factory with five thousand employees. They had a beautiful house and two daughters, nine and ten years old. She was an ex-fashion model, a beautiful woman aged thirty-nine or forty. When I showed up there, he said "I'm not certain I can do it in front of the camera, but you can use my wife. She would like to do it." So she came up to Stockholm and did the set, one lesbian scene and one with a young guy. She didn't ask for any money; I paid for the trip up to Stockholm, the hotel and food and so on. It's not unique, really. On another occasion I had a marvellous guy and a beautiful Thai girl. He was a fashion designer with one factory in France and one in Thailand. He met his wife over there. They wanted to come over to Sweden and pose for the magazine, for *Private*. So, I brought them over and we had a marvellous time together. Later she was pregnant, and he wanted her to be photographed together with him and another guy, making love when she was heavily pregnant. They came up to Stockholm, and we shot the set. They did it because they liked the magazine.'[13]

Once the money was flowing in from the magazine, Milton succumbed to the temptation to try his hand at making films. The experience was not a good one: 'I started with films many years ago. But they were so good they were copied by the Danish and the German companies. When I sold a thousand, they sold ten thousand! A man from England came to Sweden to buy my films. My latest film, the best one, was ready and I had 200 copies. When he arrived, I put it in the projector and he said, "Yes, it's a fantastic film you've done, but I saw it a few days ago in Amsterdam." So before I'd even sold the film myself, it was copied in Amsterdam. Then I said to myself, no more, I'm going to do magazines. OK, they can make imitations, try to do the things I'm doing but at least they can't just push it in a machine and copy it.'

The only other magazine Milton ever published was an occasional deviation into saliromania: sex involving urges to defile, usually by means of urination and defecation. It was called *Pirate*, the typestyle of the masthead aping that of *Private* in the manner of the magazine's many copiers. 'Yes, it was meant as a kind of joke. But there is a certain demand for things like that: let's call it what it is – shit and piss. I can tell you about one person who phoned me from Colombia in South America and asked me if I could arrange to photograph a girl shitting in his mouth. I said I could and he came over. That is not unique, because lots and lots of people are involved in shit and piss and things like that. I came across a couple in France who were involved in that, you know, shitting and pissing on each other. I bought a set from a photographer who couldn't sell it to anybody else and published it in *Pirate* No. 1. The response I got from all over the world was tremendous! I couldn't believe it! The fact is, sexual angles are so varied that you can't believe what people want to do and are really doing. We've stopped it now, because I didn't like it.'

In the early 1980s Milton bought a villa high in the hills at Costa Mijas and close enough to the fashionable Costa del Sol marina at Puerto Banus for him to moor his yacht. Swedes have a special relationship with the sun that can come only from living through eight-month-long icy winters. Milton had in any case been a regular visitor to Spain since before the death of General Franco, and the increasing summer flood of tourists from Northern Europe merely provided the extra cover he needed to shoot pornography sets.

It was a hazardous business and meticulous planning was

essential to stay one step ahead of the infamous Guardia Civil who at that time were prepared to patrol the beaches in helicopters to locate and arrest women sunbathing topless. 'I always have my walkie-talkies, dogs and things like that. I remember one time in particular, in Las Palmas [de Gran Canaria], we rented a red car from Hertz for one day. The next day we rented from Avis, and it was a yellow car and we parked it in a different place. And the third day we had yet another car. The Guardia Civil riding around on their motor bikes would see the red car one day and say "It's some stupid tourist out shooting pictures." You see, if they'd seen the same car parked in the same space every day for two, three, four days, they would start thinking. But because we changed the colour of the cars, we managed. My girlfriend would sit on the top of a hill with the walkie-talkie and when the Guardia Civil was coming she sent beep-beep-beep-beep! Then we stopped everything!'[14] Franco died in 1976 and the repression died with him. Today, topless sunbathers are only bothered by optimistic waiters and the public smoking of marijuana is legal. So is pornography.

After a few years of wintering at the villa, Milton, now aged sixty, decided to move the printing of *Private* to Spain. The prices quoted were attractive, but he needed to find a company that could guarantee the high quality he demanded. 'I work together with a man who runs thirty-six print shops – big ones. He said that the printery in Barcelona would be the best for our requirements. So I said OK, we'll start there and see what happens. In the early days, we had a lot of problems. If you can imagine the amount of aspirin I've taken!' Once the problems were resolved, the benefits became apparent: 'People in this country want to work. In Sweden, if you say on the Thursday: "Would you like to work two or three hours' overtime on Friday?" one guy will say "Sorry, I can't because I promised my wife we'd go out collecting mushrooms on Saturday"; or "I'm going to paint my wheelbarrow green, so

I can't work." Here they say "Yes, I'll do it. I'll work!" It's a little bit cheaper and I like people who like to work.'

At the beginning of 1985 the transfer progressed another stage and Milton moved permanently to Spain, taking his production operation with him. The villa is now equipped with a small design studio, the walls of which are covered with the page layouts and flat-plans for the next issue of the magazine. Milton still does much of the photography, but naturally the technology has come a long way from that first Baby Brownie: 'I'm using the latest Canon T90. That's because we have to work fast. We can't manage with something like a Hasselblad. We also use motor drives and electronic flash systems. Usually I work with three cameras loaded with Fuji 50 film. We can get it processed here in twenty-four hours. With Kodachrome, we needed two weeks because we had to send the exposed films up to Madrid and half of them were stolen. For Fuji we have a local firm that we can trust.' Even after more than two decades, Milton's attention to detail is still there: 'I still personally check every issue. First they come down from Barcelona to show me the check print. When they have made the corrections, I go up to Barcelona and check the print.'[15]

His new lifestyle has established a routine. The mail keeps him in touch and he enjoys opening the noon delivery of letters. He hates writing letters himself but is an avid user of the telephone and many an unsuspecting correspondent half-way around the world must have been taken aback to hear his voice. In 1987 at the age of sixty he has inevitably slowed down a little. He occasionally visits Stockholm to see his family and check the status of the marketing operation – the only part of the business still based in Sweden. His health is not all it used to be, but he enjoys the warmer climate, a girlfriend considerably younger than himself and frequent trips on the yacht.

It is unlikely that Milton is short of money. The bimonthly circulation of *Private* is at least 100,000 copies and, allowing for all language editions and those printed by agents, it could be as high as 200,000. It is thought to sell some 40,000 copies in West Germany alone. This compares with his main competitors, *Foxy Lady* and *Color Climax*, neither of which is thought to exceed total sales of 50,000. Berth Milton's present annual profit from the magazine could easily be in the region of $500,000.[16]

Unless one of the bridges over the Kalveboderne channel has been raised for a passing ship, even the Danes themselves might fail to notice the southerly encroachment of Copenhagen on to the island of Amager, a featureless extension of the city into the district of Øresund.

A left turn off the road that goes to Kasterup international airport leads into an equally drab industrial estate dominated by the multinational names of Renault and Philips. Beyond a derelict plot, the scene is brightened by the yellow-brick building at Strandlodsvej 61. Across the main entrance door, a large sign in red letters reads 'Rodox Trading'.

From the exterior, the building could be on any industrial estate in the world. But the entrance lobby is characteristically Scandinavian. Large plants dominate and deep leather chairs are positioned beneath net-curtained windows. A counter bars visitors from just one part of an extensive warehouse. From a glass-walled office to one side, a receptionist emerges to greet guests and ask, in good English, whom they have come to see. A clip-on identity badge is supplied.

The administration offices are on the next floor and a short walk along anonymous corridors and through a softly lit staff cafeteria decorated with Warhol prints leads to the editorial offices of what possibly ranks as the largest pornography publishing house in the world.

The vital statistics of the company's twenty-year history are astounding: more than ninety million magazines, nearly nine million Super-8 films and over one million videos cassettes.

When Peter Gruntvig Theander was born in Copenhagen on 5 December 1941 the German occupation was twenty-one months old and full-blown Danish resistance merely a storm brewing on the horizon. On the day his younger brother, Jens, was born – 22 January 1944 – the Allies landed at Anzio and the days of the Third Reich were numbered. Peter was still only twenty-five when, after an undistinguished start in life driving taxis, the two brothers invested their savings by opening a modest second-hand bookshop in the centre of the most cosmopolitan of all Scandinavian cities, Copenhagen.

It was 1966 and those were the 'black money' years of Danish pornography. However, increasingly liberal social attitudes were encouraging a growing demand on the part of the buying public. The brothers freely admit that their window displays of strictly legal naturist and pin-up magazines were there primarily to suggest to the passing trade that what was available 'under the counter' was much more interesting. The police seemed satisfied at the time so long as genitals were concealed by 'peel-off' strips of paper, but hard-core material was still illegal. Yet such was the scale of demand that it far outstripped supply. Peter soon saw that the growth of their new business was being inhibited by its dependence on the availability of suitable hard-core magazines produced by other companies. At this point he took his second major business decision – the brothers would become producers as well as retailers.

Jens would be the photographer, Peter would be responsible for the design of the magazines and for marketing the resultant product. If they couldn't find a printer, they would buy their own printing press. That way they could control both the quality and quantity of the product. There was, however, a substantial barrier to the plan: they had no money and it wasn't the kind of business proposition that could be taken to the neighbourhood bank manager.

There was only one solution. All their original working capital was tied up in the shop's stock. To free it, they would have to stop ordering new magazines and let the inventory diminish until they had enough cash for the publishing venture. It would be a risky step – if anything went wrong with the plan to publish their own magazines, they would be drained of all income. They stopped ordering fresh supplies, Jens started taking photographs and Peter designed their first magazines. As they had predicted, the cupboard under the counter was soon bare and the shop was down to selling the mediocre window display when help came from an unexpected quarter.

Under pressure from moral pressure groups, the police launched a campaign of attrition against Denmark's growing band of pornographers. Their intelligence was good; truckloads of hard-core books and magazines were seized and porn publishers and traders dragged before the courts. The only disappointment was the raid on the Theanders' shop. It was only a matter of days before the brothers realized the scale of the good deed the police had done them.

The raids had been so effective that all the Theanders' main competitors had been put out of business and the Danish market had been drained of hard-core books. If they pressed ahead with their own publishing plans, they would be able to corner a huge share of the growing market. But to avoid the heightened attentions of the police, it would have to be a clandestine operation.

'And so began an exciting game of cat and mouse with the law,' they boasted twenty years later in the anniversary issue of their magazine *Color Climax* – first published in 1968. 'Two trying, but rewarding years of using secret warehouses, false identities and anonymous printers, which came to an end in 1969, when public pressure led to the reform of the Danish pornography laws. This meant that the firm's formerly illegal activities could at last be carried out openly, like any other legitimate business.'[17]

Sales soon exceeded by far the local catchment area of the Copenhagen shop. For Peter the next logical stage in the marketing side of the business was to go into mail order. The production side had already moved into a converted house on Kastrupvej in the city centre. But even that wasn't big enough and he had to find another house on nearby Rodosvej – from which came the name 'Rodox'. Within a year, this part of the company alone was employing over forty people, a figure which was boosted as Rodox's reputation became international and customers unable to obtain pornography in their own countries mailed money to the grateful Theanders. Regardless of local laws, the Danish brothers dispatched the goods by return. It was during this period, according to Rupert James, the Theanders' English editor, that the business 'was in a real boom state and overnight people were becoming millionaires – literally!'[18]

The mail-order business was not without its problems. Although the Theanders were no longer breaking Danish law, this was not the case for traders who were buying their products for sale in countries like Britain. Rodox did co-operate in the smuggling operation, and the regular fleets of lorries carrying Danish bacon to English supermarkets provided a convenient cover for products designed to satisfy non-dietary needs. 'We stopped sending stuff in Danish Bacon trucks in 1969 or whatever,' Rupert James pointed out. 'It was no longer part of the company's policy to get involved in areas of legality in other countries.'[19]

There were good reasons for that change in policy. The London porn scene in the 1960s and 1970s was dominated by hardened criminals who were circumventing the law by bribing Scotland Yard's Obscene Publications Squad. 'We got a visit from one of the "Jewish Mafia" in Soho,' James recalls. 'He had been busted by UK Customs for illegally importing some of our material that he'd bought in Holland. He wanted to get off the charges by claiming that the stuff wasn't imported but had been printed in England. To prove that, he wanted us to supply him with the original artwork of the magazines concerned. The guy begged and pleaded, saying that we were going to cause him to lose three years of his life inside. More to get rid of him than anything else, Peter said he could have the stuff for £50,000. The guy was really pissed off and, because he was having to deal with me instead of Peter, he convinced himself that I was the cause of all his problems. Anyway, the next day I got a telephone call from him: "You're in big trouble, sunshine," he said. Why? I asked him. "Because if you don't hand over those plates, you're going to get a 'deep-sixing' [be killed by being drowned in a river]." That really pissed *me* off and I went to see Peter about it and complained. I'm only supposed to be an editor around here! In the end, John Lindsey sorted the problem out.'[20] Lindsey operated hard-core porn cinemas in London during a brief period of confusion in the interpretation of Britain's various laws.[21]

Problems with criminals did not always result in death threats, but did occasionally bring a change in business plans: 'We used to own our own trucks for making deliveries,' Rupert James recalled. 'One of the drivers found a way of getting an extra pallet put on for each trip. A pallet load of our magazines is worth a lot of money: especially on a regular basis. Anyway, the German cops found him making the transfer in a lay-by and called us to find out if it was legit. It wasn't. Peter was really angry, so he closed down our transport department and subcontracted it.'[22]

Magazines were no longer the mainstay of Rodox's business. As far back as 1969 the brothers had made a move characteristic of their enterprise; they diversified. To meet the demand for the moving image, they set up a film studio in the heart of the city at Ny Adelgade doing business as Candy Film. Although it was not in the grand style of the major Hollywood studios, it soon became one of the world's biggest producers of 8mm films. Indeed, with a ready supply of mostly Danish performers and Jens's ability to keep the cameras turning, Rodox's output of exposed film soon exceeded local processing capacity. So the following year the brothers bought an existing film laboratory and renamed it Rodox Color Teknik A/S (RCT). Both Peter and

Jens were preoccupied with the question of quality. Some years later, the younger brother expounded this philosophy:

> Despite the very difficult and specialized demands that our customers expect with regard to the story content of our films, there is always one thing they insist on – perfect technical quality: knife-sharp pictures, a 100 per cent correct colour balance and, in the case of sound films, a very precise soundtrack. For this reason we started our film laboratory, Rodox Color Teknik, seven years ago, because we were by no means satisfied with the results we received from companies processing our films.
>
> At the best of times we managed to produce only a hundred reasonable copies a day. However, by tackling the difficulties immediately we managed to resolve the problems and improve the quality of the developed products.[23]

The policy was well founded, because the studio had to be moved in 1973 to more modern premises on Baldersgade, for both filming and stills photography.

Business continued to boom, but the continual moves were disruptive and it seemed preferable to have everything together under the same roof. Peter Theander commissioned a new building on an industrial estate out of the town centre. The design studio, the production facilities, the warehouse and the administration and editorial offices were all to be relocated to Strandlodsvej 61. The move took place in June 1975. Rodox Color Teknik did not move in until the following year, but Jens was gleeful; he was now in charge of one of the most up-to-date film laboratories in Northern Europe:

> . . . we are now one of the world's largest Super-8 film laboratories and can easily produce between 3,500 and 4,000 copies daily (approximately 200,000 metres) – on a yearly basis more than one million copies.
>
> Today we have the benefit of the most modern machinery that money can buy – seven optical copying

> machines and four double-spool developing tanks which naturally facilitate continual operation. A large part of the system is controlled electronically but ultimately we rely on the skill and attention of thirty-four specialist operators to maintain and indeed better our very high quality standards.
>
> This has of course cost an unbelievable amount of money, but increasing sales have shown that to invest in quality pays high dividends. We hope that this trend will continue with respect to our latest introduction, a very expensive, sophisticated electronic colour analyser that is able to correct the colour of each new scene. This will no doubt encourage an even greater number of satisfied customers.[24]

In 1979, while Jens – looking for all the world like a 'mad scientist' with glasses, long blond hair and beard – was poring over the test tubes and retorts of his colour laboratory, Peter was poring over the financial pages. Hitting the headlines daily was the name of a Texan millionaire who presented a threat to the business: Nelson Bunker Hunt. Silver is an essential ingredient in all photographic film and Hunt had initiated a grandiose plan to buy up the world silver market. Peter, fearful of the implications for Rodox, nearly panicked. At that time, they were using the best part of 70,000 kilometres of colour film stock a year. Theander called Fuji for a quote on one million kilometres of stock.[25]

Their enthusiasm for the enterprise was encouraged and stimulated by the unsolicited reaction of their growing band of readers. Letters flowed in with each mail delivery and, today, Peter Theander has a stock of negatives, slides and prints which contains some three million items representing two decades of photographic material contributed by clients.[26]

Rodox was so well managed that it was able to respond to market demands. As the company noted in the anniversary issue of *Color Climax*:

> . . . we were able to meet the most specialized requirements of customers who wanted very specific erotic themes. We were able to keep pace with a lot of these requirements, due to the fact that we responded to customers who wrote to us, often criticizing things as well as offering suggestions for changes or improvements to our products.[27]

But this net was cast too wide and Rodox began to publish material which later attracted widespread criticism and caused a few short-lived problems with the authorities (see Chapter 9).

The big change in media that took Rodox into its third decade of operation was the rise of domestic video. The film processing laboratory was closed down and replaced by one of the most sophisticated video facilities houses in northern Europe. Editing suites, graphics and special effects computers were moved in alongside a copying system with the capacity to produce 2,400 video cassettes a day. Rodox Color Teknik changed its name to RCT Video.[28]

The cost of such an investment could be met only by making the facilities available not just to other pornographers, but to producers of conventional video material. For many years, Hollywood box-office successes such as *Rambo, Terms of Endearment, Police Academy* and *Raiders of the Lost Ark* were reproduced under licence on Peter Theander's video systems.

But even that was not enough. Although the pornography side of the business continued to flourish, RCT Video was soon losing £1 million a year until Peter sold the company to a consortium of managers and businessmen in the summer of 1987. Only his business skills and the accumulated wealth of the company enabled him to ride this financial storm. Even before Jens's departure in 1985, Peter had concentrated on production and distribution. All photographic material and video masters were bought in from other production companies throughout the world.

With capital investment now minimized, he could concentrate on the development of now famous and very profitable titles such as *Blue Climax, Rodox, Teenage Sex, Anal Sex* and *Lesbian Love* as well as the original *Color Climax*.[29]

What are the Theander brothers like? In an industry dominated by the extremes of flamboyant extroverts and publicity-shy recluses, the brothers definitely fall into the latter category. 'They are ordinary people,' Swedish men's magazine editor, Bengt Lénberg, revealed, 'ordinary people who have made a lot of money. Jens didn't make any impression on me.'[30]

Local journalists have found Peter's unwillingness to give them access frustrating. 'Theander refuses to give interviews, will not allow photographs of himself, and journalists who visit the concern's HQ on Strandlodsvej must sign an undertaking that Theander may approve the article before it is printed. The freedom from censorship which supposedly made the Theander brothers multimillionaires since 1969, does not include – according to the Danish porno king – an inquisitive press,'[31] wrote the tabloid *Ekstra Bladet* tetchily. 'He is more difficult to interview than Queen Ingrid,' conceded a source at Rodox.

Should they ever persuade Peter Theander to agree to an interview, they are likely to be disappointed. Peter is variously described in terms like 'cold', 'dull', 'humourless' and even 'boring'. In a world often dominated by drink, drugs, partying and the jet-setting high life, Peter Theander's great passions in life – apart from the business – are opera, classical music, modern art and his extensive wine cellar.

What really makes the Theanders interesting to the press is their money. Considering that they started with nothing and everything they have made is attributable to their own efforts, they are now very rich indeed. The first substantial clue to this wealth came when what had proved to be the most most effective and profitable partnership in the history of porn ended in the summer of 1985.

To some degree, the break-up was inevitable. Since the earliest days, Jens had concentrated on photography and the technical aspects of production. As the porn industry expanded and matured over the following two decades, the younger brother's 'creative' contribution became subservient to Peter's business acumen. Rodox's expansion into the production of 8mm films had been relatively painless. But the ten-minute loops it turned out were almost entirely devoid of plot and the visual content easily outweighed any artistic intent.

The problem came to a head with a new consumer demand for more sophisticated story-lines, exotic settings and attractive performers. From the mid-1970s onwards, such material became available in the form of feature films originally made for cinema release. Germany, France and – predominantly – the United States were the primary sources of such pornware. Rodox would be able to survive for some time by systematically transferring the inventory of 8mm loops to video cassettes, but that was unacceptable as a long-term strategy.

For Jens Theander, the cameraman, the solution was simple: they would expand the Candy Film studio again and start making their own hard-core feature films. Peter, the businessman, had a much simpler solution: Rodox would close down the studio and buy the European rights to the films that would be needed. That was the plan which made sense from both the financial and practical points of view. By closing the studio, overheads would be substantially reduced and the rights to films would amount to a mere fraction of the cost of production. In any case, Copenhagen had never been a major film production centre. Where would Jens find a professional 35mm film crew and the performers who could act credibly between the sex scenes? 'The time had run out for small-film porno showing 10–12 minutes of *gunga-da-gung* in the studio,' declared Keld Madsen, Rodox's production manager.[32]

It had become clear that Jens no longer had a meaningful

role in a business that had been his whole existence for half his life. For a time the heady atmosphere of Rodox turned sour as the brothers argued acrimoniously. In the end they decided to go their separate ways. Jens would receive a cash settlement for his shares on the understanding that he agreed not to set up a new business in competition with Rodox. Estimates of the amount he was paid vary, but no one sets it lower than £1.8 million ($2.7 million) and it could be as much as £3 million ($4.5 million). Jens is now out of the porn business and lives in London.

Three years on from the date when the brothers went their different ways, Peter must now be worth substantially more than that – even in net terms. Before security at the Rodox building was tightened, it wasn't unusual to see teenage children around the premises; they were there to meet their parents after school. Peter has a small apartment at the back of the building which he uses from time to time when he is working late. Two boys who were not supposed to be in the building broke into the apartment and stole Theander's wallet. It was later found discarded in a park on the opposite side of the road. It had contained DKr 150,000 (£15,000 or $23,000) in cash. 'That's like small change for Peter Theander,' said one of his associates.

The diversity and complexity of Peter Theander's business interests would probably make it difficult for his own accountants to calculate his net worth. But he lives in a £3 million ($4.5 million) house in Copenhagen and owns the biggest non-bank finance company in Denmark. Rodox itself is probably achieving annual sales revenues in the region of DKr 100 million (£10 million or $15 million). In 1986 Peter Theander wrote a thank-you letter in *Color Climax*:

> Dear Readers,
>
> It is with both pride and regret that I present this Jubilee issue of *Color Climax*. Pride, because the quality of the magazine before you is undeniably better than that of

the magazines I originally issued when I started this firm under very humble circumstances twenty years ago. Regret, because since that time things have happened so quickly that the years have simply flown by.

Nearly all the firms that began at that time have since disappeared, whereas Rodox Trading rapidly expanded, to become probably the largest pornographic publishing house in Europe. The secret behind the success is quite simple. From the beginning, I gave quality priority over quantity, and during the years that have followed, I have consistently tried to improve the firm's products. I will continue to do so, and look forward to issuing a better, even bigger Jubilee edition five years from now.

Peter Theander.[33]

Clearly, porn baron Peter Theander has no intention of quitting – even when he is ahead.

Any doubts that Peter Theander is right would be speedily dispelled by a trip south to one of West Germany's lesser-known attractions.

West of the city of Frankfurt the Rhine is joined from the east by the smaller River Main. Here Germany's major waterway bends west between the town of Mainz and, on its north bank, the old spa town of Wiesbaden, capital of the state of Hesse. Schierstein is situated in the south-west suburbs of Wiesbaden, somewhat back beyond busy Appelallee West, a main thoroughfare which at this point follows the curve of the Rhine embankment at a safe distance.

Schierstein industrial estate looks much like any other. Little about it suggests that it is the venue for one of the most popular 'cash-and-carry' sales in West Germany. Yet twice a year since 1978 the management of the firm ZBF Vertriebs GmbH has staged open house here. During the first week of April and October retailers flock to Schierstein in hundreds, not just from all over the Federal Republic, but from most of the countries of Western Europe.

ZBF Vertrieb – the firm's title is an acronym from the German for 'Magazines, Books and Films Distribution' – has its offices and one of its three warehouses at the end of a long, dusty cul-de-sac called Schossbergstrasse, a quiet turning behind one of the main feeder roads into the estate. Schossbergstrasse runs up a slight rise, over a single-track rail crossing and then continues straight and level for half a kilometre. Lined on either side by a typical selection of low-rise industrial premises, it ends in a predictable 'banjo' turning circle.

Here, on the right, 23 is clearly identifiable by the slightly dated company logo, which features a book with the letters 'ZBF' on the cover, placed above a ribbon of movie celluloid. Two-metre-high wire mesh security gates open from the road into a large car park. At the far end of the ZBF parking lot stands a red-and-white striped marquee, easily big enough to accommodate a society wedding banquet. The marquee is set up on this spot twice a year for the five days of the great ZBF discount sale. Inside, the buffet and bar are open from early morning to 5.30 in the evening, with catering staff serving a selection of *Wurst*, cheeses, salads, beer and wine. Visitors who want to take the weight off their feet or have a relaxed business chat can pick a seat at one of the long rows of white-clothed trestle tables.

All down one edge of the car park runs the two-storey-high outside wall of ZBF's trade warehouse. Three-quarters of the way along it a glazed entrance porch leads inside through a set of sturdy plate-glass doors. The large *Herzlich Willkommen* sign above the porch reinforces the hospitality in the marquee, but there is evidence of tight security in the closed-circuit TV cameras and electronic alarm sensors on the windows.

Immediately inside the entrance stands the *Kasse*, a booth staffed by three people. It serves as a reception desk, inquiry point and cashier's office, and is a little like an informal ticket office on the London underground. A charming receptionist answers phones and makes a string of announcements over the warehouse public address system. By the *Kasse* booth a waist-high metal barrier with a one-way gate set into it admits visitors to the warehouse floor. It has the feel of a large supermarket, which is hardly surprising since that is what it used to be before it was bought by ZBF in 1978.

Inside, a babble of conversation and clatter rises to the high-peaked roof. Dozens of customers mill back and forth pushing supermarket trolleys collected from the stack at the entrance. Some of the trolleys are already piled so high with goods that some people are going back for a second.

Away to the left, rows of display racks run towards the depths of the building. Straight ahead, at the far end, ZBF staff can be seen processing orders from the racks on to trolleys and small pallets and wheeling them off to the right through a wide service exit into the yard which is the main dispatch area.

Immediately by the entrance is a small counter bar – beyond that the first book displays begin. There are customers everywhere, some browsing, some single-mindedly loading their trolleys, others systematically patrolling the displays and checking prices or examining individual items. Some are alone, some in twos and threes, some look like earnest husband-and-wife teams, and there are quite a few women. Their ages range from early twenties to late fifties. Not all the company displays are manned, but at some of the more prominent stands there are supplier representatives to drum up sales.

Half-way along the far wall, facing the entrance, a set of wide steps leads up to the second floor and a sign points to the 'Cafeteria'. The cafeteria is along to the left, the décor functional white emulsion over bare building blocks with a few large publicity posters, and the coffee and snacks are self-service. Along the corridor in the other direction are the ZBF administration and sales offices. The main ones overlook the warehouse floor. They are all light and bright with comfortable furnishings and the outward signs of an efficiently functioning business: shelving, orderly ranks of files, a photocopier and smartly dressed staff of both sexes criss-crossing between offices carrying sheaves of paper. A staff noticeboard announces the five-day ZBF sale and there is a door near the washrooms warning 'No Entry – Staff Only'.

At the bottom of the stairs to the warehouse floor, the first thing which catches the eye is a stack of 30-inch TV monitors. Beyond them is a queue of customers with fully loaded trolleys. The queue stretches back from the customer dispatch area by the *Kasse* and into the narrow aisle between display racks. It averages about a dozen people at any one time throughout the day. They pay at the *Kasse*, get their receipt, their trolleys are checked through the exit barrier and on into the packing area. Here, half a dozen ZBF staff do nothing but pack goods carefully into large cardboard boxes, then carry the boxes out into the car park and load them into the boots of the waiting Mercedes, BMWs, Volvos and Opels.

Nobody in the queue, or anybody else milling around the floor for that matter, pays any attention to the colour video running on one of the monitor screens. Which is curious – or else *they* are not – since it shows a close-up of a woman's face. She is sucking the tip of an erect penis held in one hand. The minimal soundtrack suggests that the man belonging to the penis is enjoying her attentions. The camera pulls back to reveal his identity. It is John Leslie, American veteran porn-film star. His partner is Traci Lords, likewise a star in her chosen profession. She cuts short her oral activity, straddles Leslie in a matter-of-fact way and almost casually tucks his penis into her vagina.

The graphic colour close-ups of their prolonged and vigorous intercourse continue. Still nobody takes any notice; they are all much too busy. For this is bargain time at ZBF. Pornware at mark-down rates is being bought by sex club and sex shop managers, video shop owners and small distributors who have headed for Schierstein to stock up.

'It's ZBF's boast that they stock everything,' says Uli Rotermund at Beate Uhse AG in Flensburg.[34] Another observer of the German porn scene based in Cologne remarked: 'You don't do business in the porn trade in West Germany unless you do business with ZBF.'[35] Both claims appear to be true. For ZBF is certainly the biggest wholesale distributor of pornography and sex aids in Germany, and is rivalled on a European scale only by Intex, a similar operation based in Amsterdam.

In this warehouse alone can be found shelves full of every major and minor pornographic heterosexual, lesbian and gay magazine from countless publishers all over Europe and North America, to say nothing of the literature which caters for leather, rubber, S & M and other minority tastes. All the major porn video labels from Germany, Scandinavia and the United States are in stock. Rows of cassettes line shelf after shelf, arranged by company: Caballero in Los Angeles, Mike Hunter in Cologne, RIBU – from Dr Ritterbusch in Hamburg – Rodox in Copenhagen, TABU in Bochum, UVG in Frankfurt and TVO in Hanover. Plus a hundred other labels, a thousand other titles and scores of catalogues.

VTO of Hanover has taken the trouble to organize a separate stand, with publicity leaflets, displays, video excerpts on a monitor – and a glamorous blonde behind the counter to answer inquiries. Other companies have prominent floor displays advertising the latest titles in their range. Everything is available at discount prices during these few days – a pack of ten Mike Hunter 30-minute videos goes for DM115 (about £4 each).

In other clearly defined sections across the warehouse are the dildos and vibrators, the blow-up dolls, the exotic underwear and special creams and lotions which are all part of the sex accessory trade. A peep-show booth manufacturer has installed demonstration models of the latest in his range. On a bench to one side of that someone has set up a demonstration of what was described as a 'fucking machine': its larger-than-life business end pumping away at thin air from morning to night.

ZBF is another example of a family firm in the pornography trade. It is run by general manager Georg Schmitt and his four sons, Peter, Dieter, Lothar and Günther. Of the four only forty-one-year-old Peter is on the firm's board, as deputy manager responsible for export and import. Compared with Beate Uhse, Georg Schmitt was a late starter in the trade, but when ZBF was set up in 1974 he was already running his own magazine delivery and distribution business. Some veterans of the scene say that he anticipated the change: 'There were three groups of people in the business before legalization in Germany – Horst Peter and his partner Wolf Waterschild, Charlie Brown and myself. Georg Schmitt started late – officially he didn't start until the law changed but he and his sons did take some risks between 1973 and 1975. Everyone knew it was going to be legalized in the end.'[36] So ZBF's transition to specializing in the porn sector was not difficult to make. ZBF's phenomenal growth and success are graphic evidence of the scale of the West German pornography market that has grown up since it became legal in 1975.

'We are not great seekers of publicity,' admits Peter Schmitt, sitting behind his system furniture desk and looking out over the expansive interior of the warehouse.[37] And it is probably true that few outside the porn industry would know of the enormous influence exerted by the firm. Yet every week a fleet of twelve large green Mercedes trucks loads up from the dispatch yard at Schierstein and carries an average of DM300,000 (£100,000) of ZBF stock for delivery far and wide across Germany. To keep the Schierstein warehouse at optimum inventory levels, ZBF has two back-up stores in nearby Mainz-Kastel.

ZBF has negotiated distribution deals with many of the big magazine and video producers. Around 70 per cent of the pornware they distribute is on this kind of exclusive deal.[38] Deliveries of videos alone account for 30 per cent of

ZBF's annual turnover of DM100 million (£30 million).[39] Even the Uhse organization arranges for some of its sex shops to receive selected supplies direct from Schierstein, rather than from Flensburg.

'I would estimate that overall the German sex industry, including every sector, turns over about DM500 million a year,' says Peter Schmitt. 'Of the countries we supply where pornography is legal, West Germany, with a population of 60 million, accounts for about 80 per cent of our turnover. Then come Scandinavia, Holland, France, Spain and Portugal.'[40] ZBF currently employs seventy staff and many of them have been with the company since the early days.

The Schmitt family at ZBF has made a solid profit over a twelve-year period of growth from legal trading in a country which is affluent enough to afford explicit sexual material as an offshoot of the leisure industry. 'Every week,' Peter Schmitt says, 'ZBF sends out between forty and sixty new items of merchandise. There are probably seventeen new video titles a week for us to distribute. Every week. Can you imagine what that means?'[41] ZBF may not seek the glare of publicity or see itself as a pioneer of greater sexual freedom, but it is a properly constituted limited liability company with a known market sector and an observable business profile.

Much less is known about the career and business of another porn baron whose activities have become almost as legendary as his dislike of publicity – Reuben Sturman. Based since his early beginnings in Cleveland, Ohio, Sturman is reputed to head a porn empire that covers the United States from coast to coast.

Now sixty-two years old and rumoured to have retired from full-time involvement, Reuben Sturman ran his magazine, film-loop and video distribution business for more than two decades from the offices of its original parent company Sovereign News, at 2075 East 65th Street, Cleveland, Ohio.

The open nature of pornography distribution in the broad sweeps of legal market territory throughout Europe, combined with the general willingness of leading figures there to discuss financial detail, makes it a relatively straightforward task to map out the contours of supply and demand, price and profit. In the United States, where interpretative definitions of 'obscenity' and 'pornography' have created a legal minefield, the opposite is true.

As a consequence, even the estimates made by law enforcement agencies about the turnover from the US sex business – usually given as anywhere between $4 and $7 billion a year, are almost impossible to verify, let alone quantify. But the structures which have evolved over a number of years remain much as they were described by detectives from the Washington DC Metropolitan Police Department in 1978, when after a year's undercover investigation, they reported:

> The pornography industry [in America] is characterized by a vertical distribution and pyramid structure with a limited number of documented distributors within individual states . . . Pornographic material is initially supplied to [US] national distributors, who then sell to inter-state distributors, who in turn distribute to intra-state distributors.[42]

The business career of Reuben Sturman is a living demonstration of this pattern. Indeed, Sturman must be seen as both a prime mover in, and a major beneficiary of, the haphazard growth of the pornography business in America, reflecting as it does a bewildering patchwork of differing law, from the Supreme Court, down through state legislation, city and county statutes to neighbourhood zoning regulations.

Sturman is the son of Russian émigrés who settled in the United States in the 1920s. He was educated in Cleveland and studied business at Case Western Reserve University. His first venture began after the end of the Second World War, when he went into the business of second-hand comic books, selling them out of the back of his car until he had accumulated enough funds to take over a small Cleveland tobacco and confectionery store as a more permanent base.

During the 1950s he began to stock and sell 'girlie' magazines. David Friedman, an American film producer and distributor has done business with Reuben Sturman: 'I'll stick my neck out. There was one publication that probably had more to do with the creation of the pornography industry as we know it today in this country than any other. That was *Playboy*. *Playboy* took the industry away from the sleazy backroom types selling "Tijuana Bibles". Reuben started selling *Playboy*. He had news-stands in Cleveland in hotels and other places and he suddenly sees how well this magazine is selling compared with other things. So, *Playboy* immediately had twenty or thirty cheap imitators and from there it was just a matter of time before someone was publishing something a little stronger. And Reuben would sell them because they were good business. I even used to write some of the stuff he sold – porn pocket books [paperbacks] which I wrote in two nights for $300 and they would sell for 75 cents each.'[43]

Before long, Sturman had set up the first of what eventually became a chain of warehouses to service his distribution network. He expanded on the basis of a mosaic of small, locally registered firms in Ohio and neighbouring states, giving them names that sounded like news agencies and reflected the high-sounding title of his holding company, Sovereign News: names like Noble News (Baltimore, MD), Crown News (Camden, NJ), Imperial News (Depew, NY), Majestic News (Pittsburgh, PA), and Castle News (Butler, WI) are just a few of them.

The registered personnel of such companies would not necessarily reflect the ultimate focus of control in Cleveland, though that does not mean that Sturman's name did not figure on the registered board of at least some of his subsidiaries. At least one company in downtown Toronto, Ontario, had him listed as a director, and there is a case of an English company in the early 1970s which featured Sturman for a time as its majority shareholder. Sturman is certainly the sole stockholder of Sovereign News of Cleveland and his ex-wife Ester was for a long time the company secretary and treasurer.

A 1977 US Department of Justice report attempted to give a picture of just one Sturman company chain operating in the state of Wisconsin:

> The primary distributor of hard-core pornographic material in Wisconsin is Castle News Co Inc, Butler, WI. Castle News directly controls at least thirteen retail outlets in Wisconsin and Illinois and also distributes to dozens of other retail outlets in Wisconsin, Illinois and Iowa. Reuben Sturman is the sole owner of Castle News . . . Pornographic materials are received directly from publishing firms on the West Coast or from the Sovereign News warehouse in Cleveland.[44]

The essence of Sturman's operation, at least in the magazine business, has been the ability to distribute in bulk. So, functionally, his enterprise parallels those of Georg Schmitt (ZBF) and Charlie Geerts (Intex) in Europe. Where he has invested in publishing, he has established no single, long-lasting titles like *Private* or *Color Climax* or even like *Playboy*, *Penthouse*, *Screw* or *Hustler* closer to home. He cannot even boast a distinctive house style for magazines – which rarely get beyond volume 1, number 1. Returns are rebound into 'bumpers' and sent out again. Though carrying material as explicit as any European counterpart, the magazines lack the qualities of imagination and innovation which made *Private* and *Color Climax* market leaders. Those who have met Sturman describe him variously as a gentleman, 'great company' and an entertaining raconteur: 'He is a very well spoken, very polished gentleman,' insists Dave Friedman, 'a very brilliant man.'[45] Porn film-maker Lasse Braun agrees, and adds 'I think he is funny. He likes to play games.'[46] For his part, Sturman is said to dislike thoroughly what he calls 'flamboyant people'.

As a businessman always seeking new opportunities, Sturman was never solely interested in distributing hard-core magazines. He soon diversified into 'peep-show' booths – where the customer could view short segments of a complete hard-core looped film by feeding 25 cents into a slot machine. Booths like this began to be offered to adult bookstores on a standard Sturman deal: his company would meet the installation costs – varying between $22,000 and $60,000, according to one estimate – and the store manager or owner would be entitled to 50 per cent of the takings, in cash, on the spot. Sturman acquired a company which built the booths and also tied up a supply of 8mm film loops which would run in the projectors.

By the mid-1970s the Cleveland operation had tentacles stretching as far as Los Angeles where Sturman was said to have taken control of three local companies producing pornographic loops. And, according to a Los Angeles police report at that time, '580 of 765 video arcade machines are owned by companies controlled by Reuben Sturman'.[47]

Sturman also saw the potential of sex paraphernalia and he purchased the Doc Johnson Love Shop chain – America's equivalent of the Beate Uhse shops in West Germany. The manufacturing facilities include Marché Products in North Hollywood, Los Angeles. The economics of this slowly expanding corporate structure gave Sturman access to considerable sums of money which he used on several occasions to bankroll the production of loops for his peep-shows and also, during the 1970s, full-length porn feature films using established directors.

These ventures may have been something of a risk, but the arrival of the porn video cassette provided a cast-iron money-spinning certainty. Sturman's interests in the porn video industry now seem to be centred on a Los Angeles-based production company called Vidco and a network of distribution companies centred on General Video of America in Cleveland. He earlier had an interest in Caballero Control Corporation (the producers of the *Swedish*

*Erotica* titles) but pulled out of that. More recently, he tr
ferred to Caballero his interest in a New York comp
called Leisure Time.

Belated media interest in the Sturman organization began to emerge in the wake of grand jury hearings in Cleveland during the summer of 1985. The indictments filed on 27 June 1985 alleged that Sturman had evaded payments of millions of dollars in federal taxes by laundering money through offshore bank accounts in the Cayman Islands, and one local reporter summed up his findings as follows:

> [Sturman] structured his many companies, from retail stores to video production firms, in a honeycomb of nominees, false names and dead associates to avoid local obscenity prosecutions . . . the corporate structure has grown hydra-headed over the years, apparently with the more serious intent of avoiding taxes.[48]

Yet over the years, Sturman has been no stranger to the attentions of law enforcement. The FBI regularly listed him in its reports on the porn trade in the United States with the specific aim of connecting him directly to organized crime. But the Bureau seemed reluctant to go beyond the general assertion:

> Although La Cosa Nostra does not physically oversee the day-to-day workings of the majority of pornography business in the United States, it is apparent that they have 'agreements' with those involved . . . in allowing these people to operate independently by paying off members of organized crime for the privilege of being allowed to operate in certain geographical areas.[49]

The US Department of Justice had reluctantly come to the same conclusion the previous year:

> Reuben Sturman . . . though not directly connected to La Cosa Nostra, is a key figure in the pornography industry and seems to be well established in California.[50]

The nearest Sturman has come to the inside of a gaol was his arrest following the massive FBI 'MIPORN' (Miami Porn) sting in 1980. Charges against Sturman were subsequently dropped, and although a number of his business associates including Sovereign News executive Scott Dormen have been gaoled, Sturman has so far managed to stay free.

In early October 1987, as research and writing on this book were in their final stage, the District Attorney's office in Las Vegas, Nevada, announced that Sturman had been named as a principal in a grand jury indictment against a local pornography distributor. No date was fixed for the court hearings.

Sturman lives in the up-market Shaker Heights district of Cleveland. Now divorced, his three children grown up, one son David is a partner in Sovereign News. A reputed fitness fanatic, Sturman Sr occasionally leads a lunch-hour callisthenics class at a YMCA gymnasium in the city, which even sports a wall plaque thanking him for his contributions to the organization.

Whatever the basis for any criminal charges against him – and his companies have been fined more than once in the past for transporting obscene materials over state lines – it is clear that Sturman has been at the centre of a highly lucrative empire which has carved out areas of operation from the mid-West to the Pacific Coast of the United States. It has achieved an affable commercial *modus operandi* with major East Coast firms such as Star Distributors of New York, which appears to be under the direct control of the Mafia.

For its part, the Internal Revenue Service (IRS) alleges that between 1978 and 1982 Reuben Sturman had a personal income of $3.4 million, though Sturman disputes this and puts the figure at a mere $384,000. IRS charges of tax evasion amount to a total of over $1.6 million for that five-year period alone. At the time of writing, these charges are yet to be heard in full but, whatever the outcome, it is unlikely that Reuben Sturman will fade away into poverty. The contradictory strictures of US law have undoubtedly made him a rich man, though his power as a porn baron may be on the wane.

There is a strong establishment of European figures who qualify as porn barons in terms of the influence they have had, the products they have sustained and the money they have made. Any of the following would relate colourful and entertaining tales of deals done, of illegal shipments delivered, battles with the authorities and fortunes accumulated. Leif Hagen and Rolf Rahm have major publishing and distribution empires in Scandinavia. Charlie Geerts' Amsterdam-based Intex is second only to ZBF, and veteran West German publisher Horst Peter of Essen who recently took over the European distribution of Caballero videos from Geerts.

One man who looks as though his fortunes are very much in the ascendant is Hans Moser who operates out of the heartland of Anglo-Saxon bourgeois respectability: the staid province of Brunswick in West Germany. In the course of five years Moser and his wife, sex model Teresa Orlovski, have made the firm VTO – and its brand name Foxy Lady – a force to be reckoned with, not just in Germany, but in the international porn video and magazine business.

'If we're talking about pornography, we're not talking about eroticism – because eroticism is nice, but naïve. It's not realistic, it's bullshit.' Hans Moser, forty-two-year-old German pornographer, born at a time when Beate Uhse was delivering planes for the Luftwaffe, is indulging in a little philosophy. 'Erotica is nice to have, but you can't keep it. The realistic in life is more important.'[51]

He is sitting in an armchair in his office at the headquarters of VTO (Verlag Teresa Orlovski – Teresa Orlovski Publishing). Looked at from the street, the big house on Dammstrasse is just one more quiet suburban detached home in Winnhorst, Hanover's well-heeled 'green belt'. Moser's parents came to Hanover from Romania towards the end of the Second World War – his father was Hungarian and his mother German. They settled and he never left.

On one side of Moser's office is a huge video monitor

with a studio-quality sound system and speakers to match built into a custom cabinet. On the screen Moser is playing the trailer for the latest VTO porn feature *Born for Love*. By every technical measure its quality is outstanding – and the VCR itself is only VHS standard. There is imaginative use of some of the most expensive digital effects in the title sequences and the split-screen trailers for the sexual encounters in the film. All the visual proof of what many people in the porn industry say about Moser. The man is dedicated to the perfection of quality in his products. Just as he is devoted to the person and the packaging and promotion of the woman who stars in many of his videos and VTO's leading magazines, his wife Teresa Orlovski, the woman who has given her name – and growing reputation – to the company they run together.

'I'm a craftsman,' says Moser. 'If you are naïve and live only in dreams, then you are no use to this society in this world. An artist has the right to certain naïvety, certain dreams, but he's not a good artist if he doesn't see the reality on the other side. He has to split off his personality. I don't even like the word "art", because so many artists are unable to make a living for themselves. If I can make a living, be myself and keep my creativity, then I can be an artist . . .'[52]

Moser began his working life as a carpenter, then changed to dealing in furniture and became a salesman for a big warehouse. He married early, in 1965, and started to take an interest in photography 'out of a kind of frustration'. He bought a camera and his new-found hobby led him to do some freelance work. He came across adverts for mail order model shots in *Vu*, a Danish 'girlie' and nude magazine published out of Copenhagen by Sven Nielson. They triggered off Moser's ambition to take erotic pictures and sell them in the then illegal German market.[53]

Before long Moser was tempted to visit Copenhagen. There he found not only the glamourized nude shots he was familiar with: 'Picture sets, slides, and 8mm films – all of them in black and white. The films were made in Soho using prostitutes there, and they were the best films I've seen in my life, they were so horny and natural. I was very young and this was the first contact I'd had with such material. I was in the in-between stage of being a naïve person to one with experience. I was a young, green boy, wet behind the ears. I still had a certain illusion about eroticism.'

It is Moser's conviction that the pornography trade as it has developed in Europe had its origins in England. Much of what was produced in Soho during the 1960s was sent over to Denmark, which was the first country that changed its laws to accept such pornware. Sven Nielsen had a laboratory in Copenhagen which helped 'the gentlemen of Soho' to process and duplicate their film loops.

Moser began to take still pictures in Germany and transport them in person to Copenhagen for publication in porn magazines there. On his way back into Germany he smuggled magazines and films for clandestine sale in his home country. He is reluctant to talk about this stage in his career which pre-dates the legalization of pornography in the Federal Republic:

> At my age it was a kind of naïvety, but it was stupid. It was an adventure, in a way, and sometimes when I remember it, it makes me laugh. But I tried to forget that period. I have to concentrate on what is happening now.[54]

This is an understandable reaction because Moser was – by his own account – arrested four times and served short gaol sentences for smuggling or distributing pornography. When he was not having trouble with one side of the law, Moser managed to get himself into difficulty with the other side. During one smuggling trip from Copenhagen back into northern Germany, he was robbed on the train.[55] The effects on him and his immediate family of this irregular way of earning a living were naturally disruptive.

Moser resolved to concentrate on production and leave the more hazardous business of distribution to others. With minimum funds to pay the bills for the expensive processes required for colour printing, he decided to cut costs by setting up his own facilities to do this, teaching himself such complex operations as colour separation.

Between 1973 and 1976 he learned many of the skills on which the success of VTO has grown. He secured finance from Denmark to shoot colour film loops – probably from the Theander brothers – keeping the stills that he shot on the set for publication in his own magazines in Germany. By 1982 it was clear that he was not going to survive economically in such a hand-to-mouth existence. He went bankrupt.

But 1982 was also the year when he was contacted unexpectedly by an unknown model from the town of Bochum. She enclosed a Polaroid photograph of herself and offered to pose for him. The approach was to change his fortunes dramatically and bring stardom to a Polish divorcée called Teresa Orlovski. An English artist who contributes to one of their magazines later observed:

> Hans had searched all his life for a woman to be his partner. Of the succession of beautiful ladies I've seen him with, none of them would really put anything into the business. They'd take things out, but none would put in. But Teresa absolutely lapped it up![56]

Hans Moser himself praises Teresa as a strong woman with many talents. Apart from a sultry sensuality which was to transform the style and content of his magazines, Teresa also proved to have a good head for business:

> Hans had bought himself a house that year just on the outskirts of Hanover. It had belonged to the man who virtually built Hanover, his company was called Hanamag. It was a gigantic nineteenth-century firm which still exists, but of course much smaller now. It builds

lorries and ships, cranes and railways and bridges and viaducts and hospitals and harbours and . . . It's huge! A veritable Krupps!

He built this house on a little hill, an enormous granite house of five floors, like a castle with a tower at each corner. His office overlooked the railway sidings and the factories and the other side of the house opened on to the countryside.

And this is what Hans bought as his headquarters. He started turning it into an absolutely spectacular place. About a third of the way through this, having spent about a million pounds on it, Teresa came along. She said, 'It's too big! We'll never get it done. Cut your losses, sell this place, we'll find somewhere smaller, because this is going to cost another £5 million to get it finished.'

So that's what he did. But he remained a partner in it and sold it to a brothel. So now it's a very smart bordello! It doesn't actually feature in *The Great Bordellos of the World*, but in the coming edition it must! So what he's got instead is another place which is a huge house, but very much a suburban German *Haus*![57]

In August 1982 the new company was registered in Teresa's name, since Moser was still an undischarged bankrupt, and the two partners sat down to thrash out a new formula for success. Moser refused to be restricted by the conservative demands of the major distributors like Georg Schmitt's ZBF. They resolved to devote all the funds they could raise to hiring the best creative talent and to acquiring the most sophisticated print and video publishing technology. The result was a stable of new magazines with titles like *Foxy Lady*, *Sweet Little 16*, and *Lady Domina*, side by side with a range of video cassettes packaged to the same high level of merchandising.

Looking back, Moser says: 'The concept was right. It took a year, but we went for the highest quality then attainable.' That strategy also demanded an original marketing approach which would be centred on Teresa as corporate president, Teresa as magazine publisher, Teresa as leader writer, Teresa as sex counsellor, Teresa as publicity package and – most crucially – Teresa as the on-camera sex superstar.

Such a determined commitment to quality does not come cheap. VTO's current five-year capital investment programme is geared to the construction of a purpose-built video studio complex which will be equipped with high-tech recording and post-production facilities from top world suppliers in this field: Ampex in America, Abekas and Questech in England and Sony in Japan. The hardware already installed has attracted interest from a visiting team of experts working for Richard Branson's Virgin empire. The money invested so far amounts to DM3 million (just over £1 million) but the final balance sheet will show a sizeable commitment of DM30 million (£10 million).

Henry Hayler and his wife made their mark on the porn photography scene of nineteenth-century Europe. If any of the present generation of pornographers is going to threaten the hitherto unchallenged dominance of Berth Milton, Rolf Rahm, Peter Theander, and the American porn video mills, it is the unusually dynamic husband and wife partnership of Hans Moser and Teresa Orlovski.

If there is any clear recipe for success as a porn baron, it does not include a disregard for the law (some have never been awarded so much as a parking ticket), or even an imposing or outrageous personality (although Beate Uhse would be a valued guest at most dinner tables, most of the Schmitt family would pass their time at parties standing in a corner). The essential ingredients would seem to be perseverance and business acumen – but neither of those is special to the porn industry. What is certainly indispensable is an ability to motivate others to participate in the business: especially those who will appear at the pointed end of a camera – the foot-soldiers of porn.

# 3

## *The Monkey Inside Yourself: The Foot-soldiers of Porn*

'My first hard-core experience was on 1 October 1972. The film was made with a friend of mine who made me write the movie – I was not paid for it. I starred in it and I was blown by a girl named Sue Kay on a rug in a garage in Venice, California.'[1]

Bill Margold's experience may well be typical. The models who pose for sex magazines and the performers who gyrate in X-rated videos are the foot-soldiers of the porn industry. Without them, the porn barons would have no empires. But how are they recruited? Do they really volunteer? A willingness to perform sexual acts for the cold lens of a Panasonic video camera is beyond the imagination of many people. So how closely do the movie stars of the porn industry match the popular conception that they must be drug-crazed or (merely) deviant? Are these people seduced, bullied or even kidnapped into the trade?

Undoubtedly it is a special kind of person who will suck a penis or ejaculate over a woman's face in the full glare of studio lights. Many people might even be reluctant to admit to performing such acts in private. So what is the motivation if it isn't coercion? Perhaps it is no more than old-fashioned greed? Could it be the sex itself? Or does it have something to do with ego or the desire to make some mark in the world, no matter how?

Certainly a dash of exhibitionism would not be overlooked on the job application form, but is that any different from the role it plays in the psychological make-up of a performer in any other branch of show business? And whereas most movie stars positively revel in off-screen publicity, how do their colleagues in the X-rated genre deal with public and media attitudes to their extraordinary vocations?

What are the specific physical attributes required for the job? Is personality more important than the mere engrossment of anatomical statistics?

Bill Margold, *enfant terrible* of the porn video industry, lives in a small, comfortable West Hollywood apartment which betrays little evidence of high living. Visitors will note the scores of teddy-bears occupying all available spaces before they spot the 'his and hers' archives of porn videos.

Draped across an old armchair is the taciturn and unglamorous figure of 'Viper', a sophomore of the business. Margold warns guests that his companion is both shy and suspicious. The warmest welcome is from an old black-and-white cat called Hard Core.

Handsome is the last thing Bill Margold would claim to be. Six feet tall with reddish-brown hair and an untidy moustache, he wears frame spectacles which look like a relic from the wardrobe of some 1950s nostalgia movie. His face is punctuated with the occasional mole or wart. But his fulsome recollections tumble out with practised ease, for in fifteen years in the porn movie industry he has never shunned publicity.

> I originally intended to be the George Plimpton of pornography. I wanted to live out people's fantasies and write stories about them.
>
> After getting my college degree in journalism, I spent two and a half years working as a probation officer at

Central Juvenile Hall. For six years I sold dog food door-to-door. Now I am an actor in X-rated films. So my life has been diverse, to say the least.

I stumbled into the business when I was writing on an underground newspaper called *Spectrum West*. There was a gentleman who ran a model agency, called at that time Sunset International. He called up saying that we hadn't put his ad in the paper. I indignantly rushed off to defend the honour of the paper only to discover that the man was a 220lb ex-Hell's Angel. I decided that discretion was the better part of valour and said I'd write an article about him and he was thrilled.

I got interested in what he was doing and said I'd run his office if he left me alone. At the same time I wanted to be in an X-rated movie. At first, only in order to *die* – I simply wanted to get killed in a movie – cowboys and Indians, cops and robbers – I just wanted to get killed on screen.

Well, eventually, I was shot in a thing called *The Goddaughter*. Shortly after that they said do you wanna do a sex scene? These were the days of simulation – not even hard core.

Margold's total recall of his experiences in the Venice garage even extends to the colour of the rug:

It was yellow, for a very interesting reason. Some cat had decided to piss on the rug. I'd thought that I was getting excited, I was sweating, I was aroused! But no, it was because of some idiot cat! I remember the cat sitting opposite, smiling at me during the shooting, because I was using his litter box as my resting place!

The very next day, I went up north to San Francisco and shot for seven hours a thing called *Sexual Stamina – The Diary of a Sex Star*. That was not a movie, that was a book. It had five cum shots and the guy asked me at the end 'Why did you go off so much?' And I said 'No one told me not to.' I was very naïve about all of this.[2]

Over the intervening years, Margold has tried a little of everything; directing, writing, criticizing, reviewing, and publicizing as well as acting. For ten years he also ran what he claims was the biggest nude-modelling agency in the world. Included among his 'discoveries' were Seka, Serena, Kelly Nicholls, Jennifer West, Pat Manning, Tiffany Clark, Mike Ranger, Renee Summers, Bunny Bleu, Maria Tortuga – all familiar names to the *aficionados* of video porn.

Another person who made her own way into the porn business was Paula Meadows. In stark contrast to Margold, Paula is English and frightfully middle-class. That background had a lot to do with her decision. In London she shares a flat within sight of Tower Bridge with writer Frank Russell and could easily be mistaken for the owner of a sensible suburban boutique. She is now known as a painter of erotic art under the name of Lynn Paula Russell, but it was as an actress that she appeared in the stage show *Hair*.

Far from being seduced into the porn business, she seems to have pushed herself into the porn scene with some determination. She explains:

> I started off doing some modelling for magazines. I needed to break out and explore – I was a bit repressed then. Some of the photographs were for export but the others were soft stuff for England. No one's ever seen them as far as I know. No one ever recognized me from them at all. Anyway, when I was modelling I met someone I'd worked with in one of the sessions and she said that a chap called Mike Freeman had just made a hardcore video and it was very good. It had been made illegally for distribution in this country. Once I'd taken my clothes off I thought, what the hell? You know, you get this feeling that it doesn't really matter after a while.

So Paula met Mike Freeman and decided to go ahead. The first of the illicit videos she appeared in was called *Truth or Dare*. The script, written by Frank Russell, was based on the children's game. 'The second thing was called *Happy Birthday*. It started off fairly conventionally with two people bumping into each other in the street. My character gets talking to this housewife and I find out that her husband wants to spank her and she doesn't like it. He's got a birthday coming up, so I say why don't I become the birthday present? I like being spanked, so he can spank me for his birthday! It was all right, but they didn't have much money to spend on it.' Paula later split with Freeman acrimoniously and decided to pursue her new career in New York.[3]

Bill Margold's proven track record for talent spotting meant nothing when he first tried to promote his friend Viper to the industry. He was confident that she had the right qualifications. 'Her background is so incredibly diverse,' he says on her behalf. 'It includes being a member of the American Ballet Theatre. She was then a marine for six years. They threw her out of the Marine Corps and she came here from the East Coast a year ago.' Viper has a slight figure and a waif-like face with only a certain hardness about the eyes to betray the rigours of boot camp. But anyone who has seen any of her forty-five hard-core videos will have a question: Where did she get the tattoo from? The tattoo is a sinuous leopard which crawls down from beneath her left breast towards her thigh.

'It was nothing to do with the marines. It took nine months and it's a gorgeous tattoo. It's something that is analogous to her own personality and she refuses to cover it up,' says Margold, oblivious of the fact that, given Viper's line of business, a cover-up would be a pretty fruitless exercise. 'The industry, in its ignorance, didn't want to use her at first,' continued Margold, 'because she is different, because she has the tattoo, and because she is pierced in many places . . .' The piercing had nothing to do with the Marine Corps, either. 'The way I finally did it, I took her to a convention and put her in the booth with me and showed her tattoo off to thousands of people! And, as the industry itself began to walk by, they noticed her. They were to find out that she was better than they could ever dream, because she was literally open to anything that came up! Now they use her. Not on an ultra-regular basis, but they use her.'

Forty-five video appearances in twelve months is not 'ultra-regular' in hard-core Hollywood. 'I guess besides being her lover and her friend, I'm also her manager – which I derive no profit from. I have great hopes for her. She's about to go off this weekend and work in San Francisco on an X-rated wrestling video. Because wrestling's in vogue, they're gonna do some kind of "Wrestle-Mania" and they'll put her in as one of the hard-bitten wrestlers who screws her opponent into submission.' It was uncertain whether the other actors knew of Viper's Marine Corps service.[4]

The only thing Brigitte ever punched was the keyboard of a computer display. Looked at one way, she is the hard-working head of a single-parent family of two children who puts in a regular nine-to-five at a local government computer centre near Stockholm. From another viewpoint, she is a statuesque Swedish blonde who has a penchant for outrageous clothes and a mischievous sense of humour. She remembered how she was 'recruited' by a local journalist.

'I met Jan Sjölin [a writer with the Swedish men's magazine *FiB Aktuellt*] in a disco. I was wearing a dress open at the side and Jan said to me, "If you can go out like that, then you can do pictures too!" Something like that. And he told me that he knew of this guy who was interested in doing some photos. So I said *ja*, I can try. Then I started to take small jobs. That was many years ago, now.'[5]

For Brigitte, it was as simple as that. But is this always the case? Are there as many jobs as people who want them, and what are the qualifications? Bill Margold talks about the situation in the porn movie business: 'There are probably only about a hundred X-rated performers who do this as a regular way of life in the United States. Out of that one-fourth of them are men. The rest are a continually changing body of women.'

He goes on to explain that the long-term prospects are better for men.

> A girl can last as little as a year, but you have to understand something about the males in this business. The predominant – the King [John Holmes], Harry Reems [the male lead in *Deep Throat*], Jamie Gillis, Eric Edwards, and myself – have been in the business fifteen years or more. Then you have John Leslie, Paul Thomas, Herschel Savage, Joey Silvera, Mark Stevens – there are a dozen or so men that have been in over ten years. You can't say that about the women. Once a guy gets his dick into this business, and it functions even marginally, it stays in! There are only so many 300-hitters [in baseball] each year. I'm blessed to be able to survive as long as I have.
>
> Girls don't last that long, I think it's harder for them, but there are exceptions. Georgina Spelvin must have started a lot later than the age of thirty and she lasted about ten years, maybe more. Vanessa del Rio's been in it maybe ten years now, but has not done as much as everybody thinks. Her screen presence is phenomenal – she's just larger than life. Seka, for all the touting of her, has not even been in the business ten years yet.[6]

So it seems that, given the higher rate of turnover, there are more opportunities for women. Many – including Paula Meadows – started relatively late in life and brought a more mature attitude to what they were doing. But Margold does not advise waiting: 'America wants to see youth. Not under-age youth, but they want to see the eighteen to twenty-one-year-old, the baby-faced one. They appeal to the "dirty old man", supposedly, who wants to dream about going to bed with his daughter. So if he can see a surrogate daughter rolling around on the screen, more power to him. I don't question anybody's fantasy. I try and satisfy as many as possible. So, the younger the better. A lot of these kids can't even read their names – so how are they ever going to be able to play any role other than bimbo?'[7]

Of course, the means by which performers get into the business do not explain why they choose such an unusual career in the first place. Margold said he wanted to live out other folks' sexual fantasies and then write about them, and people might speculate how long the research will take before he sits down at the typewriter.

'I didn't go after being a star in the industry. I got into it not for sex and not for money, but for glory – I got into it to become immortal! Essentially,' he insists, 'the X-rated performer is a shy person who gets a chance to be what he or she has never been before, when the camera goes on. The ultimate thrill is walking into a theatre and seeing yourself on the screen. On the *big theatrical screen*, you're up there HUGE! Ultra-bigger than life and you hear the audience get off behind what you're doing. And I've never, ever had such a reward in my life! I've lived out the American fantasy. I spent part of last week being blown by an assortment of lovely women, and getting paid for it. I'm not flaunting that, it's just part of my act.'

As the ovation by the 'shy' Margold subsides, Viper makes her first contribution to the discussion: 'Most of the guys wanna get laid.' Margold concedes the point: 'OK, so the guys want the sex – which is going to be constant, and the girls want the money. Those are the overt reasons. The subverse reason is simply this – they want the attention. They are starving for attention and this is the way they're going to get it.'

In London, Paula Meadows was far from happy with these arguments. 'I don't think this is a very penetrating assessment actually. It's helped to strengthen my ego, I think. I haven't got that much money out of it. And as far as sex is concerned, I can get sex without getting it in front of the camera. I think there are different reasons for everybody.' Paula's individual motives certainly turned out to be different: 'I'll tell you why I started, why I made my first film. And why it had to be in front of the camera. It once occurred to me that I was very much aware of eyes on me and wondered what the eyes were. Whenever I was actually doing anything that was a bit sexy or a bit naughty, I always imagined someone looking at me.' Appearing in pornography would have the effect of bringing up and working through an emotional barrier. But wasn't it all a bit drastic for someone from her background? 'I woke up one morning and asked "Who am I *not* doing all these things for? I don't give a shit about them! Why am I not doing all these things?" And that started it off.'

For Paula, the experience was as rewarding as it proved to be remedial. 'I think I enjoy sex more in private, but I enjoy the performing in an exciting and narcissistic sort of way.' Is it important to be an exhibitionist? 'I think there is a great need. It's all very naughty! But there is no socially acceptable way of doing that. The fact that it might be illegal gives it more of a *frisson*.'

In Bill Margold's West Hollywood bear cave, Viper was now in full flow. 'You have truly to be an exhibitionist. I'm talking about a sexual turn-on, they're naturally exhibitionists. They *want* people to see them fuck. A lot of the men want people to see them fucking gorgeous women. They want to make people jealous. A lot of women want men to lust after them. They want men to think "Wow! I'd like to really stick my dick in her mouth!" They want that kind of attention, because most of us look like him [pointing to Margold] and me. I mean, we're just not the kind of people who you just walk in on and have like instant lust!'

And Brigitte's recipe for success? 'Well, you should love it! You have to be an exhibitionist. That's very important. When I started with this, I liked to see the beautiful pictures . . . You know, I'm not so bad looking. I have quite nice tits. To see this, you know, it was nice . . . When I see these beautiful girls in bed and the – how do you call it? the milieu? It looks so soft and so nice. I wanted to be like them.'

Viper dismisses the view that the desire for fame is significant. 'Most people in the industry don't care if they're stars. They want to be accepted within the X-rated industry, but they don't necessarily want to be accepted elsewhere. They are not like Seka who was on a marketing trip from the very beginning. Most of the women will come in, make their money and leave.'

So, if the performances are not for the fame, perhaps they are for the fortune? Brigitte agrees: 'Most of the girls I have met in this business do it for the money. They don't care how dirty the jobs are they do, just that they get good money for it. You know, the producers can use these girls as they like. They can pay them under the rate because they know they will do *anything* for the money. But if you know what you are doing, if they can see that you are good, they will pay what you want. If they pay me well, I shall also do a good job.'

Of course Brigitte has a full-time job and only appears in porn productions when she feels like it. She admits that she couldn't do it all the time, but that has as much to do with the size of the market for her talents in Scandinavia as it has with her willingness. 'It's easier to work like I do, just sometimes. There aren't any models in Sweden that are full time, I think. In that case they go around the world for so many months a year and then come back home for a couple of months. But I don't think I'd like to do it all the time – even if I didn't have any children. Sometimes when they call me, I can say "No, not this time. I'm not interested." Next time I can call *them* and say, hey, have you got something? I have to feel excited to do it.'

If those are the essential tools of the trade, and good motives for sitting around the agent's or producer's waiting-room, there must be as many wrong reasons for contemplating a future before the pornographer's camera. Viper: 'Yeah, there's a lot of people like Linda Lovelace. They'll like the idea when they start, they'll see nothing wrong with overt sexual activity and taking home money for performing sex. Then, all of a sudden, they'll grow morals, all of a sudden they'll believe – like 90 per cent of America – that sex is dirty. Someone'll say "You did that?

Oh! You and a puppy-dog? You gotta be kidding!"'

'And Linda *did* fuck a dog . . .', Margold added.[8] After her leading role in *Deep Throat*, Linda Lovelace became the industry's first major star, her name constantly on the lips of dinner guests at early 1970s cocktail parties. But Lovelace was to leave the industry and campaign vigorously against pornography. She is on record as insisting that she was forced to perform in the movie, a gun being held – literally – to her head while she performed the acts of fellation. Those involved in the production have strongly denied that she was in any way unwilling. Brigitte is typical of those denying any coercion: 'Nobody forced me to do what I do, nobody. I do it because I like it!'

Once inside porn's magic circle, what can the novitiate expect? Some performers come from fringe theatre, fewer from the conventional movie industry, though they at least should be familiar with the organized chaos of a film set. Others are likely to find it bewildering. 'They're not going to get the scripts until they walk on to the set. There's no pre-production and planning of these things,' warns Margold. In tones reminiscent of the late Alfred Hitchcock, the former director describes the shooting in uncompromising terms: 'I would just take a herd of cattle into one room and say "Ok, bang your brains out!" And they'll say, "What movie is this?" and I'll say, "It doesn't matter, go ahead and bang your brains out!"'

'First night nerves' are not unknown and under the pressures of a low budget, it is understandable why reliable blood is preferred to fresh blood. 'We're scared of trying to break a new guy in and find that he's going to lie there dead on the bed waiting patiently for something to happen,' says Margold. 'Under the pressure, very few rise to the occasion!' In view of that, it is hardly surprising that some would-be performers never actually perform at all. 'Women don't show up, men don't show up. It doesn't have anything to do with first time or hundredth time, they just decide not to be there. You just adapt the script. Some of the regular performers double book or triple book their days. I've had to go and get people and baby-sit them all the way to the location and then baby-sit them through the shooting.' Apparently that need not be a speedy exit for the newcomer: 'They're given many, many chances to continually hang themselves because they are very valuable.'

Even when the roll-call of crew and cast is complete, things may not run smoothly. Bill Margold again: 'I usually bring toys to the set to pacify Jerry Butler. I'll bring little plastic men, or little dolls for him to play with, to pacify him, because he needs his toys or he goes nuts! He's a nice person, and he is a very good performer. But the man will disrupt the set faster than anybody else I've ever met – he just starts rolling around and making noises and jokes. I bring toys for him and he chews the heads off them or something. That's just Jerry for you, though, there's only one Jerry Butler.'

The experiences of Paula Meadows in New York were a little more encouraging, but she pointed out that it hasn't always been like that: 'A lady I liked very much was Gloria Leonard. She will tell you that in the early days conditions were appalling. The money was appalling and they were often shooting in places with no running water – just someone's back garage or something. They were pushed around, touched up by everybody. But conditions are nothing like that now! When I worked in the States I was very pleased to find that things were totally different from Europe. It was very professional. I mean there was no groping of people backstage or any mucking about. God! Those girls wouldn't stand for that at all! No extraneous people were allowed in to ogle.' Of course, in the United States, production levels are so high, the stars have to work with each other on a regular basis. Unprofessional attitudes would get in the way of making money and would not be tolerated. 'I mean, we had scripts, proper scene breakdowns,' Paula enthused. 'We even had a dialogue coach! He used to come round and take us through our lines. Well, all the people who work in reputable porno, those who work with the well paid, with the *good* producers, with good directors, feel they're a cut above those who slum around. There are things they definitely won't do and they pride themselves on good performances and being well turned out.'

Everyone in the industry – men and women – agrees that the male performers have the most difficult task. Even Bill Margold concedes that the visible evidence of the effectiveness of his talent is the thing that worries him most. 'Just recently, after a long lay-off while I was married [to porn actress and director, Drea], I've gotten back in front of a camera and can perform hard core again. It's a mixed blessing, because I always wonder if I'm going to be able to function and wouldn't like to work with the same person each time. It's always this "first time in the back seat of a car" mentality, so anything that happens is usually going to happen by sheer attrition, if nothing else.' Even working with his live-in companion doesn't necessarily help: 'The only time Viper and I have worked together is a blow-job sequence in *The Devil Does Debbie in Dallas* – or *Debbie Does the Devil in Dallas* – they're all the same. Because I'd not gotten a chance to get myself up – I like to get myself up – Viper sucked on a marginally limp cock. But my cock is among the top five in size in this business and, even limp, it's bigger than most. When it does want to play it fills a mouth and a couple of hands and everybody's happy. Of course, I have the requisite ability to come on cue. I'll give you a cum shot in ten seconds, with absolutely *no* emotion. I'll just crank out a cum shot. But it's *not* for physical pleasure! No guy should have to go off more than twice a day because, if he does, he may leave his dick on the floor the third time.'

Margold illustrated the work rate of an established male star: 'I had one of the great people in the business, Joey Silvera, living here – he's a very close friend. He did like five videos in seven days and he didn't know what video he was in! He got up one morning, "What am I doing today? Who am I screwing today? Where am I going?" That's sort of sad.' Such a work schedule would seem to demand high levels of overall physical fitness and Margold continues to worry about becoming worn out.

> If there's not going to be a face shot, it's going to be up over the ass, doggy style. That's very easy to shoot, although my knees don't like it any more! When we did *Debbie Does the Devil in Dallas*, I had a sex scene in a bathtub, and it's not fun in a bathtub! I cracked a little bone in my kneecap, you can hear it on camera – they left it in there! Ah-hah, that's your knee! I said 'We're not doing much of this . . . I'm beginning to hurt. She's uncomfortable too!' But she said 'Oh, no – I'm enjoying it!' I said 'Shut up – you're uncomfortable!' I'm certainly not like the King when he was in his prime. To watch him work was like watching a surgeon. He would prepare the person and then it was an art to watch him work. I am not that artistic, I am a lumbering, uncoordinated ox when I do this stuff.'

From the earliest days, the porn movie industry has employed women called 'fluffers' to help male performers prepare themselves for on-screen action. Says Margold:

> I was in a thing called *The Young Like It Hot*, where I was flown into San Francisco specifically for one single scene and an hour and a half later I went home. It was like a hit man! I came in, did my job, and went home. It was a masturbation scene and the director said 'Do you want me to bring in a fluffer to get you ready?' and I told him, 'I've been doing this since I was twelve years old.' Now, fluffers are a lot less common. In the old film industry there were girls who used to help out, because the female stars thought it was beneath them to do that.
>
> I've done a few 'inserts', where the guy can't get up or get off. Of course, if you look real close, the size of the

poor man's cock must have changed immensely, but no one cares! In *Hot Chocolate* Tony El-Ay had six cum shots because the other guys couldn't do a thing. They were all having trouble and he had to keep on punching in everybody's shot! He got $25 every extra pop-shot. And the guy who failed had to pay him that. It had to come out of his pay. That's only fair. If you can't fire your rounds and you have to use someone else's bullets, you gotta pay for it. I've done it a couple of times, but it's very demeaning to the guy who can't function.

Given the circumstances, there have to be moments of high comedy. With or without Jerry Butler. Margold recalls the first time he encountered John Holmes:

> The King has the biggest dick in the business and proves that all men are not created equal. I had known of the King for years, but I'd never met him. We were doing a movie called *Disco Dolls and Hot Skin in 3D* and I was on the ground being blown by Lesllie [*sic*] Bovee and the King was above me being played with by three girls. All of a sudden, his dick came out over my head, it just hung out over my head like the space ship in the opening shot of *2001*! I'd never seen anything like that in my life. It is truly the most awesome-looking thing I have ever seen!

Most of the problems are caused by the contortions the performers are expected to undertake. 'We were shooting a video,' Brigitte recalls with a smile. 'One of the guys was lying on the floor in a bad position. He was almost starting to shake – because his muscles were tense. I was starting on this guy, I was licking his ass. They didn't want to stop the camera because it looked so good, everything! My fantasy was going on, and I was turning around on this guy and saw that he was red in the face because he didn't want to say "Stop now!" because everything was so good . . . And he said after, "Oh shit! I got horny and it hurt! Everything was bad at the same time that it was good."'

Where do the performers draw the line? What sort of things won't they do? 'Some things are obscene,' judges Paula Meadows. 'It doesn't mean you musn't do them but they are obscene because they're ugly. It's the context they're used in, I think. And if you want to fist-fuck somebody, generally you want to give them a bit of humiliation and pain. People might want to have humiliation and pain but I don't necessarily want to see that.' Paula went on to describe an incident in 1985 during the shooting of the video feature *Young Nympho* in New York.

The director was Lasse Braun, the European porn scene's equivalent of Orson Welles. 'The men said he was disgusting, because he wanted anal scenes. We don't want to do that, it's disgusting! Even the cameraman thought it was disgusting. He thought Lasse was a terrible director and that everything was awful. They do it now, but they didn't do it when I was there. When I was doing it, they weren't doing it at all.'

Bill Margold has a possible explanation for this culture clash. 'People would come into my office and I would say: "Will you do anal sex?" "Oh, yeah, I do that all the time . . ." I'd say "Really?" I'd ask this to *guys*! "You'd take a dig up the ass?" "No! *No!*" "Would you fuck someone in the ass?" "Oh, no *no!*" So I'd ask "So what's anal sex?" "Going to the bathroom?" They don't know! They're so incredibly uneducated in the United States!'

This seems to imply that the demarcation problem is an American one. Swedish actress Brigitte thought perhaps it might be, then qualified her view.

> I do everything! They haven't asked me to do something that I wouldn't like. I have dirty fantasies myself, so I do things they wouldn't dream of! For example, I can lick a guy's asshole. I say to them 'Hey listen, can I do this in the movie?' And they'll say 'Oh yes, do that!' And you know, I shock the public who are there watching. I like to shock, you know. It's enjoyment, of course, but I also like to shock people.

However, would she do a scene involving urination, for example?

> No! Even I have my limits! Kent Wisell [the Swedish publisher of *Q* and *Bohème* magazines] asked me to do some pictures. I don't remember the magazine's name now, but they wanted photos where I had to piss in a glass or put a banana in my asshole. I said 'No, I'm not interested.' I want beautiful pictures of myself, not pictures which people will sit and laugh at. If they see me in a photo, at least they'll get horny!

But Brigitte would probably be happy with the anal sex scenes: 'Yes. But I've never done it on film. If it was the right guy, then maybe I'd do it. I do what *I* like to do, what feels good for me.'

A regular feature of all mainstream pornography is some element of lesbianism. Brigitte found this to be a problem, even though she was willing enough.

> I have only done one. That was with a Finnish girl and she was so drunk that I had to take care of her. And she wasn't as experienced as I'd thought. I'd been thinking that *she* would help *me* and she would take the first step to make the contact and touch my body, because that was very strange for me. I wanted to try, so I took the chance. But she was quite dirty and I couldn't even think of licking her pussy. It was almost terrible to touch her pussy with my hands. I'd told her before, hey, go and wash your pussy because I can't touch it. If she had been *good*, then I could have enjoyed it, a hundred per cent. Still, I don't regret what I did. I would have liked to do it.

What cultural differences there might be can be overridden by personal attitudes and preferences, as Viper pointed out: 'Most of the videos are so *clean*! I mean they're just such mundane boring stuff. I try to be as dirty as possible and get edited out every time I do something that's really good. It's become antiseptic eroticism. The girls will sit there and say "Well, how long do I have to suck his dick for?" So they're very careful about how much they have to do, how far they have to put themselves out. They act like your classic Jewish American princess! I mean they're very concerned about not putting themselves out for the eroticism, but just to collect their paycheck.' Bill Margold agreed: 'They're becoming carnal cash-registers. You can tell in the videos who is really into the sex and who is really into "When can I collect my money and when can I go home?" When you watch a fuck film, you want to see people who are really into the fucking.'

Certainly in this environment nobody is forced to do anything they don't feel inclined to do. 'I've been very lucky. I've only met very nice people in this profession. They'd never expose us to anything that would make us feel bad. And they always ask us if we were happy doing this, before the scene. "This is what we want you to do. For goodness' sake, if you don't want to do it, say!" In fact even before you'd agreed to do the film, they'd tell you what was required. Otherwise, just don't get into it.'

The money to be made from the X-rated economy is such that no one seems willing to take any risks that a stills or movie-shooting session might be aborted by a performer being upset at the prospect of having to perform acts he or she considers unsavoury. The same view is taken when it comes to ensuring that the performers are reasonably compatible. Brigitte said:

> If it's a new photographer, I always ask what people I'm working with. I'm very careful. Then I go to this person and he tells me what we will be doing in the film. And then he can ask me 'Do you mind?' And if I say 'Yes, I mind, because I don't like it,' then he will say 'All right.' He can change it.
>
> I'm never forced to do it and I would never do it just because he pays me. When I come to the meeting, I'm

always very natural, and we start getting to be friends. If I feel that I can talk with this guy, he's normal-looking, and he sounds quite normal, then I'll say yes. But if I feel, ugh! I would die if I were to do something with this guy, then I say straight that I won't do it. And they have to accept, because I don't do shit work.

There was this guy who was a pizza deliverer. I didn't have to do so many things, just take his trousers off and maybe touch his cock. But it was enough just to see the guy – I said no. 'All right,' they said, 'we'll keep him out.' Two words and he was out, you know. But I might say 'This guy, wow!' and we had eye contact and were able to talk. Everything was totally OK, so they didn't even have to ask me. I don't care if he has a big cock, or if he has a beautiful body, he must have something in his head. Be sympathetic.

This aspect concerns female performers much more than their male counterparts. Viper admitted:

You do run into people you don't particularly want to work with. There are people who say 'I won't work with this person and I won't work with that person.' And there are other people who say 'I can work with anyone.'

OK, well, I will work with anyone, but there are people I don't like. You can use that to your advantage. For example, I really hate Ron Jeremy, he makes me puke. I can use that so I can fuck him as though I really hate it. Which is, you know, kind of interesting.

But you can't consistently work with somebody you don't get along with, because when you're in make-up, they're sitting there babbling away and it just turns you off all the time. I mean this guy's such a moron, but you've got to fuck him in ten minutes. So in ten minutes you fuck him, and you go back into make-up to get a touch-up and he starts all this garbage again. He's a moron but you know you gotta go work with him again.

Assuming that a porn movie performer has the right physical attributes and attitude, is he or she going to be called on to stretch any acting abilities? 'People who think they are serious actors are such a hassle to deal with; they want everything to be acting,' Viper noted. 'They want to act their sex and that's not the point of sex films. The sex, at least, should be real. It's hard to be real with some director yelling in the background and with a camera up your backside, you know. But you can at least attempt to put some reality into it.'

Surprisingly, Paula Meadows, who has been trained as an actress, agrees:

> You see, the trouble is the dialogue only lasts as long as you are acting and then you get a bit of sex. This is why I don't really think that pornography works as drama. The moment you start performing a sex act for real, you become yourself. You have to! Otherwise you can't function in it and you are not thinking of your character. Perhaps women can act while they're doing it. Men can't because they've got to concentrate on what they're doing: keeping a hard-on. Otherwise everything falls to pieces! I think that's why you can't get any really good drama followed through to the sex.
>
> I don't think you should expect people to act while they're screwing! Actually, filming a lot of dialogue scenes requires rehearsal and a good deal of care. Ron Sullivan [Henri Pachard] takes that care. He choreographs every little bit of it and I think that's right. You have to cast people properly, so they are acting something they feel happy with, natural with. The whole build-up to it has to be properly choreographed.

Paula's friend Frank Russell wrote the script for her first video and he backs her judgement with an example: 'A much better film than *Deep Throat*, made by the same people, is *The Devil in Miss Jones*, because it had brilliant acting. Georgina Spelvin had been Shirley MacLaine's understudy. You can even see her doing it in MacLaine's style – it's almost better than Shirley MacLaine on the screen is. She'd worked with her for so long.'

Accepting that he is not as pretty as the studs in the business, Bill Margold has made his mark as hard-core Hollywood's Walter Matthau: 'I have no idea how I am going to play a role until I get on the set. I've been all kinds of characters. Last Thursday – I played a 'Dr Bernard Burmese' in a thing called *The Cat Club*. I had everybody laughing because I had no idea how I was going to play it and just developed the character straight out. I've played probably more characters than anybody else in this business; raving lunatics, priests, senators, judges, the devil a couple of times – they seem to think I'm a good devil . . .'

On the question of drugs, there was equal consensus that too much cocaine was blowing around the business, but little agreement on the reason for this. Brigitte denies ever using drugs: 'No, never in my life. I don't even drink alcohol.' But she did know of other people in the pornography business who use drugs: 'Yes. Too many. I think sometimes that I am the only one here who doesn't do it!' The cocaine culture is at its apogee in Los Angeles, but Viper denied that it was a reason for getting into the business: 'They don't start out on dope. It's just what do you do if all of a sudden you're getting paid a thousand dollars a day and you never had more than $5 allowance before. I think it's easy to get into drugs in our business because the money that you make you don't always pay income tax on. If you put it in the bank, you're going to have to pay tax on it, so you might as well spend it. How many cars can you buy? I don't think it's the pressure at all. I think it's because they have to spend their money on something. There isn't any more drugs than there is alcohol abuse.'

Unconvinced about the availability of money being the sole excuse, Bill Margold offered an alternative explanation: 'It's also a reverse-punishment situation, because some people cannot handle the fact that they're doing this for a living. Look, I *hate* narcotics. I'm vehemently opposed to any form of drug! My background in juvenile hall meant I quickly lost my interest in drugs . . . after watching kids die. Yes, there are drugs in our business. There is as much drug involvement in our business as there is in the professional sports world and, of course, the professional entertainment world, where it flows like snow. Those poor people cannot handle their fame, so they get high to try and relieve themselves of some of the pressures of being famous. And that's very sad.' Viper was adamant about her own analysis: 'Most performers aren't so much into the success and so the pressure doesn't hit that way. The ones who do drugs, do drugs just because they feel like doing them. It's also peer pressure. If all their friends like to do it, they'll do it. They're not doing it because they have excessive pressures.'

Both of them agreed that the use of cocaine was unprofessional: 'If you're on dope, you can't work! A guy, if he's all doped up, ain't gonna function.'

Regardless of the strength of individual performers' personalities, they will all admit to experiencing some social pressures about the work. Even Margold, who sees himself as something of an *ex officio* publicist for the industry, has lived through plenty of social disapproval:

> I have an interesting time with the people I play football with, accepting me for what I do for a living. The women look aghast at it. I explain to them that no one forces people into it. No one ever forced a woman to make $1,500 a day – they do it willingly. The men sort of look upon me as special and say: 'Gee, you can do that?' I've played with a lot of different teams and one of them, they were all cops. When they found out, they were a little miffed that they had a 'criminal' on their team. But because I was good, they decided to keep me.
>
> The other time, in 1980, I couldn't find a team to play with and I finally ended up on an all-black team! I was the

> only white person on the team. I was their snowball! They called themselves 'The Saints' and were a religious team. They prayed in the huddle and they prayed before the game, they prayed after the game – and they had no idea what I did! Then they found out and didn't know what to do about it. I said, let me play, I'm not doing anything bad, it doesn't rub off! They were totally shocked and said: 'You're going to go to hell!' They sent me off to another team the next year. That team fell apart.

Women are undoubtedly subject to greater pressure than men, but the experienced performers are well versed in responding to the familiar accusations: 'Yes, but I like to be a sex object,' admitted Brigitte cheerfully. 'If I go out now, I know that everybody will see me. I also walk with my head high and look around to be sure that everybody has seen me. I enjoy it, you know, it's a good feeling. Many would say, oh shit! how is she dressed? Now I'm not shy and don't get embarrassed if somebody sees me and says: "Hey, I saw some pictures of you!" I need to be proud of what I'm doing.'

The most vociferous and public attacks come from campaigners against pornography, especially the feminist groups. 'I hope I never come face to face with them because women when they're in that frame of mind are quite ghastly!' said Paula Meadows, who considers herself a feminist.

> When women are aroused and defensive they become very vicious. I was once helping Tuppy Owens [the English sex guru] at a swing party. I was wearing just a G-string and going around sitting on men's laps, adjusting their ties and getting things warmed up a bit. I think Tuppy was doing something similar. Suddenly I was aware of a pair of glowering eyes and there was this gorgeous-looking blonde lady standing there and looking at me as if she could murder me. I still remember that look, how glacial it was, uncompromising and prejudiced. Only a woman could look at me like that. Withering . . . So I immediately got up and said 'Is this your husband?' She

said 'Yes'. I said 'Do you mind?' And she said: '*Yes!*' So I said 'Why are you here, madam? This is a swing party!'

Many women have got that side to them, I may have had myself, at an earlier stage, before I saw the light and began to explore myself a bit more. The more you're like that, the more defensive you are about changing or doing anything. I really react strongly against that kind of woman. They are aggressive and close themselves to anything that might come in and disrupt their lives. I hate the thought that women feel that insecurity – they should be coming out of that now. I can understand them feeling insecure about fifty years ago when there weren't that many opportunities.

I don't mind being the subject of a sexual fantasy! I like to be a sex subject! To be an object is to be just passed around and not considered, and I'm not happy with that.

The only thing more difficult than living with yourself is living with your mother. Does Paula's mother know what she does? 'Yes, it was brought to her notice by my brother-in-law! I think a video I was in was advertised in some magazine. She went dead white! Absolutely numb! My response was to rush over to her and put my arm round her and say: "Mum, it's all right, I haven't changed, I'm still me!" And we had a drink and we talked about it a bit. In the end, the colour returned to her cheeks and she started talking away like mad. She said "I wish I'd had the courage! Yes," she said, "you've become so brave!"'

Perhaps the best form of defence is attack. In 1980 Bill Margold appeared on the NBC show *Tomorrow: Coast to Coast*. Host Rohna Barrett asked him the question which must have been put to all members of the porn fraternity at one time or other: Would you put your daughter on the porn stage? What would happen when your daughter turned eighteen years old? Would you allow her into the industry? 'I'm not going to tell any eighteen-year-old what to do – I might even work with her myself!' Margold replied with studied wickedness. Barrett was appalled: Do you mean you'd sleep with your own daughter? That you'd work with your own daughter? 'Yeah,' said Margold with a straight face, 'but she's not my type, she has bad teeth . . .'

Paula Meadows took a similarly undefensive line when she was visited by her local vice squad: 'The police always ask you, "Aren't you a prostitute? What's the difference? You're performing sex acts for a film and getting money for it." And I would always say: "I'm not a prostitute, because the 'prostitute' who is fucking me is not paying for it! I'm being paid to act in a fantasy and the fact that it involves a sex act is another matter." But it's a fine point, isn't it?'

Few of the female performers seem to have problems with criticism from women. Approaches from men, however, can be one of the penalties of the profession. Viper insisted that even someone as commercially exposed as Amber Lynn would not want to be recognized in her neighbourhood shopping mall: 'Because if they ask "Are you Amber Lynn, the porn star?" what is she going to say? What happens if she says yes? And then what are they going to say? "Come to my house and give me a blow-job for five hundred dollars?" They're gonna ask you if they can sample your wares and you're not a streetwalker!'

Surviving in the porn business has as much to do with coping with self-doubt as it does with resisting social chastisement. 'I think girls fall by the wayside because they're not thinking at all, they damage themselves by not being selective enough,' insists Paula Meadows. 'Then they get resentful against men and start to get into a fury. I've not been damaged because I've always been in charge of what I do. I think you have to minimize the number of things you are going to regret later on. I've done one or two things that I don't particularly want to see now, but you've got to think ahead a bit if it's going to keep coming back at you. That particularly gruesome fist-fuck that you did, or the horses or whatever it was that you weren't sure of at the time . . . Don't do it, for God's sake, because you are going to spend the rest of your life brooding and wishing you hadn't. You've got to be very careful. I've done no physical action that I regret. It has a lot to do with the atmosphere that you work in. If you have to work with unsympathetic people – get out!'

Margold advises would-be porn stars not to get in in the first place: 'I tell them *don't* become a member of the X-rated industry because it is the end of your life. "What are you going to do ten years from now," I would ask the women, "when your kid brings home a video with you lying there with a candle shoved up your ass? Are you going to tell them you played the part of a birthday cake?" It's immortal. It's indelible. It does not go away. It's the rest of your life. I don't think that I'll ever be accused of having a guilty conscience about ruining anybody's life. Because even the legends like Serena, and Seka and Kelly Nicholls and Pat Manning were all given the same warning.'

Is there life after pornography? A common topic of debate in the industry is the 'cross-over' issue; is it possible to move on to the conventional sector and be a star of the big clean screen? Porn veteran Georgina Spelvin appeared in *Police Academy* – looking very much like the Shirley MacLaine she used to understudy for. She played the part of a prostitute employed to give the commander of the academy a blow-job while he was giving a lecture to some foreign visitors. Margold takes the view that this is typical of what happens when a performer tries to cross over: 'She played a whore! She obviously learned well, didn't she? Practising her art. She looked good under a table.'

Paula Meadows spoke of another failed attempt and the repercussions: 'Harry Reems is just a complete wreck, poor man. We met him in London and New York and it was really tragic. He's tried to cross over into straight films and it didn't work. And now he is full of reproach and resentment. "I'm paying my dues to this goddamned business!" he told us.'

Margold doesn't rule out cross-over, but argues that most cases of its being done successfully are limited to people who have worked *behind* the camera.

> A lot of technicians use the X-rated industry as a way to learn their art. Indicative of this is a man called Joao Fernandez who – if I'm not mistaken – was the cinematographer on *Deep Throat*. He was definitely the cinematographer on *The Story of Joanna* and a number of other *high-class* X-rated films. He is now the cinematographer on a whole lot of legitimate movies and television programmes. So he came from our industry into the real world.
>
> The earliest examples of 'cross-over people' would be the famous ones like Bogdanovich and Coppola who nibbled at the periphery of the X-rated industry. None of them can be openly accused of having done a hard-core film and I'm sure they wouldn't want to admit to it.

Margold himself insists that he will stay in the business as long as he can continue to perform. He is, however, varying his activities: 'Right now I'm teaching a class called "Writing Erotica for Dollars" – but I go beyond that. I talk to them about the X-rated industry, I give them a crash-course in the ABCs of X. I've had a good time in the industry, it's been very rewarding. I've been in a fifteen-year recess and the school bell never rung. So I thought: "What the hell?" I only recently had the opportunity to give back something of what I've learned and that's at Santa Monica College. They said "We can get you an honorarium", and I said "Well that doesn't make any sense because I went here for three years and got thousands of dollars of education. I'm going to pay some of it back." It's only fair. You know, if you take, you give.'

Having solved the problem of the unexplained eyes, Paula Meadows has now retired, but conditionally: 'I'm out of it now, I don't want to do any more. I think I've come to the end of my tether with it. It was a nice experience, very nice indeed. I'd been out to New York three years running and for the last two years I haven't been to the States at all. I haven't made many films. I should say I've made ten films in all. I kept it down because I only wanted to work with the people I liked. So I didn't really launch myself wholeheartedly into the industry. I'm not primarily an erotic actress. I wanted it to be all part of my lifestyle.'

So, if she was made an offer she couldn't refuse, would she consider going back to do more? 'Well, if it was an offer I couldn't refuse, it would have to be something very special, I think. I certainly wouldn't want to do any more hard core . . . Unless it was going to be very well directed and interesting. That desire to show myself is no longer with me. I've done that now and so I'm fulfilled, utterly fulfilled. I'm happy now! To go on doing your thing in front of the camera is going to get monotonous, unless there's something different behind it.' Paula's uncertainty later resolved itself into a commitment to get back into the business with control of her involvement by becoming a producer.[9]

Meanwhile, Brigitte plans to stay in the business but, like Bill Margold, has taken on new challenges: 'Yes, when they asked me to do strip-tease, I took it as a challenge. Wow! This could be something new, something different, and maybe I'd like it. I didn't know! I asked if I just have to dance on stage or if I have to go on the side with men, do some dirty jobs. They said no, you have to dance and show your body and nothing else. That's why I accepted it. I did it first in Helsinki. They wanted to see me live because I did one of these lesbian films in Finland. Many of them called at the club to ask, do you have more films? They have seen me live and they want to sit at home and remember they have talked to me, like to a star, you know. They go home and see me on film and do what they want in front of it.' In this way, Brigitte is following a tradition established in the United States where porn stars appear on stage as a promotional activity.

Perhaps the key question of all is, can it be worth it financially? How much of the porn gold is won by the performers? Rates of pay vary by country, by sex, whether the material is for still or moving pictures and according to the sexual acts required. They vary upwards from about $100 an hour for hard-core stills, but there are as many variations of terms and conditions as in any other job.

Certainly Brigitte proved to be an effective negotiator. Did she get paid enough for what she did? 'Well, sometimes yes, sometimes no. But if I start with a new person, like when I did a video, I say I do a short part in a long film, and you pay me so much, and if you're satisfied with my acting, then I want double next time.' So she makes a special offer? 'Well . . .' she laughs at the double entendre. 'First he tells me what I shall do and so on. He says one price. Normally they pay double [for hard-core sex], but I can go down to half-price for a shorter part. If I do a whole film then I want double, because I'm worth it, but in this business, you can't ask too much.'

So can a woman get rich by being a model in the porn business? 'No! You can't get rich in this business! Not by being a model. If I do a good job, I want to be well paid, but the money is not the most imporant part. I also like what I'm doing.'

Perhaps the performer has to go to Hollywood to make it big financially? Bill Margold explained the system in Los Angeles: 'Men get paid less. The women get more. An established woman can get $1,000–1,500 a day. Most of the men are getting $750 a day or even $500 a day. I only get five a day when I work. I've never really asked for any more. I figure five a day is not bad for doing what to me comes naturally.'

But not everyone is happy with those rates of pay and even newcomers have been known to complain – but with little effect. 'We were doing these *Divorce Court Exposé* episodes – hard-core versions of the *Divorce Court* TV series,' Margold recalled. 'A new girl called Candy Evans hired on and she agreed to $800 for her sex day and $200 for her acting day. Well, after the sex day was over, she said "I want $800 a day whether fucking or not." I told her "You gotta be crazy! We'll simply kill you!" And she started to cry. She didn't understand what I was talking about. What happened was we wrapped her body – or rather that of Jeanna Fine – in plaster of Paris and had her come into court as if she had been in a serious accident. Candy never got another cent for being in the movie and we just had her character continue totally wrapped in plaster of Paris! So she wound up losing the $200 and she'll never work for us again. It was hilarious. Jeanna Fine didn't even have to sound like her. She just comes in with these black holes for eyes: "Mumble, mumble, mumble," she says. I was playing the judge and I say "Well, I'm sorry you had your accident and I appreciate your being here." And she says "Mumble, mumble, mumble," and she's wheeled out again!'

According to Margold's figures, a man well established in the business might be able to average two working days per week; say a hundred days over the year. This means he could be making $75,000 (about £45,000) a year, mostly tax-free. A featured female star could be making twice that. What are the superstars likely to earn? 'Well, there are rumours that Seka and Vanessa del Rio get paid $25,000 a day. I don't believe this. Marilyn Chambers is reputed to get $100,000 for a package and gets a percentage on top of that. I don't believe that either, but if she does, more power to her. I think that the top common rate is about $1,500 a day. That's usually good to get you two scenes out of the girl and maybe they'll toss in a lesbian scene on the side.'

Margold explained that although a man can work less often and gets paid less, the effective working hours are not bad. 'A guy like John Leslie, when he's really up to his earning capacity, can make a thousand dollars a day and only do one scene. But then that's John Leslie, he's very special. Most of the men should be good for two scenes a day and get about $750 a day for it. Which isn't bad. When you look at it, it's about two and a half hours' work a day which can last fifteen hours – they're only really going to be working two and a half hours. Most of the time they are sitting around waiting to go to work.'

Do they have problems with the Internal Revenue Service (IRS) over income tax? 'Nobody tells anybody anything,' Margold whispered. 'Nobody really keeps records. I think they're going to try to by paying some of these people by cheque, but the performer's so far down on the earnings totem pole that the IRS has bigger fish to fry. The production companies, *per se*, have to keep some semblance of records. I think they look upon the performer as nothing more than an extension of the product itself, so the performer's another box of tape, or a roll of film, or Xeroxing. By the time the performer gets hassled, who knows – unless it's a performer who has earned so much that he has a lifestyle of ten Rolls-Royces or something, then you notice it!'

So Hollywood porn movie stars could earn anything between $50,000 and $500,000 a year according to their promotional appeal and their enthusiasm. But what do they do with it all? Margold:

> Most of these kids are so unused to earning large amounts of money that they throw it away. One way or another, they throw it away. Some of them have invested their money; Sheri St Claire bought a whole bunch of houses – which was very nice. If she can manage her life, more power to her. But most of them are so thrilled by the amount of money they make, they get rid of it as fast as they can. My warning to them when they'd come into my office was to take half what they make, and stick it away and forget about it. Then, when they do decide to quit, they have a nest-egg. But they don't listen. They should really have managers, somebody to watch over the kids. But they don't and I wouldn't trust the managers anyway, because they'd be tempted to steal from the kids. I

guess in the long run these kids are living on the road to nowhere, so they wanna enjoy it as best they can.

Brigitte summed up the attitude of many porn stars: 'Many people think that all girls who do strip-tease or films or photos are dirty girls or bad girls. But, I don't think that I'm a bad girl. I know what I'm doing, I like what I'm doing. I don't do it because I need the money and I don't do it because I need drugs. I think that what I'm doing is like any other work . . .'

But in one further major respect it is not like any other job. Regular intimate sexual contact with a wide variety of partners now requires a degree of caution which may not have been so paramount in earlier years. Where AIDS is concerned porn industry performers are inevitably more at risk than most. Yet in many ways the attitude of the porn industry to AIDS reflects that of society at large. Views are polarized between well-meaning concern and reckless disregard.

Torben Dhalvad, formerly the editor-in-chief of a number of men's magazines in Denmark makes a serious accusation of neglect against that sector of the business: 'The men's mags in Denmark – and I would say also in Sweden – are so scared about AIDS that I don't think that *Rapport* and the other magazines like that have even mentioned AIDS.'[10]

But this charge could not be levelled against the Finnish magazine *Kalle* – which prints regular gay porn features and contact ads for homosexual readers. The editor, Juhani Salomaa took early action: '*Kalle* was the first in Finland to publish the truth about AIDS. We even distributed a free condom with every magazine. The newspapers objected to this, for some reason. *Kalle* also published an "Illustrated guide to safe sex". This was pioneering. Even the Finnish Ministry of Health admitted that it included everything they knew about AIDS.' In most of *Kalle*'s gay photo-spreads and stories, the hero now uses a condom. 'We have some responsibility to our readers,' said Juhani. 'When we go on the magazine's annual trip to Majorca, we advise them to take packets of condoms with them.'[11]

Bill Margold, a veteran of hundreds of on-screen sexual encounters, takes a different view: 'My whole feeling about "safe sex" and about disease in general is that if you are unhealthy, you deserve to be dead! So I can sum that up real fast! Secondly, people are not interested in going to see X-rated films coated in rubber any more than they are interested in going to the Coliseum to see the Christians against the tabby-cats – or the LA Raiders playing touch-football . . . There have been studies on the X-rated industry which have basically concluded that the X-rated performer, *per se*, is psychologically programmed much the same to a bullfighter, a sky-diver or a race-car driver. There is a built-in death-wish . . . Yes, there is a built-in death-wish for the future . . .'[12]

Bill Margold's porn-movie actress companion, Viper, points out the more general problem of promoting safe sex in societies where the conventional media find the subject difficult to handle: 'You know, on American TV they don't like condom ads. They want to broadcast all the warnings they can about AIDS, because they really believe it's a faggot disease, and it's filthy and faggots are perverts. But they don't want to accept condom ads on TV, they don't want to say that this is a safer method and it's a good thing, because it will bring sex to the attention of the public. That's ridiculous.'[13]

At least one dedicated hard-core porn magazine has started to show the use of condoms in its photo-spreads. *Pleasure* is one of Europe's bestselling porn magazines. The first photoset in issue No. 75 features a three-way set involving an English barrister in wig, gown and pin-striped suit with the National Maritime Museum in London's Greenwich starring as a court-house. It is only when the reader reaches the final spread that he realizes that something different is going to happen. The story is titled 'Einem Job –

Um Jeden Preis' ('A job at any price'). It has establishing exterior shots in an American city and follows the 'casting couch' plot-line: 'They're going to hire me no matter what I have to do to convince them I'm their woman!' declares the female lead, Claire, in the accompanying text. When it is decided that sex will be part of the interview, the story takes on a 1980s variation.

> 'Hey, boss!' cautious Claire remarks. 'As long as we don't know each other very well, I don't see any reason why we should take any chances where sex is concerned. Let's use a rubber!' And before Gerry realizes what's happening, she has rolled the thing down over his stiff rod. 'Well, I suppose that's a reasonable request these days!' Gerry grunts.

And the condom stays on throughout the rest of the story, even during the final obligatory cum shot. Perhaps the most 1980s element of the spread is that it is Claire who is carrying the condom.[14]

Apart from the possible educational benefits of pornography and the contributory role it might play in making the use of condoms more acceptable, it has been argued that no one has caught AIDS by masturbating. The logical extension of this is that pornography might encourage safe solitary sex at the expense of high-risk casual encounters.

This point was made by Rodox's production manager Keld Madsen in an interview published in the Danish tabloid newspaper *Ekstra Baldet*. The article is headlined: 'WE BUY PORNO LIKE NEVER BEFORE – Fear of AIDS stimulates sales in one of Europe's biggest pornomakers, the jubilee-celebrating Danish Rodox company.'

> While a Danish porno giant celebrates its 20th Jubilee, fear of the deadly AIDS-virus amongst concerned people is in the air. AIDS will boost sales in the European porno market and porno boss Peter Theander expects to benefit substantially. Rodox production-manager, Keld Madsen:

'Fear of AIDS causes people to reduce their sexual activity and that will, without doubt, create the need for porno stimulation. Both between regular partners and for onanists.'[15]

Health and safety at work have always been a concern of models and performers in the porn industry. This does not, however, necessarily make them experts on sexually transmitted diseases, as one of Viper's experiences reveals: 'I recently appeared with a snake in an X-rated video called *Traci Takes Paris*. It was a baby boa constrictor. They accused me of contracting gonorrhoea after I worked with the snake. A lot this industry knows about gonorrhoea and snakes!' Some misunderstanding, surely? 'No,' Viper confirmed. Gonorrhoea? From contact with a snake? 'Yeah, virulent gonorrhoea after having worked with a snake! And then I instantly gave it to one of the three guys I fucked.' What about the snake? Did they have to trace all the snake's previous sexual partners? 'No, the snake displayed no symptoms.' But where did the story come from? 'A guy I fucked in the video. He said he got the clap because I rolled around with the snake before I fucked him!'[16]

Viper's temporary embarrassment by a clap-carrying boa may now be no more than an anecdote to dine out on, but some in the trade are prepared to take the more serious message about AIDS to their audiences directly. A US West Coast company, Catalina Video, has even put together a three-minute programme called *Safer Sex* which it will add to the beginning of all its cassettes. Made in association with the Gay Men's Health Crisis group, the video features actress Sheri St Claire and is directed at heterosexual and bisexual audiences as well as gay men. The programme will be available for use by other producers.[17]

Nobody would argue that there have not been a few casualties among the foot-soldiers of the porn industry. They are the most expendable factor in a high-turnover market: whether it's moral revulsion, physical breakdown, illness, drug addiction or plain old-fashioned exhaustion, the financial rewards of the good times are probably no compensation for the bad. But this is equally true of life beyond the confines of the X-rated economy.

# 4

# *One-Handed Magazines: Pornography in Print*

'I suppose the essential nature of pornography is repetition. The ideal form of pornography for one individual is his favourite fantasy replayed in ten million variations.'[1] The perception of the English porn illustrator who works under the name of 'Erik von Goethe' is surely corroborated by the enormous quantity of stereotyped images being replicated in the 1980s by the world's pornography industry. But it is an industry which lives off the variations.

The first challenge facing any would-be porn publisher is the choice of subject-matter. It is not enough to say that a porn magazine will contain pornography, any more than it would be to say that a car magazine will contain pictures of automobiles. Although a few car magazines will attempt to cover every aspect of motoring, there will be many others that will specialize: motor racing, rallying, sports cars, vintage and veteran cars, and special conversions. The essential formula is common to the two fields; the more generalized the product, the greater will be its potential and actual audience. Therefore, less ambitious and less wealthy aspirants will search for unexplored niches; the readership will be smaller but, with good market research, better management and a sprinkling of luck, the newcomer might get there before the opposition. The more well-trodden the market, of course, the less likely the explorer is to find an uninhabited nook.

And more challenges will inevitably follow. The time when quality was of little consequence to the success of a pornographic magazine in an expanding market place has long gone. "Curth Hson-Nilson was the first one in Sweden,' remembers pornographer Kent Wisell. 'They call him "The Legend". He started with magazines called *Peter* and *Pat*. They were a smaller size than *Private*, *Q* and the others and had lots of rubbish text and black and white pictures. But they sold in huge quantities.'[2] But Hson-Nilson was never a legend outside Scandinavia. That honour fell to the Swede who addressed the problem of quality: Berth Milton.

Few publishers would deny Berth Milton's contribution in establishing *de facto* minimum standards for content, photography, layout, reproduction and even size. Although he prefers to see his life's work as the Rolls-Royce of the industry, it is really much more like the Volvo, whose selling strongpoints are reliability, longevity and quality of design; combined with a loyal following, this ensures an acceptably high level of circulation. But *Private*, though still recognized as the value-for-money benchmark, is under pressure from competitive products such as *Pleasure*, *Blue Climax*, *Ero* and, especially, the relative newcomer *Foxy Lady*.

Unless the newcomer is going to put together yet another title for the relatively small 'bizarre' market, he has to keep in mind that all the bestselling porn mags are still in the style refined by Berth Milton from the end of the 1960s. They are 90 per cent pictorial sex with a little supporting text, as shown by an analysis of Milton's *Private* No. 79.[3]

The magazine has 124 full-colour pages and is printed on good-quality art paper. Following the contents page and house furniture is an editorial by Milton headed 'Moral?'.

The first feature is a photo-set of a single girl called 'Greta' covering eight pages (ten pictures) and with text in German, English and French. After this is what purports to be a personal reminiscence by 'Roxanne T' of Bristol headed 'It happened to me!' This is carried initially in German but is repeated in English and French later in the magazine. Next is an eleven-page spread showing sexual activity between a white woman and a black woman, culminating in the use of dildos and what is known in the trade as 'fist-fucking'. The 'problem page' is also covered in three languages with a former porn star called 'Mlle Baiser' acting as agony aunt. The photoset which follows is in the regular 'Amateur Photographer's' department. The pictures are credited to a 'Tom Evans' in the UK and there is nothing amateur about them at all. The threesome of two women and one man was certainly photographed in London with the establishing shots being taken on the concourse of Paddington Railway Station and the sex action in a hotel room.

The only way in which Milton 'recycles' material in *Private* is in the 'Reader's Request' section. In issue 79, this is a man–woman set from *Private* No. 42 featuring 'Stacey' and an anal sex scene. The trilingual sex-counselling page is supposedly written by a 'Dr Steven Roles MD' whose qualifications are spelled out fully as: Bachelor of Medicine, Bachelor of Surgery, Bachelor of Science, Fellow of the Royal Academy, Fellow of the Royal Society of Medicine and Member of the New York Academy of Sciences. How all this qualifies him to give advice on the excitation of the anus during female masturbation is not made clear. The next page invites readers to participate in *Private* by sending in ideas, photos, art, writing, fantasies and letters.

The next regular department is the 'Cunt Contest'. The three 'contestants' – who receive 'prizes' of $250 – each have a page dominated by a photograph of their sex organs with labia pulled wide plus an inset portrait in the corner of the page. Next comes the 'centre-fold' (Greta from the earlier set) and the subscription and mail order form. After the letters pages (explicit sexual experiences) is another full photoset headed 'Franci's Freaky Fuck' covering fifteen pages. It is an interior-shot man–woman sequence with no establishing pictures and concentrating mostly on anal sex. Another threesome (two men and one woman this time) takes up the next pages, with a story-line that follows the 'lonely housewife' plot stereotype; the two males are removal men. The text of 'Sandra's Sandwich' starts: 'Move it? Are these guys in for a surprise! Sandra is the fastest mover ever. She'll have them in bed quicker than they can pick it up.' Having dealt with plot in four sentences, the text gets down to business: 'Not half I will! I'll suck their bleeding cocks as dry as two pairs of prunes.' Some respite from 'Sandra's' fellatio of both their penises at the same time is granted the two men in succeeding sets depicting simultaneous vaginal and anal intercourse: the 'sandwich' of the title.

A double-page spread provides a trailer for *Private* No. 80, the right-hand page being a reproduction of the cover. The final feature is the regular 'Personal Profile'. This starts with a reproduction of a form allegedly completed by the model, in this case Vanessa Coburn, a twenty-year-old Englishwoman whose interests and activities are said to include swimming, tennis, Ernest Hemingway, Arthur Miller, drinking red wine at dinner and masturbating every lunchtime. She claims she lost her virginity to her mother's brother when she was fifteen. She also claims that she is turned on by 'tough, working-class men', which is fortunate, because the set involves her driving into the hills in a white Golf GTi convertible (the Yuppie fleet car) only to be held up by two young men repairing the road in the hot sun. After 'she gets a whiff of their animal sweat', she wants their bodies – badly, the text tells us. The sequence that follows is classic Milton; intimate sexual behaviour against panoramic views.

Apart from the single-girl set at the beginning of the magazine, all the features culminate in external 'cum shots' on the faces of the female participants. The photography is first class – so much so that it is noticeable at the end of the 'Vanessa' sequence how the light must have been fading at the mountain location, because the film has been 'pushed' so far that the 'cum shots' are grainy.

It is this formula and his obsession with quality which has enabled Milton, over two decades, to build the circulation of *Private* to something like double that of his nearest competitor. But it is that very success that attracts others at least to try and emulate what he has done. Milton's former sales manager, Kent Wisell is one of them. The burly and bespectacled Swede looks every bit the businessman, as he confirms: 'I worked for a Japanese trading company, a long time ago, and saw an ad in the paper, by Private Press – that's Milton – and I started working for him in 1978. Before that I was a normal businessman responsible for the sale of the Japanese products to Scandinavia and Scandinavian products to Japan.'[4]

By 1986 Wisell had left *Private* and was ready to test his own skills in porn publishing, but he had no illusions about the uphill task of competing with his former employer: 'I cannot use the same formula as Milton. He's a tremendously good photographer – which I'm not. I work with two photographers in Sweden and we work together. Say we have found two good-looking girls and we decide to photograph them together and decide it should be this or that place. We choose the outdoors because that sells better – apartments always look the same.' So, consciously or unconsciously, Wisell really is being influenced by the precedents set by his former employer. But Wisell has at least decided to give his magazines a specifically Swedish flavour, to capitalize on the old myth of 'Swedish sin' against the current trend for magazines to be multinational in flavour. 'We get our models mostly from Sweden. It is now hard to get Swedish girls, but it is worth the trouble, absolutely.'

But the titles of the magazines were not Swedish and

Wisell soon realized another mistake; that of spreading his limited resources over two titles: 'I just do two mags, *Bohème* and *Q*. I took over *Q* from No. 2. First of all, I didn't like the title, it sounds silly: "*Q*" magazine. So I registered the name *Bohème* and came out with No. 1. I was not so happy with the printing, I think it was too dark. Now I have material for three more magazines. I don't know right now whether I'll just drop *Q* and only do *Bohème*. Then do a very, very good magazine after that instead.'

That uncertainty does not bode well – especially in view of the capital investment involved: 'What you need – more or less – is between ten and fifteen thousand pounds. Costs for printing, layout, models, etc. Perhaps even more – perhaps up to twenty. It depends on how much you print, but I would say that material costs with the model and layout is the same. What differs, of course, is the printing, depending on the print run. In order to make a *good* magazine, you need at least four good sets in it. Say one single, one lesbian and two other sets with men and women. I think you need to pay, three, four or even five thousand pounds for those. Then comes the layout, someone to write the text, the translation, then typesetting – that's the minor part. Then comes the big part which is the photo-composition and the printing.'

Of course, that commitment does not stop with the first issue. 'I plan to publish between five and six numbers per year – the target is six,' said Wisell. 'I think it should be normal to have the magazine out every second month, so the customers know what to look for – they recognize the logo, the trademark, and the profile of the magazine.'[5]

Regardless of the increasing strength of the porn establishment, there is no shortage of people willing to try to enter the market with a new product. In an attempt to do something really different, two Englishmen teamed up in early 1986. They wanted to commission an artist to produce a pornographic strip-cartoon magazine. Hard-core comic strip magazines are popular in France, Spain, Japan and

Italy. They are, however, of little appeal outside these countries, as porn entrepreneurs Roger Hawse and Peter Baldwin were to discover. The artist they approached was an unlikely character; a quietly spoken former advertising art director who lives in West London and works in the porn business using the name 'Erik von Goethe'.

'Von Goethe' recalled how he became involved in pornographic art: 'I started using the name "Erik von Goethe" when I worked for an advertising agency. We were a little nervous about how some of the clients might react to the other side of what I do. I said: "Well, after all, advertising is just the same as pornography . . . They are both there to solicit a response!"'[6] In the early 1970s he became involved with the London 'scene' sex guru Tuppy Owens:

> I designed *The Sex Maniac's Diary* with Tuppy and that was great fun for a few years. I stopped working with her two or three years ago. I've been working entirely on my own for four and a half years now, having departed from advertising; that's a young man's business. The publishers of *The Sex Maniac's Diary* then were Gold Star, who are undeniably the biggest publishers and distributors of erotic material in Britain.
>
> I started a cartoon strip magazine called *Torrid* in 1979. It was originally Gold Star's idea. They said 'We've seen this magazine in Holland and we've got a title and we'd like you to do something like this.' I've always loved strip cartoons, but I never imagined that I'd ever do it professionally. As it happened, I never really did anything worthwhile in *Torrid*. It was certainly as hard as you could do in this country. And because you have the advantage of combining images and words, you can make the images work much harder from a sexual response point of view – photographs are just for contemplating.
>
> It appeared as often as I could produce it. There were sixteen between 1979 and 1986. Seven years. Sixteen in seven years. Heavy going that was! It was fifty-two

pages. The stories were pathetic, and the drawings were slapdash. I wrote them, I did everything from front cover to back cover and it was a hell of a lot of work.

Then I discovered when I'd just delivered issue 15 [of *Torrid*] that Gold Star were getting the same money for selling second rights in France that they were paying me! They were getting all the *Torrid* material free, in effect. So I came to a halt on *Torrid* No. 16 because I felt outraged that I'd been ripped off.

'Von Goethe' had also contributed a strip to a few issues of Hans Moser's *Foxy Lady*, but became frustrated at having to put both German and English text in the bubbles and thus making his characters stereophonically bilingual. 'This is why I gave up working for Hans Moser, because it was essential that the balloons appear in two languages! English and German.

'Then Roger Hawse rang me up. Out of the blue. And said would you do a little strip cartoon of say four pages or six pages in a magazine we're going to publish in Holland? I said, yeah! And his partner, a man called Peter Baldwin, then called and said, "Why don't we do a hard core version of *Torrid*?" He thought that would be an entertaining and interesting thing to do. I don't think it was actually. There is no future in the sort of thing that this Dutch project *Toren* represents. Starting again with it now, I would take a very different line about it altogether.'

'Von Goethe' agreed to the assignment knowing that he could minimize his risks by working from the original drawings for *Torrid*. Such is English law that it allowed him to show penises so long as they weren't erect. Just as Hollywood's 1930s Hay's Code dictated that couples on beds had to keep one foot on the floor, the ends of English penises had to point in the same direction: downwards. The deft pen of 'von Goethe', a slight, quietly spoken Englishman in his early fifties, soon brought new life to the limp members of his earlier creations.

Although the artwork was done in a 'picture postcard' cottage long since swamped by London's urban sprawl, the magazine was printed in Holland and distributed throughout Europe. 'I'm not at all sure that was a good idea, but I must say that the last news I heard of *Toren* was that 900 had gone in the airports in Holland. Just in Holland alone. And those 900 had gone in under a fortnight. And that's a hell of a lot of magazines. You know, at five quid a time.'

But the project was short-lived and *Toren* No. 2 was never to see the light of day. In spite of his enthusiasm for the art form, 'von Goethe' was not really surprised:

> The important thing about strip cartoons is that they can't compete with photo-magazines. If you want to see details, a drawing can never achieve what a photograph can. All a drawing can do is create things that a photograph can't. And I think that what *Toren* tried to do is compete with photo-magazines. This is something that I discussed at length, argued I suppose, with Roger and Peter who were saying 'more juicy pussies, more big cocks . . .' and I'm saying but I can't compete with photographs! It's silly! Why not use photographs? They'll be much more effective whereas drawings can create alternative realities, alternative worlds. And this is very much what the French are interested in. You know, the French are terribly keen on surrealism. Surrealism is really a French art form and probably always has been. If you think of English painting, it's very realistic, and very down-to-earth; Constable, Gainsborough, Turner. And they even thought that Turner was a raving loony! Because he was creating alternatives to reality. So it's nice working for the French.[7]

Von Goethe's porn strips now appear regularly in French magazines such as *BéDé Adult*. *'BéDé'* is short for *bande dessinée* and in France this is a huge industry. There are something like thirty magazines currently devoted, either completely or mostly, to strip cartoons. Across the board. In

France, they treat strip cartoons as a minor art form!

The experience of Roger Hawse, Peter Baldwin and 'Erik von Goethe' does not rule out the possibility of new ideas for porn magazines. A relatively new sector is the market for video review magazines such as VTO's German-language *Video Star*, the US *Swedish Erotica* and the Spanish *Video*.[8] These have been launched in response to the video revolution and capitalize on the growing interest in this new medium. Essentially they are derivatives of the more basic, but often bestselling product catalogues published by the distributors of porn videos.

In the 1970s, Rodox produced a flimsy, sixteen-page guide to its 8mm film products. This developed into the same format as its other magazines and the last issue – for 1984/85 – had eighty-four pages, though it was dull fare by Rodox standards. It was aimed mainly at dealers, consisted of little more than reproductions of the box covers, a product code and a description which rarely stretched beyond '2 girls + 1 man' or '5 girls + 8 men'.[9] This has now been replaced by the *Video Index* which has 116 pages and a considerably better layout.

Although the products are described more fully and illustrated with as many as eight stills each, it is still little more than a catalogue. (But the appeal for the consumer with good eyesight and an interest in no more than the hard core shots is clear; with over 900 pornographic photographs for about £5 (or $7.50), it represents unsurpassed value-for-money.)[10] The same formula is employed by Mike Hunter Video in West Germany with its *Hardcore-Programm '86*, the larger format of which permits a more imaginative layout – fewer large pictures, rather than many small ones – but still concentrates on the product at the expense of all else.[11]

The breakthrough to a more interesting and comprehensive magazine for the porn video enthusiast is best represented by Hans Moser and Teresa Orlovski's *Video Star*. Setting aside the nature of the contents, the quality of this publication is such that anyone in publishing would be delighted to be associated with it. The format is larger than that of the traditional porn magazines (being a centimetre short of A4) but it is in full colour and printed on heavy art paper.

The material is all in some way derived from the porn video industry and its products. Typically, the contents of video review magazines will include: reviews of current releases; interviews with performers; photosets of the female stars; reports of trade shows and award ceremonies; and features on the leading production companies. A representative issue of *Video Star*[12] included: a cover portrait of Teresa Orlovski; an editorial about the German Video Kongress '86 (signed by Teresa); Teresa's 'Readers Corner'; an illustrated profile of sex star Karin Schubert (including a friendly handwritten note from Richard Burton, signed 'Richard Bluebeard' and adding 'Good luck from Elizabeth too'); reviews of the latest releases from Hohmann Video, Tabu and Love Video, RiBu Video, Paradise Visuals, and Video Teresa Orlovski; a short story; an article on the Mosers' latest trip to Italy; a joky 'Show report' on Video Kongress '86; a review of soft-core videos; a photo-spread on Chicago-born video star Jeannie Pepper (with the obligatory centrefold); an extensive feature on American veteran porn actress Nina Hartley; an article on retailer Raimund Schneider and the Schmitt family's ZBF company; more reviews and a 'potpourri' of news items including a two-page update on the California scene called 'Porn in the USA' by Jeremy Stone. Naturally, there's also an extensive set of stills from one of Teresa's latest videos. Regardless of the expansive and expensive style of the magazine, it is unremittingly and unapologetically hard core.

There are signs that such video magazines may be the first pornographic publications to attract conventional advertising in addition to advertisements for other porn and sex products. The same issue of *Video Star* includes three pages of advertising by the Japanese consumer electronics giant,

Sony. These promote their low-cost, compact Video-8 camera systems, the implication being that they are the ideal thing for amateur productions such as *Hausfrauenpornos* (see Chapter 1).

Although the ratio of pictures to text in such magazines is much lower than in traditional porn magazines – perhaps 60:40 instead of 90:10 – they are still essentially hard-core pornography and will be used as much for the 'solitary vice' as for the promotion of videos. In view of the success of these magazines it is becoming increasingly necessary for video producers to ensure that plenty of stills are available to illustrate reviews as well as for conventional promotional materials and packaging.

In the latter case, the photographs will normally be soft core, but the video magazines will demand hard-core shots of the action in the programme. Where these are not supplied, attempts will be made to produce colour transparencies directly from the video tape or, even worse, by photographing a television screen. The quality of this will be poor – an unattractive proposition for both the magazine publisher and the production company. However, as the technology of video advances, the quality of stills produced from tape is expected to increase significantly.

These magazines are here to stay, but it will be difficult for new entrants to the market to match the quality of *Video Star*, which probably sells 20,000 copies per issue.

Another characteristic of Berth Milton's business which sets him apart from the rest of the porn establishment is that he is a single-product company. The others have gone through a successful process of diversification. 'Rupert James' is the name used by an ex-guitar player, ex-advertising executive, old-Etonian Englishman who works as an editor for Peter Theander:

> Rodox started with one magazine – *Color Climax*. We publish all the main titles – about twelve of them – four or

six times a year. So we have about fifty magazines a year of what we call the large format, and then various reprints plus cheaper mags which are cut-down versions. Not to help on mailing, it's simply a business logistic, getting the most mileage out of material as possible and keeping the price down – 'Pocket-size for the penny-wise' was the sales slogan for them. But that was when they were literally pocket-sized A5. Now we now do the economy-sized magazines in the larger format with thirty-two pages instead of 68 to 116.

The most popular outside of *Color Climax*, which is the flagship mag, are the 'Teenage' titles; *Teenage Sex* and *Teenage Schoolgirls* – of course all with models of legal age, that has to be. But, for some reason, these 'teenagers' have some sort of charisma . . . We have done various market-teasers, but I don't think we've had any titles which could be described as failures. In that context we prefer to describe them as having been 'not as successful as we would have wished'. Our market policy is to follow sales trends. We don't go deeply into market research, we stick with what looks safe. In that way we are like the BBC, we stand back and count up to ten before taking any plunges.[13]

Rodox has one of the most well-developed product lines in the porn business and it is worth examining in more detail. The company, usually trading as the Color-Climax Corporation, has four magazines which can be viewed as being well within the mainstream style established by *Private*. To the inexperienced eye, there may be little to choose between them, but Rupert James explained the key differences: '*Color Climax* is the flagship magazine, the original bestseller. It is published six times a year and the print run is about 50,000. *Blue Climax* is a similar publication but is more elegant and sophisticated in terms of photography and content. *Exciting* has more solid action. Fewer establishing shots and less ancillary material. *Rodox Special* is even more vulgar and hard-hitting than the above three titles.' It should be understood that in the context of pornography, terms such as 'more vulgar and hard-hitting' are strictly relative.

Even to non-consumers of pornography, the popularity of magazines featuring young women may come as no surprise. Certainly Rodox's *Teenage Schoolgirls* and *Teenage Sex* sell as well as any in their range (see below). 'Here the appeal is in the titles,' Rupert James confirmed. 'The original title was *Teenage Sex* and this was so successful that we followed it up a few years ago with *Teenage Schoolgirls*. Younger models are featured.' But this is not child pornography; the women are well beyond puberty and care is taken to check their ages. 'Of course they are all above the age of consent, some of them very much so. Unless the photographer produces release forms and evidence that the models are over sixteen, they don't get paid – it's as simple as that. But it's amazing what you can do with a pair of little white socks.'

Peter Theander's early success in capitalizing on the appeal of youth has been noted by other mainstream pornographers, especially in Germany. The formula is straightforward enough; the right title and the youngest-*looking* models that can be found. Apart from that, the sexual action depicted is essentially the same as in any other mainstream magazine.

A major competitor of the Rodox titles is Horst Peter's *Teenager*. Issue No. 32[14] featured: a boy-girl set titled 'Teenager in Love: Helene's Hot Hole'; a single-girl spread of 'Olivia'; a long three-way set featuring a white couple and a black woman; another boy–girl set and a double-page montage trailing Peter's other magazine in this genre, *Schulmädchen* (*Schoolgirls*). Not to be left out, Hans Moser's Verlag Teresa Orlovski has *Sweet Little 16*. This is much like *Foxy Lady* in style, content and quality. Of course, the women have to look younger and this restricts the ubiquitous Teresa to the editorial column.

Considering the recent uproars over child pornography and the exploitation of women in South-East Asia, Germany's most borderline magazine must be *Thai Lolitas*. Subtitled 'Original Sex from Bangkok', issue No. 13 comprises three sets, each of which shows hotel-room encounters between European males and one or more Thai prostitutes (if the text is to believed).[15] *Thai Lolitas* is distributed by Georg Schmitt's ZBF Vertrieb.

The porn publishers are running out of ages for magazine titles. Doing two years better than Rolf Rahm's Swedish *15* but only one year better than Moser's *Sweet Little 16* is the Dutch *Seventeen*. Although the 'Collectors item' subtitle is a clear signal to child-sex enthusiasts, it does not include pre-pubescent children. However, some of those shown in issue 7 of the magazine[16] seem likely to come close to the American age limit of eighteen. Perhaps, for once, the title is being honest.

As noted in the opening chapter, lesbianism and anal sex are common fare in today's mainstream pornography. This is reflected in the success of two of Rodox's top titles. '*Lesbian Love* is exclusively lesbian in its content. Of course, it is not a magazine for lesbians – although some might like it – but for a male readership. It sells very well,' James observed with a nod of satisfaction. '*Anal Sex*, as its name suggests, is the application of the "Greek technique". Another best-seller.' Sales of over 40,000 per issue puts a porn magazine into the bestselling category.

James explained the rationale behind *Cover Girls* and *Sexy Girls*: 'We like to boast that these magazines include all the single-girl shots that the other magazines wouldn't dare publish. They include solo girls, spread shots and masturbation.' The unbeguilingly titled *New Cunts* is what is known as a 'depilation magazine'. 'It still includes a lot of that: shaven cunts. Again, single girls.'

Rodox now publishes only one magazine which falls into the 'bizarre' classification. '*Sex Bizarre* is our specialist magazine which covers things like S & M and bondage,' said

James. 'It does not have a massive circulation – about 25,000 to 30,000.' Interestingly enough, if Rodox's well-refined product range is in any way a reflection of the market for pornography, this places the mainstream material at much more than 90 per cent of the total. The company does occasionally try new titles in this area if demand can be identified. One recent magazine depicted transsexuals engaged in a variety of sexual activity with differing combinations of male and female partners. It was called, appropriately enough, *Transexual Climax*. 'We've dropped this now,' added James. 'We originally started publishing it in 1983 or 1984, when there was this big thing for transsexuals in Paris. But interest seems to have dropped off and we do have problems getting good material.'[17] This may seem hardly surprising.

Kent Wisell has also studied the market structure: 'Mainstream porn is much more than 90 per cent of the total volume of the business. The bizarre stuff is a very small percentage. Animal sex and child sex is completely forbidden. S & M, bondage, etc. has a certain clientele, *Lady Domina*, *Sex Bizarre* and so on, but it's still a very small percentage – perhaps 10 per cent at the very most. The Germans seem to go for a lot of S & M, but you should ask Hans Moser about it, because he's the publisher of *Lady Domina*. But in Scandinavia we don't use that material.'[18] This is a view which seems in conflict with the product lines of Swedish sex shops and mail order houses. It seems unlikely that they would stock and advertise such material if there were no buyers for it. But Wisell is right about Moser's product mix; out of thirteen titles, five specialize in bizarre material.[19]

Theander's *Pussycat* and *Darling* were 'mini-mags': Rodox's attempt to make high quality porn available at moderate prices. They were in a smaller format with just thirty-two pages and bore the slogan 'Porn for the pennywise' on the cover. 'We no longer publish them in this small format,' noted Rupert James. '*Sexorama*, *Inspiration* and *Sexual Fantasy* are the current titles in our economy range.

They are still thirty-two pages but the same size as the standard mags. It is important to say that the lower price comes from the fact that there are fewer pages – the porn is still the same high quality as in the other Rodox products. We use fewer pics from the same sets and then do a new layout and rewrite the text. We like to make that clear – these are quality products. It's exactly the same printing lithos that are being used to produce the dearer ones. Once we've finished a run on a mag and it's had its reprint potential played out then we'll consider putting it into a cheaper version. But the actual quality will never diminish.'[20]

This rationalization is based on the recycling of earlier material. For example, *Teenage Sex* No. 7[21] included a single-girl set of a very slight and young-looking girl called 'Tove' (she is also on the cover). James describes her as 'The *Teenage Sex* mascot. She is not, of course, as young as she looks.' Tove's first set covered six pages and thirteen photographs. The mini-mag, *Stimulation* No. 22[22] includes a reworked version of the same Tove set. This time it covers only four pages and nine photographs. The text has been rearranged as much as rewritten.

Once the topic of the magazine has been chosen and the target market identified, the next step is the detailed design of the magazine – starting with the title.

Some time after the launch of his two magazines, Kent Wisell was still undecided: 'No, I haven't changed my mind about the names of the magazines. I will do something about it. When I took over the company, the magazine was called *Q* and I'm not so bloody pleased about it. It doesn't tell you anything about the mag. For instance, Rolf Rahm has *Ero*. *Ero* is the best name – everyone who buys a magazine called *Ero* knows exactly what it is. The name is no problem really, so long as the quality is there, but it does take time to get reader identification. If I came out with a new magazine called *Something No 1*, and that could apply for instance to *Bohème No 2, 3, 4* or *Q No 5, 6, 7*, they don't know what it is. You are starting again from the point of view of the buyers. *Bohème* was a better name than *Q*. The guy who does my layouts sings opera. He came up with the name *Bohème*, so we thought of other opera names like *Rigoletto* and God knows what . . . *Carmen*! So I think that the next magazine that will come out will be called *Carmen*. *Carmen No. 1*. Perhaps in the summer [of 1987].'[23] In practical terms, publishers of magazines to be circulated internationally prefer explicit titles in English.

The size of porn magazines is usually 6.5 inches wide by 9.25 inches deep (165 x 230 mm). Like many things, these dimensions were pioneered by Berth Milton: 'It's a peculiar size, the magazine. It relates to the size of the sheets the printers use on the litho presses. And all the magazines being made now use this size. We would like to print the same size as *Penthouse* and *Playboy*, but it doesn't fit on the roll.'[24]

Although a larger format gives greater scope for varying the layouts, most porn shops are now fitted with shelves designed to display the product of this accepted size. Any variation could mean that a magazine does not get the prominence its publisher would prefer.

The number of pages to include is purely a function of the amount of money available to be invested. The more pages in the flat-plan, the more sets can be included – the more saleable the resulting product. Carl Delvert remarks:

> If you take a typical German product like *Pleasure*, in a magazine about the same size as *Private* they have three sets. That is a lot of pictures which are very similar to each other. We have eight in this issue of *Private*, eight different stories. That increases production costs, it is more expensive to do it that way.[25]

It is also necessary to keep up with the trends, says Rupert James: 'The structure of the photosets has changed in recent years. These used to be one-third establishing shots and two-thirds action. Now they have two double-page spreads to establish and then straight into the sex. If [the layout artists] don't like the location shown in the establishing shots, they have been known to montage the models on to library shots of other locations.'

Other trade secrets in design include having a soft-core or even non-pictorial cover which can be folded back to reveal a second, hard-core cover. Issue 79 of *Private,* referred to above, has a cover which describes the contents in text and can be displayed – where legal – in regular bookstores. When this is folded back the inside cover shows a girl licking semen from her face as she looks directly into the camera. This, clearly, could be used only in porn shops.

Another trick is to include the cover of the next edition of the magazine on the back or inside. Rodox resists doing this because unscrupulous dealers will fold the magazine to this page and seal the product in shrink-wrapping so that unsuspecting buyers think they are getting a new issue of the magazine.

Once the magazine has been designed and the artwork completed, it is ready to go to print. Few publishers – not even Peter Theander – now have their own printing press and the work goes out to tender. Now that the European market has opened up, it is possible to send the magazine out of the country of origin to the lowest bidder. So some Swedish publishers are printing in Finland, Berth Milton, Kent Wisell and Hans Moser are printing in Spain. Wisell explains why: 'I've printed in Spain. I don't know where to continue; whether I should go down to Spain again or if I should continue in Sweden. I went to Spain in the first place because I'd received a good offer, but I was not so satisfied with the mag they printed. OK, it was perhaps a big mistake because they were working in a hurry to get the magazine ready, so they didn't get the correct paper. I know they can do the mag better. They've approached me and want to print it again. The printing costs in Spain are so much cheaper than here. And now since they joined the Common

Market, they get paper from Germany, better paper.'[26]

Berth Milton has been printing pornography in Spain longer than most other publishers: 'If anything gets held up, it's usually the layout, the printing, I'd reject the print and reject the print. And have them re-do their lithography until I was satisfied. I still personally check every issue.'[27]

A critical decision must also be made regarding the print run. Deciding how many copies of the magazine to produce – especially in the case of the first issue – will influence the future of the magazine: too few and not enough money will be generated for investment in future issues; too many and capital will be locked in perpetuity in a warehouse stock of unsaleable material. The perfect number will be exactly that quantity consumers will buy over the life of the issue – a figure which is impossible to determine without the benefit of hindsight. In any case, the publisher will not be selling to the public (other than by mail order), and what he really needs to determine is what he can sell to distributors.

As the one-time sales manager for *Private*, Kent Wisell was well aware of the problem he was facing with *Q* and *Bohème*: 'My aim from the beginning has been not to print so much that I have to keep a large stock. It's better to print smaller quantities. I cannot afford to keep a stock of say 20,000 magazines – it's impossible, since I'm working on my own. Being conservative on initial print runs is very important.'[28]

Wisell had the advantage of already knowing the major distributors such as Boksenter for Scandinavia, ZBF for Germany, and Intex and Calvista for the Netherlands. A preliminary discussion with them about the design of the magazine being proposed would have been very helpful in planning his print run. The nature of the product will also be a factor; a mainstream porn magazine will sell more than those specializing in the bizarre. So will the multilingual publications. Assuming a certain minimum level of quality in content and reproduction, the number of pages in relation to the price will be a factor; will the magazine *feel* bulky when the customer browses through it in the shop?

Over twenty years, Rodox has probably put more thought into the print runs of its various magazines than any other publisher. The well-established *Color Climax* usually has a first print run of over 40,000 and the more up-market *Blue Climax* is not far behind that. The other major titles like *Exciting*, *Rodox Special*, the *Teenage* series, *Lesbian Love* and *Anal Sex* print between 35,000 and 40,000. *Transexual Climax* – now defunct – and *Sex Bizarre*, into which Theander now puts all his non-mainstream material, sell between 25,000 and 30,000 copies on the first print run. *Sexorama* and the other economy magazines sell about 20,000 on the first printing.[29]

Berth Milton's *Private* is far ahead, with a bi-monthly circulation of well over 100,000 copies, but Hans Moser has admitted to print runs of 40,000 plus for *Foxy Lady*, and *Ero* and *Pleasure* probably do just as well. All the same, 20,000 copies of a brand new magazine, even one of exceptional quality, is certainly ambitious, if not plain foolhardy. One solution is to start low and budget for a speedy reprint if the distributors begin to reorder. Wisell does not seem enthusiastic about this: 'I don't have any intention of reprinting the magazines, which some people do. Of course, if I had 20,000 back orders, I should print more! That might happen when the mag reaches number 18, 19, 20, something like that.'[30]

That is certainly the experience of the porn establishment, for which reprints are a way of life and can soon come to represent the bulk of sales of the more successful issues. *Lesbian Love* No. 11 from Rodox is a case in point. The magazine was originally published in June 1982. Between then and November 1984, 61,650 copies were produced. (The odd numbers occur because the printers have clearance to go to the end of a batch of paper.)

Even more successful was the twenty-fifth issue of *Teenage Sex*, first released in 1982. Its print history is as follows: August 1982, 44,150 copies; January 1983, 20,050;

and January 1984, 21,780. The total of 85,980 must have been enough; no more were printed after that.[31]

Other key criteria in the financial equation are the cost of production and the selling price to the distributors. It has been estimated that, for a print run of 5,000, colour magazines of these dimensions cost between 50p (80 cents) and £1 ($1.60) a copy depending on the number of pages. These figures decline as the print run increases because the costs of the photographs, artwork and typesetting are spread over a higher production volume. When sold in moderate quantities to distributors, the price will be about four times that amount, say £2 ($3) a copy. For example, *Teenage Sex* currently sells at a wholesale price of DKr19 for orders between 100 and 999.

If this can be taken as a reasonable average price, Rodox's revenues to date from *Teenage Sex* No. 25 referred to above are 85,980 × 19 = DKr1,633,620 (or more than £150,000, say $225,000). If total production costs are less than DKr5, the gross profit on that issue alone must be more than £120,000 ($180,000)!

The benefits of the 'mini-mag' format can be deduced from similar figures. *Stimulation* is a thirty-two-page publication with a wholesale price of DKr6.50 for quantities between 100 and 999. ('It sells very well in Brazil,' says Rupert James.) The print run is usually just over 20,000. No new photography is required (that has already been paid for) and the magazine has only a quarter of the pages of something like *Color Climax*. Even so, the profit must be lower – DKr100,000 (£10,000 or $15,000) for one edition. Rodox is probably grossing £500,000 ($750,000) a year on each of the major bi-monthly titles and as little as £100,000 ($150,000) annually on each of the minor magazines.

Porn gold? Probably not; that profit margin has to support the overheads of Rodox Trading and its eighty employees and make a contribution to the tax coffers of the Danish government before any net figure is arrived at. In reality, the figures are not out of line with those of a successful publisher shipping more conventional magazines; and they have the benefit of being able to carry lucrative advertising.

What money is there to be made further down the chain of distribution? The retail price will largely be determined by the competition and the figure there may vary between £3 ($4.50) and less than £7 (say $10). The subscription price for six issues of *Private* is £35 ($75 for US customers), but that includes the mailing cost. Certainly, it will be an outstanding product which can be sold at a higher price than *Private*, the market leader. The average retail price in Europe for a porn magazine, therefore, is probably £5 ($7.50). From that, the retailer will get about £2 ($3), the distributor £1 ($1.50) and the publisher £2 ($3). The distributor gets the least because he will be handling the largest volumes and will undoubtedly require some degree of exclusivity to keep that volume high. That explains why *Private*, for example, has only two distributors in Sweden, one in Germany and two in Holland. But if the German distributor – ZBF – is shipping 50,000 copies per issue of *Private*, then on six issues a year the deal must be worth something in the region of £300,000 ($450,000) a year.[32]

So who are those key distributors? Many budding pornographers will be seeking nationwide distribution of their magazines. Even more – especially those aiming to compete with the high-quality products of the porn establishment – will be seeking international distribution aimed at the widest possible market. Two of the biggest potential markets will be difficult if not impossible to penetrate: the United States of America and the United Kingdom. To the manufacturer of more conventional consumer items, the US market with its ready wealth and refined infrastructure beckons tantalizingly. Pornographers, however, view it as a difficult country in which to do business, not merely because of attempts by the US Customs Service to keep outside what is readily available inside, but because federal laws and variations in obscenity statutes make the market so fragmented.

This phenomenon is best illustrated by the problems faced by American magazine publishers. Dave Patrick is editor and chief photographer of *Spectator*, probably the best of the soft-core 'adult newspapers' published on the West Coast. Issued weekly, *Spectator* covers the San Franscisco Bay area sex scene from its base in Berkeley – it is a descendant of the now-defunct 1960s underground paper, *The Berkeley Barb* – and is often bought by out-of-state visitors wanting to know where they can leave their hearts. 'A guy living in Oregon sent in his $29 subscription, but we had to turn him down,' Patrick remembers. 'Then he called and we explained that we could not mail the paper out of the state. "But I only live twenty miles from the California state line!" he said. We suggested that he opened a mail box this side of the border and collected it from there. That was the only way it could be done.'[33]

*Spectator* would not pass for hard core in continental Europe, the New York-based *Screw* certainly would. *Screw*'s infamous publisher, Al Goldstein, can include hard core material for the Big Apple, but when he launched *National Screw* magazine, he had to limit it to the kind of soft-core material common to other nationally distributed publications. Patrick, a former worker in the Goldstein empire, described it as 'a poor man's *Hustler*'.[34] Indeed, in order to stay as raunchy as possible for those states where 'raunch' is acceptable, *Hustler* often appears in a variety of editions, the softest for the Bible Belt.

This situation goes a long way towards explaining why the American porn magazine business is much less impressive than that in Europe. Carl Delvert, the marketing manager of *Private* tipped his hat in the direction of Larry Flynt's magazine: '*Hustler* is first class,' but was less generous towards the others. 'The quality of American mags is generally poor. Maybe the Americans are not used to good print and paper quality.'[35] For a company so preoccupied with quality, lack of it in the local opposition represents a business opportunity.

Carl Delvert looks and acts more like a clerk than the chief salesman for the world's top porn magazine. Tall, stocky, and with dark hair, he wears a moustache and horn-rimmed spectacles. From behind a desk covered with shipping documentation, invoices and sales statistics, he talks about the company's attempts to break into the US market:

> We've tried operating through an agent, but he was not doing very much. We can't ship into the States in large quantities, so we have to find a way of printing over there. But the people who have approached us are talking ridiculous figures. They are talking about five or ten thousand and I'm not going over there with the printing material for that figure! We were very close to making a deal with Al Bloom [Caballero Control Corp, producers of the *Swedish Erotica* video series and magazine], but it just sort of died. So availability [of *Private*] is very patchy, just a few copies going in by mail order. I know a Swedish guy in America and he is trying very hard, but that is again mail order. American law is very strange, because you are more or less allowed openly to sell pornography, but it has to be produced in the States. I am not even sure I can send in the printing plates. But if we go over and shoot the pictures and so on, we can easily publish *Private* there. It's a problem of customs more than anything. It's odd.[36]

Kent Wisell, Delvert's predecessor at *Private* would agree. Both are Swedes, a nation still in delayed shock over the assassination of Prime Minister Olaf Palme and universally horrified at the violence prevalent in American society. Wisell confirmed Delvert's experience: '*Private* never made it in America. It should be printed in one place and distributed to all the other states, but this couldn't be done. That's the big problem – moving stuff across state lines. Economically, it's impossible, otherwise. There has been big mail order business into the US. I think most of it gets through – it should do.'

Like many Scandinavians, Wisell is baffled at what he sees as the confused morality of the country: 'America is a crazy country in my opinion, because in some states you are free to go out and buy a hand-gun and shoot down anyone in the street. But magazines showing a normal act between two people? It's banned! It's crazy, a crazy country. It's the same double morality which exists in England. I saw something when I was over in March; dwarf-throwing. You couldn't show anything like that here. It should be banned!'[37]

With or without dwarf-throwing, the British Isles are the last vestige of porn-free Europe; trading in hard-core pornography is illegal under the Obscene Publications Act and the officers of Her Majesty's Customs can seize more or less anything they don't like the look of at points of entry. It is hard to believe that the British and Irish are any less interested in porn than any other Europeans, and pornographers eye the last potential growth area on the continent hungrily. 'England is difficult to ignore because it is so big,' says Carl Delvert, 'you have so many people. But it's stupid, ridiculous, the English law as it is. It's the only country that is so strict. You can't sell into the UK, you just can't. I'm sure that if it was legal, our turnover would double the next day. But pornography will not be made legal there in my lifetime.'[38] So it seems that readers of *Private* will have to take their chances that the mail will get through the combined customs and postal inspection at six separate UK centres.

Rodox in Denmark is less concerned about penetrating the British stronghold. English editor Rupert James explained their position: 'We don't sell directly into the UK ourselves because we're not in the retail end of the business any more. There are mail order companies who do send our products into the UK but, as we point out to people, we are a manufacturer, not a distributor. This is a *manufacturing* company – full stop. Responsibility for distribution lies entirely with our wholesalers.'[39]

In the two decades following the decriminalization of pornography in Sweden, the rest of Europe and Scandinavia has opened up to the porn barons. Although Sweden itself is no longer the insatiable market it used to be, there remains a nucleus of enthusiastic consumers who can obtain sex magazines with ease. There are three main avenues of distribution to this market: through the national magazine distribution company Presam; via Boksenter, a company owned by Rolf Rahm, the general factotum of Swedish porn; and through mail order companies such as Hagen Import.

'In Sweden we use the state-owned Presam and Boksenter. They [Boksenter] distribute on to stores specializing in this kind of material,' says Delvert. The idea of a national distributor delivering all types of publication to all outlets throughout the country on a regular basis might appeal to any publisher. It does, however, have its drawbacks.

'No, I don't use Presam,' Kent Wisell reveals. 'They are difficult to work with in the beginning. They only pay after twenty days and, anyway, they don't sell so much. What happens with Presam, they have lots of outlets, all over Sweden. Many times they send it out to small places in the north or south of Sweden and there is an old lady standing in the kiosk. She puts it down – I don't want this. Then they send it back after a few months and I get all the returns. It's better to sell directly, because I don't sell on a sale-or-return basis. I get a better deal with Boksenter.'

The nature of this deal demonstrates the benefits of a good relationship with a distributor: '*Bohème* carries advertisements for Boksenter's own products. They plug my magazines and I have ads in the mag for their videos. I'm a very good friend of the owner of Boksenter, Rolf Rahm. I'll scratch your back, you scratch mine.'[40]

Distribution to the news kiosks and bookstores which will stock pornography has become increasingly essential in

Sweden (and Denmark) as the number of specialist porn shops has declined. This development has given added importance to mail order as a means of distribution and specialist companies have been established to service this need. Norwegian-born porn baron Leif Hagen owns a porn shop in Stockholm, but his main business is centred on Hagen Import AB (founded in 1980), a mail order company which trades as LH Postorder AB and is based in the suburb of Solna near Stockholm. The highly efficient, computerized operation is managed by an affable young man called Viggo Berggren. It employs fifteen people who process over 50,000 orders a year, generating sales revenues of about £2 million ($3 million) annually.

In an astute piece of 'vertical integration', Leif Hagen expanded his mail order catalogue into a men's magazine called *Aktuell Rapport* (see Chapter 5). A typical issue of this high-circulation weekly carried as many as ten full pages advertising 463 hard-core magazines and videos as well as some audio cassettes and sex toys such as dildos.[41] Hardly any of these products are made in Sweden and most come from Denmark, West Germany, Holland and the United States (via porn baron Charlie Geerts at Intex in Amsterdam).

The full scale of the inventory, and the need for a computer, can only be appreciated when it is seen stacked high on the hundreds of yards of shelves in the spacious modern warehouse. There are 8,000 magazine titles – all hard core – with some two million copies in stock at any one time. This is supplemented by 2,500 video titles, a quarter of a million cassettes for the Swedish market only.

About one in a hundred and fifty Swedes orders something each year from this source alone. On the walls of the company's small cafeteria are a number of huge photographs showing what appears to be the result of an explosion in the warehouse. What actually happened was that when LH Import first moved into the building, the timber shelving failed to support the weight of the porn.

The end unit toppled over and knocked down the next one and so on until the domino effect had wrecked the whole storage system.[42]

Sweden is a lively, but small market for pornography. West Germany, which decriminalized pornography in 1975, is probably five times larger and could be the biggest in Europe unless or until the law changes in England. Its importance is underlined by the fact that 80 per cent of Peter Theander's output from Rodox heads south into the Federal Republic.[43] You cannot be a major porn publisher in Europe without doing business in Germany. And you cannot do business in Germany without doing business with ZBF and the Schmitt family (see Chapter 2).

Georg Schmitt and his four sons dominate the distribution of porn from their three massive warehouses in Wiesbaden, near Frankfurt. Making use of their infrastructure is essential; although the German market is much bigger than all of Scandinavia, it is much more tightly regulated. In addition to the material itself being regulated (child sex is strictly forbidden and acts of violence are frowned on), pornography can only be sold through licensed shops. These are allowed no external display of the product and people under the age of eighteen are forbidden entry. Sending pornography through the post is also banned, thus making mail order impossible. But within those rules, West Germany is a thriving and healthy market, where the porn industry has achieved more of an aura of respectability than anywhere else.

ZBF publishes a full-colour product catalogue the size and weight of a local telephone book. Its latest, *Europa-Erotik-Totalkatalog No. 6*, was published in late 1985, and Peter Schmitt says that it was by no means comprehensive. Since then, so many new products have been added to the range that the catalogue needs a thorough review – an expensive and time-consuming task.[44] Shop managers can place orders by mail or telephone. Deliveries are made by the company's fleet of twelve Mercedes trucks which also carry a stock of all the fastest-moving lines. Each driver has his own territory to cover and between deliveries, he makes calls at other shops. The company also ships into Switzerland and Austria. The driver/salesman aims to visit each shop at least once a month and to sell goods from the back of the truck.

ZBF performs the classic distribution function. The firm buys the best products from all over the world and sells on to the porn shops and video cinemas. It does not sell to the public, nor is it involved in producing pornography. Beate Uhse's operation in Flensburg is more vertically integrated; it makes films and videos and distributes these and other companies' products to its nationwide chain of nineteen shops (Beate Uhse Läden), fourteen Dr Müller shops and sixteen Blue Movie Kinos from its Flensburg headquarters.[45]

Second only to Germany in the size of its porn market is Spain, a relative newcomer and the first of the south European countries to liberalize the publication of magazines showing explicit sexual acts. Kent Wisell experienced this aspect of the radical changes that took place in Spain after the death of the repressive dictator, Franco:

> It is a very big market. Spain has a population of 36 million, plus millions of tourists going there every year. It was not a steady thing since Franco died – it exploded in 1980 or 1981.
>
> At that time I was working for *Private* and we were approached by a big company who wanted to print *Private* in Spain, although it was not legal at that time. But they went ahead and printed a Spanish edition. The first sold out in about eight hours. Then they printed No. 2, but the police confiscated it and the case was in the newspapers and on television. Some years passed, a year perhaps, and it started again.
>
> Now you can buy anything. In the beginning it was pure curiosity because they hadn't seen anything like

these magazines. Now they have so many tourists in Spain, people from all over the world.

The English particularly see something they can't find at home and they're interested in it. I think the tourists are a big part of it.[46]

But the Swedish porn publisher was quick to point out the problems of Spain as a market: 'Even a poor-quality magazine can sell 20,000 copies there, and there is so much competition that the prices are the lowest in Europe – only 600 pesetas (£3, $4.50) for something like *Private*. The magazines they publish there themselves are awful. There are lots of domestic producers, but it's lousy stuff. There are four or five different companies buying photographs from France, mainly. Also domestic material. But they are always in a hurry, their layout is done in a rush, printing in a rush, bookbinding in a rush. So the final result is poor.'[47]

Spain is also important as a gateway to the expanding porn markets of South America. 'I lived in Argentina for a year in 1970, working down there. Then even *Playboy* was in a black plastic bag, so you couldn't even check what was in it. Now the political climate has changed a bit – perhaps very much in Argentina and I notice that magazines are being shipped over from Spain to South America. Brazil is a big market.'[48]

'A lot is happening in South America,' agrees Carl Delvert. 'I'm not sure which countries, because that area is obviously looked after by our Spanish distributors. There is a Spanish version of *Private* for Spain, so they will get that, but I'm not sure if they will do a Portuguese version for Brazil. There are no legal problems down there at all. It all happened only a couple of months ago.'[49]

Of the remaining countries in Southern Europe, pornography is now legal, or at least unhindered by the law, in Portugal, Greece and Italy. Italy gained the unusual distinction of being the first country in the world to elect a porn star to political office. As a candidate for the unorthodox

Radical Party, 'La Cicciolina' (Little Chubby – better known as Ilona Staller) was elected to the national Chamber of Deputies in the general election of June 1987. Her propensity for pulling down the top of her dress ensured maximum turnout for her campaign meetings and only her party leaders won more votes.[50]

Further north, the Dutch market – augmented by tourist sales in the porn shops of Amsterdam's notorious red light district – is dominated by two competing distributors. 'Fat Charlie' Geerts whose Videorama company was the major importer of American X-rated videos for many years, also operates a general porn wholesaling concern called Intex, based in Amsterdam. Its leading competitor in Holland is Ari van der Heeul whose Calvista International distributes out of Rotterdam.

For the porn magazine publisher these are now all established and well-refined sales channels for the stable European market. But pornography now circles the world thanks to an ambitious and personable forty-five-year-old Australian called John Lark. Lark's business is now based at Fishwyck in the Commonwealth Territory of Canberra and employs twenty staff, fifteen of them women. Lark has been dealing in 'adult' material for years, starting in the book trade, progressing to hard-core 8 mm films, which originated with Rodox in Copenhagen, and now does his main trade in video and mail order. He has operated against a background of inconsistency in Australian federal and state law and, more recently, concerted attempts to strengthen the statutes governing the import, duplication, distribution, display and sale of pornography.

'*Private* is the biggest line of magazines we've got,' Lark confirmed. 'In fact I specifically targeted *Private*, because Milton's been publishing it for twenty years now and it has to be the biggest-selling hard-core magazine in Europe, so there's got to be a market for it in Australia. I flew out to see Milton and he agreed to give me the franchise.'

Lark's area of operation covers Australia, New Zealand

and the South Pacific Basin. He can't make any headway into the 'islands', Papua New Guinea and Fiji, because of the strict censorship there. Nor does he trade with Hong Kong, for the same reason. Singapore, Manila, Tokyo and Taiwan are places where he might be tempted to take up the potential, particularly for video, but only if the law changes.

'*Private* has gone very well,' says Lark. 'It's the style of the magazine, even the early issues going back to No. 20 and No. 30 still sell – and he's now on to No. 80. It's the stock line for an adult shop, so we just keep replenishing. We import just under 5,000 per issue, which is quite a lot for the size of Australia's population. It takes about a year to sell that many. The initial distribution is around 2,000, after that it's only a question of topping up the shelves.'[51]

The bread in the thick European porn sandwich is represented by Britain and Ireland to the west and the Soviet bloc to the east. Pornography certainly exists in those countries, but is very illegal, as one Swedish truck driver discovered to his cost: 'We never tried sending stuff into the Eastern bloc,' Carl Delvert recalled. 'You should never try and smuggle it there. We knew a truck driver going regularly to one of these Eastern bloc countries and he came up here and said "Can I buy something? I'll take them in." Of course he knew that if he could get them in he could make a fortune. So he bought ten or fifteen magazines. He had been going regularly for five years into that country without any problems and – believe it or not – that particular time, they caught him! He went through some very nasty experiences and he's no longer allowed to go back to that country. He lost his job with the trucking company but it was his own risk. There is a market there, but I wouldn't advise anyone to do it.'[52]

The same advice could apply to the Middle East where pornography is popular with expatriates and the wealthy ruling families alike. Such are the risks involved in smuggling magazines, that it is possible to sell individual pages of *Private* for £10 [$15]. A whole magazine could attract more than £500 ($750) – and a public flogging.[53]

Although hard-core magazines are available in Iceland and Greenland, the Faroe Islands seem to be a troublesome market. Torben Dahlvad was once editor-in-chief of *Rapport*, a Danish men's magazine which occasionally includes porn spreads (see Chapter 5). For him the Faroes (half-way between Scotland and Iceland) became something of a battleground between himself on one side and the local chief of police on the other: '*Rapport*, a legal Danish magazine, is banned on the Faroe Islands. And that is part of Denmark! When you pass a law in the Danish Parliament, they normally say this law doesn't affect the Faroe Islands because they are more or less independent and have another legal structure. So pornography was never free on the Faroe Islands. Three years ago, the police chief in the Faroe Islands banned *Rapport* and all the other men's magazines. The figures weren't that high, but if you looked at the per capita figures, we had one of our densest readerships there; it was 1,500 magazines per week.'

The Irish monks who discovered these bleak islands in the eighth century would have been appalled; only 42,000 people live there today. If Dahlvad had only 50 per cent of the market, more than one in five of the male population was buying a sex magazine every week. His response was prompt: 'We had to campaign for subscriptions, because there was no way they could stop the mail. We started an ad campaign in a weekly paper that was distributed to every household on the Faroe Islands and that went OK for the first week. The second week, the police visited the printing plant and told the owner of the paper that if he ran the ad again, the whole circulation would be banned. So he had to take that out. Then we did a direct mail campaign to all the households and that resulted in some strange letters from priests and others!'

It was not the small loss of circulation which preoccupied the Dane, or even the principle too much: 'We got a lot of press coverage. And a lot of time on radio and television. They loved it! The Faroe Islanders, they are either drinking or not drinking, they are fucking or not fucking. It divided the whole population! Some took it very seriously and said, well, you are bad boys and the others, they laughed at it! We got about 400 subscribers. That's not bad.'[54]

Before porn magazines became universally available in continental Europe, a subscription was often the only way that customers could gain access to the product. That situation has now changed. 'Mail-order has gone down considerably and we only have wholesalers, agents throughout the world instead. They handle subscriptions themselves. We have a mail order insert which they take and put their own name and address on. This is all right by me, because Swedish postal charges are increasing – it's very costly to mail out of Sweden. We ship in bulk from Spain and then they send out the individual copies. There is still a big mail order business going into Japan, though.' But many customs officers still see a need to protect their countries from foreign porn and will seize anything they can intercept. 'The customer knows that he takes a risk,' warns Delvert. 'About 20 per cent is intercepted. With the US it depends on which state. With California we don't have any problem, for example. We know about the mail intercept operation, but they have not been checking stuff from Spain. Anyway we are not mailing stuff out of Spain now – we have found a solution to that as well. Let's see how long it will last.'[55]

Now that the law is only exceptionally a hindrance to a free market in pornography, most magazines are bought over the counter at specialist porn shops or at regular bookstores and news kiosks. In Holland, Denmark and Sweden hardcore magazines can be bought at any retail outlet that cares to stock them. For example, the bookshop franchise holders in the duty-free area of Amsterdam's ultra-modern Schiphol Airport stock magazines such as *Private* and *Pleasure* along the top row of the shelf immediately under the cashier's desk inside the store. Any innocent buyer of *Fortune* magazine, the *Frankfurter Allgemeine Zeitung* or a love story by

Barbara Cartland cannot fail to notice them.

In Sweden a major distributor of pornographic magazines is Presam, the national wholesaling company owned jointly by publishers. If you join the association of publishers, there is no way in which Presam can refuse to distribute your product. Although many news retailers – at railway stations, for example – will stock sex magazines, they usually keep them on the top shelves out of the reach of children and insist that they have relatively innocuous covers.

Most hard-core magazines, however, are sold through specialist porn shops where customers have a wider choice and need not feel embarrassed about making a purchase. In some countries, porn shops have to be licensed and are required to bar young people under the age of eighteen. In West Germany pornography can only be sold through such licensed outlets.

In many cases these shops have now become little short of lavish in their ambience. The Soho Sex Shop in Stockholm is owned by Curth Hson-Nilson, the veteran of the Swedish porn scene who, according to one local journalist, 'invented fucking'.[56] Soho is located at Birgar Jarlsgaten 15, a few blocks from the $12-a-drink Grand Hotel overlooking Stockholm's harbour. In keeping with the locale, the shop has a discreet frontage with none of the usual neon. Only by looking carefully can you see a window display showing magazines, videos and a few sex aids. The visitor is greeted by piped music, and a wide, sweeping staircase which leads down past the door of the kino/strip club (open evenings only) and into the main store.

Many interconnecting rooms have been made to appear like the grottoes of a cave through the use of a curving, fake-stone ceiling. There is even the occasional potted plant. In various corners are a dozen or so booths for 'previewing' videos. In the centre of the main room are three small *rive gauche* café tables complete with parasols at which clients can drink a coffee or beer while considering their purchases. Everything legal in Sweden seems to be available – including animal sex – but with gay, S & M, and even the old *Janus* series of English bondage magazines prominently displayed. Soho is very clean, carpeted and has a pleasant and relaxed atmosphere. This is one of the few porn shops left in Sweden, but is probably one of the classiest in the world.

Berth Milton has a theory for the decline in Swedish porn shops: 'It is because Sweden is more open, more outspoken, more free. It's not a big step any more to go into a sex shop, but now you don't have to. You can go into any tobacconist and say "I want *Expressen*, I want *Aftonbladet*, and I want *Private* . . ." Now this is normal behaviour, it is no sensation.'[57] Perhaps so, but without the porn shops there is a limited choice. This, and the ability to shop from the comfort of your own home, explains the rise in mail order porn in Sweden.

The 'Postorder' in the name of Leif Hagen's company is the Swedish equivalent of the cash-on-delivery system used in most countries – but not quite the same. This is how to place an order. Each advertisement concentrates on a particular type of porn, or on a particular brand, and has a fairly standardized layout; a headline strip across the top, order details and coupon across the bottom. The body of the advertisement is a set of small colour reproductions of the magazine or video cassette covers. Underneath each of these are product codes, sometimes the price and sometimes the title. To order, tear the page out of the magazine and circle the products you want to buy. Enter on the coupon your name, address, postcode, and name of local post office. Then sign to confirm that you are over eighteen years of age and post the advertisement to LH Postorder. Send no money!

At the Solna warehouse, order details are keyed into an Ericsson multi-user computer system. This prints out 'picking lists' for the warehouse staff, address labels and an itemized invoice. At the end of each day, the Swedish Post

Office sends a truck and picks up the shipments. These are distributed to the customer's local post office. The post office delivers a standard card telling him he has a parcel and how much to pay. He takes this note and his money and hands them over at the post office to get the goods. The post office then transfers the cash collected to Hagen's account via the Giro (national banking) system. It is an efficient system which obviates the need for Hagen staff to handle cash. The Swedish Post Office is well aware that it is carrying hard-core pornography, but there is no law to prohibit that and it is pleased to have the business, as is the Giro Bank.[58]

But mail order is not suitable for the walk-in tourist trade. At the opposite end of Europe (and the scale of retailing standards) from Curth Hson-Nilson's Soho is the last porn shop in Europe before the South Pole. Before being mugged by the tourist industry, Los Christianos was a remote fishing village on the south coast of Tenerife.

Situated off the north-west coast of Africa (in the same latitude as Florida and Cairo), the volcanic, sub-tropical Canary Islands have belonged to Spain since the fifteenth century. The British attempted a sea-borne takeover bid for the islands (credited by some as the remnants of the lost continent of Atlantis) in 1797 but withdrew after a thrashing, Nelson leaving his arm behind in the process. A more successful invasion came in the twentieth century, this time borne by the Boeings of the package-tour operators. The results are predictable: hotels, bars, discos, night clubs, restaurants, time-share property agents and junk souvenir shops. The British were first – and they still tend to dominate – but the islands are now also patronized by the Germans, French, Belgians, Italians, Dutch and Scandinavians.

On Calle de Juan XXIII in Los Christianos between John L. Gardner's Indian Restaurant, the Carniceria, the Café Bar la Bohème and opposite the El Rancho de Don Antonio Restaurant–Bar is the Sexy Shop, as advertised in *DA Here and Now* ('The Canary Islands' only English newspaper').

On the shelves of this furthest outreach of porn Europe are copies of *Foxy Lady* from Germany, *Private* from Sweden, and *Color Climax* and *Teenage Sex* from Denmark.

A dwindling warehouse stock will not be the magazine publisher's only sign of success; the customers will write to him or her. Berth Milton has a heavy postbag:

> I get thousands and thousands and thousands of people who write. I can't understand how they spend their time, writing eight or nine or ten pages. I can only recall one letter – probably written by an idiot – which said that you're showing filth. But all the other letters are positive. I remember in particular, one letter from an English couple. This said, 'When we happened to come across *Private*, we put it in the bedroom. We dress up, we go out, wining, dining, dancing and so on, and when we get back, she puts some very sexy outfit on. Then we turn the pages of *Private*. We try the positions and the ideas we can get out of the magazine.' That was a very, very beautiful letter.
>
> In No. 62 I had a questionnaire with twenty-four questions – English on one side, German on the other – and we got 13,000 answers! I put these in the computer so I know exactly what people would like to see and what they don't want to see. From Spain, from Germany, from Austria, from Luxembourg, Switzerland, Scandinavia, Holland. If you compare it with the *Hite Report*, they sent out 100,000 questionnaires only to get 3,000 back. We got 13,000 from something like the same distribution! They were mostly men. But very, very often, the man is writing here in English and his wife or girlfriend has used the other [German] side.
>
> People are more open now, more sophisticated in their taste, that's what you have to consider. And that's what I'm trying to show in my magazine. Interesting stories which include sex. Not just 'in and out' because that's out of date today.[59]

Artist 'Erik von Goethe' had a similar experience: '*Torrid* got more letters than any other Gold Star magazine . . . Curious, isn't it? Tuppy Owens once said to me, she felt responsible in producing magazines, because her magazine might well be the nearest that many of her readers, maybe most of her readers, would ever get to the real thing. Which is horrifying! And flabbergasting. The thing is, about the role of pornography in people's lives, the reason they become loyal readers of yours is, when they buy your magazine they're not just buying sex pictures, they're buying friendship. And this is absolutely what Teresa Orlovski has picked up and run with. She's so honest in her editorials. I can remember one in which she says, "Life is a little difficult at the moment, I'm sure we all know what it's like – I've gone off sex! I know it's only temporary, but I've gone right off it." What a thing for a sex publisher to admit! But it's also something where everyone will say, yeah! That happened to me last year!'[60]

So it takes considerable effort and resources to launch a new and successful porn magazine in a crowded and competitive market. Will Kent Wisell succeed? His former employer, Berth Milton doesn't think so: 'Wisell will not succeed with his new magazine. It is impossible to start a new magazine these days.'

Perhaps Wisell learned enough during his time with Milton to realize the perils, but he is not short of enthusiasm and ideas:

> My own dream is to make some sort of combination of *Penthouse*, *Playboy* and a magazine like *Q* or *Private* or whatever it is. Some editorial stuff, make a hard-core magazine in A4 size. That would be the best. And that's what people want to see. You don't see many sex magazine in this size. There are a few American ones like *Swedish Erotica* [the magazine]. But they are just forty-eight pages. If you make a magazine like *Playboy*, *Penthouse*, *Hustler*, and put in some editorial stuff, so people

can read something, not only just look at pictures – and have lots of good sexy pictures. But you must carry advertising. That's the big problem, because I think there are companies who want to take out ads. We would be looking for ads from people like Marlboro, Prince, Johnnie Walker.

Wisell is even prepared to consider the more rapidly growing market for porn videos:

That's why I should start doing the videos very soon. I'll call them the *Carmen* series. I'd probably shoot magazine material at the same time. So the same material is in the magazine and vice versa. That's the smarter thing. If you make a ninety-minute movie for instance, you can perhaps make three still sets for the magazine. And you can carry ads for the videos in the magazine and put ads in the movie as well, for the magazine. I think that the people who are going to buy the magazine, if they see some good-looking model, they would like to see her working. It would help to consolidate the name *Carmen* – whatever it would be.[61]

The cross-production method described by Wisell was first established by the Theanders in the early 1970s when they were making film loops, but is no longer available to them since they began buying in material. The technique has now reached refinement in the hands of Hans Moser and many *Foxy Lady*, *Sweet Little 16* and *Lady Domina* sets are available both in the magazines and on video cassettes.

The earlier estimate (in Chapter 1) of 250 million hardcore sex magazines printed in Europe and Scandinavia since the end of the 1960s is a conservative one. Production is accelerating as more countries liberalize their censorship laws. On a world scale, there are more than 1,000 porn magazine titles being published at any one time. If the average annual circulation of these is only 50,000 copies (including reprints), the global inventory of pornography in print is being engrossed by at least 50 million magazines a year. This represents a consumer expenditure in the region of £250 million (or $400 million) every twelve months.

Little wonder that relative newcomers like Roger Hawse in England and Kent Wisell in Sweden snap at the heels of *Private, Color Climax, Foxy Lady, Ero, Pleasure,* and all the other leading titles consumed so avidly by the collectors of hard-core magazines.

# 5

# *The Secret Pages: Men's Magazines in Scandinavia*

Men's magazines everywhere have a familiar set of ingredients: adventure, crime, war, travel, cars, motor bikes, sport, humour, competitions, gossip, show business, personal finance, gambling and even a seasoning of politics – especially if a scandal is involved. They also include women and sex.

The successful recipe will inevitably be conditioned by the culture and laws of the country of publication and will vary according to the traditional profile of the target audience: the key factors being age range and level of disposable income. When a circulation war breaks out, it will also be influenced by the editorial decisions of competitive periodicals.

Many such magazines have a long-standing and up-market reputation for being a source of well-written stories about travel, adventure and sport for the discerning male reader. American *Esquire* remains the definitive example of the genre. Even the more recent, more sexually orientated entrants to the market place – notably *Playboy* – have tried to emulate *Esquire*'s respected status by publishing the work of some of the world's best writers. However, Torben Dhalvad, one of Denmark's leading editors, describes such articles and stories as 'alibi material'.[1] In its pioneering decades of the 1950s and 1960s, it was probably safe to assume that the 'Playmate of the Month' was winning *Playboy* more buyers than any number of contributions by Isaac Asimov, Norman Mailer and John Updike. The same must be true today.

What has changed over the intervening years in all men's magazines is the quantity and quality of those pages dedicated to photographic spreads of (mostly) young women in various stages of undress. These have followed a steady progression from innocent outdoor shots of smiling, healthy girls in swimsuits and bikinis through coy nudes to today's studio photographs of women, legs akimbo in exotic sets, vaginal lips on provocative display.

In Sweden in the mid-1970s, magazines for men were at their apogee. The market was dominated by three titles: *Se* ('Look'), *Lektyr* ('Reading') and *FiB Aktuellt* ('FiB News'). Each was then published weekly and their respective circulations were 120,000, 253,000 and 279,900; a total of 652,900 for a population of only 8.25 million. Scaled up for the US market, this is equivalent to more than 17 million copies per week for those three publications alone. But it wasn't to last.

Bengt Lénberg, a writer working for *FiB Aktuellt* in the 1970s, played a major role in a circulation war where the combatants took no prisoners. Lénberg, a career journalist who cut his teeth on Sweden's provincial newspapers, is in his early forties. A fair beard of uncertain geography fails to cover the worst that acne can inflict. He frequents bars but drinks only Coke. 'Never have drunk alcohol. Except a glass of champagne at New Year and a schnapps at Midsummer. They're kind of traditional.'

Tenstoppet ('The Pewter Tankard') on Dalagatan is a favourite post-deadline meeting place for Stockholm's journalists. Indeed, so good was their trade that when the city's equivalent of Fleet Street closed down, the owner moved lock, stock and barrel to a more suitable location. The regulars insist that from the inside of the bar there is no visible evidence of the move having taken place. As dictated by the country's tight drinking laws, Tenstoppet is part bar, part restaurant, but the bar part is much bigger than the restaurant part.

The doorman takes guests' top-coats; good cloakroom management is a necessary feature of Scandinavian efficiency. Lénberg's usual Coke is already waiting as he approaches the beer-stained bar. Before he has taken the second pull, a stocky, genial character slips up to him, whispers in his ear and, in almost the same movement, slips a couple of large-denomination bills into the top pocket of the journalist's shirt. They shake hands and nothing further is said, but it is clear that a short-term loan has just been repaid in full. The owner of the bar-restaurant stops by to exchange pleasantries. Lénberg is just one of the regulars.

'Men's mags are fantasies like James Bond movies,' he says. 'You need the right formula of cars, travel and sex. *Se* wasn't really a men's magazine. It always had a cover-girl, but no naked girls inside. It was really like a Swedish version of *Life* – a vehicle for photo-journalism.' As he expounds his theories on magazine journalism, it becomes clear that he remains an enthusiast for the high standards represented by the *Life* magazine of old. 'But,' he goes on, 'it became impossible to sell men's mags in Sweden without nude girls. Something in the format of *Life* would not sell more than 10,000 copies today.'

So, even in 1977 *Se* was terminally ill and ceased publication before the end of the decade. But Lénberg denies that the continued high circulation of *Se*'s two main competitors was solely due to their willingness to print plenty of 'glamour' material: 'At *FiB Aktuellt* and *Lektyr*, we had a journalistic idea about exposing politicians . . . about revealing how they were travelling around the world or around Sweden, eating and drinking. We could get access to their expenses claims because we have this Public Information Act. For example, I went to Sundsvall [a port on the

Gulf of Bothnia in the north of Sweden] to interview a hockey player. While I was there I also went into the municipal offices and took out the receipts of the local politicians to discover how much they'd been spending at restaurants over the previous fourteen days. Well, they were always out spending 1,600 crowns [about $380 at the time] for two persons. And then we put it in the magazine, we'd put those stories on the front page with a big banner: their drinks bill! Ordinary people loved it! Because they knew their local politicians. They read the magazines for those revealing articles. And we did a lot of investigative journalism – environment scandals and so on. *FiB Aktuellt* and *Lektyr* were pioneers in that field in Sweden. That was why the circulation was so high in 1977.'

It did not stay that way: 'You cannot have copyright on an idea,' Lénberg explained. 'We'd done those stories for five or six years without anyone stealing the idea. In 1978 the daily newspapers took the idea over and started doing it day after day. That led to a change in the representation rules for politicians. Now they can't drink liquor, they must drink wine and so on. But that was a very big thing. And they did it day after day. In the magazines, we could only do it when we had the complete story. They could begin and within one week they could kill a politician! Those stories were a big image thing for the men's magazines.' But then they were gone.

Rapidly running short of ideas about developing the product, the combatants took the traditional route of concentrating on the promotion. 'In the late 1970s when *Lektyr* and *FiB Aktuellt* were really competing we made records, we made cassettes, we made everything! We had T-shirts, we had lighters, we had shows, we had vans – everything! But somehow during those years we *killed* selling magazines with those ideas. It was too much . . . And there has been a new generation who don't fall for the same gimmicks.'

Perhaps it was inevitable that someone would try telephone sex as a sales gimmick. To get the special number you had to buy the magazine and that would result in an increase in sales. Or so the theory went. Bengt Lénberg was there to witness the resulting farce:

> The first time it was tried in Sweden, it wasn't in the general idea of phone sex, a taped recording on an automatic machine. There was a Swedish girl called Marie Vorso who made porno films under the name of Maria Lynn. She made a film with Harry Reems [the male lead in *Deep Throat*] called *Bel Ami*.[2]
>
> We had Marie as a sex adviser and one of the ideas was that you could phone her. That was in 1977 when *FiB Aktuellt* was still owned by the Bonnier company [the biggest publishing house in Sweden]. That first night we blocked out the local telephone system! More than 20,000 people didn't have any telephone! That was the first time you could call a girl and talk about sex. They'd tried it on *Expressen* with doctors and so on, but this was the first time you could call a girl who fucked publicly and Sweden went mad! Only three phone calls got through! On the first, all you could hear was heavy breathing, just 'huh, huh, huh . . .', and then, 'Thank you!' Then the next. After the third phone call Marie couldn't stop laughing and all the lines went dead.

Lénberg grinned as he relished the memory: 'I was with her because I was going to write a story on what they were talking about. I was trying to dial out and couldn't get anywhere! Everything was blocked! The day after, we read in the morning newspaper that *FiB Aktuellt* had ruined the telephone system, so we didn't do that anymore. We got into a lot of trouble with Televerket [the telephone company]. It finally cost over Kr100,000 [about $24,000] because the magazine had to pay to fix the system. We tried to do it again with an extra number, but they wouldn't give us one! *Lektyr* tried the same thing two years ago and also blocked out the telephone network! So, I think there is potential for phone sex, but I don't think there is a potential for selling magazines from it. OK, you could hide the number behind a patch that people would have to scratch away . . . but they would just scratch it away in the store!'

If the failure of the promotional campaigns wasn't bad enough, the market began to shrink dramatically; the results of the postwar baby-boom began to grow up. By 1985 no fewer than 190,000 males who had previously been in the fifteen to thirty age range were being counted among the thirty- to forty-five-year-olds. Even the demise of *Se* didn't help, for two new magazines appeared on the scene: *Stopp* and *Aktuell Rapport*. In 1980 a new circulation war broke out for what remained of the contracting market and a new weapon was wheeled on to the battlefield: hard-core pornography.

Explicit sex was not new. '*Lektyr* started it,' Lénberg recalled. 'Historically, they were one week before the old *FiB Aktuellt* back in 1973. *Lektyr* made the first hard-core pages in the men's magazines in Sweden.' Did he mean *FiB Aktuellt* was one week behind? 'Yes. There was editorial misbehaviour by other editors,' he conceded stuffily, 'and then we all had to do it. And once you put it in, you can't get rid of it.' Little of the material which had been appearing in the late 1970s was particularly strong. The magazines were being sold in news kiosks and bookstores and the publishers were nervous about frightening off their established customers. Their concern was to prove well founded.

What upset the balance of power was the appearance of a magazine with no pretence of being anything like the traditional publications. *Aktuell Rapport* ('News Report') was originally launched by Norwegian porn baron Leif Hagen to promote his expanding business in Sweden. It was little more than a mail-order catalogue with the advertisements for hard-core magazines, 8 mm films and videos interspersed only by illustrated reviews of the same material. To make the magazine editorially viable, Hagen needed a staff of professional journalists. His first recruit was Bengt Lénberg who left *FiB Aktuellt* to become editor-in-chief of *Aktuell Rapport*.

'When *Aktuell Rapport* arrived, it was a pure porno magazine,' Lénberg recalled. '*FiB Aktuellt*'s owners, Baltic Press, responded by launching *Stopp* which contained even more sex material. The porno war had really started!'[3]

During that same year, 1980, in the Danish capital of Copenhagen, another journalist was about to change jobs. Tall and ruggedly good-looking, Torben Dhalvad could have stepped down from the advertising pages of one of his own magazines. He joined *Rapport* as a writer but was soon promoted to editor-in-chief of all the magazines in the A & L International publishing group with the specific brief to stop the rot in the old-established men's magazine. Under the same pressures the sector was experiencing in Sweden, *Rapport*'s circulation had plummeted from a 1978 high of 185,000 to a mere 85,000 at the turn of the decade.

Lighting one of his extensive collection of briar pipes, Dhalvad described the events leading up to his arrival.

> What happened in Denmark in the mid and late 1970s was that a lot of amateurs – you know, entrepreneurs, dubious characters – they saw the big market and they said 'Well, what's *Rapport*? *Rapport* is nude girls, fantastic stories, and big pictures . . . We will do the same!' And so, at home, they put together something that looked more or less like *Rapport*. The layout was crap and the text was nothing and the pictures were bad: but they had the girls! You can get the girls from anywhere. And they can always get someone to sit down and write the fantastic stories. I wouldn't say that it affected the circulation, but it screwed up the market. Suddenly, there were four, five magazines on the news-stands. Then the people at *Rapport* at that time made their first major wrong judgement. They were market leaders, but suddenly they went after the small ones, in content and in style. So the small ones responded by putting in hard-core material.
>
> Then the *Rapport* people said, oh, how do we fight

them? We'll fight them on their own ground! They did that instead of keeping to the proven formula. Of course they'd already seen that, if once in a while they made a special issue with a little hard core – reviews of sex films and things like that – then it sold reasonably better than the previous issues. So they started to put in pornography on a regular basis. And, as Lénberg said, once you've started, it's very hard to stop it.

The problem with pornography is it's very hard to get rid of. But also to do it fifty-two times a year . . . That's impossible, because you end up doing it stronger and stronger, because you always want to do new things with it . . . And there are not that many variations.[4]

While Bengt Lénberg busied himself in Stockholm with the daunting task of turning *Aktuell Rapport* from a porn mail-order catalogue into a real magazine, Dhalvad was trying to revitalize the flagging circulation of the Danish *Rapport*. Though certain in his own mind that it was too late to remove the porn entirely, he was equally reluctant to experiment too much; the operation could be a success, but the patient might die. Instead, Dhalvad got clearance from A & L to launch a quick-fire series of new titles, each with a different mix of ingredients.

From the publisher's rabbit-warren of an office building on Sankt Anna's Plads, close by the dock from where ferries sail each day to Sweden, Norway and Finland, Dhalvad launched the first of the new magazines. '*Rapport*'s formula was 80 per cent stories and 20 per cent girls and sex,' he explained. '*PS* was launched in January 1982, shortly after I became editor for the group. I gave it the reverse formula to *Rapport*: 20 per cent stories and 80 per cent girls and sex. Quite honestly, the 20 per cent was just alibi stuff!'

The opening salvo found its target. The first issue of *PS* was a great success, selling 119,000 copies. This has now stabilized at an average 75,000 every month. The November 1986 issue is typical of the magazine's style. The sex content is very heavy, with even the '20 per cent' stories concentrating on sex topics (the main feature is an illustrated survey of the sex scene in Vienna). Although the 'glamour' material would be acceptable in most countries, page 53 carries a stark banner: *He kommer de Hemmelige Sider* ('Here come the secret pages'). No less than thirteen of the so-called 'secret pages' carry hard-core material, including a feature on the controversial American porn star, Traci Lords. The photographic material is supplemented by three pages of Japanese erotic art showing explicit sexual acts.

But Dhalvad was far from finished: 'We first published *Extra* at the end of 1982 and it is still issued six times a year. We originally wanted it to be wrapped in plastic and to include a free gift every few issues. I got this idea from women's magazines and the sort of things they included – shampoos, combs, knitting patterns and so on. We seriously considered including a packet of condoms . . .' There was a twinkle in Dhalvad's eye as he paused for dramatic effect. 'But we ruled this out on the grounds that the old family owners of the business might not consider it in good taste. In the end, what we did was to include another magazine! One mag carried the stories and the other the girls and sex. Perhaps we were looking for a "his and hers" approach? Anyway, it worked for a while, but it is now all in one magazine and we dropped the plastic wrapper to reduce production costs.' *Extra*'s circulation varies between 90,000 and 100,000 per issue. But there was more to come.

*Express* was launched in February 1985. The formula here was based on having lots of shorter stories, gossip, small news items, humour and curiosities. 'In style,' Dhalvad explains, 'it is rather like America's *National Enquirer* or West Germany's *Bild Zeitung*, but with 'contact advertisements'. I saw that *Ekstra Bladet* [Copenhagen's evening tabloid newspaper] and the Blue Newspaper [the local equivalent of *Exchange and Mart*] were making a lot of money from contact ads. So, *Express* carries contact ads. It appears monthly. Oh yes, it also has "girls and sex". At the start, the circulation was 70,000. That dropped and then recovered to 70,000, which is where it is today.'

In the autumn of 1985, A & L launched *Album International*, perhaps Dhalvad's most ambitious project. This is a stylish publication printed on heavy art paper and employing plenty of 'impact white space'; it even has a little good taste. The articles are long and the women beautiful. In the tradition of *Playboy* and *Penthouse*, they try to feature personalities and the main article in issue 6 of 1986 is an interview with Tina Turner – who kept her clothes on during the experience. On launch, the circulation was 55,000. But at DKr34.85 (about $5) the magazine was expensive and sales soon dropped to 40,000. It is now back to 55,000 again. 'The main problem with *Album*', said Dhalvad, 'is attracting the classy advertising – Braun, American Express, Bang & Olufsen – not contact ads. It's hypocrisy that is holding the advertisers back. I thought the British and the Americans held the monopoly on hypocrisy but there are vestiges here in Denmark.'[5]

Initially, Dhalvad's promotion of the magazines was conservative: 'The main way was through ads in the daily newspapers – in *Extra Bladet* and so on. They were full-page ads but they had to be low key. Even *Ekstra Bladet* censored the ads! We couldn't say "Lolita". They wouldn't allow it – even if the girls were twenty-two! It didn't matter. You have to come up with new ideas all the time. We discussed of course the idea of getting into video. If we'd started breaking into the video scene five or six years ago [in 1980–81] we could have had an enormous market. But the owners didn't want to get involved at that time. It would attract too much attention to the name of the publishers; a little conservatism was coming in there.'

In spite of Lénberg's experiences in Sweden, Dhalvad wanted to try something else: 'The phone sex was the big thing. *Express* also offers a free phone-sex service. The idea originally started in *Rapport*. We bought five answering machines and put some heavy-breathing recordings on them. We used a double-page spread to launch the service in *Rapport*; it included some nude shots of a girl and the number to dial to listen to her talking sexy. On the first day so many people called in that the telephone system in Copenhagen collapsed. On the second day the PTT [the telephone company] took the number out of service and made special announcements on radio and television asking people not to call the number any more. Inevitably, this was fantastic publicity for *Rapport*. Eventually, we did a deal with the PTT who installed seventy-two lines.' The service is now featured in *Express* instead of *Rapport* and Dhalvad claims that it receives over 500,000 calls a year.

Although members of the Nordic Union, the Finns are quick to remind visitors that they are not like other Scandinavians, essentially because they are not Scandinavian. Few real Scandinavians would argue with them about this. The Finns live in a climate which is hostile eight months of the year and idyllic the rest. They are fortified through the winter months by two kinds of spirit; the sort that comes out of a bottle and the sort that comes out of their hearts. This they call *sisu*. John Wayne would call it 'True Grit'.

The Finns view Swedes in particular as a staid ascetic bunch. There is an apocryphal story told in Stockholm concerning a bored English visitor. 'Where can I get a decent drink at this time of night?' he asks the head porter, after giving up as the sole customer at his hotel bar. The porter suggests a place two blocks away. It is mostly frequented by Finns. As the Englishman walks in, he is hit first by a roar of noise and then by the fist of a massive drunk who staggers at him from the bar. From a horizontal position on the floor, the horrified visitor demands in English to know what he did wrong. The large Finn apologizes profusely, 'My God, I'm sorry! I thought you were Swedish!' He gently helps his victim to his feet, finds his displaced teeth and attempts to replace them.

Tampere, a hundred miles north of Helsinki, is the main city of Central Finland. The proximity of vast reserves of pine forest led to the growth of the paper mills whose chimneys dominate its skyline. That in turn led to Tampere's growth as a major centre of printing and publishing. The main thoroughfare, Hämeenkatu, is quiet except for the Russian tourists who seem to move around in flying wedges. Off Hämeenkatu on Puutarhakatu stands the modern office building occupied by the publishing group Lehtimielmet. The cuckoo in this highly respectable nest of commonplace magazines is the subsidiary company of Suomen Miestenlehdet Oy which occupies three small offices on the third floor.

Suomen Miestenlehdet Oy publishes three men's magazines which even Bengt Lénberg and Torben Dhalvad feel obliged to describe as 'raunchy': *Ratto, Kalle* and *Jallu*. The first office is occupied by the editor of *Jallu*, a magazine in which the girls and sex easily exceed the 80 per cent in Torben Dhalvad's 80:20 formula. And about half the 80 per cent is hard-core material showing single girls masturbating, straight-sex threesomes, oral sex, anal sex and lesbianism. The editor is a young woman called Arja Utriainen.

'*Jallu* was started in 1958,' she explained. 'It has always featured girls and sex, but the hard-core material was not introduced until 1981 when the circulation started to decline. In 1986 the official audit figures showed that the magazine had average sales of 22,858 a month [for a population of less than five million people]. But that was half the circulation we had in 1982.'

Arja first joined the magazine as a secretary in 1980 and has been editor-in-chief for the last five years. 'I get lots of calls from men to confirm that I really am a woman.' She also gets calls for other purposes and had to interrupt her exposition of the magazine's philosophy to explain patiently to a caller that she would rather not walk on him, with or without high heels.

'Our readers are very conservative. The magazines include a "reader preference coupon" which encourages them to tell us what they like,' Arja says enthusiastically. The completed coupons presumably supplement the telephone calls. 'Our typical reader is a working-class character living in the forests, rather than the cosmopolitan types of Helsinki.' *Ratto* of May 1987 even features an article about Erwin, 'our typical reader'. It jokes about him in an affectionate way and conveys the impression that he is into booze and women. This is very Finnish. It is also probably true.

Arja itemizes Erwin's preferences: 'For example, text is always included with the photosets – the photosets are mostly imported, mainly from the Mario Costa Agency. Anyway, new ideas can take two to three years to get established. It is important to get a really good girl on the cover. And it is essential that her eyes look to the camera. That's what makes people buy the magazine – a good cover.'[6]

But when Erwin has been seduced by the eyes of the cover-girl and carries *Jallu* off into the tundra, he will find that some changes have been made; the magazine has softened a little bit recently. This was done under pressure from Finland's monopoly distributor who wrote to the chief executive of Lehtimielmet and threatened to cancel their order unless they softened the material in *Kalle, Jallu* and *Ratto*. This was done, but it required a careful analysis of the magazines before and after the ultimatum to determine the exact nature of the changes. None of the bizarre sex had been eliminated, but it seems as though they took the cum shots out.

That change was more of a wrench for *Kalle* than it was for *Jallu*. Throughout Scandinavia, *Jallu* is considered to be the more restrained of the two. Even Jan Sjölin, *FiB Aktuellt*'s roving correspondent of the world of sex, expressed bemused horror:

*Kalle* is strong in a kinky way, I would say. I don't understand how Finnish people are thinking. Sometimes they are totally . . . Look, I can give you an example. In one of their magazines they had a competition for guys, for readers. They had to stand up and masturbate in front of the camera. The winner was the guy who came first! And they had a stupid reporter there who fucked around with everything. One week, he took a cow from the backside – you could see it in the pictures! Standing there with a T-shirt and fucking the cow! That's Finnish stuff!'[7]

Juhani Salomaa, the editor-in-chief of *Kalle* is the stylistic opposite of Torben Dhalvad. He carries an expression of vagueness and uncertainty in his body as well as his bearded face. He regularly shows up in the pages of *Kalle*, apparently as a familiar for Erwin. This can occasionally lead to problems: 'I once appeared in the magazine in my underwear, standing with a naked girl. The boss was rather mad about this and told me to stop doing it. I told him that it was to encourage the readers . . . that if a fat, balding and ugly guy like me could have a beautiful girl, perhaps they all could!'[8]

Juhani started off his career in literature and the arts as a dramatist and then became a newspaper journalist. Before joining *Kalle*, he used to write romantic fiction for magazines published in the north of Finland. 'All good writers in Finland come from the north,' he states confidently. 'For me this is fun. It is also work – but I enjoy my work.' His magazine, *Kalle*, was started in 1972 and by 1986 was enjoying an average bi-monthly circulation of 29,576 copies. It has been publishing hard-core material since 1979, but the density of mainstream hard core has become so high that the eye of the casual browser is more likely to be drawn to the photo-spreads which feature the activities of two grossly fat lesbians, a transsexual engaged in oral and vaginal intercourse with a woman, and the scenes of male homosexuals indulging in oral and anal sex. *Kalle* could well qualify as the only fully integrated gay/straight hard-core magazine in the world.

Juhani explained why each issue of *Kalle* carries a large section of gay porn: 'Public attitudes to gays in Finland are still a little out of date. Unlike Copenhagen or Stockholm, many homosexuals here find it embarrassing to buy gay sex mags at a kiosk – I'm not even sure there are any in Finnish. However, *Kalle* is known as a "girlie" magazine and that makes it possible for gays to buy the mag without having to declare their sexual interest. The idea must increase our sales by a good few thousand.'

Whatever is happening to the circulation of men's magazines in the Nordic area, *Kalle, Ratto* and *Jallu* are considered to be very profitable by the Lehtimielmet group. Indeed, *Kalle* is the seventh best revenue-earning magazine in Finland. 'The news magazines like *Ratto* are under most pressure and we have more problems with that than with any of the others,' explained Arja. 'Much of the pressure comes from the shift to special interest magazines; magazines about cars, about ice hockey, about hunting. So we have to publish magazines for people whose special interest is sex. *Kalle* and *Jallu* are for everyone who is interested in sex.

'The magazines are not allowed to carry ads for cigarettes or alcohol and that puts pressure on us to keep the sales high,' Juhani added. 'Many of the ads we do carry are for sex shops and mail order pornography.' Of course profitability is also helped by keeping the overheads down: 'Here we have one and a half persons per magazine. We measure our staffing levels in kilos.'

But what was it like to edit a magazine like *Kalle* in such a small community? 'I never hide what I do,' Juhani replied. 'If anyone asks, I just say I am doing my job. We get a lot of students in the local bar and the girls often argue about the magazines. But afterwards, they sometimes come up to me and ask how much I pay for the stories.' At that point, Arja intervened: 'Women write better sex stories than men. Finnish men always start their stories by saying: "On the way home, I bought two bottles of vodka . . ." Women are much better, they put more emotion into the stories. A woman writes as a woman.' Stories are still important to the Lehtimielmet magazines and Juhani discounts the influence of video: 'Finland is a very literate country. There are still not videos in every home. If you watch TV and videos day and night, you will soon tire of it. We find that readers over the age of forty are often more interested in reading than watching videos.' But Juhani and Arja are clearly not going to ignore the problem; their next magazine will be called *Sexvideo*.

Although it publishes really hard material – even by Scandinavian standards – the company has not had any trouble with the law in recent years. In some parts of the country, kiosks will not stock *Kalle*, but the 1924 national law concerning publishing standards has fallen into disrepute and the police seem to limit their activities to raiding the sex shops in Helsinki. These are usually prosecuted if the shop is stocking material 'smuggled' from abroad – a strange phenomenon considering that the imported pornography could rarely be harder than that being published in Tampere.

The magazines are promoted through cross-advertising between the publications and by placing small advertisements in the national newspapers. In 1982 they tried the telephone-sex idea from offices in Helsinki and Tampere. The results were, perhaps, predictable. In Helsinki they had problems with the telephone system: they had more than 40,000 calls in the first night and the telephone company told them to stop – the network couldn't handle it.

A more original idea was described by Arja: 'For the last three years we have organized a trip to Majorca for our readers. This takes place every February and about forty readers come with us. Forty drunken Finns – imagine that!'

Arja is as unrepentant as Juhani about her unusual job. She flicks at the fancy garter draped over her desk lamp and identifies two major beneficiaries of the business: 'By charging 19.5 per cent MOMS [value added tax or sales tax], the government does very well from sex magazines. So does the church. In Finland, many companies as well as individuals pay levies of 1 per cent to the church. Lehtimielmet hands over such a levy to the Lutheran Church.'

The publisher, the Finnish government and the Lutheran Church are not the only organizations to benefit from the pornography trade. 'Actually, we have our printing done in Finland, it's cheaper than in Sweden.' Back in Stockholm in the mid-1980s, Bengt Lénberg was busily building up the circulation of *Aktuell Rapport*. 'We use a company called Hel-Print which is supposed to be northern Europe's biggest photogravure printing firm. Their head office is in Helsinki, but their printing plant is in Mikkeli near the Russian border. We send the artwork out by plane and the printed magazines come back by lorry. Baltic Press (*FiB Aktuellt* and *Stopp*) also print there and their mags come back in the same container. Baltic also uses another big company called Laakapaino who are in a town called Borgå [the Finnish name is Porvoo].'

So the Finns print the pornography for a Swedish company and send it back to Sweden, but the magazines are not supposed to be sent back to Finland again. 'That's right,' Lénberg admitted wrily, 'not the hard-core "secret pages". That's why the wrap-around supplement is useful – we can take them off before the main part of the magazine is shipped back to Helsinki again.'

In his years as editor of *Aktuell Rapport*, Lénberg steadily increased the news-feature content. Expounding the magazine's editorial policy, he referred once again with affection to *Life* magazine 'as it used to be', and that pioneering style was certainly reflected in *Aktuell Rapport*'s news-spreads. They even have the same international flavour – 'Not much news in Sweden,' Lénberg comments – with excellent coverage of the Waldheim case, the downfall of 'Baby Doc' Duvalier and the murder of Prime Minister Olaf Palme prominent in the spring of 1986. Under his guidance,

*Aktuell Rapport* became the bestselling men's weekly in Sweden. He built the circulation up from some 60,000 in 1981 to 75,000 in 1986 with some issues peaking at 100,000. All this at the expense of *FiB Aktuellt* and *Lektyr*.

'But without the pornography, the circulation would be as low as 40,000,' Lénberg said. 'The porn is worth that 40 per cent difference. No, we can't get rid of it, not in the short term. And publishers only think in the short term.' So it's a necessary evil? 'Yes, a necessary evil, I guess. But in a journalistic rather than a moralistic sense. It is not the case that more porn leads automatically to more sales. You can have too much porn. The more porn you have, the more you attract a readership which buys it only for the porn. Then you are also competing with hard-core magazines and – especially – videos. The trick is to get the balance right; a good crime story, but only one, some sport – an interview with a hockey player for example, a test of a car or motorbike. Between each of these might be some glamour material and then, towards the end of the mag, a hard-core porno spread. Just one, perhaps two, but more than that and the nature of the magazine changes – it becomes something else. We also begin to compete with our own more explicit products.'

Lénberg thought about all that for a moment and then continued. 'Look, it's probably possible to make a men's magazine in Sweden without pornography. But you need money to take a loss for two years, to get back the readers who don't buy men's mags because of the porno, because they can't take the magazine home, because they dare not buy it in the store. And it will take two years to get it generally known that it is nothing dangerous to buy it, that no one will look strangely at you any more, as if you're a pervert or something.' So there would have to be a very big promotional campaign? 'Yes. And you also have to make a hell of a lot better magazine.'

Lénberg compares producing a magazine to something like building a house. If you do something wrong in the building process, sooner or later it will fall down:

For example, the crossword puzzle also means a lot in these magazines. I didn't think so at one time. Two years ago, I cut out the crossword puzzle in *Aktuell Rapport*. We only got about fifty answers every week, so I cut it out. One month later, when the first magazine without the crossword was published, twenty-seven people phoned and wanted to know where the crossword was! I had to say there'd been some technical mistake and another would follow in three weeks – then I had to phone Finland and tell them to get the crossword back! Somehow we should never underestimate those items, you have to get the balance right.

The cover of the magazine is especially important. This has been tested. The flickering moment when you see it in the bookstore is all-important. For men's magazines two elements about the cover-girl are very important. First, there's the eyes; the cover-girl is always supposed to look at you, telling you whatever you're thinking she's telling you! Secondly, nipples always sell better than no nipples. And two nipples sell better than one nipple!

So the nipples should be looking at you as well? 'Yes – four eyes! Because in our culture, in the last hundred years, nipples or big tits . . . oh, we men would like to play a lot with those!' There is also, as Lénberg puts it, a particular type of girl which is good for a cover. 'She has to be beautiful and fairly young. In Sweden, blonde girls generally sell better than brunettes or black or redheads and so on.'[9]

Not satisfied with the runaway success of *Aktuell Rapport*, owner Leif Hagen decided to expand. One year after Baltic Press launched *Stopp*, Tre Mag introduced an equivalent monthly magazine called *Cats*. This enabled the company to carve themselves an even bigger slice of the market. By 1984 *Cats'* sales had stabilized at about 60,000 when Lénberg and a management colleague packed their bags and flew to the United States. They were going to buy the European rights to *Hustler* from its publisher and editor, Larry Flynt.

The American edition of the magazine had been on sale in Sweden some years before. For a while it had been distributed by porn baron Berth Milton and his erstwhile sales manager, Kent Wisell remains an enthusiast for the magazine: 'Flynt is smart. I admire his work, I must say . . . *Hustler* is a very good magazine. It was even better when he took care of it, before he was injured. I would say that the first *Hustlers* I saw in 1973 or 1974, whenever it was, were perfect. Fantastic. The best sex magazines I've ever seen! With lots of very, very good cartoons. We marketed it in Scandinavia in 1979. We had a contract as the sole agents and appointed distributors. We had the contract for two, two and a half years more or less, but it was taking too much time and we didn't have the resources to do *Private*, *Pirate* and *Hustler* as well. So we left it to the national distributor in Sweden, Presam.' But *Hustler* is a very American magazine. What is its appeal in Scandinavia? Wisell was uncertain: 'I don't understand it, either. I think *Hustler* was a tremendously popular mag when it first came out in the early seventies, when Larry Flynt had a clear mind – before he was shot. He had lots of dirty jokes and very, very good-looking girls. Now it's just boring, no innovation.'[10]

But why would Tre Mag want to get involved with *Hustler*? Lénberg retains a clear picture of how it all started:

> Originally we wanted to use the cartoons of a guy called Duane Tinsley. He really made *Hustler* big. Our executives at Tre Mag thought it might be a good idea if we published the whole magazine here in Europe. In autumn 1984 we went to see Larry Flynt. At the time he was still recovering from being shot and was popping pills of every conceivable colour. During the fifteen hours of negotiation he sacked his two nurses at least twice and the rest of his staff at least once. Flynt was originally a pimp in Cleveland, Ohio. He owned two bars and a strip club through which he ran the girls. He started publishing a duplicated

news-sheet for the girls which became so successful that the clients wanted to read it. Eventually he started binding it in a colour cover and it developed into *Hustler*.'

We now publish it six times a year as *Svenska Hustler* ('Swedish *Hustler*'). I think Tre Mag are really more interested in getting *Hustler* launched in West Germany and Spain. Those are very big markets if you translate the magazine.

However, the Swedish market for Flynt's publication does not seem quite so exiting and sales probably languish below 40,000 per issue.

Of course, Tre Mag's successes were at the expense of the other magazines, and in the late summer of 1986, Lénberg returned to Baltic Press to apply his magic formulas to the ailing *FiB Aktuellt*. The circulation of *FiB Aktuellt* itself had fallen from about 140,000 in 1981 to a barely viable 55,000 when its new editor arrived. Stable-mate *Stopp* had dropped from the launch circulation of 110,000 to 52,000 over the same period.

Within eight months, Lénberg had reversed the trend by adding 5,000 copies to *FiB Aktuellt*'s bi-weekly sales. But when *Stopp* continued to decline to 45,000, the company took a leaf from Torben Dhalvad's book and launched a new magazine called *XL* – because of its 'extra large' format. The 80:20 ratio was now closer to 90:10.

The net effect of introducing the new title was to increase Baltic's market share. But it was unquestionably helped by another major development in the market: the venerable *Lektyr* went out of business. In the first four months of 1987 it is believed that Sweden's oldest surviving men's magazine lost 32,000 copies, bringing its sales down to 30,000 – a fraction of the 253,000 copies it had been selling ten years previously. So what went wrong? Torben Dhalvad in Copenhagen had no doubts:

It was the owner's wife! You know, last year she tried to modernize *SV* [a women's magazine] and succeeded in bringing that down from 120,000 to 90,000! And, you know, a lot of people have done wrong to that magazine over the years, but they never succeeded in bringing it that far down! She modernized it so it looked like a magazine from the 1960s.

Then she took over *Lektyr*. Last year they ran a lot of inserts with hard-core material. They were more or less forced to do that by *Aktuell Rapport*, because *Aktuell Rapport* was getting stronger and stronger. Then they tried to put in small inserts with *Hemmelige Siden* [secret pages]. Well, on a short basis that worked, but then they went completely the other way – they even took out the naked girls! On top of that, it wasn't even a well-designed magazine – it was a crap magazine! It was terrible! So they took out all the interesting girl material and they didn't make a good magazine – an adventure magazine – instead.[11]

In Stockholm, a few weeks after *Lektyr*'s demise, Bengt Lénberg was equally critical: 'Everyone is amazed. They bragged that they'd taken the pornography out and almost all the girls too. They try to make a clean magazine – and the circulation went from 60,000 to 30,000 in three months!' So his prediction of doom for any magazine taking out the porn had been proven? 'It's not only because they've cut the pornography and the girls – the entire magazine is dull! Look, everything is dull! You just can't do what *Lektyr* did – cut out the pornography *and* make it a very poor magazine!'

Disdainfully, Lénberg pulled a copy of the last issue of *Lektyr* from his desk and examined it. 'First of all, the cover. Since January, since they changed the magazine, they changed the cover so much that you can't recognize it any more. In Sweden 40 per cent of all magazines are bought in stores where you have two hundred magazines on the stands. There is an instant moment – only about half a second – when you are looking at it and you have to see it *immediately*. There's a lot of impulse buying. If you don't see it – you don't grab it. This is especially important for men's magazines, because you can't ask out loud for it in the store. You can't go to the young – and it's always young ladies in Sweden – and say: "Where is my *Lektyr*?" There are always others who might be your neighbour and so on. You have to see it immediately! To grab it and put it in *Expressen*!'

He flips through the pages and continues to describe the comedy of errors: 'The idea of having a contents page is wrong for a weekly. You don't want the reader to be told, you want him to find out. They've wasted a page here. It's probably because they've sold this advertisement and they don't know what to do with the rest of it. It's a lack of ideas. An old tradition in Swedish men's magazines says that one is always supposed to begin with a strong first spread. The lead story is very important. It must be very strong. They have made the mistake of not starting the magazine properly. They have wasted six pages here with small and weak items. It never really starts. Also they are using spot colour but no colour pictures. The impact of pictures is important, because they hit the eye when the buyer browses through the mag in the store. Impact white never has the same effect. Impact white was modern four years ago. When our readers see this, they wonder if three pictures have fallen away here! This spread about music has far too much text. It needed more smaller items. Not all the photos are very good anyway. The general idea is to start with the strongest story or to start with the strongest pictures . . . or you could start with the strongest headline, but that only happens once or twice a year.'

He stands up and turns the magazine. 'I have to show you something. You have taken yourself into this magazine. There is a man winning money . . . here is a man, a TV personality . . . *they are standing . . . they are not doing anything*!!! We are now on page 17 and we haven't had our first girl! Page 17 is the first action picture. But it's not even captioned – captions are essential. They are very bad on editing their magazines. Still no women . . . still no action. Here are pictures of cars, but still no action. At least have a man driving the goddamned car – or a woman draped across the front!'

*Lektyr* has now been bought from the liquidators of Saxon's – the company which published it – by a group of employees and Lénberg and Dhalvad have both wished them well. But the recovery of the lost ground will be a major challenge for them.

What about the future for all the men's magazines in Scandinavia? Dhalvad is pessimistic:

> Well, I think the time has gone for these magazines, you know. Let's just go back to the ingredients of the magazines when they started. It was photo-journalism and girls. They were both new things. We introduced some rather special journalists that the readers could follow and they loved them. *Rapport* had maybe four or five. Some of them were crazy, they did crazy things, but they were also doing really good investigative journalism. But they were personalities and after having done that for six, eight or ten years, they got fed up with it! Or they died! Or they switched to other magazines. The new ones often become replicas of the old ones. Then the daily papers started – not just investigative reporting – they also started writing about sex. The damned editors there! They saw that sex sold! So now you can see sex stories in all the papers – even in the women's weeklies, they write about sex! They have columns with sex and they have a letter box where you can write in and get advice about how to handle your sex life! So they took away that part of the market where people just wanted to write a little bit about sex.
>
> And then came the videos and it's not only the sex videos that affected it. People bought a video machine and they had to fill the time, they had to get their money back. So they rented Clint Eastwood movies – instead of reading crime stories – and they got all the bang-bang they needed for that week. And on Friday night a guy

says, what am I going to do? He goes to the video shop, or to the service station and he takes home maybe three or four videos and a six pack or whatever. Then he sits down in front of the video and watches the TV.

Another thing is that these magazines were selling damned good over a long period of time. They made so much money. But nobody ever thought of developing them, changing them, keeping them up with the times. They got fat and lazy because they thought they could sell *anything* during the 1970s. And if you look at the magazines, the magazines that sold 200,000 in those days, how the hell were they so bad? Compared to what we did later? You got fat and lazy because it didn't matter what you did – it just dropped! And the publishers didn't have the courage to go in and say 'Well, we'll change it, we'll try to build new magazines and try to live with the times' . . .

Now the names of the magazines are smeared by the sex image and I think it's impossible to change that. But why not create new magazines without the sex image? I believe in a whole new kind of magazine. For example, Springer Verlag [of West Germany] has put out this new one called *Ja* [in March 1987]. That has a lot in common with the old *Rapport* and they also steal a little from *Stern*. They always have one or two sex-related stories but not hard core. I don't have the sales figures, but I think it's been *very* successful.[12] But for the others, it's the end of the road.[13]

In Stockholm Bengt Lénberg blames the poor prospects of the men's magazines on all the earlier 'editorial misbehaviour':

Of course the porno war scared off a lot of ordinary readers. They couldn't take the magazines home because of their girlfriends. We did a survey in 1977 which showed that *FiB Aktuellt* had 279,900 buyers a week, but we had three times that many readers which is . . . let's say 800,000. But out of 800,000 readers, 286,000 were girls – women! Because of the investigative journalism. But when the porno war started, they disappeared almost immediately, because very few girls are interested in this kind of porno. A lot of those 286,000 women *bought* the magazine and read it with their boyfriend or with their husband because it was fun. But suddenly, they weren't interested. Even if the man said he didn't look at the girls, his girlfriend would say we are not getting this magazine any more because it is dirty! The porno war made a lot of ordinary readers disappear and today the market is still going down a bit and in my opinion that is because of the porno.

Today you can get a lot of video porno. And those who were interested in porno have found that porno that moves is much better – even if it is more expensive. I think they save their money to buy or rent porno videos. It is only between 30 and 50 crowns here for overnight video rental. When the mag costs 22.50, it is only three of these to get a real porno movie. And last year [1986] was the year of the real video explosion in Sweden when Swedish people bought video machines in big numbers. At the end of 1986 there were 400,000 video machines in Sweden. But last year they sold another 400,000 in the one year!

If these magazines still exist in ten years, they will probably be without porno or as we have done it sometimes, with special magazines, so we don't have it as a standard thing. In five years really it will be low. They've done it wrong and too early and too bad. My idea is not to do any big stuff with the porno here because we have this special section called 'Sexy Sweden'. But when we do these, then we go for it all the way. If we promise, we fulfil! You can't take it away suddenly.

The problem with *Lektyr* was that the whole formula went wrong. They had some kind of dream that if they just cut out the porno and made a different magazine they would sell a lot more advertisements, but they didn't do that. And the second idea was that they would lose a lot of porno readers, but they would get a lot of the others. But the others haven't read these magazines since 1980 when we first put the hard-core stuff in.

Lénberg's cautious optimism stems from a little-known fact about the readership of *FiB Aktuellt* which perhaps puts them and the porn issue in perspective. The magazine carries a page called 'The Wonders of Nature'. This is the most popular page in the magazine and it has been since 1965. It is an educational drawing strip with detailed notes about some interesting facts of nature – usually animals or plants – by Charlie Bood. Five times, different editors have tried to cut out this page and they have failed each time. Every year a book is compiled from these superbly drawn pages and these sell between 75,000 and 100,000 copies. Lénberg is full of admiration: 'In the years when we had regular reader evaluations, that page had . . . well, the girls were second. They had a rating of 70 per cent. Charlie Bood's 'Wonders of Nature' always had 99 per cent!'[14]

# 6

# *Out of the Porn Ghetto: Alternative Hollywood*

'I'm a youth in Babylon!' says Los Angeles film producer David Friedman, waving a fat, but unlit, cigar. Friedman, a youth in Babylon for most of his life, is also a walking history book of the glory days of X-rated Hollywood.

Appropriately far from the lots of the major studios, the headquarters of Entertainment Ventures Inc, a production and distribution company, is in what Friedman describes as 'the Korean Sector' near the intersection of Vermont Avenue and the Santa Monica freeway. The area has the two-dimensional feel of a dilapidated movie set, the clapboard frontages covered with graffiti of the late spray-can school. Entertainment Ventures occupies a faded yellow building with parking to one side and, to the rear, a loading bay which has doubled as an exterior lot in earlier years.

Any production designer could have won an Academy Award for coming up with Friedman's room as the archetypal producer's office. Wood-lined and windowless, it is dominated by a cluttered desk no smaller than a king-sized bed. On the desk at the front is 'DAVID F FRIEDMAN' spelled out in carved wooden letters and a collection of jokey mugs: 'Whistle for your beer', admonishes one of them. In a corner of the office is a dusty and forlorn slimming machine – the type with a wide belt that sends shock waves through the flabby regions; next to it is a director's chair. On a cupboard by a small television and VCR are a number of erotic film 'Oscars'. But the unsuspecting visitor's eye is drawn inexorably to the poster-covered walls – screamers for early 'splatter' movies such as: *She Freak, The Defilers, Brand of Shame, The Notorious Daughter of Fanny Hill, The Brick Doll's House, Two Thousand Maniacs*! An entire town bathed in pulsing human blood! they read; Gruesomely stained in blood colour! Madmen crazed for carnage!

Friedman himself is a genial character. Aged about sixty, he has a stocky build which boasts victory over the infernal slimming machine. He habitually chews a handsome cigar but, having given up smoking, never lights it. He is everyone's idea of the Hollywood producer – a showman, expansive and larger than life, with a well-massaged ego, and skilful with the *spiel*. David Friedman represents the 'theatrical' side of the X-rated industry which is now losing out to the up-and-coming video merchants.

If anyone was born to the task of unceremoniously shoving back the boundaries of taste in feature films, it was Dave Friedman. Born in Alabama, his father was editor of the conservative *Birmingham News*. With his brother (Friedman's uncle), his father owned a chain of movie theatres and, in a remarkable parallel with that other pioneer of porn, Berth Milton, an amusement park. Although qualifying as an engineer, Friedman's first career move after the Second World War was into show business. 'I bought into a circus, "Biller's Circus".' But the big top of the movie industry beckoned and he worked for many years as Paramount's distributor in Atlanta, Georgia, before forming his own production company in 1956 to make what were known then as sex exploitation or 'sexploitation' movies. His first claim to notoriety was achieved by distributing a film called *Mom and Dad* (made by Kroger Babb). It shocked

America, not by showing a sexual coupling, but by displaying a possible result: the birth of a child.[1]

The late 1950s saw the rise of what the industry calls 'tits and ass' movies which used documentary-style coverage of nudist colonies as their *raison d'être*. *Garden of Eden* appeared in 1957, followed by *Daughter of the Sun* the year after. Friedman recalls making at least ten of these. By 1959 the world had had its fill of naked colonialism and strictly simulated sex was in, with Russ Meyer's *The Immortal Mr Teas* and Ted Paramore's *Not Tonight, Henry*. David Friedman did not miss out on the trend and 1959 was also the year he made *The Adventures of Lucky Pierre*. For a few years he jostled with the rest on the 'T and A' bandwagon – even a young Francis Ford Coppola jumped aboard with *Tonight For Sure* – before deciding that what was missing from all that flesh was buckets of blood.

In 1963 Friedman teamed up with a director called Herschell Gordon Lewis to make three films that were to set the tone for the likes of *Texas Chainsaw Massacre* and *Friday the 13th*. In three days and for a budget of $24,000 they shot the gruesome tale of the ancient Egyptian Fuad Ramses, using the Suez Motel as the main location. That's the Suez Motel in Miami Beach, Florida. *Blood Feast* shows a woman having her tongue ripped out so it could be thrown into Ramses' evil 'elixir of life', and the public queued at the box office to see it happen: 'I think it has now grossed about $35 million,' says Friedman cheerfully. Spurred by the success of *Blood Feast*, the Friedman/Lewis partnership quickly moved on to make *Two Thousand Maniacs* and *Color Me Blood Red*. 'Ashamed of them? Yes, I am – I'm ashamed at the appalling crudity of them. I used to go with Herschell to the butcher's shop and buy sheep and chicken entrails for the effects. Now you see retrospectives of these things on college campuses.'[2]

While Friedman and Lewis were making contributions to the historical archives of motion picture arts, 16mm black-and-white 'stag movies' showing explicit sex were still being produced underground. Creations of the 1930s had included such silent classics as *The Dentist, The Casting Couch, The Daisy Chain* and *The Plumber Does a Little Plumbing*. The last of these, a production credited to the 'Master Arts Picture Company', preceded *Deep Throat* in its use of a little light humour. The screen captions were written as limericks:

The name of our plumber is Lee
The girl in the story's Marie
She said 'Stop your plumbing,
I hear someone coming!'
Said Lee 'No one's coming but me!'[3]

Under way by the turn of the century, the stag-movie era lasted until the end of the 1960s. In view of the illegality of such enterprises, few of the production companies gained any public prominence, though some of the creative people (on both sides of the camera) stayed on to become part of the industry producing porn features for public showing in cinemas. What certainly did live on was the 'stag' format as the line for 8mm plotless shorts for both the home market and for use in automatic peep-show projectors. These loops were shot on 16mm film and then printed in high volume on to 8mm reels by companies such as Caballero in the US and Rodox in Denmark. They sold for up to $40 for ten-minute sequences.

The two hundred 'art houses' in the United States which specialized in showing foreign films had long since recognized that a fleeting glimpse of Brigitte Bardot's naked flanks in releases like *And God Created Woman* boosted attendances enough to justify the occasional matinée. According to Friedman, this 'bare-assed, good-looking French broad' could boost the weekly box office from $2,500 to $10,000. Under pressure from television through the 1950s and 1960s, art house programmes shifted increasingly to 'T and A' and 'nudie-cuties'. These were soon joined by many of America's 'neighbourhood' cinemas, badly hit by new distribution policies imposed by the major studios, which favoured prestige modern theatres for their high-budget conventional releases. These exhibitors began to show pornographic films in the early 1970s. But they no longer served coffee in the lobby and the vernacular 'art houses' was dropped in favour of 'scratch houses' and 'shooting galleries'.[4]

With the release of *Deep Throat*[5] in 1972 and the virtual collapse of restraining laws, a certain chic was bestowed on the porn movie business. Its producers and artistes achieved the distinction of appearing in the columns of *Time* and *Newsweek* magazines, if not exactly on the covers. They were given the fashionable notoriety today afforded to the stars of pop and soap rather than respectable fame and glory: Linda Lovelace appeared on the Johnny Carson Show. She, Gerard Damiano, Harry Reems, Georgina Spelvin and John Holmes, among others, bore the popular faces of a porn industry newly promoted from clandestine currency.

Like *Blood Feast*, *Deep Throat* was shot in Florida and became the first porn movie to reach a mass audience. It has been suggested that it ranks as one of the top ten box-office successes in the history of film-making, along with conventional Hollywood output such as *ET* and *Star Wars*.[6] (It was almost given the stag title of *The Sword-Swallower*, which would have robbed a generation of journalists of one of their most useful pieces of jargon.)

*Deep Throat* was certainly not the first hard-core feature film to win a public showing (that credit goes to Mike Henderson's 16mm *Electro-Sex '75*[7] which was made in 1970) nor was it the first 35mm movie to achieve national distribution. That distinction probably goes to *Man and Wife*, a 'medical documentary' showing sexual penetration, made the same year by Marvin Miller and Matt Cimber, Jayne Mansfield's first husband.[8] It was a sign of the times, though a temporary one, that *Man and Wife* was distributed not by the expanding porn cinema network but by the conventional Man chain which now includes the world-famous Grauman's Chinese Theater on Hollywood Boulevard.[9]

The plot of *Deep Throat* is something of a protracted (62-minute) joke about the predicament of a woman, played by Linda Lovelace, whose clitoris is located at the back of her throat. Harry Reems, her doctor, is forced to resort to an unorthodox remedy to treat her resulting physiological and emotional problems. So, the sex is legitimately delivered within the framework of a plot, the actors try to act, and the whole thing is handled light-heartedly. None of this was new to conventional films, but it certainly was to pornographic movies and – with the novelty of Lovelace's 'sword-swallowing' act – probably accounted for the success of the production.

After various prosecutions had brought *Deep Throat* to considerable media attention it became *de rigueur* viewing for yuppie couples wishing to keep up with the latest cocktail gossip. As well as creating a chic new audience it also marked the start of the porno-star system, with Linda Lovelace and Harry Reems. With initial production costs of less than $25,000, *Deep Throat* is thought to have grossed a staggering $100 million worldwide. But is that mostly unquestioned figure realistic? David Friedman believes it is:

> I was a partner in the Pussycat chain at the time and we opened *Deep Throat* at the Pussycat theatre on Santa Monica Boulevard. The *Los Angeles Times* would not allow the title of the movie in our ads. So we had '*IT* is here!' I think we took $24,000 in the first week. The next week, it was down to $18,000 and by the third week only $15,000. Vince Miranda, the president of Pussycat, said 'You know, this is a big disappointment.'
>
> Well, *Time* magazine that week came out with a whole page about *Deep Throat* – this phenomenon! The guy from the *LA Times* calls me up and says, 'OK, if it's good enough for *Time* magazine, it's good enough for the *LA*

> *Times*. If you want to put *Deep Throat* in your ads this week, fine.' So, that Friday the ad read: '*Deep Throat*. 4th Week. Now.' The gross shot up to about $50,000 – in a 450-seat theatre! The following week it went up to $90,000!
>
> I know that Pussycat paid the Peraino brothers [the distributors of *Deep Throat*] $3 million in film rentals. Those figures are good because Pussycat is a very legitimate operation – they paid cheques! And that $3 million was only for showing the picture for about a year in one cinema and about six years at another.
>
> I would say that the total amount of film rental paid to the Perainos was somewhere in the neighbourhood of $35 million. If an established distributor had handled the film, it would have been more like $50–60 million. Now, 60 per cent rental translates down to 40 per cent after publicity and distribution costs. The net figure is 40 per cent, so *Deep Throat* must have taken at least $100 million at the box office by now. That excludes video.[10]

*Deep Throat*'s reputation and durability is such that it is readily available in England today in the form of privately pirated video cassettes.

Of equal durability is its director Gerard Damiano who is still making X-rated films. If the porn critics are in consensus over the historical significance of *Deep Throat*, few of them agree on the quality of the movie. But New York-based Damiano did not have to wait long for accolades. Later in 1972 he returned to Florida to shoot *The Devil in Miss Jones*.[11] The plot is more metaphysical than physiological, concerning as it does the plight of poor Justine Jones (played by Georgina Spelvin) after she commits suicide. She cannot go to heaven because she just killed herself, and she can't go to hell because she hasn't sinned enough. Trapped in this limbo, she decides that her only chance is to head for Hades. Harry Reems (fresh from solving Linda Lovelace's problems in *Deep Throat*) is appointed to help boost Miss

Jones's sin count. The sex scenes are almost encyclopaedic; anal, oral, lesbian, masturbation and a threesome as well as encounters with bananas and a snake. One critic said that 'Damiano's view of hell . . . is most inspired',[12] and another observed that the film 'epitomizes Gerard Damiano's continuing Catholic conscience'.[13]

Damiano was well able to live with that conscience. Over fifteen years he managed to get four movies in critic Jim Holliday's 'Top 40 Best Adult Films'[14] and made two of the top three *Hustler* magazine's bestselling porn videos[15] over the same period: *Deep Throat* was first, *The Devil in Miss Jones* was third. Hard on the heels of *The Devil* in sales, but at the very top of Holliday's 'Top 40' is *The Opening of Misty Beethoven*.[16]

Directed by Radley Metzger (who sometimes uses the name Henry Paris) in 1976, *Misty* is an early example of how the X-rated movie industry rips off plots from anyone and anywhere. This one came from George Bernard Shaw's *Pygmalion* (or at least Hollywood's *My Fair Lady*). Metzger seems to have done his version of the story justice, and porn critic Jim Holliday pulls no punches in justifying *Misty*'s current status as the best porn movie ever made: '. . . lavishly produced, superbly scored . . . no film has ever been edited so brilliantly . . . sheer cinematic genius'.[17]

Well over ten thousand hard-core films and full-length videos have been made since 1970. In terms of quality and consistency, the same directors' names keep cropping up: Gerard Damiano, Anthony Spinelli (real name Sam Weston, the younger brother of the actor Jack Weston), Henri Pachard (Ron Sullivan who, like Spinelli, has six films in the Top 40), Henry Paris (who, as Radley Metzger, made the 1978 remake of *The Cat and the Canary* in London with Honor Blackman and Edward Fox), Alex deRenzy, Howard Ziehm (Linus Gator), Robert McCallum (also with many credits as a cinematographer) and Chuck Vincent. In true American tradition, the X-Rated Critics Organization (XRCO) – which counts Jim Holliday and Bill Margold among its founder members – has opened up a 'Hall of Fame'. As well as 'film creators' David Friedman, Gerard Damiano, Radley Metzger, Alex deRenzy, Anthony Spinelli and Howard Ziehm, it lists performers Georgina Spelvin, Tina Russell, Rene Bond, Marilyn Chambers, Sharon Thorpe, Annette Haven, Lesllie Bovee, John Holmes, Harry Reems, Jamie Gillis, Eric Edwards, John Leslie and Paul Thomas, most of whom still appear regularly in the credit sequences of porn films and videos.

By the 1980s the number of cinemas showing porn had peaked at about nine hundred. The American X-rated industry was reputed to be grossing well over $500 million every year and much of that was being recycled into new productions. Gone, for the time being, were the days of $25,000 products like *Deep Throat*. Fearful of losing their new-found middle-class markets, many producers invested more in the quality of the productions. An early example of this was *Take Off*,[18] made by Armand Weston. Stylishly photographed on expensive sets, the story-line is borrowed from *The Picture of Dorian Gray* and includes short pastiches of classic Hollywood movies with look-alikes for Cagney, Bogart, Brando and Gould. To broaden its market place, *Take Off* was made in three versions; hard-core, soft-core and 'R'. The $225,000 investment reputedly returned $4 million after costs on a box office gross of $20 million. The film appears as number five in Holliday's Top 40. Another appeal to the 'sophisticated' audience which might not have been exposed to pornography was attempted by Chuck Vincent with his 1982 film *Roommates*. This appeared at a few genuine 'art houses' as well as the regular porno theatres and won two 'Best Film' awards.[19]

As the American porn industry strove for returns and respectability, Europe was not idle. In Germany, Jon Sanderson made *Born Erect*,[20] 'laughing sophistication' was used to describe Lee Hessel's Danish production of *Bordello*,[21] even the British hard-core feature called *Diversions*[22] won some plaudits. But the only European director to gain the acclaim afforded to the likes of Damiano and Spinelli was an Italian called Alberto Ferro, later dubbed 'The Pope of Porn'.[23]

Ferro was born in 1936 in Algiers, the son of a diplomat. Like Berth Milton, he had an unsettled childhood. Unlike Milton he still seems unable to stay in one country for very long. After a wartime childhood in Frankfurt am Main and Belgrade, he returned to Italy to attend the Leo XIII Jesuit college in Milan. 'I have been interested in sex since I was seven years old,' Ferro declared many years later. 'I have always loved sex and I've always masturbated.'[24] This attitude tried the patience of the priests who promptly expelled him.

After an equally unsuccessful sojourn at the local school, his father secured him a place at the select Montana Zugerberg International Institute high above the sleepy Swiss town of Zug, twenty-five miles south of Zurich. Ferro flourished in the Institute's liberal climate and by 1954 was selling copies of Hugh Hefner's nude calendar photograph of Marilyn Monroe to his wealthy fellow students at grossly inflated prices. He added Spanish to his repertoire of Italian, German, English and French under the tutelage of Alfonso de Bourbon, a claimant to the Spanish throne.[25]

Ferro did well enough at the Institute to gain entry to the Modern Philosophy School at the Sorbonne in Paris the following year. He was impressed and influenced by the existentialism of Sartre and by Camus' hedonistic view of life: 'My philosophy is the philosophy of pleasure,' said Ferro.[26]

By 1961 Ferro was back in Milan unenthusiastically studying law and writing a thesis on censorship. For some years he had spent each summer working as a tour guide throughout Europe, improving his knowledge of the continent, his languages and his record of sexual conquests. He admitted to having to pay for fourteen abortions since 1956, but shrugged it off: 'Fourteen mistakes out of two thousand ejaculations is not bad going!'[27]

A news item in *Il Giorno* of 30 September 1961 caught his

attention. It was headlined: 'International gang of pornographers arrested in Genoa'. One of those arrested had the same name as his current girlfriend: Ferro called her in Rome. She was distraught: the man was her brother. He and a friend had been smuggling pornography to Genoa from Monaco in order to raise money for their gambling debts. Ferro made them an offer: he'd give them as much legal and financial support as he could if they cut him in on the action. He would need to know the name of their supplier. They were appreciative but apprehensive, how was he going to help the smuggling operation? 'My father is a diplomat,' he told them, 'so I have CD [*Corps Diplomatique*] plates on my car.'[28]

By 1962 Ferro had traced the source of the pornography back through Monte Carlo and Paris to two men operating from behind a tobacco shop in Brussels. Now he could get the best prices for magazines such as *Paris-Hollywood*, *Studio*, *Revue* and *Eldorado* (mostly supplied by a Dutchman based in Copenhagen) as well as some scarce and, at £150 a copy, expensive 8mm films. He gave up studying law in favour of breaking it as a professional pornography smuggler. He crossed borders almost on a daily basis, sometimes carrying the bigger shipments in the open passenger seat of his small Triumph TR3 sports car. He had hundreds of regular retail customers throughout France, Spain, Germany, Switzerland and Italy. He was known to customers as 'Al Harvey', 'Miguel dos Passos' or 'Charles de Rossi'. Portugal was too far to drive in the firmly sprung roadster. It was also too small for the increasingly large shipments, but his income was now high enough to trade the TR3 for a more comfortable Mercedes 280 saloon. This had a large boot and enabled him to take a girlfriend and a dog as occasional extra cover.[29]

By the mid-1960s, he co-operated with his Belgian suppliers in publishing in Denmark a magazine called *Shadows*. The demand for films was increasing and he heard about a possible new source. In London's Soho, a tall Welshman called 'Big Jeff' showed him some black-and-white 8mm films. Ferro was disappointed with the quality of these 'Climax Film' productions, but bought some anyway and left Big Jeff with the suggestion that they start shooting in colour on 16mm stock.[30]

After a close shave at the Alpine railway tunnel between Mondane in France and Bardonecchia in Italy, Ferro decided to retire from smuggling having made five hundred 'porno-diplomatic' border crossings between 1961 and 1967. Publishing magazines did not interest him nearly as much as film, which appealed to his creative instincts.

While on holiday on the island of Elba, off the western coast of Italy, in July 1967 he made his first fully produced porn film. His girlfriend 'Laura' borrowed her father's 8mm camera and starred in the leading female role. They tried some simple nude scenes first in order to determine how diligent the staff were at Kodak's Milan processing laboraory. When the film came back uncensored, they filmed themselves in a well-lit oral scene and even that came back without any problems. The Kodak laboratory was too overworked to be looking at what was going through the system. Ferro decided that it was worth going ahead with a proper production which he would then try to sell to Big Jeff in London. Laura's almond-shaped eyes gave him the idea of casting her as Madame Butterfly in a hard-core interpretation of Puccini's opera.

With occasional breaks, the film was shot over two weeks – a schedule which gave Ferro a chance to experiment with many different camera angles and movements. He later admitted that the most difficult part of the job was maintaining an erection for the benefit of Laura and the camera while having to think about the technical aspects of what he was doing. Only when he got the films back from the laboratory did he learn that all his exertions had not been in vain: Kodak had done an excellent job. After teaching himself about editing as he assembled the final version of *Golden Butterfly*, he was faced with deciding how to reproduce it and sell it. He changed his mind about handing it over to Big Jeff in London and resolved to establish his own marketing company in Stockholm, where he was unlikely to be harassed by the law. In the meantime, he would live in Portofino.[31]

By the end of the year the Italian adventurer was president of the AB BETA corporation of Stockholm. The company's objectives were to produce 8mm porn films and sell them by mail order in other countries – starting with Italy. A trip back to his homeland was needed to persuade some men's magazines to carry advertisements for a catalogue. The advertising managers haggled over the wording, but eventually agreed to this:

> Swedish film-production company seeks contacts with Italian collectors of 8mm films. Adults only. Request a catalogue by sending 1,000 lira to:
> AB BETA, Postfach, Stockholm 3, Sweden.[32]

The advertisements appeared in *Playmen* on 4 January 1968 and in *King* a week later. In optimistic anticipation, Ferro opened a numbered bank account in the town of Chiasso, just across the border in Switzerland. With the catalogue sent to inquirers he would include a payment form addressed to the bank. The manager was happy with that.

Three weeks later it seemed that his plans had gone awry: Ferro had received only one batch of twenty orders from the mailbox in Stockholm. He was seriously considering new marketing ploys when he got a message from the Portofino post office to collect some mail, about a thousand letters in all, each containing 1,000 lira (about £3) for the catalogue. In his excitement he failed to spot the reason for the delay: the packages had been opened and resealed by Italian customs.

Ferro hastily printed a brochure which offered five 'Eros films' for sale, ranging in price from $150 to $250 – payable in American currency direct to his numbered Swiss bank account. Apart from *Golden Butterfly*, no films had yet been made. The idea of selling the brochure was to raise money for production and now it looked as though it might work. Ferro and Laura, now his wife, folded the leaflets, inserted the order forms and wrote the envelopes by hand.

In February he visited his bank in Chiasso to open the replies and count the money: it totalled $50,000.[33]

Over the following weeks the money continued to flow in and Ferro made plans to find actors and shoot some more films. Before he could get started the lucrative porn operation through Sweden stalled. On 31 March 1968, in a club in Portofino, Ferro was approached by a friend, a lieutenant in the *carabinieri*. The lieutenant's concerned expression foretold bad news; Italian customs in Genoa had pieced Ferro's operation together from the mail intercepts, and details of a warrant for his arrest had been telexed to *carabinieri* stations throughout the country.

Ferro and Laura loaded the Mercedes and drove to the border north-west of Milan. Dressed like one of the local mountain people, Ferro hiked through the wooded hills taking care to avoid border patrols. Laura was not named on the arrest warrant and so had no trouble getting through the official crossing with the car. They met up on the Swiss side and continued north towards Sweden. It would be twelve years before Ferro could go back to Italy.[34]

The first film he made in Stockholm was called *Chains*. As his network of contacts expanded, he was able to boost production and *Suzie la Blonde, Blow-up 69, Sex on the Motorway* were finished in June 1968 to complete the promised set of five 'Eros films'. He was now able to fulfil the orders from Italy – at the buyer's own risk.

Business boomed well enough to raise sufficient funds for a trip across the Atlantic. After visiting some possible distributors in New York, Ferro and a camera assistant flew south to the Caribbean. Following a short stay in Barbados, they travelled on to Trinidad. Ferro always heads for the nearest discotheque when hunting performers. In this case he found just what he was looking for at a disco on a beach near Port of Spain. On hearing a tale that he might have had sex with twenty-four local girls in as many hours,[35] Ferro was at pains to put the record straight: 'That's ridiculous! Impossible! It was only about nine. You see, I really love eating pussy and these girls hadn't experienced much of that before. So they would tell their friends and before long they were coming to proposition me.' The trip ended with a wild sex party to see in the New Year of 1970.

The edited results of the footage shot on this trip became his *Tropical* series of 8mm loops which went into production for distribution through AB BETA. Life was looking good until the Swedish police visited him with the news that the *carabinieri* had circulated details of the arrest warrant over the Interpol network. Although the police were only curious and had no intention of taking him into custody, Ferro was disturbed. He decided he would move again and perhaps change his name to avoid this kind of harassment. The latter was arranged almost immediately. When the police visited his apartment, a local workman had been carrying out some repairs.

'Do you travel a lot?' Ferro asked the carpenter.

'No, I like Sweden too much. I sometimes go to Finland because that's where my wife comes from.'

'What's your name?' the bearded Italian asked.

'Lasse Braun,' said the puzzled man.

'If you don't travel much, can I borrow your name? I'll pay you a fee for it.' The Swede agreed and legal papers were subsequently drawn up and signed.

Alberto Ferro moved to Copenhagen in Denmark where he opened a studio at Vesterbrogade 27 near the railway station. The 8mm loops which he shot were distributed throughout Europe by the likes of Peter and Jens Theander and Ferro soon achieved worldwide notoriety for the erotic and raunchy films made under the name of 'Lasse Braun', a Swedish carpenter.

He began to package the material in trilogies of ten-minute films, an arrangment pioneered with the original *Tropical* productions. Output from the Vesterbrogade studio included the *Top Secret* series (with *Little Jane Bond* as one of the titles), the *Viking* series (shot in Sweden) and the *Casanova* series (including *The Kinky Adventures of Casanova*).[36] 'He made lots of money,' said an Englishman who met him in Copenhagen at the time, 'it was then that he started behaving like a Hollywood movie king.'[37]

A regular visitor at the studio was an ambitious, red-headed young German called Hans Moser, who was laying the foundations of his own porn empire by buying Lasse Braun films and smuggling them home over the border to the south.

In 1970 Ferro received a telephone call which signalled the start of a new phase in his career in pornography. The American at the other end of the line had been excited by his first sight of a 'double penetration' in the Lasse Braun film *Delphi in Greece*. He was very interested in buying the US rights to the loops and asked if it would be possible for them to meet when he got to Copenhagen. Well aware of the huge potential income from 'store-front' cinemas showing 16mm films and from peep-shows, Ferro decided on red carpet treatment for the man from Cleveland, Ohio. The party was held at the Italian's house in Copenhagen and featured an immense amount of food and a floor show. 'It was a renaissance party! He couldn't believe his eyes,' Ferro reminisced.[38]

When the discussion got down to business, Reuben Sturman told Ferro that he had business associates who were seeking to acquire good negatives which could be printed on to 8mm for their extensive and growing chain of peep-show booths. The deal was struck. Ferro was already able to supply thirty films, another twenty would follow: 'The deal was incredible. Over the next four years, they made a million copies of each one of them. Fifty million copies in all!' Ferro recalls with awe. 'This was before Caballero even got started. For all those years, the top thirty or so short films were *my* films!'[39]

Ferro is right to be impressed: if Sturman's associates used all those films in peep-shows (and that is the only conceivable explanation for the number of copies involved), then the 'slot-machine' gross must have exceeded $2 billion. *Deep Throat*'s $100 million gross seems inconsequential by comparison.

It was time for the Italian pornographer to move again. Although large amounts of money were flowing into his organization, little of it stayed for long. He sold the European rights to his negatives to Peter Theander of Rodox and in 1973 moved to Breda in Holland. 'My ambition was to make a hard-core feature film that would be shown at the Cannes Film Festival,' said Ferro. 'At that time there were warrants for my arrest in France as well as Italy, and Breda was as near as I could get to Cannes.' He set up an 'academy of erotica' and held open house in his spacious premises at Boschstraat 148 for anyone interested in what he was doing. One of his earliest visitors was an English film-school graduate called Falcon Stuart who had been involved with the short-lived 'underground' newspaper called *Suck* and Amsterdam's 'Wet Dream Festival'.[40]

Stuart proposed that he shoot a documentary film of Ferro practising his art as a pornographic film-maker. Ferro agreed enthusiastically. In it they cast a resident of Boschstraat, Brigitte Maier, an Austrian woman born in Linz in 1953, but now a US citizen and former *Penthouse* cover-girl. The documentary opens with a hard-core cartoon sequence drawn by the famous French cartoonist Bob Siné. It also introduced to a wider audience the doyenne of French domestic porn stars, Sylvia Bourdon. '*Penetration* was a spoof on how and why to make a "porno" movie,' Ferro subsequently argued. '[It] was naturally more funny than erotic.'[41]

The result was an idiosyncratic, quasi-biographical work originally called *Penetration* but later renamed *French Blue* for US distribution, and *Lasse Braun's Liebesgeflüster*[42] (*Lasse Braun's Pillow-Talk*) in Germany. Finished in November 1973, it was exhibited at the Cannes film festival in 1974 – the first hard-core film ever to be shown there. An American distributor who saw it spoke with Falcon Stuart –

Ferro's ambassador – and went up to Breda soon afterwards to sign the American rights. *French Blue* opened at the Lido cinema in Times Square, New York City, in December of that year. 'I went to the première of my film, it was wonderful,' said Ferro.[43]

Reuben Sturman had never made much headway in the theatrical side of films, and had preferred to concentrate on peep-show operations where the money flowed continually.[44] Ferro had tried to put enough finance together to back his own plans for a feature film before, but without success. Now *Variety* newspaper had reviewed *French Blue* and pronounced that though sex and comedy did not usually work, in this film it did. Sturman was impressed by the review and Ferro flew to Cleveland to see him. '*French Blue* is only an experiment, it's not really erotic,' the Italian admitted to the porn baron, 'you cannot get a hard-on, in my view, but we did not do it for that! But I promised that if he backed my proposal for a full-length 35 mm feature film, I would deliver a movie that would make the whole world horny, but be very serious and beautiful and all that.' Reuben Sturman caught the infectious enthusiasm of the Italian director and agreed to back the film with an initial funding of $100,000 to make a 35 mm hard-core film which could also be distributed in the United States. This initial round figure had to be increased by $50,000 after Ferro had drafted a more considered budget.[45]

The film would be called *Sensations*.[46] It was shot in England, Belgium and, mostly, Holland in January and February 1975. Ferro and Brigitte Maier were inseparable by the time *Sensations* was being made and it was a foregone conclusion that she would star as Margaret from Minnesota, on a sexual Grand Tour of Europe. The rest of the casting was not quite so straightforward. To deliver what he had promised, Ferro needed an attractive and interesting cast who could both act and perform sex on camera. Help came from an unusual quarter:

> A Dutch millionaire collector [of pornography] called Albert van Dam telephoned me when I first arrived in Breda in 1973. Some scenes in the film *Modesty Blaise* were shot at his beautiful home. At the time van Dam wanted to introduce me to a marvellous French woman called Sylvia Bourdon. She came up with a friend and we all fucked and had a great time. I shot her in some of my small films. When Sylvia was back in Paris she started to send me some wonderful people, many of whom hadn't appeared in pornography before.[47]

This explains why many people have assumed *Sensations* was French. Members of the cast recruited from Paris by Sylvia Bourdon included Véronique Monet, Fréderique Barral, Pierre Latour, Nicole Velna and Jean Villroy. Villroy, who is also credited as Robert Le Ray, was over sixty when *Sensations* was made and is probably the oldest man to 'perform' in sex scenes.

Appearing in the opening sequence at the rail of a Sealink cross-Channel ferry in the cameo role of Lady Pamela was the British publisher – best known internationally for her *Sex Maniacs Diary* – sex guru and 'swinger', Tuppy Owens. Owens's research for her books and 'educational' films has brought her into contact with many people in the porn industry, one of the closest encounters being with *Deep Throat* star Harry Reems. On a visit to London, Reems obliged Owens's penchant for al fresco anal sex in Blackfriars underpass under the unconcerned gaze of a City of London police constable.[48]

The sexual adventuress first met Alberto Ferro in London and agreed to help him find producers prepared to back his films. She also thought she could sell some of his 8 mm loops but rather distressed him when she insisted they had to be severely edited for the English market. They remained friends, however, and when he invited her to play Lady Pamela, she concurred readily enough: 'It was small "lie-on" part – I wasn't very good, really.'[49]

Many of Ferro's friends wanted to be in his new movie, albeit avoiding the explicit scenes. During an episode shot in a Brussels fashion boutique, Falcon Stuart can be seen in the background, as can one of Ferro's pornography suppliers from his earlier smuggling years.[50]

Although the film was shot in Holland (on Kodak's Eastmancolor stock), it went into post-production in London because that was where Ferro believed – as he still does – that he would find the best technicians in the world. It was edited by Ian L. Rakoff – who had previously worked with the major British director Lindsay Anderson – and dubbed by Alan Bell.[51] The original music was composed by another Englishman, Roger Moore and the lyrics written by Falcon Stuart.

A clandestine preview took place in a top central London viewing theatre in Wardour Street, home of the British film industry. 'It was a strange experience,' remembers one of the people who were there. 'When I was in advertising that was one of the cinemas where I used to go and see rough cuts and finished prints of commercials. Then, one day, I was sitting there in this same cinema watching Alberto's film. It was very funny, because many of the people I knew in the film business and advertising world were there too.'[52] Because Brigitte Maier had played an American woman, her voice had to be dubbed for the German version. This was done by a well-known Munich actress, Uschi Wolff, for a fee of DM300. She subsequently revealed that she had achieved the best results for some non-verbal parts of the sound track by sucking a sugar cube close up to the microphone.[53]

Back in Cleveland, Reuben Sturman was alarmed to learn that Ferro had gone $20,000 over budget on post-production, but not too alarmed – *Sensations* was clearly going to be a major success.

That success was virtually assured by a series of showings at the Cannes International Film Festival in the summer of 1975. They took place at the Olympia on Rue d'Antibes –

now converted into a multiple cinema called Les Ambassades. Twelve years later Ferro recalled:

> I will never forget the international Cannes audience's reaction to *Sensations*. My film was screened for seven nights in a row at midnight. For about an hour before, the Olympia was already packed with people who wanted to be sure to get one of its 800 seats to see my movie. Outside, every night, there were thousands of *festivaliers*, crowding the Rue d'Antibes, fighting to enter the Olympia through the inadequate police protection.[54]

The film was highly praised at Cannes and years later one of the American critics, not usually the biggest fans of European erotica, still rated *Sensations* as one of the best five X-rated films ever made: '*Auteurs* can prove that Chuck Vincent is a better film-maker than Alex deRenzy, but the trouser mouse will render them impotent theorists. Lasse Braun is in the deRenzy mould, an eccentric genius who shoots masterful sex films when he's in top form . . . *Sensations* is so sumptuous that sex is an art form.'[55] 'It was Alberto's finest hour,' added Falcon Stuart.[56] At last Ferro had achieved his objective of 'taking pornography out of the ghetto'.[57]

Basking in the success of *Sensations*, Ferro had no trouble finding his next financial backer and by July 1976 *Love Inferno* was in production for a Bochum, West Germany-based porn-film distributor called Manfred Metz. Manfred and his brother Dieter are close friends of American producer David Friedman.[58] The budget was only $75,000, but that was the least of Ferro's problems: he began to have trouble with his Dutch crew. Filming stopped for so long that the actors moved on to get other work. Ferro went to see Metz and, without fully spelling out the scale of the problems, persuaded him to contribute a further $60,000 to get the film finished.

But, knowing that *Love Inferno* couldn't be completed, the Italian director started another production, this time with an English crew. 'Falcon found a cameraman called Peter Sinclair for me,' Ferro recalls.

> Peter was marvellous – especially with lighting – and he taught me many things. When you see *Body Love*, you can see art in that picture! I think it was my very best work. At first my good friend Manfred was outraged when I told him what I'd done. A lot of work was needed to make *Love Inferno* into a complete film, but I was impressed with what was done. Manfred smiled again when I pointed out that I had given him two films for the price of one![59]

While Ferro was enjoying the rewards of porn's new-found freedom, a rival pornographer in West Germany was struggling to turn adversity to gain. In the early 1970s Gerd Wasmund had been a printer based near the German capital of Bonn. His company had already printed some pornographic magazines but the company went into bankruptcy. So financially desperate was Gerd Wasmund that he resorted to opening a toy shop, but was soon drawn back to the excitement and profits of porn.

He heard on the grapevine that the now famous 'Lasse Braun' had once more hit money problems and went to see the flamboyant Italian at his base in Breda. He went with a proposition: 'You can make films and I can handle money. Let me become your business manager.' Ferro agreed.

Citing the success of *Penetration/French Blue, Sensations* and the loops being distributed in America, Wasmund persuaded a magazine publisher from Essen called Horst Peter and the owner of a strip club in Cologne to back the production of the next series of Lasse Braun loops. They would make ten films in all, five of ten minutes' running time and five of twenty minutes'. The cast would include both American and English actors who would be directed by Alberto – it couldn't fail. The films would be made 'back-to-back', and because Wasmund would manage the production money could be saved all round. The backers put up DM650,000 (£200,000).

At the time – 1977 – the German pornography laws had already been changed. Although a loophole in English law had temporarily made it possible to show hard-core films in private clubs, production there was still highly illegal. But both Alberto Ferro and Gerd Wasmund were so enthusiastic about the skills of English film technicians that they decided it would be worth the risk: the films would be made in London. After a comic skirmish with customs officers at Heathrow Airport – who had identified the porn film-maker and refused to believe that he was taking his case full of kinky leather clothes, dildos and whips to a party – Ferro went by taxi to the duplex penthouse he had rented at Blake's Hotel, Roland Gardens, in the Royal Borough of Kensington. The luxury suite, reputedly used by Rolling Stone Mick Jagger on visits to London, became the base for a project which involved twenty days of planning and twelve days of filming.

One short segment called *Country Life* was made at a green-lawned mansion outside London, but the rest were shot in the capital city itself. The leading actors are credited as 'Marylin Courtis', 'Dennis Couper', 'Samantha Nichols', 'Helen Winters', 'Ava Mondie' and 'Mercedes Gregory'. Ferro cast Wasmund in a cameo role: 'There's a scene where I'm playing a cripple, being pushed around Hyde Park in a wheelchair by my nurse.'[60]

The last of the twenty-minute films, *Satin Party*, was made at a house in Notting Hill Gate. Horst Peter, his wife and a girlfriend arrived from Germany and asked Ferro if they could watch the shoot. Ferro agreed, on condition that they supply him with four cases of his favourite Crystale-Roederer champagne. There were twenty people in the house and the champagne and other intoxicants were liberally consumed as Ferro and his crew filmed the sexual encounters. 'I don't know how I managed to keep working. The owner was in heaven,' said Ferro, 'he couldn't believe what all those girls were doing!' The 'party' ended suddenly with the noisy arrival of the police.

Swedish photographer and publisher of *Private*, Berth Milton with the accoutrements of a successful porn baron. (*Courtesy Berth Milton*)

The prestige headquarters of Beate Uhse's porn empire at Flensburg, West Germany. (*Beate Uhse*)

One of Beate Uhse's three porn shops at Frankfurt International Airport. (*Beate Uhse*)

The youthful management team at ZBF Vertrieb, Wiesbaden, West Germany, with founding father Georg Schmitt (centre) and son Peter (second from right). (*Video Star/VTO*)

Pornographic video cassettes stacked high in one of ZBF's Wiesbaden warehouses. (*Video Star/VTO*)

Brigitte: Swedish porn photographic model, video performer and computer terminal operator. (*Courtesy Baltic Press AB*)

Porn video actress, Paula Meadows (artist Lynn Paula Russell). (*Trevor Watson*)

Ex-Marine and porn video star, Viper.

Veteran porn actor, scriptwriter, director and critic, Bill Margold in serious mood on the set of *Inner Blues*. (*Video 2000*)

Bengt Lénberg, editor of Swedish men's magazines (most recently *FiB Aktuellt*). (*David Hebditch*)

*FiB Aktuellt*'s roving sex-scene reporter, Jan Sjölin, on assignment. (*Courtesy Baltic Press AB*)

Arja Utriainen, editor-in-chief of the Finnish hard-core man's magazine, *Jallu*. (*Heikki Mattinen*, Jallu)

The 'Pussycat' porn movie theatre on Hollywood Boulevard, Los Angeles. Two doors to the right is a hard-core bookstore with video booths in the back room. (*David Hebditch*)

David F. Friedman, Hollywood producer of horror films, 'nudie cuties' and porn movies. (*Jane O'Neal*)

Pussycat Theatres' all-time top dozen porn feature films.
(*Courtesy Pussycat Theatres Inc.*)

Top American porn-film and video director Henri Pachard (Ron Sullivan) with cast on location in St Tropez, France.

US Customs Special Agent Jack O'Malley escorts West German child-porn dealer Roland Scherer from Chicago O'Hare Airport, 20 January 1987. (*Michael Fryer*, Chicago Tribune)

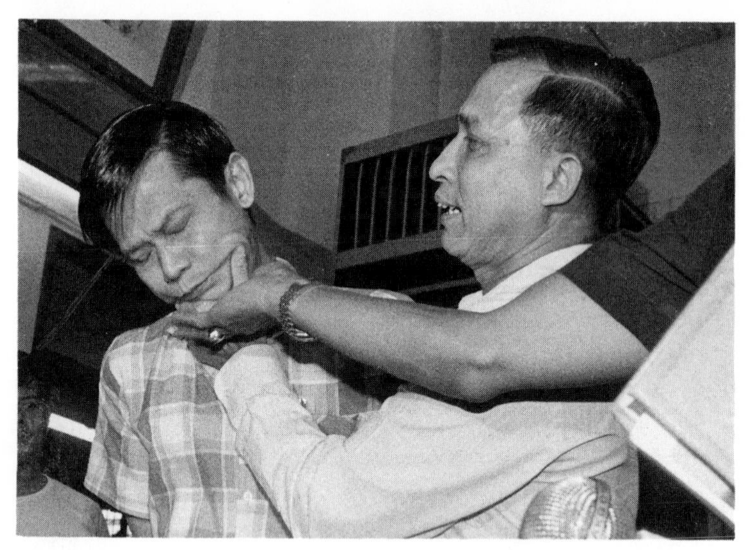

Child pornographer Manit Thamaree is encouraged to face the cameras by Bangkok police officers. (The Nation, *Bangkok*)

A Bangkok police officer displays a child-sex magazine found in the possession of Manit Thamaree. *Children-Love* was published by Danish porn baron Peter Theander. US Customs investigator 'Tuli' Tulalamba is centre, with glasses. (The Nation, *Bangkok*)

Danish child-porn pioneer Willy Strauss shows off the porn gold to be made from bizarre sex magazines and videos. (*David Hebditch*)

The Great British Confidence Trick – much bootlegging and censorship, no real pornography. An advertisement placed by the 'Private Organization' in UK men's magazines.

Under the glare of flashing blue lights and the stares of the neighbours, eight uniformed officers entered the house and dragged the startled performers – in various stages of undress – to the waiting police van. At first they failed to notice that Ferro was still filming: 'The black actress was really scared,' said Ferro with a guffaw. 'At the end of the film you can see her banging on the window of the police van protesting that she hadn't done anything wrong!' The whole thing was a set-up. Ferro had hired a specialized company which supplied convincing policemen and vehicles to film companies to carry out the raid.

Although the filming was successful, the problems began when it came to post-production. Before this was complete, Ferro received an offer to appear on television in the United States. He accepted, knowing that he would arrive a few days before his Italian passport expired at the end of July 1977. He could not renew it without returning to Italy and falling into the hands of the *carabinieri*. But the word from his homeland was that the Italian Parliament might pass an amnesty bill at any time. He told US immigration at Los Angeles International Airport that he planned to stay for three days only. The visit lasted for two years.

Gerd Wasmund was furious. He had been left with a set of unsaleable products and a group of angry investors demanding to know how they were going to get their money back. In any case, the German market was for full-length films and not loops. Ferro suggested that he shoot some additional footage of the actors talking about their sexual experiences and then use the material from the loops in 'flashbacks'. Wasmund retained an English cameraman called Paul Nicholas to shoot the extra material and had it edited into two films by a German technician called Hans Krüger. The resulting products were called *Sex Maniacs*[61] and *Sin Dreamer*[62]. Although they were 90 per cent Ferro's work, Wasmund put his own name on them as director. Both films were successful in Europe, but are virtually unknown in the United States. The whole audacious operation avoided the attentions of the British police and press, even when English actress Anne-Elise Kin, who appeared in *Sin Dreamer*, was seriously injured in September 1978 in a car crash on the M4 motorway while *en route* to Germany for the film's première.[63]

Ferro and Wasmund were not the only film-makers to use England as a production centre for pornographic films. The precedent for that is reputed to date back to the early 1960s and the activities of a character known to the pornography world as 'Charlie Brown'. 'Brown' first came to prominence in the late 1950s when he was working as a steward on the many cross-Channel ferries and the passenger boats plying the longer routes between the British Isles and Scandinavia. Few of the passengers served by the correctly spoken steward could have realized that he had a much more exciting, dangerous and lucrative job than waiting at table; 'Charlie Brown' was London's top porn smuggler.

'Charlie Brown's' real name was Walter Bartkowski. In spite of his impeccable English, he was German-Polish and had been a prisoner of war during the Second World War. In 1945 he decided that even the austerity of postwar Britain was preferable to East Germany under the Russians and applied to stay. After a period in another camp, he was released and settled in London. Contrary to popular misconception, 'swinging London' of the 1960s was not just a consumer of 'foreign porn' but a major producer for the European and Scandinavian markets. As Hans Moser remembers, 'Our kind of porn really started in Soho, not in Sweden or Denmark as many believe. Denmark was just the only liberated country in Europe which would take it. Walter Bartkowski was the main distributor for "the Gentlemen of Soho" and he handled slides, picture sets and 8 mm black-and-white films.'[64]

One of the porn film-makers operating in London in the

1960s was Mike Freeman. Freeman knew 'Charlie Brown' very well: 'Walter? I remember him – always wore a little leather hat. Walter used to phone me up from Germany and if there was a good-selling line, he used to order them in batches. They were twenty-minute 8mm prints in proper boxes with photographs on the outside. He used to get the stuff through Calais, somehow.'[65] Freeman specialized in loops, originally shooting them on 8mm black-and-white film. These were the films that 'Big Jeff' – a bulky associate of Freeman's called Evan Phillips – had shown the eccentric young Italian who drove a grey Mercedes 280 with CD plates. Freeman had not met Alberto Ferro because he (Freeman) was in prison at the time of the Italian's 1966 visit.

But on his release he took Ferro's suggestions to heart and promoted himself to a wind-up Bolex H16 camera and 16mm productions using colour and sound. 'I used to make them in London with professional models and sometimes amateurs, but mostly with professionals. The sound was over-dubbed later. I had three labels at that time: 'Venus', 'Climax' and 'Action'. I supplied all the shops in the West End as well as exporting to Scandinavia and Europe through Walter,' Freeman recalls.[66]

Another Briton making films at that time was Ivor Cooke. He was less prolific than Freeman but his output is thought to include: *Pussy Galore* (not related to the later David Friedman movie of the same name), *First Audition*, *End of Term* and *100% Lust* (which supposedly features a pre-Profumo Christine Keeler doing hard-core scenes). 'Ivor Cooke was a real gentleman in all the other shit,' is Hans Moser's recollection, 'because as is well known the British pornography business at this time was sponsored by Scotland Yard.' However, closeness to corrupt CID officers in London did not guarantee immunity outside the Metropolitan Police's 'manor' and, claims Moser, 'Charlie Brown saw the inside of just about every gaol.'[67]

But the law was changing throughout Europe and going

to gaol seemed to be an increasingly unnecessary overhead for participating in the industry. Walter Bartkowski settled in Germany and founded his own company, Starlight Films. Eventually this was consolidated into Tabu Films in Bochum, a town which was also the home base of Manfred Metz, who had backed Ferro's *Love Inferno* and, unwittingly, *Body Love*. Tabu remains today one of the continent's top producers and distributors of pornographic films and videos. Bartkowski has recently retired and is now living in Canada off a small pension in the form of royalties from Tabu.[68]

By 1975 the Federal Parliament in Bonn had abolished Article 184 of the Criminal Code and confirmed the legalization of pornography in West Germany and the porn goldrush had begun. The Uhse empire in Flensburg was as eager to take advantage of the situation as other prospective companies and individuals. Oddly enough, the most successful film made for the German market was a lavish costume version of the old Austrian story about a turn-of-the-century Viennese courtesan, *Die Abenteuer der Josefine Mutzenbacher* (*The Adventures of Josephina Mutzenbacher*).[69] It was made in the mid-1970s in West Germany and distributed by Herzog Films. Despite the success of that early venture few films are made like this in West Germany now, because of cost and the difficulty of finding actors: 'Directors say it's hard to find actors who will do the porn scenes, but you must have something in between,' says one observer of the German scene. 'You can't train German actors, although it's easy to find nice-looking girls in a place like Munich.'[70]

Gerd Wasmund took the same view. He and Alberto Ferro parted company after the making of *Sin Dreamer* in London. Exiled as he was in Malibu, California, Ferro willingly accepted Wasmund's offer for the European marketing rights to the Lasse Braun movies. In 1977 Wasmund, his own financial difficulties now behind him, set up a production and distribution company in Cologne called

Mike Hunter: 'I chose the name because I liked the sound of it, and it wasn't German.'[71] Armed with the rights to Ferro's films and new freedom under the law, Wasmund began to build one of the biggest film and video distribution empires in Germany.

Initially he did not neglect production and began to direct the films as well as fund and manage them. These included a sequel to *Sex Maniacs* called, unsurprisingly, *Sex Maniacs II* which starred Laura Martinelli. By the early 1980s Wasmund was ready to invest in a major production which would be right for the US market as well as the European one. In 1983 he took a German crew to Las Vegas where they would meet up with the cast he had recruited in Los Angeles. The American actors to appear in *Las Vegas Maniacs*[72] included many established names; Annette Haven, Richard Pacheco, John Leslie, Lisa DeLeeuw and Rhoda Joe Patty (who is billed as a look-alike for Farrah Fawcett of the *Charlie's Angels* television series). The film was shot over twenty-five days in and around Las Vegas on a budget of $600,000 and became a bestseller in both film and video formats with soft-core versions appearing on the *Playboy* channel in the United States and on cable networks in West Germany.

But the production was not without its problems – the main one coming at the very end of shooting. *Las Vegas Maniacs* was released in America as *Sex Loose*[73] and porn critic and actor Bill Margold had seen it: 'That's the murder mystery, the strange murder mystery. It starts out in a taxi-cab and goes on for ever. It has an all-star American cast with Haven and Leslie – but all the actors' voices are dubbed into English!'[74] As he was packing his bags to return to Germany, Gerd Wasmund had received a telephone call. 'We've got your soundtrack,' announced the anonymous voice at the other end, 'you can have it back in return for a quarter of a million dollars.'

The negative itself was safely locked up at the processing laboratory in San Francisco, so the sound tapes must have been stolen in Las Vegas. 'But I realized then that the Mob weren't happy with me working in the States,' says Wasmund.[75] 'I hope he told them to stick the soundtrack up their ass,' was Margold's opinion. It is uncertain what Wasmund may or may not have said to the mysterious caller, but he declined to pay the ransom money. Instead, he took the film back to Berlin where he employed American actors to redub the soundtrack. From this, Hans Krüger – who had cut *Sex Maniacs* and *Sin Dreamer* – was able to complete the editing. Wasmund was not the first and will not be the last to lose money in Las Vegas. But the experience has not put him off making movies: 'High-budget porn films are always a success; you get good actors, long playing time and good sets.'[76]

There was no porn gold in making X-rated movies for the benefit of the critics. As the fictional porn-film director in Gerard Damiano's 1978 feature *Skinflicks* says to one of his cast: 'You have to think of your audience out there . . .' The product had to reach consumers throughout the United States and Europe. Cinemas were, however, becoming available for such a purpose. As television expanded it began to win audiences from the movie houses, which could only compete by offering a continually narrowing range of box office 'block-busters', such as *Star Wars, ET* and *Raiders of the Lost Ark,* aimed at teenage audiences. The smaller cinemas were unable to compete – especially those in the run-down areas of the inner cities. So, for them, the idea of specializing in porn movies was attractive; there was plenty of material available and none of it was ever likely to be seen on the NBC, ABC or CBS television networks.

Within the space of a few years, there were over nine hundred cinemas, including many 'drive-ins', dedicated to showing the hard-core output of the Los Angeles and New York producers. The Pussycat chain run by Jimmy Johnson and Vince Miranda soon became the dominant outfit in this sector. They were perfect outlets from the porn industry's point of view. Ideally sited for audience convenience, there were no restrictions on entry (apart from requiring that patrons be over eighteen) and their methods of distribution and operation were identical to those used by the conventional motion picture industry.

While there were no restrictions on what could be shown in the kinos of Scandinavia, the situation was less satisfactory for the industry in England. Continuing pressure from 'anti-smut' groups made a liberalizing change in the law as unlikely as ever and the British Board of Film Censors (BBFC) was not going to license any hard-core material for showing in public cinemas. But none of this made the market demand go away, and while the demand was there someone would find a way of tapping it.

Two English porn entrepreneurs, John Lindsey and David Waterfield, discovered a loophole; private clubs were outside the remit of both the BBFC and the Obscene Publications Act. Lindsey started his Taboo chain of clubs and Waterfield opened the Exxon Cinema Club in north London. They openly advertised them as outlets for hard-core blue movies and they lived up to their promises. They did not underestimate the demand and the pub across the street from the Exxon Club in Islington did good business entertaining Waterfield's clientele as they waited an obligatory hour for their membership applications to be 'processed'. For many years the only way in which the law could interfere was by putting undercover officers into the clubs to discover members masturbating; this would be grounds for charges of 'running a disorderly house'.[77]

The German porn industry wanted to offer porn to 'walk-in' customers and in the mid-1970s PAM (Porno American Movies) was the first major chain to take advantage of regulations whereby clients paid a DM12 entrance fee, the cover price for beer and a sandwich. Showings of films such as *Sensations, Sex Maniacs* and *Die Abenteuer der Josefine Mutzenbacher* were thrown in for free.

In April 1975 the editor of Germany's equivalent of the

*New York Times* and the London *Times*, *Die Zeit*, sent reporter Petra Meister to investigate the new phenomenon. Her article[78] describes a visit to Hamburg's Pamkino.

At that time, although openly showing US porn films, the cinema was not allowed by law to advertise them (the *Los Angeles Times* and other American newspapers impose similar prohibitions on advertising X-rated movies). So the adverts simply ran: 'Pamkino, new programme, intimate atmosphere, tension, excitement, adults only.' The Pamkino chain had been established by a group called Bauer-Film, based in Dortmund. It had, by 1975, eighty US porn films on its list which were distributed to the chain across Germany.

According to Siegfried Bartylla, a director of Bauer-Film, it had prepared its move over the two years between 1973 and 1975 as the German legalization debate ran its course. Within the confines of the newly formulated federal law there was an exploitable loophole. Strangely, the clause in question stated that it would be an offence for anybody to organize public showings of porn films where the entrance fee was wholly or largely paid for such a performance. So, Pamkinos charged DM12 at the door and for this the customer received a drink and a sandwich which were placed in a little basket. The customer, basket in hand, then took a seat in the cinema proper. Pamkinos could then claim that they were operating eating/drinking enterprises in which porn films were incidentally shown to entertain the customers; and that was permitted under the new law.

Bartylla explained that he showed US films because, although Scandinavia exported a lot of films to Germany, these were simply 'sex films'. 'American hard-core takes over where the sex film leaves off,' Bartylla told reporter Petra Meister. At the time of the interview Bartylla claimed that Bauer had the monopoly of US porn film imports, and that business was good. The authorities had stipulated that only Hamburg, Munich and Berlin could have more than one Pamkino.[79] The film which was showing on the afternoon that Meister visited the Hamburg Pamkino was *Memories* (called *Memories Within Miss Aggie* in the United States), by Gerard Damiano.[80]

A few years later, the Cologne newspaper *Stadt-Anzeiger* reported that the Pamkino loophole had been closed. The paper referred to a ruling handed down in the fifth Appeal Division of the Berlin Federal Criminal Court in response to an appeal lodged by lawyer Gerd Joachim Roos against a judgment where the Metropol cinema was fined DM100 on fifty separate counts of showing porn films, but charging for food and drink on entry. Roos's appeal was rejected on the grounds that exploiting the loophole in the law was itself an illegal act.[81] From that point paying customers were only permitted to see porn films in late-night bars and on the premises of licensed sex shops (porn kinos).

Once the law had been clarified, Beate Uhse was able to expand her small but profitable chain of 'Blue Movie' kinos. Such was their success that Uhse made her first and only major mistake – and one that was to cost her a considerable sum of money. David Friedman remembers what happened: 'Beate Uhse tried to set up business in the USA. She was about as welcome here as a case of hives.'[82] Uhse had wanted to benefit from the retailing of pornography in America and establish outlets for her own productions. She delegated her son, Uli Rotermund, to set up the operation. According to one uncorroborated version of the story it did not take him long to discover that none of the established US chains would show their movies, so he decided that they would buy their own cinemas. A few outlets were purchased but none of the distributors would supply American hard-core films. 'Someone called Uli and pointed out how unfortunate it would be for business if he kept finding bodies in his auditoriums,' says one source.[83] Rotermund cannot remember receiving such a call but does not deny that there were difficulties which he attributes to an unfortunate choice of managers in Los Angeles. 'If we were blocked by the Mafia,' he jokes, 'then it was definitely the Jewish Mafia.'[84] The Uhse operation eventually pulled out of the United States losing a reputed $500,000 in the process.

In America the cinemas showing X-rated movies were doing good business in spite of having their heels snapped at by every district attorney with an eye to the forthcoming elections to the bench. One of producer David Friedman's earlier brushes with the law took place in the late 1960s in his home state of Alabama.

But Friedman is no soft target and he fought back by suing the governor. It was after the time when George Wallace, disabled by an assassination attempt, decided to run for state governor again, following the death of his wife. While the election was being fought, Deputy Governor Albert Brewer had taken over. Friedman recalls:

> Brewer decided it might be good for votes to try and shut down a local movie theatre. They were showing one of my films: *Pussy Galore*. The judge was called Johnson and he was what passed for a liberal in those parts. Prosecuting was a man called Carter of the law firm Hill, Carter and Hill. His partners were Senator Hill and Congressman Hill, so Carter got all the jobs. In this case he was defending the governor's decision to close the movie house. Fighting the case with us was the manager of the movie theatre, the 81 Drive-in in Selma, Alabama.
>
> In presenting his case, Carter refers to a character in the movie called 'Phil Latio'. On hearing this the judge breaks up. He asks Carter if he knew what the name meant. Carter says 'Yes' and the judge says 'What?' But Carter says he couldn't possibly say in open court. Then I'm called as a witness and the judge asks 'Did you produce this movie?'
>
> 'Yes, your honour, I did.' I used my Alabama accent.
>
> 'Do you know what Phil Latio means?'
>
> 'Yes, your honour, because I thought up the name.'

'I suppose you also thought up the title of the movie – *Pussy Galore*?'

'No, your honour, I stole that one from a James Bond movie.' The judge broke up again, he was really enjoying it. Anyway, the police didn't act legally in the raids and we won the case.[85]

Not all producers and theatre operators were so fortunate, but from 1968 they did at least have the support of the newly formed Adult Film Association of America (AFAA). Friedman was one of the founders:

At that time there were about a hundred of us involved in the production, distribution and exhibition of adult films. We were getting a lot of heat at that time from the south and the south-west of the country. The stuff was really pretty tame – today most of it would be judged 'R' or even 'PG13'. We could show no pubic hair and no male genitals. So, we said 'We must hang together or we surely will all hang separately.'

We appointed three top First Amendment lawyers to represent us throughout the country. They were Stanley Fleishman, Tom Cudgel and Harrison Graves. The problem was that an exhibitor would get busted and his local lawyer would have no idea how to proceed. So we got these three lawyers on retainer and they produced an 'advice kit' for use in the defence of obscenity trials. I admit that our original aim was somewhat selfish. Anyway, the AFAA grew and prospered. In 1968 we held our first convention in Kansas City.[86]

Throughout the 1970s the AFAA expanded. It held twice-yearly conventions in places as far apart as New York and Hawaii, it annually presented its own 'Oscars' – Erotic Film Awards – and published the *AFAA Bulletin* to keep members up to date with the latest industry gossip and legal cases. As well as holding various positions in the AFAA, from president down, Friedman was also the editor of the

*AFAA Bulletin* for many years and his own quirky style showed through. The *Bulletin* was generous enough to publish verbatim the opinions of those opposing the industry. Even long articles from the publications of the Moral Majority were reproduced without comment. But, just once, Friedman made an exception:

> 'This is very detrimental to the American home, not only for the children, but for the adults. It's a tool, possibly a Communist plot, that is making the American home decay. It's insidious.' – Barbara Stephens, Moral Majority.

Hand-written beneath the cutting was: 'No! No! Ms Stephens – we're capitalists, not communists!'[87]

The AFAA was not without its detractors in the porn business. Al Goldstein, the publisher and editor of *Screw* magazine in New York was one of them. He wrote, sniffily:

> It was that time again. Time for the august members of the Adult Filmmakers' [*sic*] Association of America to gather in their rented tuxedos and pat each other on the paunch in celebration of another successful year at the box office. And it would have been a pretty successful party too – if only there had been some sex, or some scandal, or *something* to remind you that this annual event is, after all, the West Coast's Academy Awards of porn films.

Goldstein's little sally against the AFAA drew a tart response from Friedman in the *AFAA Bulletin*:

> Thus began Al Goldstein's annual knock of the Erotic Awards in the 1 August issue of his tiresome publication. Al, we don't really mind you making a spectacle of yourself every year, but please stop boring us.[88]

Bill Margold's accusation was a more serious one: 'The AFAA was a politically aligned, economic, "buy your award", "buy your nomination"-type situation. I was affiliated with the Adult Film Association for years. I was even a member for a while, and the way they operated was that they bought the nominations and then I honestly suspect that they also bought their awards. That is corrupt. What usually won didn't deserve it . . . Sometimes, of course, it did by sheer attrition. The AFAA *is* in danger of going belly-up because they take themselves too seriously.'[89]

David Friedman vehemently denies Margold's suggestion. By the 1980s, the AFAA had some 260 members and the internal bickering was probably no better or worse than that encountered in any other industry group. Most members avoided the in-fighting and got on with making money. This included the Pussycat chain which celebrated its 25th Anniversary in 1986 with a retrospective 'Erotic Film Festival' held at its theatres in Hollywood and Buena Park, California, between 1 November and the middle of December. The choice of films was interesting because it was billed as 'Featuring 12 of the Greatest X-Rated Movies of All Time'. They were: Gerard Damiano's *Deep Throat, Take Off, The Private Afternoons of Pamela Mann* by Radley Metzger, *Inside Jennifer Welles, The Opening of Misty Beethoven* (also by Metzger), *The Life and Times of Xaviera Hollander*, Anthony Spinelli's *Sex World*, Lasse Braun's *Sensations, Debbie Does Dallas, Naked Came the Stranger* (another one directed by Metzger – this time under the name of Henry Paris), *Talk Dirty To Me* (also by Spinelli) and *The Erotic Adventures of Candy*.

In the last film (made in 1978), producer and director Gail Palmer excels by 'borrowing' from three plots; *Candide, Candy* by Terry Southern and *The Wizard of Oz*.[90] These are by no means the first twelve productions in Jim Holliday's Top 40 charts, but they probably represent the leading money-spinners for what was the biggest chain of porn outlets in the world.

In the 1980s production costs for a quality sex movie had risen to $250,000 – with an industry average of about half that sum. Only exceptionally will costs reach the $600,000 supposedly spent by Gerd Wasmund on *Las Vegas Maniacs* (*Sex Loose*). This money is invested in the cast, the locations and the amount of time available for shooting. Wasmund's twenty-five days on *Las Vegas Maniacs* is at the top end; a long weekend has been referred to as being at the other. Even when the production is 'in the can', further money will need to be invested in editing, music, printing, promotion and distribution.

So how do the investors get their money back? Across the United States in 1980, there were nearly eight hundred cinemas, some 6 per cent of the countrywide total, which specialized in showing hard-core porn movies. About three million paying customers went past their box offices each year. With over one hundred features starting each year, the ratio of new films to theatres was such that the outlets were spoilt by a luxury of choice. Consequently, distributors got as little as half the usual cut from the box office takings (35 to 50 per cent against 70 to 90 per cent for conventional films).[91]

Lower percentages notwithstanding, porn movies usually grossed $1 million in the first eighteen months of distribution. Furthermore, porn films stay in circulation longer because they 'age' much less quickly than conventional Hollywood output. Russ Meyer, the most successful producer of soft porn would exploit this consideration by, for example, always having the cast drive old classic automobiles rather than the more recent models which are liable to date before the film is out of post-production. Meyer's best-paying film, *The Supervixens*, cost $213,000 to make in 1974 and grossed over $20 million in the intervening years. But the continuing success of films like *Deep Throat* suggests that Meyer's extra care to prevent his films from dating might be unnecessary; perhaps the nature of the material itself ensures enduring appeal.

Writer Robert Rimmer reveals that a minor production called *Ms Magnificent* grossed $22,000 in the first two weeks of its release in two cinemas. *Frat House* receipts totalled

$7,993 in three days in one Denver theatre, and $11,148 at a cinema in San Diego. Robert McCallum's *Tangerine* grossed $789,532 in the first year of its theatrical release. The accounting was corroborated by Bob Sumner, the former head of Mature Pictures (the Los Angeles company which made *Take Off*), one of the porn industry's major producers. His company, Sumner confirmed, had produced or distributed thirty-seven money-making sex films: 'About 60 per cent [of the box office receipts] goes to the theatre owners and the rest is divided by the film companies and distributors.' After expenses, Sumner is left with between $300,000 and $500,000 per picture.[92] Box office receipts of the American industry as a whole in 1978 were $365 million, and in 1980 definitely exceeded $500 million.[93]

The scale of the phenomenal success of *Deep Throat* is best seen against the box office track record of a long-standing front-runner in the conventional motion picture industry. Assuming *Deep Throat* has grossed $100 million, this figure can be set against the $325 million made to date by the Disney blockbuster *Snow White*. But *Snow White* cost $1.5 million to make compared with the measly $25,000 invested in Damiano's film. (The comparison favours *Snow White* here because it was made using 1940s dollars.) So *Deep Throat* has so far grossed 4,000 times the original investment compared with a factor of 216 for the cartoon classic. Little wonder then, that the industry agreed on one thing. 'People make porn features for one reason: money – easy money,' confirmed director Carter Stevens.[94] David Friedman is equally unequivocal: 'It's a very hard business to lose money in.'

The euphoria was short-lived. In 1983 hard-core Hollywood suddenly realized that it was not immune to the advances of new technology. What was happening to the conventional film industry was about to happen to them. 'A lot of the industry, the *front* of the X-rated industry is beginning to vanish,' laments Bill Margold. 'The theatres. You should go and look at the Mayan Theatre on Hill Street in LA – one of the great porno palaces of all time. I hope it's still there. It's gorgeous! But it's gonna be vanishing soon, because there's no reason for it to exist anymore. It is the crumbling edifice that is the X-rated theatrical business. You can almost visualize the vultures sitting on the cornerstones of that building watching the theatrical business sink into the mire.'[95]

Margold was right. Throughout the world, the X-rated industry was being submerged under a giant mass of videotape, and the bonanza years of porn films were rapidly becoming the good old days.

# 7

## *Hooks to Hang Dreams On: The Video Revolution*

'There is no record of the number of men who died trying to drive home from an X-rated movie theatre with one hand,' said John Weston, counsel to what had become the Adult Film and *Video* Association of America.[1] Weston was merely confirming that no cinema patrons would want to watch a porn film while sitting next to a cop from the local vice squad, when they could be viewing more or less the same thing in the comfort and privacy of their own homes. If the decline of cinema audiences in favour of home video was inevitable for the conventional movie industry, this additional consideration – that pornography exists primarily for the purpose of sexual arousal – was a convincing extra motivating force in the case of the X-rated industry.

Many porn barons had seen the writing on the wall; Noel Bloom's Caballero Control Corporation in California was transferring 8mm loops to Sony Beta video cassettes as early as 1976.[2] However, the diehards were still convinced that the video market would be peripheral to the continued theatrical release of 35mm feature films. In 1981 David Friedman, as President of the AFAA, was cast in the role of King Canute: 'There are 894 adult theaters operating in the

United States. Despite the burgeoning of the video cassette market these theaters are still the largest source of income for producers and distributors of adult films. Contradicting the fear that video and cable will diminish theatre attendance, there has been a marked growth in patronage.'[3] Box office revenues that year were 17 per cent of the entire motion picture industry, represented by a weekly patronage of about two and a half million paying $5 each to see adult films in *Pussycat* theatres and other cinemas. This placed gross revenues in excess of $500 million a year.[4]

If the balance sheet was still in Friedman's favour in 1981, the trends to video certainly were not. Two and a half million theatre attendances may have sounded impressive, but by 1987 that figure was all but obliterated by an amazing 15 million-plus hard-core video rentals every week – an annual gross of well over $1 billion.[5]

At the end of the 1970s three million video cassette recorders (VCRs) were installed in American homes.[6] In 1981 the figure had reached five million and – suggesting a growth rate of over two million VCRs a year – 17 million in 1984. And that was still only 20 per cent of the number of homes with television sets.[7] Saturation point is now being reached with well over 40 million VCRs in the United States (44 per cent of homes with televisions) and more than 200 million worldwide in 1987. If anything, Europe has been in advance of America with this trend and in the UK alone there are some ten million VCRs (50 per cent of TV households).[8]

The only thing likely to stop this expansion is a switch in technology to another video form such as optical disc (hitherto unsuccessful). But even if that happens, the decline in cinema attendances will not be stemmed; home viewing is the new thing and it is here to stay. As a reflection of this, most former porn theatres are defunct (they now total less than two hundred in the United States) and the production of 35mm feature films is correspondingly down from a peak of about 120 to less than twenty a year.[9] In 1983 the twenty-five-year-old *Pussycat* chain suffered its first reversal of fortune: the number of theatres in the group was down from thirty-six to twenty-nine and revenues had declined by 20 per cent.[10]

The conservatism of that sector of the industry deeply rooted in theatrical distribution was no worse than in the rest of Hollywood. Indeed, there is much evidence that the X-rated video revolution confirms the historical astuteness of pornographers in embracing new publishing technologies. The advantage lay not merely in the expansion of the business to a much wider potential audience (people who would not go to a porn cinema, even if there was one in their town) but video also opened up new methods of distribution and viewing. Material in video form can be bought or rented on cassettes and discs from porn shops, video 'libraries' and, in many countries, even the local petrol station; it can be seen on multi-channel cable in 'peep-show' booths and in-hotel systems; in video 'porn-kinos'; and some governments even allow it on pay-TV and subscription cable. One enterprising company in Amsterdam will supply hotel guests with a VCR and a selection of porn videos for the duration of their stay in the city. The inherent flexibility of video over film means that its potential is limited only by the imagination of the porn barons.

Those porn barons established in the film-making industry of the 1970s were well poised to be the first to exploit the new medium. Because video was recognized as having the potential to attract a new clientele, the 'software' could be drawn from the industry's film archives. By then, after eight decades of 16mm 'stag' movies, and more than ten years of making 8mm loops and 35mm features, over 10,000 productions were available.[11] (A notable exception to this is the early 'Lasse Braun' loops made by Alberto Ferro, who still retains the video rights. He does, however expect this old material to be released on cassette 'before the end of the decade'.[12])

Although the stag films were invariably uncopyrighted,

they suffered the disadvantage of being in black and white and mostly without sound. A company called Boccaccio 100 located in Tempe, Arizona specializes in releasing its substantial stock of public-domain stags on video and such pornware can occasionally be seen incorporated in current releases where a pretext can be built into the plot.

Unfettered by distribution agreements and residuals, the loops offered the most immediate source of 'software' and the custodians of such material became dominant in the video era. In Europe Peter Theander was quick to transfer the loops made by his brother Jens and Lasse Braun to video cassette under the Rodox label. In California Noel Bloom of Caballero Control Corporation republished the famous, but very un-Swedish, *Swedish Erotica* series on video (in association with what was perhaps the first porn video company, TVX, in which the ubiquitous David Friedman had an investment). Other series which were relaunched in the same way included *Limited Editions*, the *Diamond Collection*, and *Peepshow*. Three or four loops would be copied on to a one-hour cassette and sold for, say, $39.95. Profits were good because the films had already been paid for and costs were therefore centred on tape duplication and packaging.

But such products would only suit the needs of a certain, relatively unsophisticated sector of the market. The newly won 'yuppie' audience in the United States would be demanding the more sophisticated fare they were used to seeing at their local *Pussycat* theatre. The video distributors had to start doing deals with the film-makers. Where the distributors themselves owned the rights, the material could often be transferred to tape without any more money changing hands. Where the producer was independent of the distributor (as was usually the case) a video deal would have to be struck.

But with the technology on their side, the odds were very much in the distributors' favour. Movie houses were closing by the day, and the producers were only too pleased to find new sources of revenue. This was forthcoming in the form of a royalty on each cassette sale, plus a guaranteed advance for a production with a proven box office track record. The only question was who would get which of the best money-spinning films. The real winner was Butch Peraino's Arrow Films of New York state, which holds the rights to *Deep Throat* – reputed to have sold 500,000 video cassettes – and other titles in the Damiano output.[13]

But the video revolution did not merely change the form in which pornware was distributed – there was also an upheaval in the structure of the industry. Single film products could no longer generate enough money for reinvestment in new productions on the scale of *Sensations, Take Off* and *Las Vegas Maniacs* (*Sex Loose*). The industry needed to go down-market with a wider range of cheaper products. The new generation of video distributors were ideally positioned in midfield to dominate the game and take absolute control of the market.

They took the money flowing in from the retail sector and invested it directly in productions to which they would own all the rights. To keep the product-line varied and the profit margins high, these new productions would be shot in days – even hours – for as little as $15,000, using freelance crews drawn from a reliable pool of directors, cameramen and technicians. These 'sexvids' would feature actors and actresses whose names were mostly well-known to the customer-base and the supportive publicity machine.

Producers are as little loved in the X-rated movie industry as they are in conventional Hollywood. They are universally berated for their lack of creative talent, but never praised for their business acumen. The combined productivity of American companies like Caballero, Vidco, Essex, VCA and VCX peaks at 400 porn videos a year. Every day in California a new X-rated video starts production and, more often than not, is 'in the can' before the day is out. The edited result, in the hands of people like Al Bloom, Peter Theander, Russell Hampshire, Hans Moser,

Joe Steinman, and Sidney Niekerk, means that the $15,000 invested each time can be magically transformed to $150,000 in a matter of months.

So how easy is it to break into the temptingly large video market? In 1981 producer/director Mike Freeman re-appeared on the London scene with just that intention. His reckless plan was to exploit a temporary confusion in English law over whether the Obscene Publications Act had any relevance to video. During the resulting hiatus, Caballero's *Swedish Erotica* cassettes were readily available throughout the United Kingdom and Uli Rotermund of the Beate Uhse Organization in Germany confirms that they sold 10,000 cassettes of a single title in Britain between 1979 and 1983.[14] Another observer was even more specific: 'In those years, the Americans saturated the UK market.'[15] With an eye to such sales and profits, Freeman put the word around that he was looking for performing talent to appear in hard-core, feature-length videos.

Paula Meadows, sexual libertarian and porn actress (see also Chapter 3), was one of those who responded: 'Well, I started off doing some modelling for magazines. A model I worked with in one of the sessions said that Freeman had just made a video and it was very good. It was being made illegally for distribution in this country.'[16] Meadows's telephone number was passed to Mike Freeman who called a few days later and arranged to visit her. 'I was very pleased to meet him at first,' Meadows recalls, 'I thought we might be on to a similar sort of thing.'

Freeman also remembers well his first encounter with the self-assured woman who was living with Frank Russell, an Irish writer and much older man. 'We were smoking a joint and talking about what she would do in the film. She said she liked to be a slave and have men to tell her what to do,' said Freeman. 'So I told her to lift up her skirt. To my amazement, she did, and while this funny old geezer was still sitting in the corner of the room and watching, she knelt in front of me and started to suck me off. A girlfriend of hers joined in. She looked up at me and said "I'm a phallus worshipper, you know." I thought, well, get worshipping that, girl!'[17]

Perhaps by way of compensation, Frank Russell was given the job of writing the script, 'of which they didn't use a word', he protests.[18] Meadows liked the script: 'It was a beautiful story based on something I'd been through myself. Mike said, "Look, if you've got any of your own experiences you'd like to act out, then we'll do it." So I said "Yes, I have!" And we devised a story and circulated it to all the members of the cast – we thought that was how they worked, because I'd never done it before, you see. I assumed they all worked professionally like that.'

The video was to be recorded in a flat in north London. On the morning of the first day, Meadows relates: 'I turned up with my script under my arm and I found out that nobody had even bothered to open the cover of it at all. Even the director [Freeman] hadn't actually, he hadn't got a clue what it was about!'[19]

Matters did not get any better as cast and crew sat around waiting for something to happen. 'The first thing Mike did was light up a joint, start smoking and say, "OK, let's get into all this . . . What's the first scene?" And, vaguely, "Where are we doing it?" He was an artist and a painter and he appreciated the visuals of it, but had no idea what it was all about . . .'[20]

The film did get finished and the final result was titled *Truth or Dare* after the name of the children's game. Freeman's company Videx used Meadows in another production. 'The second thing was called *Happy Birthday*,' says Meadows. 'It started off fairly conventionally with two girls bumping into each other in the street. I get talking to this housewife and I find out that her husband wants to spank her and she doesn't like it. Anyway, he's got a birthday coming up, so I say "Why don't I become the birthday present – I like being spanked. So he can spank me for his birthday!" It was all right.'[21]

Mike Freeman sold the videos by mail order. He openly promoted them as genuine hard core through full-page colour advertisements placed in British men's magazines and the suppressed market responded enthusiastically: 'I was doing really well,' says Freeman. 'I was even doing export orders to places like South America.'[22]

Seeing the need to expand by doing deals with the porn barons of Europe, Freeman visited the MIPCOM film convention in Cannes in 1981 where he counted no less than six hundred producers and distributors from all over the world, doing business in pornography. On his return he contacted Peter Theander's Rodox company in Copenhagen. Unfortunately, it seemed that much of the success of Videx's productions was attributable to content rather than class. Rupert James at Rodox took the call: 'Mike Freeman? Oh, yes, I know him. He's a fucking terrible film-maker. He had a distribution company in the West End, I think it was called Videx or something like that. All this was in 1981, about. The last time I heard from him he'd phoned to offer us his next twenty films at some ridiculous price. Not on the basis of your last showing, I told him.'[23]

James was not alone in his opinion. The hard-core strip-cartoon artist who uses the name 'Erik von Goethe' knew of the Videx venture: 'The curious thing is, Freeman is so rotten at making films, yet he's made one of the best I've ever seen! *Truth or Dare*. I thought that was the best offering of the year.'[24]

Mike Freeman was only unknown to newcomers to the British porn scene. He was actually the same Mike Freeman who had been making 8mm and 16mm porn films in Soho in the 1960s, many of which were distributed by 'Charlie Brown' and Alberto Ferro (see Chapter 6). His career in the porn film business had been interrupted by an Old Bailey judge's requirement in 1969 that he serve a life sentence for murder in one of Her Majesty's prisons. 'I fell out with some people who sent a hit man to kill me. But I got him before he got me,' says Freeman, who had also served eighteen months from 1966 on obscenity charges.[25] His opportunistic exploitation of the temporary loophole in the law naturally caused the police to take a further interest in their irascible adversary.

A year after making *Truth or Dare* and *Happy Birthday*, Paula Meadows heard a knock at the door to her flat: 'It was the police. The Vice Squad had appeared! They'd arrested Mike and they were just talking to everybody, to find out who his partner was. I mean, they weren't interested in us after they'd talked to us for a few minutes. They realized we weren't involved with him on the business side. We were just acting in the film. They'd assumed that someone else was involved, that someone else had put the money up. I don't know whether they ever found him. He was a strange secret partner.'[26]

There is good reason to believe that Mike Freeman's 'strange secret partner' may have been none other than the British government. While still in prison, Freeman had been planning to go into the growing video business, but he knew that capital funding would be a problem. Even if he hired the Hi-Band video equipment, further costs would be incurred in editing, duplication, packaging and advertising. In the early 1980s, the government was making funds available for people wanting to set up new businesses, especially those that might involve job creation. On his release, Freeman applied to the Department of Trade and Industry who administered the scheme. He was, no doubt, a little vague about the exact nature of the films he planned to make but, whatever he told them, they willingly came forth with the money.[27]

Freeman's re-established career as a porn film-maker came to an end with his arrest by Scotland Yard's Obscene Publications Squad. At the first of his trials an effective team of defence lawyers – backed by expert witnesses such as Tuppy Owens, 'Erik von Goethe' and Derek Malcolm, film critic of the *Guardian* – persuaded the jury that the Videx videos were not obscene and the case was dismissed. At the second trial, the bewigged barristers had a harder time finding excuses for Freeman's energetic self-defence during his arrest and he was sent to prison again.

While the Old Bailey was busy with Mike Freeman, Paula Meadows had started to make porn videos in the United States with directors such as Art Benn (Ron Dorfman, who works with his scriptwriter wife, Betsy), Henri Pachard (Ron Sullivan) and Lasse Braun (Alberto Ferro). This time her experiences on set were better: 'I was very pleased when I worked in the States to find that things were totally different. It was very professional. I mean there was no groping of people backstage or any mucking about. We had scripts, proper scene breakdowns.'[28]

Frank Russell's experience with the script for *Truth or Dare* was probably not exceptional in an industry which has a reputation for working from scripts written in the taxi *en route* to the studio.

But porn videos really do have scripts. *Don't Get Them Wet!*[29] was written by 'Viper' (credited as Angela Mapache) who also starred in the resulting production. The script includes pages headed 'Suggested shooting order', 'Adult encounters', 'Scene/location breakdown' and 'Characters', before the script itself begins. The plot is derived from the Steven Spielberg production, *Gremlins*.

The opening scene wastes no time in establishing how things are going to turn out. In the video itself, Bill Margold plays the part of Joe, Mike Horner is Rod and Viper is Beta, the 'nymphlin':

(ROD *enters a dimly lit sex aid store. He begins to browse around, the shopkeeper sees him and approaches.*)

JOE: Sir, can I help you with something in particular?

(ROD *starts, looks slightly guilty.*)

ROD: It's my room-mate's birthday, I was, well, trying to find him something sort of, well, unique?

JOE: Unique? I have the perfect gift . . . It is rather expensive . . .

ROD: Money is no object, as long as it is something really special.

JOE: Wait here, I'll bring it out.

(JOE *retreats to the back of the shop,* ROD *continues to browse.* JOE *returns with a large Cellophane-covered object.*)

JOE: This is the ultimate in a high-technology sex toy. It walks, talks, fucks and it can't get pregnant! It is called a nymphlin, a specially designed creature to be used as a sex toy.

(JOE *slowly unwraps the nymphlin.*)

ROD: My God, she's perfect . . . He'll love it.

JOE: As I said, it has been specially made, through genetic research, to be the ultimate in an orgasmic partner.

ROD: And it can do everything a real woman can?

JOE: They did a remarkable job on these, it is a limited edition. They only made one for sale purposes. There are a couple of things you have to be careful of . . .

ROD: This sounds perfect . . . What things?

JOE: Well, you can never get them wet . . .

ROD: No problem, fucking in the tub is kind of uncomfortable . . . What else?

JOE: Don't let her eat after midnight . . .

ROD: That's all? That's easy. How much?

JOE: For you . . . $500.

(ROD *winces.*)

Sure enough, Rod's friend Steve (played by Jerry Butler) is delighted with the gift. So delighted that he shares her with Rod:

(ROD *and* STEVE *partake of* BETA. *She claws and bites and seems to have a voracious appetite for sex. Afterwards . . .*)

What is not included in the script are detailed directions for the sex scenes. The formulas for a 'two males plus one female' encounter are well known and well-practised by the performers and crew over hundreds of film and video productions. Indeed, once Steve gets Beta really wet, he ends up with another three 'nymphlins' (played by Breezy Lane, Paula Winters and Domino) thus making more encounters possible. After Steve's and Beta's coupling, there is a four-way lesbian scene between the 'nymphlins', a male plus two 'nymphlins', followed by most other combinations.

Just as the market demands that magazine publishers include explicit text with their explicit photosets, porn videos have to include some 'dirty talk'. A typical example of this in *Don't Get Them Wet!* occurs in a later orgy scene which is reminiscent of the Victorian *Romance of Lust* (see Chapter 1). Joe (Bill Margold) is showing the others how to 'deal with the nymphlins':

> JOE: See here, fuck her face . . . See? She loves it. Use your dick . . . it is the answer to control. OK, Steve, you fuck her from behind. That's it. Use that dick . . . Fuck her good now and Rod go ahead and eat that pussy of hers . . . Yeah, that's the way . . . Come on Bongo . . . get involved.

*Don't Get Them Wet!* is neither high comedy nor high art, but the makers of this example of 1980s porn ephemera would never pretend that it was anything other than what they intended it to be: low-cost, unsophisticated and explicit pornography designed to meet a well-understood market need.

Once the script has been drafted, the video needs to be casted and a location found for the shoot. Casting can be done in a number of ways. The 'star names' will be selected at a fairly early stage and some or all of these might have long-term associations with the distributor funding the production. Other roles will be cast from relative newcomers, including the industry's 'starlets', or from performers who specialize in playing characters parts, older people or foreigners (an Englishman for a butler, a Frenchman for a hairdresser, for example). Others will be selected for particular physical attributes such as very large breasts, or transsexual characteristics. There are agencies, such as

Pretty Girl International in Los Angeles which represents porn actors and actresses. Some of the more experienced and well-connected performers operate as freelances and represent themselves.

'The days of the casting couch are over,' says director Ron Sullivan. 'I always thought that it was pretty demeaning to ask a person to take their clothes off like that. In any case, we are now dealing with a small community of performers who are well known to producers and directors. I do all *my* casting on the telephone.'[30]

Finding locations is not ranked as a major problem by film-makers, and they have learned to live with the need to shoot hard-core scenes outside the Los Angeles county line. Most locations are no more than private houses for which a 'facility fee' will be budgeted. The same houses tend to get used fairly often, but few viewers seem to take much notice of the décor or the furniture.

Bill Margold described the perfect setting: 'A good location should have its bedroom, its shootable bathroom. If you want sex in the kitchen, that's nice. A living room with a fireplace is always pretty. It would be nice if the place has a yard and even nicer if it has a pool and a hot tub. I'm really tired of shooting movies indoors but then, of course, when you go outside, you are fighting mother nature, whose cloud-cover sometimes does not wanna give you what you want, climate-wise. The ideal location should have an indoor–outdoor type of facility.' The rooms need to be as large as possible to accommodate the cameras, lights and the crew surrounding the action they are recording for posterity.

*Don't Get Them Wet!* was taped in a house in the San Francisco Bay area which is regularly used for hard-core video productions. Ron Sullivan has also worked there. Neither cast nor crew like it: the place has limited working space, is not noted for its cleanliness and there is inadequate water pressure for the showers.[31] It is not a far cry from Gerd Wasmund's lasting impressions of the house in

Kensington where a segment of *Sin Dreamer* was shot by Lasse Braun: 'It was a big cold place with no proper services or heating, the toilets hardly worked and there was only cold water there.'[32]

California became the home of the film industry because of its brilliant natural light and the predictability of its weather. But this prime advantage is a less bankable asset once away from the coast. 'A prime example is one we shot up in the mountains,' says Margold about the making of the 1979 film *Olympic Fever*[33]. 'We got up there and it was sunny, hot and clear . . . Two days later we had a fucking blizzard! What the hell is this shit? The director of course saved all his outdoor shots for the last day.' In a plot nullified by the American boycott of the 1980 Moscow Olympics, Margold plays coach to the 200-metres freestyle star of the US Olympic swimming team, the secret of whose success is 'protein injections by mouth'. The film includes two of the performers having sex in the snow.

Margold points out that a good location can make the film: 'Well, it's nice to have a location before you have a script. It's essential to know where you're gonna shoot because you can hardly write a movie around a pool if there's no pool! So once you have the location, you usually have a day or so to write a script – or at least to figure out a reason for something to happen there.'[34]

The whole system of manufacturing video pornware is now so well refined that specific management tasks can be subcontracted. A distributor seeking a new property will approach a producer, occasionally it may happen the other way around. 'Sometimes they have screenplays they want shooting – sometimes I have the scripts. We look at what is involved and we agree a fee,' says Ron Sullivan. 'My scripts are very detailed, perhaps thirty pages. When I'm shooting on film, it might be as many as fifty pages. Because the budgets are so small, I like to shoot as many as three videos back-to-back. I have even done that with films. These might be for the same client, but not necessarily.'

Less well-established producers might call on Bill Margold to help out. He explains how his support system works: 'All the major distribution companies need product at the rate of two to four a month. So they contact what amounts to an executive producer who could also become the director. He gets in touch with me and says, "I want to put together a package – fix it up!" I'll write it, I'll cast it, I'll scout the location, I'll production-manage it, I'll co-ordinate the talent, I'll co-ordinate the make-up, the stills man, the food, because we should feed these people – I love to eat, anyway. I'll break it down for them – formula video – so he'll never step on his own dick.'

The equipment used (cameras, lights and recorders) will belong to the producer/director or, more commonly, will be hired. The same will apply to the crew. This will involve – at the very least – one or more cameramen (one of whom may be the director), a sound recordist, a video engineer, a lighting engineer/electrician and perhaps an assistant director, dialogue coach, wardrobe mistress, make-up artist and hair stylist. One indispensable member of the crew is the one designated to handle the 'cooze spot' – a small pencil spotlight brought into play to illuminate crisply every intimate detail of genital interaction. One boasted:

> Without me those close-ups would look like shit . . . pussies would look like day-old liver without my trusty cooze spot. I'm providing a valuable service to mankind. I have to get right in there, tight on the action and spot the light just right. It has to illuminate without drawing attention to itself. My job is to make it subtle.[35]

The technical side of *Don't Get Them Wet!* was handled by a company called Video General which supplied a three-man crew with all the necessary equipment. Video General subsequently edited the video too.[36]

Some directors prefer to work with two cameras, because this helps guarantee that the critical – and often unrepeatable – cum shots are caught. It can also make it easier to gain the footage needed to make an 'R' or soft-core version of the finished product. This is not, however, done with the very low-budget productions. The video technology used during shooting is usually three-quarter inch Hi-Band or, more recently, Betacam which is subsequently edited up to a broadcast-standard one-inch tape for copying and distribution.[37]

A one-time director himself, Margold is more than a little dismissive of the job: 'As I told Ron Sullivan recently, directing an X-rated video is analogous to choreographing a nude traffic accident. That's really all you have to do. How are you going to tell these people who are professional pieces of meat how they should fuck? They know where to stick it! I don't really have much faith in the directors. I have directed video myself and discovered early on, who gives a shit?'[38]

All the same, it is hard to believe that it would be possible to meet such tight schedules and budgets unless the cast and crew were under the management and co-ordination of an experienced director like Sullivan: 'I always work with the same crew of freelance technicians who know what I want. That's the only way you can shoot efficiently in such a short schedule. But, in spite of what Bill Margold says, most of the time is taken up with motivating the actors to do what he says should come naturally.'[39]

In 1987 three days for shooting was considered a luxury and only a director whose name was worth having on the cassette box could negotiate more.

'A five-day shoot?!' exclaimed Margold. 'Well, the five days may include the editing. We shoot for one, maximum two days. I couldn't do anything in five days in video. You know, I'd go crazy! I'd love to have three days to shoot a video.' And the result of that intensive effort (and increasing objections to the long hours by cast and crew alike) is a feature-length video of about ninety minutes in length: *'Don't Get them Wet!* runs for eighty-five minutes. But at least sixty, perhaps seventy minutes of that is sex action.

The sex scenes – which are usually seven or eight in number – can run between eight and ten minutes apiece. You have very little time for talking. America doesn't listen anyway, they just look! You know, if you wanna hear a movie, buy a radio! The script for *Don't Get Them Wet!* is the prototypical video script. You have the key to the industry in the simplicity of the whole thing.'[40]

Shooting on *Don't Get Them Wet!* began at 9 a.m. and did not finish until 11 p.m. that night. Some of the cast drove up from Los Angeles the previous day in Margold's dilapidated old Volkswagen van and set off home down Interstate Highway 101 immediately after the 'wrap'. The supposed glamour of the X-rated movie industry must have faded somewhat after the eight-hour drive.

During his involuntary sojourn in Malibu between 1977 and 1979, Alberto Ferro was unable to make films. But as soon as his legal problems in Italy and France were resolved and he was issued with a new passport, he could get the necessary work permits and resume production. His first project was *American Desire*, an interpretation of his view of American sexuality, which was filmed in New York and Connecticut in October 1980.[41] With film-making in steep decline, he had little choice but to accept in 1984 an offer (involving the Dark brothers, producer/directors from the West Coast and, it is believed, backing from Reuben Sturman) to turn his talents to making videos.

But even the maestro had severe problems with budgets and schedules. 'A friend' of Sturman's originally proposed that at least three days could be allocated to each video. Ferro recalled the sequence of events:

> This 'friend' said he would appoint a production manager who was the very best. But it turned out that he was very confused, he didn't seem to have the accounts and didn't know what he was doing. So anyway, we started the production.
>
> The contract was for six pieces, made to a budget of

$25,000 each. They paid me a separate fee in advance – the whole amount, everything I wanted. So, I wrote six screenplays for three cheap ones and three more elaborate ones – we had fourteen days to make them in. I thought that was OK. So I said: 'Let's take the first seven days and make the three cheap ones, then we'll review the situation.'

But when the three cheap ones were finished, we had used practically the whole budget! I said 'God! Why? They were all broken down, there would be six sex scenes, so many ejaculations and so on.'

I wanted to stick to the contract so, in the end, he said 'We have four days to make the last three videos!' I had to change all the sceenplays, because the cheapest ones had now become the expensive ones and the last three become the cheapest.

After I'd finished rewriting these things he said 'No, it's not four days, it's three.' I said 'You're out of your mind! I can't do this!' So I start to change them again. When I'd finished that, he said: 'It's still impossible, it has to be done in two days.' He said either you call the backer and tell him we are out of budget, or you have to do it in two days.

You see, the problem was that someone had told them how much money I made and for them it was an enormous amount. But what can I say? What can I do? So we finally had two days. I'd shot four hours outside the day before and they fucked up there – no sound! So we had to re-do that with the sound. A nightmare! Now I have twenty-eight hours to do three films plus the four hours before to re-do, that makes thirty-two hours. So it's less than eleven hours each. I had to make eighteen sex scenes in two days![42]

The results included *Flasher* and *Young Nympho* which starred English actress Paula Meadows. These were mostly well received by the critics, but it is hardly surprising that they are not thought to be up to the standard of Ferro's *Sensations*. As if by way of compensation, the American X-Rated Critics Organization elected *Sensations* to their Hall of Fame in 1987.

In the case of *Don't Get Them Wet!*, the tight budget and time constraints revealed themselves in the form of unsubtle and insensitive lighting, continuity errors, largely inaudible sound, inappropriate library music and spelling mistakes in the credits. The closing scene differs from the screenplay because two of the actors joined in the four-way lesbian sequence (which they were supposed merely to watch). Consequently, they completed their contractual cum shots ahead of schedule and were 'too tired' to participate in the closing orgy. An arbitrary montage sequence of sex shots from earlier in the video was substituted.[43]

In Europe producers are still influenced by film-making and are prepared to invest much more time and money than the West Coast porn barons. In Germany ninety-minute feature-length videos are still expected to cost between DM300,000 and DM500,000 (£100,000–170,000) to shoot on U-Matic or one-inch tape formats.[44] This is not an unreasonable budget for a programme with high production values, but it will take longer for the investor to get his money back. If the production can be edited to a soft-core format, distributors such as Gerd Wasmund (Mike Hunter) can exploit the transmission rights he owns on two West German television channels plus independent US cable channels; RTR, Luxembourg and Zeppelin I.[45]

Once the director arrives back from the shoot, the tapes are ready for editing. This involves choosing the best shots (where multiple cameras and multiple takes were employed), and resequencing the material so that the story, such as it might be, is told to the best effect. The programme will also need to be 'topped and tailed' with a title sequence at the beginning and (usually) the credits at the end. There might also be a requirement for some added video effects, either within the film (to indicate flashbacks, for example) or in the opening and closing sequences. All production will have music which might be 'library material' from pre-recorded discs or specially commissioned in the case of higher-budget productions. The theme song to *Olympic Fever* included the less-than-immortal lines, taken from a US Marine Corps marching song:

> I didn't know,
> but I've been told,
> an Eskimo's pussy is mighty cold.

The AFVAA and the XRCO give awards annually to the best X-rated film music.

The editing of porn videos takes longer than the shooting and employs more expensive equipment but fewer people. *Don't Get Them Wet!* was edited in about forty hours. Time on the hardware can be rented from a 'facilities house', but technically the production levels are now at such a high standard as to make it possible for many companies to own their own editing systems. Once that investment has been made, use can be maximized, as in the video trade generally, by hiring out to other producers.

This approach was adopted by porn baron Peter Theander in Copenhagen. His RCT Video (a descendant of Rodox Color Teknik) is superbly equipped. In addition to three (JVC and Sony) editing suites able to handle a variety of tape formats, the company owns a British Rank-Cintel telecine machine for converting film to video, and 'Image Artist', Ampex ADO and Quantel Paintbox systems for computer-generated graphics and effects. It also has a 'Computexter' subtitling computer and a rostrum camera studio. In Hanover Hans Moser at VTO has gone for even more expensive machines from 'leading edge' companies to equip his huge new studio complex.

Once the final, edited version of the porn video has been assembled on to a broadcast-standard one-inch tape, it has to be copied on to VHS, Beta and Video-2000 format cassettes for distribution. In the duplicating room, RCT Video has no fewer than 220 Panasonic VHS HiFi VCRs for copying. Such is the company's output rate, that it even makes its own tape cassettes using a row of Tape Automation cassette-assembly machines. These British-made units alone cost $50,000 each. (All Rodox pornographic cassettes are made from blue plastic to avoid their becoming confused with conventional products during the later stages of manufacture. Anything purporting to be a Theander product on a cassette of any other colour has probably been bootlegged.)[46]

John Lark's Australian facility at Fishwyck in Canberra has its own duplicating centre, where copies for his mail order business are run off from standards-converted masters imported direct from Caballero in California. 'It's run by one of our women staff,' Lark explains. 'We've got seventy units working sixteen hours a day on two shifts. That might be expanded to one hundred units – which is about pro rata for what America's doing.'[47]

After the programmes have been copied at Rodox, each cassette is labelled. The variety of the product-line is such that the task of making these labels has to be trusted to a small computer system which uses a specialist label printer supplied by Printronics. This turns out labels for the video cassettes, in the right combination of title, format and language, as well as labels for the shipping cartons. After this, the cassettes are transferred to a shrink-wrap machine which is used to secure each video cassette into its printed box. The maintenance department operates from a workshop with everything from lathes to milling machines and vertical borers. The overall capacity of the Theander operation is such that they can easily duplicate and package 1,000 pornographic video cassettes in a single working day.[48]

Even before a new X-rated video is out of production, it needs to be promoted to the retail end of the industry. The bi-weekly *Film World Report*, published out of Los Angeles as part of the *Adam Film World* stable and edited by Jared Rutter, plays a key part in communications between the producers, distributors and retail outlets.[49] Above the masthead of the 13 April 1987 issue is an item headed 'Retail Tips and Promotions'. Next to a reproduction of the cover of another publication called *1987 Awards X-rated Film and Video* (a special issue of *Adam Film World Guide*), the text reads:

> Consumer action will be stimulated this month by the *Adam Film World Guide*'s new special edition: *The 1987 Awards*, spotlighting the Best of Year in X-Rated Film and Video. The Top 10 Videos, Best Performers, Best Foreign Movies, Best Directors and Best Sex Scenes, as chosen by *Adam Film World* editors, are analysed and illustrated with action colour shots. Product featured by advertisers includes: *Dirty Dreams* (Caballero), *Charmed and Dangerous* (Vivid), *Lust Tango in Paris* (Penguin), *The $50,000,000 Cherry* (Vidco), *Sweet Revenge* (Zane Bros), *Classic Swedish Erotica* (Caballero). Publication is distributed by All-America Distributors Corp. Cover price is $3.95. Copies for resale to your customers may be ordered by calling (213) 651 2650.

Here Rutter is employing the same marketing technique as German porn baron Hans Moser with his *Video Star* magazine (see Chapter 4). Heavy emphasis is placed on the use of 'action colour shots' as an incentive to buyers.

One of the eagerly sought features in the single-sheet trade newsletter is the chart listing the current bestselling porn videos. This is described as 'Current adult videotape rankings based on a nationwide survey of sales of X-rated video cassettes by major retailers and distributors'. For early April 1987, these were shown as:

1 *Devil in Miss Jones, Part 4: A New Beginning* (1987) 80 mins. Directed by Gregory Dark. Stars Lois Ayres, Jack Baker, Paul Thomas. (VCA Pictures)

2 *Deep Throat II* (1987) 85 mins. Directed by L. Vincent Revane. Stars Krista Lane, Jamie Gillis, Mellissa Melendez. (Arrow Video)
3 *The Load Warriors* (1987) 90 mins. Directed by C. C. Williams. Stars Miss Sharon Mitchell, Angel Kelly, Randy West. (Vidco)
4 *Little Shop of Whores* (1987) 80 mins. Directed by Paul Thomas. Stars Jamie Summers, Blondi, Mike Horner. (Vivid Video)
5 *Lilith Unleashed* (1987) 85 mins. Directed by Henri Pachard. Stars Tish Ambrose, Paul Thomas, Kim Wilde (Barbara Dare). (VCA Pictures)
6 *Caught by Surprise* (1987) 83 mins. Directed by Jack Genero. Stars Stacey Donovan, Eric Edwards, Cara Lott. (CDI Home Video)
7 *Broadway Fanny Rose* (1987) 80 mins. Directed by Paul G Vatelli. Stars Penny Morgan, Lori Lovett, Jerry Butler. (Caballero)
8 *Harlem Candy* (1987) 73 mins. Directed by Henri Pachard. Stars Amber Lynn, Angel Kelly, Herschel Savage. (Wet Video)
9 *Divorce Court Exposé II* (1987) 85 mins. Directed by Vinni Rossi. Stars Cyndee Summers, Jeanna Fine, Buddy Love. (Vidco)
10 *Club Ecstasy* (1987) 85 mins. Directed by Henri Pachard. Stars Colleen Brennan, Nina Hartley, John Leslie. (Caballero)

This list is supplemented by a further, less detailed chart headed 'The Best of the Rest':

11 *Phone Sex Girls* (Video Team)
12 *Careful, He May Be Watching* (Caballero)
13 *Best Little Whorehouse in Hong Kong* (Essex)
14 *Restless Nights* (SEVP)
15 *Charmed and Dangerous* (Vivid)
16 *Debbie Does the Devil in Dallas* (Essex)
17 *Dirty Dreams* (Caballero)

18 *Born to be Wild* (Essex)
19 *Sex Aliens* (Caballero)
20 *The Oddest Couple* (VCA)

The charts are compiled by Jared Rutter himself by telephone-polling distributors and retailers. Although he makes no extravagant claims for their accuracy, he does assert that they may be no less precise than television audience ratings. Their importance cannot be understated, since many of the 10,000-plus video retailers who stock pornographic tapes restrict their line to the *Film World Report* top ten or twenty.[50]

An analysis of these charts confirms some interesting characteristics of the American porn video industry. Of the twenty titles, eight are apparently derivatives of conventional Hollywood motion pictures (*Little Shop of Whores, Sex Aliens, The Load Warriors,* and so on). In April 1987 Bill Margold predicted that after the release of the film *The Untouchables,* someone would make a sex video called *The Touchables*. However, he was only half right: in the ten bestsellers listed in the *Film World Report* of 28 September 1987 there were *two* videos called *The Touchables* (the one released by Coast to Coast was doing a little better at No. 5 than its rival from Caballero, which was ranked No. 8).

A further five titles in the earlier charts shown above are sequels to older X-rated successes (the most obvious being *The Devil in Miss Jones, Part 4: A New Beginning* and *Deep Throat II*. Ron Sullivan (as Henri Pachard) directed three of the Top 10, each for a different distributor. The distributors are all established names in the industry with VCA, Essex and Caballero being well represented. New releases are also listed, along with the pornware in production:

*Big Summer Titles on Tap*

Manufacturers are already starting to promote their big summer releases, most of which will debut around the time of the Chicago CES [Consumer Electronics Show]

show (30 May–2 June). Here are some of the major sales expectations:

**Caballero** is prepping *Blow-Off,* a film with Ginger Lynn, shot several years ago but never released. **VCA** makes June Vanessa del Rio month with two of the superstar's film vehicles, *Dr Lust* and *Dynamic Vices*. **Vivid**'s summer push starts with *The Brat Pack* with Jamie Summers.

**Vidco** is promoting a Samantha Strong starrer, *The $50,000,000 Cherry,* followed by *Furburgers* (*Home of the Box Lunch*). **4-Play** is gearing up for Bruce Seven's *Loose Ends III,* with Sheri St Claire and Erica Boyer. **Cal Vista** has on tap *Grind,* a big-budget Henri Pachard video.

**Catalina**'s June blockbuster is the bisexual *The Switch is On,* with Jeff Stryker, Danielle and Elle Rio. **Western Visuals** has *Oral Majority III* and Henri Pachard's *Moonlusting* on the boards. **Video Team** will make a big deal of *Peggy Sue,* with Samantha Strong and Lois Ayres, followed later in the year by the Hal Freeman-directed *Falcon Lust*.

**Fantasy Home Video**'s June push is *Pumping Irene II,* as well as the debut of their exclusive new starlet, Angela Baron. Her first starrer, *Where There's Smoke There's Fire,* ships in May.

The column headed 'Industry Items' is a miscellany, including changes of addresses and telephone numbers:

**Candida Royalle's Femme Dist.** has moved to new quarters at 588 Broadway, Suite 1110, New York, NY 10012. Phone is (212) 226-9330. No toll-free numbers are planned at present. Royalle has just wrapped up production on two new video features, numbers 5 and 6 in her *Femme* series.

personnel changes:

**Andrew Steves** has replaced Ronald T. Daniels as national sales manager of **Great Pictures Inc**, according to president **Greg Petaludis**. Also joining the sales staff is

> **Sonja Wagner**. The Jamaica, New York, mail order firm is expanding and is now accepting inquiries about its bi-monthly catalogue newsletter. Call Steves at 1-800-445-6662 or (718) 523-0235.
>
> **Rick Olson**, formerly with **Penguin Productions**, is now part of the sales force at **4-Play Video**. He can be reached at (818) 848-7529 or 1-800-662-7529.
>
> **Perry Ross** is expanding his **Fantasy Home Video** sales staff and is looking for new personnel. He'll pay a salary plus 10 per cent commission. (818) 341-7957 or 1-800-843-9781 (California only).
>
> **Marty Krause** is looking for salespersons with telemarketing experience for his **Video Asylum** one-stop. He promises high commissions. Call (213) 931-1531.

as well as snippets of industry trivia:

> The winner of **CDI Home Video**'s video camera raffle was **Ron Bryant**, vice president of franchise marketing for **Discount Video** of Livonia, Michigan. His name was pulled from a bowl of several thousand postcard entries by starlet **Blondi**. The JVC compact video camera-player was awarded as part of a promotion for the new CDI release, *Caught by Surprise*.[51]

Apart from trade publications such as *Film World Report*, the main avenues for doing business in porn videos are the trade shows which take place once or twice a year in Europe and the United States. These include the annual Consumer Electronics Show (CES) held in Chicago, MIPCOM in Cannes and Germany's yearly Video Kongress. These are also the main trade shows for the conventional industry and the pornography side is often fully integrated (as with Video Kongress) or placed in the ghetto of a nearby hotel (as with CES for the last few years).

Germany's annual sex fair (*Sexmesse*) – held in Offenbach in 1986 – is an exception in that it specializes in pornography and sex-related products. However, most of the bigger, long-standing arrangements among producers, distributors and retailers are settled on the basis of personal contact, and the trade shows often provide no more than a vehicle for celebratory wining and dining.

Distributors are mostly interested in deals which generate the biggest unit sales for each production for the lowest administrative overheads. The advantage for the buyer under such an arrangement is that he will obtain the product at a better price. Within a country such as France, Germany or the United States the deals will either be done with national chains of retail outlets or with regional distributors. They will be supplied with a complete, packaged product ready for immediate sale.

However, the international shipment of packaged cassettes in finished form is not an economically attractive proposition. The product is bulky and has a low unit cost. In these cases, it is preferable for the producer or distributor who owns the rights to the video to agree a distribution deal with a company that can take a master tape of the programme and perform its own replication, packaging, promotion and distribution.

Caballero Control Corp, in California, for example, has distributors in Europe. One of these is Horst Peter. Reportedly one of the backers of Lasse Braun's *Sex Maniacs*, made in London in the 1970s, Peter's Silwa company in Essen recently bought the Videorama label and the rights to Caballero's videos from the Dutch porn baron Charlie Geerts[52]. Some degree of exclusivity is normally built into such contracts so that the distributor can be reasonably assured of the market for each product.

In some cases distributors may take products from multiple sources in order to build up a comprehensive line of offerings. Since Peter Theander stopped making films, he has bought in his videos. These are grouped, according to a number of influencing factors, into the main title series.

*Climax Prestige*. 'These are seventy-five to ninety-minute

hard-core feature films that we buy in from the United States,' explained Rupert James. 'We pay between $7,500 and $10,000 for a seven-year licence for Europe. We get an NTSC [the American television standard], one-inch tape and do our own standards conversion [to PAL and SECAM].' All *Prestige* videos are available with German soundtracks as well as English. Customers can have Danish or Swedish subtitles on the English soundtrack if they wish.

James explained how the distribution deal was arrived at: 'Some years ago I wrote to all the producers in the US and told them that we were interested in copyrighted material. A lot wrote back – a surprising number – so we do get what we need.'[53] The films Rodox sells under the *Climax Prestige* label are made by a San Francisco company called Now Showing. The producer/director is always Lawrence T. Cole, a veteran of the industry, who started by shooting stags and loops. One of his earliest is rated as one of the best; it is *Pool Orgy* from the San Francisco *OZ* series and features veteran actors John Leslie, Joey Silvera and Christine Kelly.[54] He was also responsible for *Dogorama* which starred Linda Lovelace some years before *Deep Throat*. Theander's deal with Cole is a good one because he does not have to pay any royalties on the cassettes sold. From Cole's point of view, the rights sale probably goes a long way towards meeting the original production costs and he has no further responsibility as far as European sales are concerned.

The twenty-one *Blue Climax* titles are one-hour feature films which have a story of sorts but, clearly, are shorter than standard feature-film length. With the exception of four old Rodox productions, these are all made in France. On the basis that as much as 90 per cent of the Theander product range is exported to Germany, all these titles are dubbed into German before they are copied to cassettes. Color Climax videos are mainly sixty-minute productions from any source (occasionally from Now Showing). Some of them are compilations of two thirty-minute videos. These are also dubbed or have Danish or Swedish subtitles added.[55]

*Danish Hard Core*, *Exciting* and *Bestsellers* are all sixty-minute compilations of two or more video programmes which have been published previously in some other form. Rodox titles are thirty-minute compilations of older 8mm film loops. The grouping is according to the specialization: Lesbian, anal sex, John Holmes or urination ('golden showers'). Rupert James insists that 'When we are reissuing material, we always make clear in the catalogues what is included. We are very concerned that customers should not feel that they have been misled.'[56]

Major releases currently being distributed by Rodox include: *Temptation* (called *Temptations* in the United States); *Illusions of Ecstasy*; *Inflamed*; *The House of Strange Desires*; the Ginger Lynn vehicle *Pleasure Hunt*, *Pleasure Hunt II*; *Future Sex*; *The Ultimate Orgasm* (released as *The Ultimate Q* in the United States); *Nasty*; *The Performers*; *Dangerous Desires*; *Battle of the Stars* and *Battle of the Stars II* (released in America as *Battle of the Stars, Round 2: East vs West*).

Although all the big names appear in one or other of these videos (Mike Horner, Ron Jeremy, Herschel Savage, Blair Harris, Grant Lombard, Ginger Lynn, Jamie Gillis, Billy Dee, Paul Thomas, Amber Lynn, Nina Hartley, Mai Lin, Christy Canyon and the notorious Traci Lords among others), the Rodox publicity machine makes very little of the 'star system'. Star names are rarely mentioned and that is only in the text in the *Video Index* catalogue.

In some cases, though, 'star names' can be promoted to the packaging as a means of attracting attention to the product – the implication being that if you like the performer, you will like the videos which she (for it is usually a she) has agreed to promote. Gerd Wasmund has always found the French videos starring Monique Carrera to be very successful in Germany. So, in 1986, his Mike Hunter Video company concluded a deal with Carrera allowing him to use her name to promote a series of videos which, in fact, are from a variety of sources and in the production of which she has had no involvement.

Confirming this deal, Wasmund said: 'Monique Carrera is a porno actress [appearing in] French productions. She let us use her name in 1986 to gain publicity for herself and us.'[57] Indeed, so loose is this arrangement that several Carrera titles feature the well-known 'Ginger Lynn' series from the United States. These include: *Ginger on the Rocks*, *Deep Hole Maniacs*, *Ginger Die Verhurte Sau* (*Ginger the Debauched Pig*), *Privatparty Bei Einer Domina* (*A Governess's Private Party*) – featuring 'Stud of the Year, Tom Byron' – and *Domina's Tower*. Several further 'Carrera' productions, thirty-minute videos, appear under a separate order code, 'VMC, Monique Carrera, Queen of Porno', in the flyer. The titles don't look exceptional (*Revolting Excesses*, *My Secret Desires*, *Schoolgirl Perversions*), though one features an explicit shot advertising a little number entitled *Piss On Me, You Sow*.[58]

International distribution agreements can work in both directions when both parties are involved in production or own the necessary rights to the films. But because European films are less popular in the United States than American video pornware is in Europe, the arrangements tend not to be symmetrical. A further complication is the exclusive nature of any other distribution agreements already in operation.

A good example of this is the relationship between Al Bloom of Caballero in the United States and Gerd Wasmund of Mike Hunter Video in West Germany. The most prominent products in Wasmund's film catalogue, *Hardcore-Programm '86*, are his tried and true classics, *Sex Maniacs*, *Sex Maniacs 2*, *Sin Dreamer*, and Lasse Braun's *Sensations*, *Love Orgy*, and *Liebesgeflüster*, and Bloom holds the US rights to all of these. However, if a German customer wants to buy Caballero products, he will have to go to a Beate Uhse shop.

There are exceptions; the Caballero production *M.A.S.H.'D* is distributed in Germany by Mike Hunter, but these are rare cases. The American products in Mike

Hunter's range come from varied sources; Arrow and Essex as well as Caballero. Of course, Wasmund might insist that he prefers the freedom to choose what he considers to be the best from the total market place, but the fact remains that distributors holding exclusive contracts will probably have first refusal.

Once the rights have been acquired and the master tape delivered, the distributor needs to decide how many cassettes to manufacture. Only companies as big in Europe as Teresa Orlovski, Mike Hunter, Intex, Beate Uhse and Rodox will have sales levels large enough to justify producing tapes in VHS, Beta and Video-2000 formats. The same is true of the American manufacturers and the VHS and Beta formats. However, VHS is now considered to dominate the domestic video market and newcomers and smaller established firms will concentrate on that.

Wholesale prices of new sex videos to retailers vary between $20 in the United States and over $50 in Scandinavia.[59] Taking the lower price, if the total production cost of a new video programme is $20,000, another $20,000 can be added to cover the cost of duplication, packaging, overheads and a margin of profit. This means that the distributor has to make and sell 2,000 cassettes to get his stake money plus a little profit back.

But the usual initial production run for new videos in the United States is 3,000 cassettes.[60] A bestseller like Caballero's August 1987 release *Traci, I Love You* will easily run to 10,000.[61] These can be sold or rented according to the nature of the retail outlet. Other income can be obtained from foreign sales and the disposal of rights to cable companies and for use in video-booth machines.

Now that many countries permit the sale of hard-core cassettes through non-specialist, non-licensed points of sale, such as regular high street or neighbourhood video libraries and even petrol stations, some companies have started to package the videos with soft core boxes. This has been the case for some time in the United States. Rodox announced its decision to do this thus:

> *Double Covers*
>
> Three of our most popular feature-length porno video series: *Color Climax, Blue Climax* and *Prestige* are now available with both hard-core boxes and soft-core covers for the books, giving appropriate alternatives, to correspond to the type of public display that is required.

In Scandinavian video shops, X-rated videos are not put in a separate 'back room' as they are in America.

The economics of retailing for sale, rental and video-booth display are quite different. In the case of outright sale, the retailer will add between 30 per cent, if he is discounting, and 50 per cent to the wholesale price, thus enabling him to achieve a profit margin of anywhere between $10 and $30 per cassette. *Don't Get Them Wet!* carries a price sticker of $79.95, but that could easily be discounted down to $49.95 or less in a 'two for the price of one' offer.

Rights arrangement for rental vary from country to country. In some cases, America being a prime example, the retailer can do what he likes with the tape once he has bought it. In other countries, the retailer has to buy a licence enabling him to rent the video to customers. In certain instances, the rental licence is cheaper than the purchase price, but a proportion of the rental fee has to be paid over to the licensor as part of the arrangement. The lowest overnight rental prices are in the USA; $1 is not unusual for a midweek hire. But it can be as high as $6 (£4) in places like Sweden. In Germany rentals originally cost DM10–15 a day, but now it's only DM5–6 ($3–4), so $1 is probably cutting the margin to the bone. The retailer may need to rent the tape out as many as twenty times before he begins to see any money back. Specialist porn stores usually charge a good deal more. Their selection will be wider and they might charge for membership of some kind of 'video library'.

Another way of using the video material is in video-booth operations. These are generally incorporated in sex shops, but are also sometimes set up as specialist operations. Video-booths are advances on 8mm 'peep-shows' which were, in their turn, advances on old-fashioned 'What the butler saw' machines. Inherent disadvantages in the older-style devices have been eliminated by enclosing the projector or television screen inside a booth – with a seat and door, giving customers privacy as they watch the programme.

The film-loop peep-show incorporated a projector and screen, usually the back of the door, which operated when a coin was placed in a slot machine. The projector then ran for a few minutes before the customer had to insert another coin. A red 'occupied' light would appear over the door while the projector was running. As long as coins were inserted the showing would continue until, after about twelve minutes, the customer had seen the whole loop. Increased revenues could be achieved by shortening the time the projector ran for each coin or by installing additional projectors – if space allowed.

The latest video systems are based on installing a television set in each booth. This is connected via a multichannel coaxial cable to a bank of VCRs (one per channel) on which the operator can play feature-length videos or, more commonly, those which are compendia of old 8mm loop material. At the end of the tape the cassette is rewound and started again. In the booth the user can feed coins into a slot machine which will display the amount of credit remaining as the video is running. A channel selector enables the customer to choose the video programme he wants to watch. A choice of eight is generally available, but some newer systems offer twenty, and technology to enable the user to choose any of up to 200 channels of non-stop pornware is being implemented.

It is presently estimated that there are some 3,000 video booths in West Germany, 350 of which are being operated by the Beate Uhse company. They yield gross revenues in the region of DM100 million a year.[62] The equivalent figure for the United States has been estimated at $3 billion. Video-booth operation is a guaranteed source of porn gold.

It is not quite that simple, however. Video-booth facilities need to be based in central downtown sites which incur high rental or outright purchase costs. The construction of the video booths and the installation of their accompanying equipment also needs to be paid for. The customer base is largely itinerant and it is certainly the case that the most popular locations for such facilities tend also to be tourist centres; San Francisco's Tenderloin district, New York's 42nd Street, the red light district in Amsterdam and Kaiserstrasse in Frankfurt. Local patrons will tend to be those unable to rent a video for home consumption.

Some distributors, especially those in the United States, gained effective control of hundreds of outlets by offering retailers, usually bookstore operators with space to spare, a packaged deal. Under this arrangement, the distributor would supply the peep-show machines and even build the booths in return for a significant percentage of the cash take. Reuben Sturman concentrated on this aspect of the porn business in preference to the theatrical exhibition of films and his empire grew to include companies which built and maintained the peep-shows and collected the money.

Promotion of videos at a retail level is becoming increasingly dependent upon the X-rated video magazines (see Chapter 5). The industry also encourages the review of hard-core videos in men's magazines such as *Hustler* and *Swank*. Some distributors employ the technique of making their video catalogues as explicit as possible using illustrative material from the programmes themselves as an excuse; this approach is employed by Caballero, Mike Hunter, Rodox, Beate Uhse and Video Teresa Orlovski. It is also a standard feature in many 'contact magazines', one particularly successful example being Horst Peter's *Happy Weekend*.

Also increasingly popular is the idea of publishing this material in video form. This is one way of making the promotion pay for itself. Mike Hunter does this with a cassette called *Die Grosse Programmvorschau aus unserem Hardcore-Programm* (*The big preview of our hard-core range*). This contains thirty trailers which concentrate on the sex action, thus making the tape saleable for its content. The Beate Uhse organization does the same with its *Best of Beate Uhse* and *Highlights* series.

The next major development in video retailing will probably be initiated by the major distributors. In the conviction that rentals benefit the retailer more than the distributor, and reinforced by the view that the 'agelessness' of porn will encourage enthusiasts to collect, they will start to release pornware on much cheaper cassettes. They will start with the old loop material which has already paid for itself many times over. From there the trend will move on to the older video features – but probably not the classic movies for as long as they continue to attract higher prices.

This is a trend already seen in the conventional side of the business which has started releasing movies long seen on television like *Casablanca* and *Citizen Kane* in packages costing as little as £9.95 ($14.95). Hard-core pornography will soon be sold at such prices. Indeed, Mike Hunter has already pushed some of his prices down to previously unheard-of lows. Uli Rotermund confirms the trend: 'In Holland, Denmark and Italy everything is getting cheaper. In Spain, everything is half-price: that country takes so much material it can't absorb it. All the same, in West Germany, even without the benefit of mail order, the market for video is slowly growing.'[63]

Rodox is about to re-release some material in this new cheaper form: 'I have a pile of some two hundred 16mm master prints and an old Moviola editor waiting for me,' Rupert James disclosed somewhat ruefully. 'I have to view all the material and classify it according to subject matter and specialization before coming up with some titles. This is all very much in the tradition of Rodox: diversify and stay up with technology and market trends.'[64] Caballero, Essex and the other major US companies are in the process of doing the same.[65]

It would be unwise to assume from the above that it is possible to break into the X-rated video industry with a bankroll of $50,000 (say £30,000). Even with that kind of modest start-up money there are many other hurdles to be overcome. A cast has to be found, as attractive as those regularly appearing in the Los Angeles, New York, French and West German productions. A crew has to be hired who can work efficiently and professionally, though renting the equipment needed would not normally be a problem. Once at the stage of having a good master for duplication and packaging, there is still the problem of promoting and distributing the cassettes, since many if not most retail outlets will already have some kind of exclusive deal with other, established distributors.

But once those distribution deals have been made, the money can start to flow back fairly quickly and the growing market could be big enough to attract competitive newcomers. If the success of the established producer/distributors is anything to go by, there is plenty of porn gold in making X-rated videos. Assuming average production, duplication and packaging costs of $40,000 and average sales of 5,000 cassettes per production (at $20 each), a company releasing only four new titles a month to the US market is achieving annual revenues of $5 million, $3 million of which will be clear profit. To this has to be added the income from all other forms of rights sales. This goes a long way towards explaining why as many as one sex video a day is being made in Los Angeles alone.

Few industry observers seem able to agree on the overall scale of the US and world markets for X-rated videos. The most conservative estimate was made by *Newsweek* magazine: 'The market is growing explosively. *Newsweek* estimates that the total annual revenue generated from video rentals and sales could reach $5 billion in 1988, with "adult" materials accounting for 8 per cent of that total.'[66]

At one time it had been variously estimated that porn videos represented more than 50 per cent of the total video market. Indeed, of more than 14,000 cassette titles on the market, an estimated 7,000 were X-rated. This early dominance was caused by the tardiness of the conventional film industry in getting their products to this new market place.

Once it had reacted, the figure could be revised: 'Hard-core pornography accounts for a hefty share of the cassette business. X-rated movies were among the first to be released for home video and once made up about a half of all sales and rentals. That share has dropped to around 15 per cent by most industry estimates . . .'[67] Of course, it should not be inferred from this that sales of porn videos are declining; they are certainly on the increase, but not by enough to prevent them being swamped by conventional Hollywood output.

Some estimates of the US industry's annual gross – especially those made by US law enforcement agencies – have been as high as $7 billion, but it is hard to substantiate these figures. 'They claim we are a $7 billion a year industry: who are they kidding?' asks David Friedman. 'I wish we were! Based on one billion cassettes sold and twenty rentals each – that makes our revenues at something like $1.5 billion a year. At best.'[68] But even $1.5 billion makes a very big cake and the smallest slice can provide ample sustenance.

The difficulty of estimating present revenues and forecasting growth is illustrated by Rimmer's attempt – with yet another method of calculation – to scale the 1990 market: 'Assuming a combined annual market of at least one sexvid per owner (disc or tape), I think it is a safe estimate that by 1990 more than 20 million sexvids will be sold per year – and that estimate may be low. If only a few of the proposals for "reforming" sex on regular network television become a reality, a "frustrated viewer market" of 50 million tapes and discs annually would be a much closer estimate.'[69] If Rimmer's measure of one porn video per VCR owner is safe, and it does not seem unreasonable, annual sales must already be approaching 50 million in the United States alone and will certainly have exceeded that by 1990, with or without the establishment of a viable videodisc market. It certainly adds credibility to his prediction that 'Based on an average price of $25 for sexvids by the end of the decade and despite inflation, the production and distribution of sexvids could be a multi-billion dollar industry – and could even represent the biggest segment of the video and film industry in the United States.'[70]

It is conceivable that America's 12,000 video stores are handling at least $1 billion worth of porn videos each year and those revenues represent the livelihood of a large group of people: 'While there are no accurate statistics,' says Rimmer, 'I would guess that more than 10,000 people in the United States earn a good living from the production and distribution of X-rated films. This would include producers, directors, financial backers, actors, actresses, screenwriters, cinematographers, adult film theatre owners and employees and retail video dealers.'[71]

On the world scale the number of VCRs installed amounts to twice the figure for America. An equivalent number of people – 250 million – live in areas where pornography is unhindered by the law. This suggests that the market outside the United States grosses at least another $1 billion – and probably a good deal more than that. By the end of the decade, total worldwide revenues in hard-core pornographic videos will probably exceed $3 billion.

# 8

# *The Collectors: Inside the Child Porn Rings*

Close by the freeway to Bangkok International Airport stands the unassuming Sakuntala Restaurant. Away from the central tourist attractions of the Thai capital, it is mostly patronized by the local middle class.

Shortly before nine on 7 August 1985 their evening was disrupted by the arrival of a party of seventeen unexpected customers. Half-eaten meals were politely but firmly removed from under guests' forks as seven commandeered tables were put together in the restaurant's central area. No one complained.

As the guests were being reseated, US Customs Attaché Tom Winker waved his spectacles to clear them of condensation. The group had been welcomed by the management with the traditional bow of Buddhist greeting. The Sakuntala is owned by the family of a young police major on the Bangkok metropolitan force who had been part of the surveillance team. He acted as *maître d'* for the evening.

Police Colonel Thawee gestured for Winker to sit at the head of the table. The rest of the party organized themselves more or less by rank. On the bandstand, the

Thai singer with the Atlas Trio was doing an acceptable impersonation of Elvis Presley performing 'Heartbreak Hotel'.

As the party settled, Winker surveyed the extended table. This had been the first-ever case of direct, official co-operation between the US Customs Service and a local police force in pursuit of an international criminal. At his right was Colonel Thawee who had headed the team from the Bangkok police. Next to Thawee was the undercover customs agent from Chicago and then Thawee's three lieutenant colonels, Padet, Arthut and Sunchai. To Winker's left was the undercover agent from Detroit and next to him Tuli, employed by Winker as a local investigator when the US attaché's office had opened in Bangkok that April. Tuli had lived in Britain and had adopted the lifestyle well enough to play club rugby. His sister was married to Colonel Thawee.

Further down the table sat Major Somsak. He had been in charge of the surveillance team at the apartment and had made the arrest. Now he was careful to sit close to his prisoner. Beyond them were Lieutenants Eddy and Cherdchai who had been given the job of providing armed protection for the American undercover agents. Eddy spoke good English. He had been at college in Albuquerque and still carried a New Mexico driver's licence. Five police NCOs from the surveillance team sat at the end of the table, obviously enjoying the occasion. The only female member of the group was the beautiful, young second wife of one of the senior officers. The admiring agent from Chicago had earlier mistaken her for a policewoman.

Fish dishes were the house speciality and the orders were soon agreed. The Chicago agent, a self-confessed meat-and-potatoes man, struggled unenthusiastically to get the Kai Haw Bye Tevy chicken pieces out of their wrapping of dark green herb leaves. He was to drink a lot of beer that evening. Winker could not help noticing his colleague's bemused glances at the special guest.

The arrested suspect sat nervously, his chin on his chest and his handcuffed wrists beneath the table. Some of the younger policemen flicked pieces of bread and threw disparaging remarks at him. The more experienced officers, in the longer-term interest of developing him as a source of information, attempted to reassure him.

For the previous eight years, Manit Thamaree had been producing and distributing child pornography. Described as one of the world's leading suppliers, Thamaree had personally taken thousands of photographs of European, North American and Australasian men performing sexual acts with Thai girls, most of whom were under the age of twelve. He had sold photographs from his collection to a worldwide underground network of child-sex enthusiasts. Sets of his pictures had also been published in child-porn magazines printed in Denmark, Holland and West Germany and which had a large market in the United States.

Thamaree was the only one who ordered anything different that evening. Still handcuffed, and apparently oblivious to his law enforcement hosts, the man who had once worked as Ogilvy and Mather's chief advertising copywriter in Bangkok[1] forked boiled rice and shrimp into his lowered mouth.

Much later, as the party left the restaurant, Winker touched Somsak's arm.

'Keep an eye on him tonight. In the US we've had some problems . . . He might try to kill himself.'

'So what?' Somsak shrugged.

In the background the Atlas Trio moved on to their own special interpretation of Presley's 'Jailhouse Rock'.

The bizarre dinner party at the Sakuntala Restaurant[2] was worlds away from the routine preparatory moves made six months earlier in the American Midwest which had set the operation against Manit Thamaree in motion.

Jack O'Malley's window looks out over one of the bleaker vistas of Chicago's south side towards the University of

Illinois. The late January snow did little to improve the view.

The sixth-floor room used to be the evidence lock-up; the door still had a combination lock. So much seized contraband had been stacked in there during the previous year that O'Malley had eventually moved in with it. Some wag had taped to the door a printed legend which read 'Father O'Malley'. It was the only indication that the room was occupied.

Among the general clutter of O'Malley's desk was a telephone message slip which simply read 'Chaivat, PO Box 10-1006, Bangkok 10311, Thailand'. From a drawer O'Malley pulled a plain sheet of airmail stationery, took up a pen, thought for a moment, and then began to write. It was the first in a protracted exchange of letters.[3]

MR CHAIVAT, *January 29, 1985*

I hope you don't mind me writing to you directly but I was recently advised through common friends at *Wonderland* of certain products you have for sale. Could you possibly send me an advertising brochure and price list. I prefer magazines (*Lolita*, etc) but films and photos are OK. Some of my orders sent to Holland have been confiscated. I hope the same thing won't happen with you. If you charge for ad matter, please advise.

Sincerely,

*Jack Negus*, P.O. Box 735, Tinloy Park, ILL. 60466, USA

O'Malley folded the airmail sheet, slipped it into an envelope, sealed it and wrote the Bangkok address on the front. On his way home from work that evening he stopped by his local post office and mailed it.

The reply was prompt. Less than ten days later O'Malley collected from PO Box 735 an airmail letter addressed to 'Jack Negus' posted in Bangkok on 5 February. He waited until he had reached the office before opening it. Inside was a single sheet of paper, on one side of which was a photocopy of eight prints showing adult Caucasian males in sexual acts with very young Asian girls.

Each photograph had been overstamped with the words 'AIR MAIL' in blue and carried neat annotations in red block capitals. These stated: 'THAI 12 VS. A DUTCH', 'LAOS–THAI 11 VS. SWISS–ITALIAN', 'LAOS–THAI 11½ VS. BIG DUTCH', 'CHINESE 10 VS. A FRENCH-RUSSIAN', 'THAI 12 VS. AUSTRALIAN', 'THAI 10 VS. NEW ZEALANDER', 'THAI 11½ VS. AMERICAN' and 'CHINESE 9 VS. CANADIAN'. The numbers referred to the children's ages.

The photographs were little more than snapshots taken inside an apartment using simple direct lighting. All the subjects were naked. The girls were shown holding the man's penis, engaging in sexual intercourse or, in one case, sucking the penis. None of the men was making any attempt to conceal his face. A distinctive striped bed-sheet featured in two of the pictures. The men were between thirty and sixty years old.

O'Malley turned the photocopy over. On the reverse was a letter written in a tidy hand.

DEAR MR NEGUS, *February 4th*

Thank you for your welcome letter of Jan. 29th I received today, sir. Would you please kindly let me know to whom given you my address. Mr J. B. in Chicago or Mr J.H. in Caseyville, etc., sir? His (their) full name(s), please. In this field I must be discreet, hope you understand. Thanks.

As you requested, some samples is in the back of this letter, sir. The price of 12 (colour postcard size) sexy nude girls (open pussies and many positions etc.) cost US$50. And set of 12 (colour postcard size) exciting action girls with men (licking, sucking, fucking pussies or asses, rapes etc.) cost US$100, sir. Hope you send money to order its soon, as they are very exciting and rare. Most of my clients who bought the first set, they ordered for more and more, some of them even bought all I have. I have about 300 pix in nudes, also about 300 in actioned.

Sending orders by wrap the biggest banknote(s) safely inside your next letter(s), seal well, and mail to me by Airmail, if possible REGISTERED, sir.

And I'll send you your order pix the same day I get your money by Airmail, in each envelope of 4 pix each, sending every two days seperate [*sic*], sir. And your money will not be confiscate as in Holland, as I received about 2–3 orders every week, even one today the same time I got your letter from my Post Box, sir. If possible, please also indicate what kind of pix you wanted to have: sucking, fucking or rapes in the pussy or ass etc., sir. What age of the girls you prefer most? V. or Non-V.? (V. = Virgin. Age of the girls please always plus 10 more years. 11 = 21 etc.) etc. etc.

Wish you were here in Bangkok now! Two of the new ones are waiting for you to enjoy, sir. A Canadian–Thai V.18, and a new N-V of 20. I am sure you'll like them!! All kinds of sex games are available, if you could pay the prices, sir. When, then? Sometime in 1985? Did you ever been to Bangkok before?

This is all for my first letter to you, sir.

Please kindly reply and write to me again soon (with some orders?), all your questions will be answer, sir.

All my best to you and your family, dear Mr Negus, and take good care of yourself from the coldest Winter this year in USA. May I wait for your next letter soon. Thanks, sir.

Yours sincerely,
*Chaivat.*

(P.S.) Please underline my: BANGKOK 10311

O'Malley opened a file on Chaivat and placed the letter in it. He decided against replying immediately but made a call to his colleague Ray Martinez in Detroit.

As a result, on 26 February, 1985 Chaivat received a letter from a new contact in the United States. It was typed.

| | |
|---|---|
| CHAIVAT | 30 W. Cross St, |
| PO Box 10-1006 | Ypsilanti, MI 48186 |
| Bangkok 10311 | February 11, 1985 |
| Thailand | |

DEAR SIR;

I have been informed, through some very close associates, that you may have certain merchandise for sale or trade that may interest me.

I am particularly interested in youthful pursuits and would like to correspond with you further, if you have literature available on the subject. I am more interested in the purchase of such literature, as my personal collection is somewhat limited at this time.

Films and/or photos on the subject would also be welcome additions to my collection.

If you are of like interest, and are able to provide me with the opportunity to purchase the material I've described, I would appreciate hearing from you.

Thanking you in advance.

Sincerely,

*Roy Morgan*

Chaivat replied immediately.

DEAR MR MORGAN, *February 26th*

Many thanks for your welcome letter of Feb. 11th I just received today, sir . . .

In this kind of business we must be very careful and discreet in all ways possible, sir. So I would be very appreciated if you let me know to whom you got my address from, sir. Thanks.

On the back of this letter are some samples of my action photos, all in colour postcard size. One set of 12 exciting action photos (licking, sucking, fucking pussies and asses, rapes etc.) cost US$100. And one set of 12 nude photos of many girls (open pussies or with dildoes etc.) in all positions cost US$50, sir. If interested, please wrap your biggest banknote(s) possible safely inside your next letter and send to me by Airmail (if possible please REGISTERED), and as soon as I get your money, I'll send you your ordered photos (I have also boys') in each envelope of 4 pix, sending every 2 days seperate [*sic*] to you by Airmail also, sir. These photos – especially the action pix are very exciting and rare, most of my clients sent money to ordered and ordered again after they got the first set I sent! Please order it soon, you sure will be very fond of it also, sir. And if you interested in the 'Real things', why not come to Bangkok sometime this year and enjoy my new YOUNG ONES! Also a new young virgin I just got last week are all waiting for you to use and enjoy in any kind of sex games you like, sir. When, then?

As to the books of Pedophile, yes I have some in my own collection, they are stories (without drawings) of girls under 13 being used and raped and fucked by men, of course they were printed before 1977 which available to buy these books; old books printed before 1977 or 1978 are much better than now. The best book I have is 'Little girl Lovers' by Anonymous. With more than 200 pages of stories of rapes of young girls under 13, very exciting! And if you really want to have this book, I would gladly to send you IF you would send me two of your best books (fiction pocket books) soon by Airmail Printed Matter, I'll do the same as soon as I get yours, sir. I like books of girls under 13 rapes and fucks by men.

For your next letters you could also sign your name as '126', sir. Girls age always plus 10 more years (11 = 21 etc), V. = virgin. N.V. = non-virgin etc., sir. Girls of which age, and V. or N.-V. you prefer anyhow? All your questions will be answered.

All the best to you, dear Mr Morgan. Please reply me soon, and perhaps with an order for my exciting photos. Thanks, sir. Please write soon.

Yours sincerely,

*Chaivat.*

(P.S.) You have very nice names, sir. I like the names of Roy or Ron etc. But I prefer your last name Morgan, sir. How I like to drink Morgan rum!!

The airmail service between Thailand and the United States could be erratic. Interceptions by US postal inspectors in the Midwest certainly did not help. Although it could have taken as little as five days, Chaivat's letter did not reach the Ypsilanti address until more than six weeks later. When he arrived at the local post office to collect any mail addressed to 'Morgan', Ray Martinez was surprised to see a message written on the back of the airmail envelope. It read:

Do you know James A. Scott in Detroit 48227, sir? Please write soon, as I'll have new address after March 29th.
Mr Brandy

Martinez certainly did know James A. Scott of Detroit. He had been charged in 1981 with conspiracy to mail obscene materials, and mailing obscene visual material involving the use of a minor child. The indictment named Scott's supplier as an 'M. Lee' of Bangkok.[4]

Chaivat did not go without mail from the Chicago area during March 1985. A letter he received at the end of that month was, in due course, to produce many new names for his mail order operation.

#25-B, 2520 N. Lincoln
Chicago, Illinois 60614, USA
27 March 1985

DEAR MR CHAIVAT:

I am a bit confused by your letter. A dear friend in Canada had asked me to send a subscription to Wonderland to a "M. Marnit" at your same identical box number. I don't know if you are sharing the box with someone else, or if this is another name for you. In any event, I have sent the last two issues of *Wonderland* to

M. Marnit by first-class airmail. Unless these have failed to reach Thailand, I don't know why you first learned about my publication through a contact in Caseyville. (I have no subscriber in that town, so have no idea who your Illinois friend might be.) If you have had trouble getting your mail from the U.S., perhaps you might have suggestions as to a safer way to send future issues.

As for your photos, my interests are only in legal nude materials. Almost all the photos you included with your letter would be considered 'child pornography' in the United States. It is now against the law to *receive* such photographs, even if you did not order or request them. NEVER send any such photos to anyone in the States who did not specifically request such materials. I don't think any collector wants to go to jail because you think you are doing them a favour!

In view of the stringent penalties of the new US law against such materials, someone would have to be bereft of their reason to purchase your materials and try to sell them here. The only place where such photos can be legally sold is the Netherlands, and I suggest contacting Delta Boek in Ridderkirk about your negatives.

If you might like to try selling very 'tame' nude photos, I would be willing to give you a free ad in *Wonderland*. On your one page you sent, with girls by themselves, the two 'Thai 12 (non-V.)' and the 'Thai 6' photos would be legal. The ones labelled 'Thai 11' and 'Canadian–Thai 8' would be illegal, since that is considered 'lewd exhibition of the genitals'. If you arranged a set of such legal photos, you would have numerous customers, especially if you priced it more reasonably. Perhaps only 6 photos instead of 12 and only about $20.00. I could not run any ad that offered illegal material, but what happens between you and your customer after they contact you is none of my business.

You might tell your contact in Caseyville that I need subscribers. I also sell various stories and artworks to help pay for publication of *Wonderland*. If only half the collectors who get their copies from a friend would order from me directly, I might be able to break even on the publication instead of losing money.

Kindest regards,
*David Techter*

David Techter is the American publisher of a quarterly magazine called *Wonderland*. Produced from Techter's Chicago address, *Wonderland* describes itself as the 'Newsletter of the Lewis Carroll Collectors Guild'. There had been twelve issues by early 1986. The magazine is typeset and consists of articles – mostly written by Techter himself – reviews, letters and small-ads. None of these could be classified as being pornographic in any way. *Wonderland* is illustrated with naïve line drawings of naked boys and girls with exposed genitals. The advertisements offer a variety of mainly nudist materials from suppliers in Europe and the United States.[5]

On 17 April, the day after receiving his first letter from Chaivat, Martinez wrote back thanking him for the sample prints. He deferred placing an initial order until Chaivat had confirmed his new address. The mention of James Scott on the back of the envelope gave Martinez a chance to deepen his cover: 'I noticed on your envelope that you asked me about Mr Scott,' he wrote. 'It was not very discreet to put his name on the outside of the envelope. I understand that he had some trouble a couple of years ago and that he may be being watched. As you can tell, I am very paranoid about being caught. It is a shame that honest emotions such as mine cannot be as open as they are honest . . . I would really like to visit you and your "family" in Bangkok. Unfortunately, I don't know how soon it could be arranged. If I was to visit you, would you meet me somewhere? or would I have to arrange to find you?' He signed the letter '126'.

Coincidentally, David Techter, publisher of the

*Wonderland* newsletter, sent a letter to Chaivat the following day (18 April). In it he sounded a cautionary note to his new-found correspondent in Bangkok.

> DEAR FRIEND:
>
> I got your aerogramme, which explains various matters that had puzzled me. I'm pleased the copies of *Wonderland* had reached you safely . . .
>
> While I'm sure a market exists for your photos in the States, I don't have the funds for a dozen negatives at $15.00 each, let alone 100 of them. Further, I don't have the means for printing from negatives even if I wanted to go into the business of selling photos. Currently I cannot find a single processor in this country who is willing to print photos of minors nude. A contact on the West Coast was raided and all his equipment and addresses seized because he was selling photos of little girls in panties. These of course would be completely legal, but the authorities in this country don't care about such niceties. They're going to crack down on anyone who displeases them, legal or not. I've had dear friends who have subscribed since issue #1 ask to be removed from the mailing list because they are terrified of getting into trouble. This is definitely not the time to try to sell photos in this country.
>
> I'm surprised you need to ask the address of Delta Boek (PO Box 92, N-2980 AB Ridderkerk, Netherlands), as their ad appears quite prominently in each issue of *Wonderland*. They are probably the largest porno house in the Netherlands. The items in *Wonderland* are almost the only things they sell that are NOT pornography. Another possible buyer for the 'tame' nudes is Kings Cross Mail Orders (PO Box 238, Waverly 2024, NSW, Australia). They are selling photos of nude little girls for $7.00 each and might well like having a few more choices available. A Mrs Hanna Strum seems to be the one in charge there.
>
> I'd also suggest getting off a quick note to PO Box 7214,

Emmastraat, NL-4800 GE Breda, Netherlands. The gentleman who runs the sales from that address (a Belgian rather than a Dutchman) seems to be a frequent visitor to your country and seems to be planning another visit shortly. I'm sure he would be happy to negotiate about your photos. He might even serve as a front person for orders that would be forwarded to you. This is how he supplies the Japanese books he is selling . . .

I also gave your address to a friend in California, Don R., who had asked me for someone in Thailand interested in photography.

Kindest regards,

*David Techter*

Techter's caution about Chaivat's product was not misplaced. In a brush with the Chicago police a few years previously, Techter was eventually acquitted on charges of sending child pornography through the mail. Unbeknown to him, his mail was still being intercepted. On 24 April, Chaivat wrote to 'Roy Morgan' at his Ypsilanti box number.

DEAR MR MORGAN, *April 24th*

Many thanks for your welcome letter of April 17th I received today, sir . . . Please kindly send money to order soon. And as soon as I get your money I'll send you the pix ordered in each envelope of 4 each and send to you every 2 days as I did to the other clients in the USA and all were safe. Please always seal all your envelopes with money inside safely, thanks sir. And may I wait for your first order SOON.

I am glad to learn that you would come to Bangkok to enjoy the young ones. Of course I would [meet] you at the Airport or your hotel here on your first evening, if you could inform me your flight number and your hotel staying here, and your real name to check with the hotel etc. 100% sure.

I'll gladly meet you to make some money as usual, sir.

As to the prices (girls or boys you prefer?), and information in details to all your questions, as you did not reply me *from whom you got my name and address?* So may I replies [*sic*] the details you wanted to know, after I know to whom you got my address from, sir? Please forgive and kindly understand that I must be very discreet and careful for my risky position now.

Sorry that I put the name of Mr James A. Scott on the back of my last envelope, sir. I did not hear from him since 1980 and wonder how he is now, and would like to contact him again. Do you know him, sir? What is his address now? I would be very appreciated indeed, sir. As he was such a wonderful man to know. So friendly, frankly, generous and a well-paid American.

As you would be in Bangkok to enjoy 'its' someday in the near future (1985?), please kindly let me know some about you and your likings (girls or boys? age you prefer most. – sucking or licking or fucking or deflo. rape etc. etc.), so I could arrange for your arrival. Though I have now 2 Gs a N-V. and a V., sir. You can trust me, and sign your name as 126 always . . .

All my best to you and your family, dear Mr MORGAN. I would very appreciated if you could replies my questions. All your questions would be replies in my next letters too. And may I have your reply with your first order of exciting action pix SOON. Thanks, sir.

Yours Sincerely,
*Chaivat.*

(P.S.) What is the meaning of 'paranoid' as written in your letter?

That letter was not picked up by Martinez until three weeks later, on 14 May. In the meantime, Chaivat had received a frantic letter from David Techter.

DEAR FRIEND, *3 May 1985*

I received your latest letter and got quite a shock. I feel

very remiss in not warning you against the advertisers in *Wonderland*. Nearly every personal advertiser is known or suspected of being a government agent. This is especially true of EVERY name on page 9. The gentleman you cite as 'generous' is probably the most dangerous one in the pack, as he has had myself and friends fooled for months, until I happened to check with an unfortunate collector who had been arrested and found out who had been responsible for his legal problems. PLEASE, DO NOT ANSWER ANY FURTHER ADS UNTIL YOU CHECK WITH ME FIRST!!! I don't know how much trouble a postal inspector in the US can make for a resident of Thailand, but if they can do it somehow, believe me they will stop at nothing to put you in jail.

By now you should have heard from Don. He wrote he had sent a letter to you shortly before departing for Europe. He [hopes] a reply from you will be waiting for him on his return. As for others you should write, you must appreciate that most of my contacts are very wary of my giving their names out to anyone. Plus you desire people with money, which leaves out most of the collectors I know. One man you might try is: Richard Rogers, PO Box 1321, Ontario, California 91762. An overseas contact is: P. M. Geddes, RFA Olna, B.F.P.O. SHIPS, London, England. These two have let their subscriptions expire, so I don't have much interest in protecting their identity.

On a happier note, I was startled today to receive another letter from Thailand. It turned out to be an ad order (accompanied by a very generous money order) for Japanese photo volumes. It was from a Bill McGee, Bin #504, 521/3 Soi Sriayudtaya, Bangkok 10400. He mentions a 'mutual friend in the Houston area', so I think I can guess who he is. But I think it quite likely the two of you are unaware of each other and might have fruitful interactions.

Thank you for the names of contacts. I will send them

the application form for *Wonderland* and see if they respond. This is a very unpredictable matter. A contact sent me perhaps 15 names of collectors he was trading with throughout the US. I sent off information to all of them, without a single response. Then I will get a list of two or three from someone else, and every one of them will subscribe. One never knows.

I heard via another contact that Gerd Berendt, the German nudist publisher, is seeking sources of nude photos of Asian children, mentioning specifically Thailand. He would of course only be interested in what he could legally publish in Germany, but you could likely help him out. . . . [H]is address is PO Box 344, D-8111 Tauting bei Murnau, West Germany.

Kindest regards,

129

A few weeks later Chaivat received a further letter from 'Roy Morgan' in Ypsilanti. In it, Martinez began laying the basis of the plan to entrap the Thai pornographer.

DEAR SIR, *May 21, 1985*

First, to put your mind at ease, I was given your name by Mr Jack Negus. . . .

Secondly, I am very happy to include $100.00 (US) for the pictures . . . I am sorry that I do not write in more detail, but I am still afraid of people looking at my mail.

As for Mr Scott, I do not know where he is now. All I know for sure is that he had some trouble with the law. I doubt that he is in a position to correspond with you.

My trip to visit you may be sooner than I expected. My company is sending me to Hawaii on business. I will be there for several weeks, as it looks now, and I believe that I shall have enough time to fly to Bangkok for two or 3 days. I should be in Hawaii sometime in August of this year. I will let you know more specifically as the time draws closer . . . I should also let you know that a very close friend of mine is also interested in your pictures. If it is all right with you, I will invite him with me to visit you. You should know that he is very well 'connected' and that we have often discussed going into business, as you have. I believe that, if your pictures are as good as you say they are, he may wish to make a considerable investment. As you may have guessed, this is a fairly unexpected situation, and I am very excited about it.

Sincerely,

126

P.S. 'paranoid' means that you are afraid of being caught because someone is after you, even though they really aren't. There is a lot of pressure right now on people like us, and I always wonder who is watching me. But I am very discreet, and I know that it is unlikely that I will be 'caught'.

David Techter's next letter to Bangkok was written on the same day.

DEAR FRIEND, *21 May 1985*

Overside is the note I received today from Bill McGee. He apparently had not received my letter suggesting changes in his ad. He is not a friend of Jim L. as far as I know. He is a close friend of another Houston contact, Mad Hatter.

I also today received a letter from Don R. from Sweden, on his European trip . . . He had tried to contact the contact using the Breda address, but was told the latter was leaving for Thailand on May 15. So he may well be in Bangkok at this moment. Too bad he did not have your address before he left.

I'm really sorry I did not stop you before you contacted Carl D. Happily you did not answer his questions. Don't expect to hear from Jim L. for some time. He has been arrested on various charges resulting from a government set-up. Quite possibly Carl was involved in the trap. Rudy Ciano is another contact I'm very leery of. He did not write to me at all for over a year after subscribing. Now he wants a very explicit ad run. I would be very careful with Negus and Morgan also. If they don't say where they got your name and address from, it likely was from a postal inspector.

Do NOT write anyone on page 9! That's why they are all grouped on that particular page. I don't know enough about Peter M. (Marx) or Rodan to make any judgements. Bennan is a postal inspector, and so is Layor.

Robin Spring is an old correspondent. Very sincere but, as he says, on a very limited income. 'Ray Handcock' is a dear friend, but again almost no money. Others I can vouch for are: White Knight Productions; 'L. Arthur'; 'T. Mco.' (Terry Mcorey). But, again, no money.

I wrote the five US names you sent me. The letter to Dan Collins came back marked 'No such person at this address'. J. Lind just sent me a subscription. No response as yet from the other three . . . Hope you make contact with Bill McGee. I gave him your address when I wrote, so possibly he would contact you.

No, I do not want any photos at the present time.

Kindest wishes,

129

At the end of the same month, after a long delay, Jack O'Malley – again using the name 'Jack Negus' – wrote his second letter from Chicago to Chaivat in Bangkok.

DEAR MR CHAIVAT, *May 29, 1985*

I'm sorry it took me so long to return your nice letter from February. I'm very interested in your photo sets. They look better than anything else for sale at this time. Enclosed is money order for $100.00. I would like the VIRGIN set if you have available.

I have referred several persons to you including R.M.

from YPSILANTI, Michigan. I think he might be ordering as well.

I appreciate your offer to meet in Bangkok and I might take you up on it at a later date. If you ever visit the US please let me know so I can extend the hospitality. I'll be awaiting your photos and letter.

Thanks,

*Jack Negus.*

While that letter was on its way, Chaivat was responding to the order placed by 'Morgan' in Ypsilanti.

DEAR MR MORGAN, *May 30th*

Thanks for your kind letter with $100 (Registered Airmail) of May 21st I received today . . . I enclose 4 pix inside this letter, and another 2 more envelopes of 4 pix each will follow in every 2 days, sir. My special offer for you is order at the same time of $300 instead of 3 sets of 36 action pix you'll get 40 pix! A rare chance, sir . . . Thanks, sir. Please order SOON.

Surprised to learn that you got my address from Mr Jack Negus, as I got his only letter early of February and after I asked him to whom he got my address from, since then no news from him. Hope his answer was not 'from Mr. Roy Morgan'! Wonder why he could not reply my sincere question.

Glad to learn that your friend also interested in my pix and wish to make a considerable investment. Please ask him to write me SOON with his address to reply and perhaps an order.

Chaivat was beginning to nibble at the bait. His natural fear of being caught, nurtured by Techter's warnings, was being suppressed by his desire for dollars. The letter continued:

Surprised to learn that you'll come to Bangkok so soon in August, and perhaps with your close friend! So soon, you must be a hot-blooded man indeed, sir. I had never entertain 2 friends at the same time before, just one by one would be safer and more fun I guess. As we are still strangers to each other, I afraid I must 'think' about it through and thoroughly, wonder if my 143 IQ tested in London on 1970 could help me! At the moment, the best way to make me trust both of you and make my decision is to send me 2 full-length photos of you and him to me soonest possible (its also help to remember you when you come. Polaroid also OK), I mean if you and your friend are REAL and TRUE and GENUINE, sir . . .

Yours sincerely,
*Chaivat.*

(PS) When you are in Thailand, would you and your friend be interested in heroin or hashish also, sir? And two for one? quite unfair indeed!?! – HOW PARANOID am I now –!
'Anonymous & nobody'

As promised, Chaivat sent the remaining photographs in two batches of four each on 1 June and 3 June, 1985. The set was the one featuring a 'Laos–Thai' girl of eleven years old and a Swiss–Italian man who appears to be aged about forty. He is stockily built with short dark hair and clean shaven. In photographs showing the two on a bed covered with striped linen, a number of sex magazines have been prominently placed in the foreground. One of them is clearly identifiable as an issue of *Lolita*. This is a well-established child-sex series founded and published by Joop Wilhelmus from the town of Breda in Holland.

Included with the final set was a further handwritten note from Chaivat urging 'Morgan' to place another order. On the reverse was a postscript.

(PS) . . . You seem to be so worried and so fear and so PARANOID. If really so, why should you using your home address so openly and not use a P.O.BOX as all the genuine Pedophiles always do, sir!?

Of course, you can trust me for sure. Wonder if I can TRUST YOU also?!

The last of the twelve photographs shows a girl aged about ten lying face down with a pillow under her hips. The man is penetrating her from behind. The girl appears to be in pain and is crying.

Once Martinez's order had been sent, Chaivat fired off a tetchy reply to O'Malley. There seemed to be problems.

DEAR MR NEGUS, *June 5th*

Many thanks for your welcome letter of May 29th and money order of US$100 I received today, sir. But I must send your money order back to you immediately, because I cannot accept any cheque or money order at all, as Chaivat is not my real name. The only way you should is just the way I TOLD YOU BEFORE . . .

Roy M. already sent me $100 banknote last week with his long letter, and I already sent him the ordered 12 pix in 3 envelopes. Even though I don't trust [him] for some reasons. Few days ago I also written you a short letter just to warn you. But perhaps you are his friend also!

I enclosed inside this rush letter your money order back to you, sir. Sorry . . . And may I get your reply and cash SOONEST.

Yours Sincerely,

*Chaivat.*

(PS) *From whom you got my address from, sir????*

Although Chaivat had still not received the reassurances he had been demanding that Negus and Morgan were genuine members of the international network, another problem of a technical nature had Chaivat reaching for pen and paper the very next day.

DEAR MR NEGUS, *June 6th*

Hope you by now have received my replied letter and the return of your money order of US$100 I sent to you yesterday . . .

You mentioned that you wanted to have photos of virgin set, which I don't understand, because action photos are licking-sucking-fucking-rape, so how could they still be virgins in action set? Or do you want the nude photos of the virgin girls? Please explain with your order (or do you mean the rape of a virgin etc.). What do you like with the girls, sir?

Thanks for your kind wish to entertain me if I ever go to U.S. I was there in 1981 for some weeks visited many states . . . Very large and most wonderful country indeed. Perhaps I'll go there again in 1987 or so . . . Where could I find the little girls in the USA, sir? Very dull there indeed for your 'FREE WORLD'.

I hope you now could tell me that 'WHERE DID YOU GET MY NAME AND ADDRESS FROM, SIR?'

All the best. And look forward for your next letter with order (in cash, please) soonest. Thanks, sir.

Yours sincerely,
*Chaivat*
(PTO)

On the reverse of the aerogram, Chaivat had added a desperate postscript.

(PS) Is Mr Roy Morgan a cop or your government agent, sir?

And you? – (EXPLICIT ANSWER, PLEASE.)

During the second week in June, Chaivat in Bangkok busied himself with a mail-out of a promotional offer to a number of his regular clients. Techter's next letter to him was more businesslike than the previous one.

*9 June 1985*

DEAR FRIEND,

Got your letter of 29 May. I also heard (from Thailand) from our Breda contact that he had met you. I gathered that he was not terribly interested in your photos. I'm surprised at the attitude of Delta Boek. But perhaps you'll unload some photos with Mrs Strum . . .

I'm going on 53. I'm employed as a telephone surveyer at present . . . It's enjoyable, but not very lucrative. My collection is about 95 per cent preteen girls, 5 per cent preteen boys.

While I do not make any judgements about sexual activity so long as both partners are willing, I do not see that as the end all of existence. I'm much more interested in stable affectionate relations with youngsters. At the moment I'm emotionally involved still with Christopher, as you can read in *Wonderland*. He is now 13½ and much too old for my being sexually attracted to him, but I'm in love with the contents not the package.

I don't know any of those people whose addresses you have lost . . .

Kindest regards,

*David Techter*

Techter was now providing an important stimulus to Chaivat's business. He wrote again six days later.

DEAR FRIEND, *15 June 1985*

Got your barrage of letters . . . Your reply to Roy Morgan was about as well as could be done under the circumstances. Since I don't know if what you are doing is against Thai law or not, I don't know if a US agent could cause you trouble.

His approach certainly is bold, but then some sincere people are exceedingly bold also. I would be certainly hesitant about an address with a PO box in the western suburbs (such as Tinloy Park), as that is the prowling ground for the notorious John Ruberti, the postal inspector who had me arrested on trumped-up charges in 1982 and has also trapped several other contacts.

You are not the first to suggest that I must be a sting operation since I operate so openly. The reason they leave me alone is precisely because of those ads you object to; they find it much more useful to use a genuine periodical than to concoct their own just to trap unwary collectors. I offered you an ad for precisely the same reason that I give free ads to Gerd Berendt, Delta Boek, Pojkart, and Box 7214. My readers are eager for any source of legal materials, and most suppliers will not pay for an ad. (Our friends with the postal inspectors office are happy to pay for ads.) . . .

The type finally returned from the typesetter, so #10 is partly in press now . . .

Kindest regards,

*David Techter.*

On 17 June O'Malley picked up another letter from Bangkok. He had already received Chaivat's letters of 5 and 6 June. The new envelope contained the Thai's promotional offer. Even O'Malley was shocked by its contents. The postcard-sized colour print showed a girl no more than ten years of age. She is shown lying on a bed with her legs spread towards the camera. She is smiling as she holds the lips of her vagina apart. Painted across her abdomen are the words: 'FUCK ME'. A note was also enclosed.

*June 9th*

Here is a FREE PHOTO for you, dear Mr Negus. Hope you like it! As you like – she is a V. waiting for your KIND deflo., sir! – When, then? There are many more of her sexy nudes and sucking men's cock photos.

Please send me soon $100 to replace your 'money order' I could not cash, for the exciting and rare 12 exciting action photos of young girls vs. men. SOONEST, PLEASE. THANKS.

*Chaivat*

Covering the embarrassing mistake in his last letter, O'Malley wrote back immediately enclosing a $100 bill and confirming that he did indeed want the 'action' photographs.

MR CHAIVAT, *6/17/85*

I'm not sure which letter I should answer first. I recd. all your letters in about one week's time . . .

As I mentioned in my letter of 1/29/85 I received your name through common friends at *Wonderland*. I must admit your letters of 5/31 and 6/6/85 were rather strong – if you'd rather not do business with me please say so. I have referred a number of persons to you including Mr Morgan from Michigan. He is a friend, paranoid yes, but with good reason – I'll explain at some later time . . . I must also be discreet – the stakes are a good deal higher in the US than in Thailand. You are certainly aware of the laws here – very very tough – but only for us and not for you – are there no regulations at all in Thailand?

Please remember that many Americans like myself and Roy were in Southeast Asia during the war and still have many 'pleasant' contacts there . . .

In closing – don't be so tough on Roy and I – Roy has his reasons for being a little paranoid.

Sincerely,

*Jack Negus*

Chaivat filled the order promptly. The letter enclosed with the first four of the twelve prints read as follows:

DEAR MR NEGUS, *June 25th*

Many thanks for your welcome letter of June 17th with $100 I received today, sir . . .

I am sorry that I have written rather rude to you and Mr R. M., that's because I think he and you (or Carl David) are your government agents etc., and trying to make troubles for us – Pedophiles.

Anyhow, you still did not reply me THE NAME of someone who given my address to you, sir? Please, if you want me to trust you. Or perhaps you could not?! Anyhow, the most dangerous (fake Pedophile) is bad Rudolph Ciano from TX 77473. Do you know him, sir? But I think you know John Ruberti!! I lived near Tinloy Park for sometime though. And he was quite notorious! . . .

As to your kind questions, may I answer after you inform me THE NAME of the man who given my address to you, sir.

All the best to you and your family, dear Mr Jack Negus. Hope to hear from you again with new order soon. Thanks, sir.

Yours sincerely,

*Chaivat*

(PS) Which photo you like most?

The balance of the photo set arrived over the next few days. At the bottom of the note included in the last envelope was a now-familiar question.

FROM WHOM YOU GOT MY ADDRESS FROM, SIR?!

Fear of entrapment by US postal inspectors was well founded. Chaivat had just received his second indictment from an American court. That month he had been charged by a Los Angeles Grand Jury with conspiring with a Donald Stephenson to commit offences under the 1984 Child Protection Act.[6] The indictment claimed that Stephenson had been sending obscene drawings to Chaivat in exchange for the latter's photosets. The Thai had also asked Stephenson to send him books, the titles of which included *Jungle Rape Squad*, *Bloody Encounters*, *Raped Captives* and *Thy Neighbor's Little Girl*.

Stephenson was known to the Thai as 'Dan Collins', a name Chaivat had given to David Techter the previous month. When Ray Martinez learned that a Thai national was involved in the Stephenson case he arranged to look at the files. The letters written from Bangkok seemed to use a real name and the handwriting matched that in the letters received in Detroit. Martinez had now discovered the true identity of 'Chaivat'.

Keen to keep up the impetus and to divert Chaivat from his own dubious credentials, O'Malley ordered a $300 batch of photographs. The letter took a firmer line than the previous ones.

> MR CHAIVAT, *7/10/85*
>
> . . . I have sent you cash (at the risk of losing it) and advised I received your name from an associate of *Wonderland*. If you are sincere (and not an agent) and a *true* pedophile you should know that *less* said is better. Loose lips sink ships! Mr Techter should keep that in mind before he talks to *TV reporters*. As you might know many persons in the US are weak and give up others to help themselves out of trouble. I have no control over what people say in their letters to you. The names you mentioned – Ciano, Ruberti – mean nothing to me. Should they? If someone is notorious, let me know ahead of time . . .
>
> I'm sorry that our relationship seems to consist of angry letters. I'm sorry you do not trust me, but there's not much I can do. Mr Chaivat, you have no idea how difficult things are in the US re: our interest. People open mail, listen to phone calls, etc. Disclosing names, etc. puts people in jail – think of Mr SONNENSHEIM from AUSTIN, TX. I hope you will rethink your feelings about me.
>
> Sincerely,
> *Jack Negus*

The following day, from his home a few miles north of O'Malley's office, David Techter wrote his final letter to Chaivat.

DEAR FRIEND, *11 July 1985*

Hope that #10 has reached you by now. On page 9 you will find the article about Jim L.'s arrest. It sounds almost certain that the Cianos were responsible . . .

Mr Geddes is in the British navy; *Olna* is the ship he is stationed on. I haven't heard anything from him in over a year, so he might have a new address by now. The only name I have from Spain is: R. Cooke McSorley c/o Fernandez, Pueta Canseco 49, 3-3, Edf. Jamaica, E-38003 Sta. Cruz de Tenerife, Canary Isl., Spain. I only heard from him once. I know no one in Scotland, Ireland, Iceland, or the Socialist countries. Mr Veltri, of Studio Veltri that advertises has wide contacts throughout Europe and might well know collectors there.

The letter you received from 'Negus' only heightens my distrust of him. The only 'mutual friends at *Wonderland*' he could have gotten your address from is one of the government agents you wrote to from an ad, John Bennan or Carl David. Be very cautious in dealing with him.

. . . Our Canadian friend continues to send me donations from time to time, so I will continue sending you the newsletter. My total pressrun is now only 400 copies. I have had few funds for advertising in recent months, so I have not been able to get new subscribers to replace those who drop out . . .

Trust all is well with you.

Regards,

*David Techter*

Chaivat's dilemma remained. Techter's continued warnings were being countered by the lure of more money from O'Malley and Martinez. He acknowledged O'Malley's $300 order gratefully:

DEAR MR NEGUS, *July 15th*

Many thanks for your kind and long letter of July 10th

with $300 I received today, sir. Of course you can trust me for 100% sure, because I am honest and sincere to all my clients always.

May I say 'sorry' again if I was so rude to you and Mr Morgan (he did not write again since, please ask him to write. Thanks). The reason as told in my letter, and also till now you cannot tell me the NAME of the man who given you my address! Please, if you are real and want me to trust you please name it . . .

I enclose the first 4 pix inside this letter and'll continue to send you envelopes of 4 pix each to you about 4 or 5 envelopes each week, there still 36 more action pix or 9 more envelopes to come, sir . . . And if you are interested, I would like also sell all about 600 negatives (action and nudes) altogether for $5,000 fix price. (Please compare the price of the negatives and pix. It's cheap, almost same price!) . . .

Yours sincerely,

*Chaivat*

(PS) Please inform the NAME I asked so many times and I'll trust you, sir!

O'Malley certainly was interested in the $5,000 offer; if Chaivat was prepared to take the risks he was taking for a few hundred dollars, what would he be willing to do for five grand? The reaction from Bangkok had been positive and, after many meetings and telephone calls to headquarters, it was decided to go ahead with the next stage of the operation; Chaivat had laid his own bait.

In the third week in July, Martinez resumed his correspondence with Bangkok. After some discussion, he and O'Malley had agreed to adopt differing roles. O'Malley would be a businessman interested in publishing Chaivat's photographs. Martinez would not claim to be anything more than an enthusiast for sex with children. This time he had what he hoped would be good news for Chaivat.

DEAR MR CHAIVAT, *July 15, 1985*

Very happy to receive your letter and the photos. All three sets arrived safely. They were everything you said they'd be. I am enclosing $300.00 for the special set of 40 photos . . . I am sorry it has taken so long to respond. I have been out of town on business . . .

I have received word that my trip to Hawaii (and then, of course, Bangkok) may be sooner than I expected. It may be as soon as the last week of July or the first week of August. I asked my associate about the photos you requested. He is not at all interested in being photographed or sending a photo due to 'security' reasons. He has advised me not to send a photograph as well. As he has offered to pay for the visit to Bangkok, in the interest of putting together a business deal, I promised him I would comply with his wishes. He was particularly interested in your offer to provide 'candy' during our visit. He is always looking for new sources for H— or H—, and has expressed interest in this part of the business as well. In this country, though, there is a ready and lucrative market for photos of the young ones. [My friend's] plans stand to make us all a lot of money . . .

Please note that the address you've been writing to IS a post office box! I call it 'Apt. #C-14' in order to fool the authorities. I may not have a 143 IQ, but I am capable of being clever . . .

Hoping to see you very soon, and hear from you sooner.

Yours very truly,

126

In the weeks prior to the trip to Bangkok only one job was outstanding: to obtain US passports in the names of Negus and Morgan. They already had state and international driver's licences in the false names. They even had Diners Club charge cards which worked – Martinez complained that this caused him to receive twice the usual amount of junk mail.

But getting fake passports was not so straightforward. At first, State Department required them to change their names before a federal judge. They could not find a judge who would agree to this. Applications to US attorneys and circuit court judges also failed. They asked another federal court judge to issue an order authorizing the use of the phoney names. When he refused, it looked as though the operation would have to be cancelled. Only last-minute negotiations with the Departments of State and Justice enabled the fake passports to be issued.

O'Malley and Martinez arrived in Hong Kong en route to Singapore on a flight from Chicago. It was in reality the first trip to Asia for both undercover agents. As they entered the transit lounge at the colony's Kai Tak airport, they spotted two men wearing fatigues and blue berets and carrying Heckler & Koch machine pistols. The two policemen, members of the élite anti-terrorist squad, walked right up to them.

'Mr O'Malley? Mr Martinez? Please come with us.' As a matter of routine, the Hong Kong authorities had been forewarned that they would be taking contraband through Kai Tak and the assumption had been made that the Americans were carrying drugs. In the event, they were ushered into a side room where they were greeted by a senior British officer of the Royal Hong Kong Police.

'Special Agent Jack O'Malley, US Customs Service, Chicago,' said the taller of the two Americans as they shook hands, 'and this is Special Agent Ray Martinez. Ray's based in Detroit.'

Their host did not press them for details of their assignment. They spent a pleasant hour in his company drinking tea. Close by O'Malley's chair was a briefcase containing Chaivat's pornography; by Martinez an aluminium custom case full of radio bugs and telephone tapping devices.

In the world at large, Holiday Inns tend to be somewhat more exotic than they are in the United States. The Royal Holiday Inn in Singapore is a case in point; it is owned by the Sultan of Brunei who is also the proprietor of London's prestige Dorchester. But the splendour of the décor was lost on O'Malley and Martinez as they checked in, bleary eyed, just before midnight on Saturday, 3 August.

They met up again the following day for a late breakfast and tried to relax out the jet-lag. Early that evening, Tom Winker arrived from Bangkok. With him was Lieutenant Colonel Padet of the Bangkok Metropolitan Police Serious Crimes Squad. The four immediately went into a planning meeting which was to last nearly six hours.

The conference started with the bad news: Padet pointed out that the publication and sale of pornography was not a very serious offence in Thailand. What about child porn? asked the American agents. No distinction is made in law, said the Thai policeman. The few cases there had been had resulted in fines of a hundred dollars or so.

'So what do we do?' asked O'Malley. 'This guy has been making a lot of money and a fine is unlikely to put him out of business.'

'Perhaps there's something more serious we can pin on him?' suggested Winker, the customs attaché in Bangkok. Padet nodded.

'If you can get him to supply you with girls under thirteen years old, that could result in a prison sentence. Try and get him to bring one to your hotel room.'

'Yeah, that might be possible,' said Martinez, 'he's offered to do that often enough in his letters . . . Come to think of it, he also offered us dope. Hashish or heroin.'

'Even better,' said Padet.

The meeting then moved on to matters of safety. The side arms which O'Malley and Martinez wore in the United States as a matter of routine had been left behind. Winker had been concerned about adverse publicity from any shooting incidents. But illicit firearms are easily obtained in

Bangkok and Martinez pictured Chaivat as an organized crime figure. Padet reassured them, saying he would assign two of his best lieutenants to give them close cover at all times. In spite of those assurances, Martinez wondered if he would have to use the weapon concealed in his suitcase. He had chosen it because it would not trigger off the metal-detectors at airports.

The only outstanding operational problem was how they would make contact with Chaivat once they arrived in Bangkok. It was decided to send a cable to Chaivat's box number.

The cable arrived at 8.30a.m. the following morning, Monday. It read:

MR CHAIVAT
PO BOX 10-1006
BANGKOK
SIR, MESSRS MORGAN AND NEGUS WILL BE AT BANGKOK PALACE HOTEL ON TUESDAY AUGUST 6TH. ANXIOUS TO MEET AND DISCUSS PROPOSITION AS DETAILED IN OUR CORRESPONDENCE. ITINERARY DEMANDS STOP IN BANGKOK FOR NO LONGER THAN 3 DAYS. WE WILL WAIT TO BE MET AT HOTEL.
126

In fact they travelled on the Monday in order to avoid the danger that Chaivat would attempt to meet them at the airport.

The flight from Singapore that afternoon was uneventful. The only problem arose while they checked in to the Bangkok Palace. At the airport Lieutenant Colonel Padet had escorted them to an immigration office away from the public areas. Here, the precious fake passports as well as the genuine ones were stamped with entry visas. But the forms which went with the visas were only completed for the real passports. When the undercover agents presented the passports in the names of Negus and Morgan, the check-in clerk was unable to find the forms he needed to copy out the visa numbers as he had been trained to do. There followed an embarrassing moment which was only resolved when Padet leaned across the counter and whispered to the clerk:

'Police business . . .'

The fact that the manager of the Bangkok Palace was a former police major helped them get the facilities they required. O'Malley and Martinez were allocated connecting rooms 8044 and 8046. As the bellman showed them down the eighth floor hallway they passed room 8041 on their left. That had already been set up as the control centre for the Chaivat sting.[7]

Waiting for something to happen is the worst part of any undercover operation. They had arrived the previous afternoon shortly before Chaivat made his routine 4 p.m. pick-up from the mailbox. It was now Tuesday, 6 August 1985.

Earlier that morning Ray Martinez had busied himself by wiring Jack O'Malley's hotel room. Using an induction coil he had connected a Sony miniature recorder to the telephone line. Another recorder was hidden under the bed with the microphone concealed beneath the bedside table.

Martinez, a former police officer on the Ypsilanti force, then installed the radio receiver from the surveillance kit behind a window curtain. He fitted the tiny Negra microphone and transmitter beneath O'Malley's shirt and had him walk around the hotel to check that the receiver was working properly. It was then that they hit the first snag: as soon as O'Malley walked into an elevator, the receiver lost him. The bust *had* to take place in the bedroom.

By late afternoon that day they had lived off room service for twenty-four hours. They read paperback books and performed keep-fit exercises. Occasionally, the local investigator employed by US customs would come over from the control centre in Room 8041. His name was Rungroeng Tulalamba but everyone called him 'Tuli'.

Armed plainclothes policemen from the Bangkok metropolitan force were placed strategically throughout the hotel. The surveillance team watching Chaivat's house had undercover motor cyclists and a taxi on call in case they needed to follow him in Bangkok's unrelenting traffic. Boredom mixed with frustration; it was a long way to come to sit around a hotel room watching Chinese kung fu movies with Thai subtitles.

From his own room Martinez heard the telephone ring and rushed through the connecting door in time to see O'Malley press the 'record' button on the Sony recorder and pick up the receiver.

'Mr Negus? This is Chaivat.' The voice was high-pitched and nervous. He spoke rapidly. 'Is Mr Morgan with you?'

'Yes, he is. We're both looking forward to meeting you. Are you in the hotel?' As he spoke, O'Malley nodded at Martinez who slipped back through the connecting door and out of his own door into the corridor. He ran the fifteen yards to the control centre. Tom Winker was there with Tuli. He waved at them and with Eddy, Cherdchai and the other police officers they followed the special agent back to the adjoining room and tiptoed in. O'Malley was talking.

'Hey, what's the problem? I've got a comfortable room here. We can have a drink in private.'

'No, no. We meet somewhere else.'

'What?' Through lack of practice, Chaivat's spoken English was not as good as his letters suggested.

'We meet somewhere else.' Things got worse. 'Who did you get my name from? Where you get my name? You not say in letter, Mr Negus.'

'Listen, just take it easy. I don't want to use names on the phone. We have to be real careful. Why don't you come up here to the room and we'll give you a contact name?'

'No, no. Somewhere else.' Chaivat was now bordering on hysteria.

At that time no one realized that he had twice tried to make contact at the hotel earlier in the day. Initially he had arrived in time to see a petty thief being arrested by uniformed police in the shopping arcade adjoining the lobby. Chaivat had scurried away.

The second occasion alarmed him even more. As his *tuktuk* motorized trike rattled around the corner into Makasan Road at the rear of the hotel, the Bangkok Palace seemed to be surrounded by patrol cars and trucks full of armed police. He screamed at the driver to turn round and get out of the area. But even Chaivat did not justify that much attention. Railway workers at the Makasan Station had called a strike and the police were there to keep an eye on the pickets.

Although Chaivat was still torn between his fear of being caught and his greed for the $5,000, the rendezvous was going to be anywhere but the Bangkok Palace Hotel. The telephone conversation continued.

'Do you have the money?' Chaivat demanded.

'Yeah, of course I have the money. Look, just relax, man. Nobody's going to rip you off.'

'Who gave you my name?' insisted the voice.

'C'mon, you don't really expect me to mention names on the phone do you? Why don't you come over here. Bring the items you wrote us about.'

'No, no, no. We meet at the Indra.' O'Malley didn't understand this.

'The Idla? What's that?'

'The Indra! *Indra Hotel*!' Chaivat was almost shouting.

'Indra?' O'Malley repeated. The Thai officers nodded and waved to show they understood. 'OK, the Indra Hotel. What time?'

'In lobby at seven o'clock. Bring the money. Five thousand dollars.' The line went dead.

'Mr Chaivat? Mr Chaivat?' Jack shrugged angrily and hung up. 'He's gone.'

'What did the man say?' asked Tom Winker.

'He asked if we had the money. And where we'd gotten his name from. Said we had to meet him at the Indra Hotel – is that it? Indra?'

'Yes,' said Tuli, 'it's not far from here.'

'Okay,' O'Malley continued, 'we're to meet him in the lobby at seven.' The four men from US Customs looked at their watches simultaneously. They had about two hours to plan the next move.

'Where is Chaivat now?' O'Malley asked Tuli. Tuli turned and spoke to the policemen. There was a shaking of heads. Then one of them said something and left the room.

'Nobody seems too sure,' Tuli said.

'I thought they had him under surveillance?'

'They have. Well, the house is being watched and they're following him when he's away. I suppose the problem is staying with him. They're going to call Major Somsak now.'

Winker raised a hand: 'Let's hear the tape.' The room fell silent. When the playback ended one of the officers spoke briefly to Tuli, who then turned to the three Americans.

'Lieutenant Colonel Padet thinks Eddy and Cherdchai should go down to the Indra fairly soon and get into position. Of course, Chaivat could already be there.'

The two lieutenants hurried off while the others sat down to discuss tactics. If Chaivat would not come to them, they would have to go to Chaivat. That realization made Winker even more uneasy; they would not be able to record the meeting. Nor would it be as easy to give the undercover agents the armed protection he had promised their bosses in the States. Although the Indra Regent was no more than seven hundred yards from the Bangkok Palace Hotel, Winker suggested that O'Malley and Martinez should travel there by taxi. That would be the obvious thing for tourists to do. The agents were happy with the idea; with the armed back-up gone they didn't relish the risk of getting mugged in a back alley before they could get their hands on Chaivat. With Tuli as his guide, Winker would go on foot.

The plan was to continue to lure the target back to O'Malley's room at the Bangkok Palace. The annoying concern was that they still did not have the full $5,000. The $1,000 Winker had managed to raise from embassy funds was barely enough to 'flash' and they now needed the additional $4,000 urgently. Tuli said he would call Colonel Thawee about it. If they had the full amount they could go to Chaivat's place and do the deal there, Martinez suggested. The attaché objected.

'Too dangerous. And the Thai police have to be the ones who make the arrest.' What Martinez had in mind was a more expedient form of citizen's arrest.

When the undercover agents reached the lobby it was already dark. They prepaid the fare at the travel desk and the cab hurtled out of the drive only to stop, stuck solidly in the city's most congealed traffic. Increasingly concerned that they would be late, they continued to rehearse the 'what-ifs' of the long-awaited encounter. Occasionally Martinez reached down and touched the knife strapped upside down to his left calf. Without their guns, that knife might provide their only protection if Eddy and Cherdchai lost contact.

A chorus of horns sounded in front and behind. The taxi could not move.

Tom Winker later spoke about his own journey between the two hotels.

> Eddy and Cherdchai had already left and must have reached the Indra a damn sight faster than Tuli and I did. They were much younger and fitter. Tuli and I ran down a street hardly wider than an alley trying to avoid the puddles from the afternoon rain. That was when I began to be really worried. Ray and Jack were unarmed and I was ultimately responsible for their safety. They were out of my sight and Eddy and Cherdchai were not with them. I didn't know where the other cops were. When we got to the end of the street we turned left and went up some steep steps to the pedestrian overpass. It's impossible to cross the main road at that point.'
>
> 'We could see one of the taxi drop-off points for the

Indra Hotel,' 'but we'd no time to look for Jack and Ray. We went down the steps at the other side as fast as we could against the flood of people trying to get home. As we walked into the hotel lobby, we looked around. I was relieved to see Eddy and Cherdchai – they'd found a table in the corner next to the travel desk.

Tuli gestured that they should go up the grand staircase in the centre of the lobby to the cocktail lounge. They found a table in the corner overlooking the central area of the lobby. From below, it is impossible to see into this bar. Winker and Tuli ordered and settled down to wait. Winker remembers:

Jack and Ray came in after about fifteen minutes. They sat on a sofa facing back towards the door. They looked a little self-conscious. Then Jack got up and took a circuit around the lobby. When he got back to Ray he asked him something. Then he walked to the lobby bar out of sight from where we were sitting. That's when Chaivat must have made the contact – we didn't even see which direction he came from. He could have been in the hotel already. Jack walked to Ray and touched him on the shoulder. They left straight away.

I threw a handful of money on the table and we hurried back down the stairs to the lobby. As we turned to the left we slowed up in case they were standing there just out of sight. We couldn't see them, but we did spot Eddy and Cherdchai running out the door.

We followed at a brisk pace, trying not to be too conspicuous. That door takes you out into a shopping arcade. At that time of night it's real crowded and busy with people shopping on their way home from work. It has to be one of the worst places imaginable for surveillance. It was like a scene from *Blade Runner*. We couldn't see any of the guys. Chaivat, Jack, Ray, Eddy and Cherdchai had all disappeared. We struggled through the crowd for a while to try and pick them up, but it was impossible. It was dangerous for us to continue like that so we returned to the lobby.

Chaivat had led the undercover agents up the escalator to the second floor and then on up to the next. He walked rapidly, weaving his way through the crowd. All the time O'Malley tried to get him to slow down.

'Hey, take it easy. What in hell's going on? Where're we going?'

'How do I know who you are? How can I trust you?' hissed Chaivat. They continued the upward climb. As they reached the top floor, the crowd thinned, but only a little.

'Slow down, man. How can we talk here?' Martinez was hard on their heels. They were heading towards a cinema. Now he was really worried they might be walking into an ambush. The agent from Detroit had a black belt in Tae-kwando but the spectacular kicks of the Korean martial art would be difficult to perform in the limited space. He fell into the rehearsed routine.

'Hey, where are the kids? I thought you were going to fix some kids for us?' Chaivat stopped and turned to face them. He was dressed in a red plaid shirt. His hair hung over his face. He was sweating profusely. The three were standing in front of a shop selling stereo systems and the music was deafening. As Chaivat spoke his eyes shifted furtively to the left and right.

'Where you get my name from? Who gave you my name?' Always the same question. 'Show me your passports!' They did. Chaivat peered carefully at the fake documents and noted the visa stamps. 'Where you get my name from?' O'Malley took a deep breath and played what he hoped would be the trump card. Leaning towards Chaivat he whispered the name of an undercover cop from San Diego who had been 'working' the Thai since the beginning of the year. Chaivat relaxed visibly and so, capitalizing on the situation, O'Malley pulled a book from his hip pocket and held it out. Chaivat took it tentatively and slipped it out of its wrapper.

'I thought you'd like this. You said in your letters that you liked books.' Chaivat nodded and flipped through the pages.

'Yes. I know of this. It's a good book . . .' The story centred around the repeated rape of a teenage girl. Then Chaivat remembered that he had a package for Martinez. He passed the agent from Detroit the last set of four photographs. Martinez slipped them into his shirt pocket.

'Great. Thanks. Did you fix the girls for us?' But Chaivat was not going to be drawn. He wanted to do the deal with O'Malley.

'Not now. Do you have the money?'

O'Malley shrugged.

'Not all of it . . .'

Chaivat grew frantic again.

'Why not? You promised five thousand dollars. Where's the money?' The American held up a hand. The one big snag was now threatening the whole operation; they needed the rest of that flash money urgently. Perhaps Martinez could get back to Winker in the hotel and organize something fast? O'Malley assumed that Winker and the Thai team were there – they had seen none of the back-up since leaving the Bangkok Palace more than an hour ago. In spite of the crowd, they felt very isolated.

'The money's back at our hotel. Look, I wouldn't even walk around Chicago with that kind of money. It's in the safe deposit. Let's go back there. We can talk and do the deal. What d'you say?' The Thai shook his head and glanced up and down the crowded plaza. Martinez touched him on the shoulder.

'Yeah. Let's do that. You can fix the kids for us. You promised us.' At that point, O'Malley turned on his companion.

'Look, I'm trying to do business. Get the fuck outa here!' Martinez got the message and, waving a hand dismissively, turned on his heel and headed for the escalator. 'I'm in charge here and I want to do the deal,' O'Malley pleaded,

'Why don't you get the negatives and we'll meet back at the hotel?'

But Chaivat was not listening. He watched with horror as Martinez disappeared into the crowd.

'Where he going?' Before O'Malley could answer, the Thai took off in the same direction. Again the agent took off after him urging him all the time to slow down.

The frantic, weaving procession eventually made its way back to the Indra Hotel. O'Malley went through the door hoping that Chaivat would wait outside for him. By now he had lost sight of Martinez, but he could see Winker standing at the lobby bar ahead of him. He walked slowly forward and pretended to look for Ray. Through his teeth he hissed frantically at the attaché.

'It's going down! It's going down now! Better get the rest of the money.' He could feel Chaivat's eyes boring into his back. O'Malley spotted Martinez and walked out with him. Chaivat was still there but, still agitated, he walked away down the street with the customs agents in tow. For two blocks O'Malley tried to persuade him to meet back at their hotel. Now the Thai was getting angry.

'Where's the money?' he demanded.

'I told you, at the Bangkok Palace.' At that Chaivat stopped and faced them.

'Five thousand dollars!' he screamed. 'Get it!' At that he ran off, leaving the Americans, faces beaded with sweat, to watch helplessly as he was absorbed by the traffic on Ratchaprarop Road.

Shortly after ten the next morning, 7 August, Tom Winker and Tuli pulled into Bangkok's Metropolitan Police headquarters. The debriefing the previous night back at the Bangkok Palace had centred on the problem of raising the extra $4,000 of flash money. Tuli had come up with an idea.

Winker and Tuli walked through the open-air food market which served as a cafeteria for the metropolitan force, and up the stone steps to the office of Colonel Thawee.

Thawee, Tuli's brother-in-law, was in charge of the Thai side of the operation for the Bangkok police and he might be the last resort for the flash money. The year before, the Metropolitan Police had co-operated with the US Secret Service in catching a Taiwanese counterfeiter who was producing a particularly good line in US $20 bills. According to officials at the American Embassy the Thai police still had the money which had been seized.

They were shown into Thawee's office and Winker got to the point of the meeting as soon as it was polite to do so. Tuli translated where necessary. Before the customs attaché had a chance to finish the story Thawee nodded and picked up a bunch of keys from his desk. Without leaving his chair he reached down to a lower drawer, unlocked it and started to stack bundles of fake bills on the desktop. Winker and Tuli were stunned. Thawee gestured that they should help themselves. They counted off $4,000; it seemed to make little impression.

Back at the hotel O'Malley and Martinez inspected the money closely. The forgeries were good – even the serial numbers varied. They shuffled the bills and O'Malley tucked them into a billfold at the back of the $1,000 of genuine money the embassy had supplied. All they could do now was to wait for Chaivat to make contact again.

That afternoon Martinez and O'Malley were again holed up with kung fu movies, *singha* beer commercials and room service. There was a sharp rap at the door. Both agents leapt to their feet, then froze. As O'Malley walked to the door, Martinez switched on the recorder under the bed, checked that the surveillance gear was out of sight and gave his colleague the thumbs-up. O'Malley peered through the peep-hole in the door. It was a bellman.

'Letter for Mr Negus.' O'Malley took the letter and hurriedly tipped the messenger. The typed envelope had been mailed from a Bangkok post office and was addressed to 'Negus', Room 8044 at the Bangkok Palace Hotel. It had been stamped 'EXPRESS' three times. Inside was a letter typed on paper bearing the letterhead of the Indra Palace Hotel. It was from Chaivat.

*August 7th*

DEAR SIRS,

Sorry that I'll not be able to phone you to make our next meeting. I was so nervous last night when we met.

And today on the way back from the Bank I had a car accident at around 10.40a.m. Very bad luck.

As both of you will be in Bangkok no longer than 3 days as mentioned, I'll not be able seeing you again, sir. Sorry.

Please inform Mr Morgan that I don't have the 'thing' he wanted at all, I have only mentioned negatives (I bought from the China-town here years ago) to sell to both of you, sir. If you really to buy its as told, and there is 'a ready and lucrative market' in the US as you mentioned before, then I'll send all the negatives to any of your addresses (Tinloy Park or Ypsilanti or etc.) after I recieve your $5,000 in my new Bank account opened for you, sir. Please hurry go to my Bank soonest today (8.30–3.30p.m.) and put in the mentioned 5,000 in my Bank account number, and I'll also send you the mentioned (almost 600) negatives soonest, sir. Thanks.

My Bank account number as following . . .

Mr Marnit
A/C Number 118-305516-7
BANGKOK BANK LIMITED (Silom Road Branch)
300 Silom Road
BANGKOK 10500

Thanks for all. And all the best to both of you, sir.

And wish you a wonderful time in Bangkok, and have a safe and sound trip back to US

Yours sincerely,
*Chaivat*

The agents called Winker and Tuli over from the control centre and went into conference again. Paying the money into the account and leaving, as Chaivat had suggested, was not the option they were going to take. They could write back, but the faster course might be to send another cable to his post office box. Tom started to work on the wording of the reply. They had gone through a few drafts when Eddy arrived and asked Tom if he would take a phone call in the control centre.

When he arrived back, he stood nervously before the undercover agents.

'I think you'd better pack your bags after all. It's all over. He's just been arrested.'

'Shit!' exclaimed O'Malley. 'Why? What happened?' Winker shook his head.

'We don't know yet. They got a message from Major Somsak that he'd arrested him near the apartment. Let's get down to police headquarters and find out what's happening.'

Asked later how he reacted to the news, Ray Martinez said 'I felt like I felt when I heard my grandmother had died.'[8]

They sat in the office of Colonel Thawee and waited. Martinez was pessimistic; they had lost the case. O'Malley thought that the typed letter might be good evidence to back up the materials they had brought with them from the States. After more than an hour, word arrived: go to Chaivat's apartment.

The suspect lived in a public housing project. The condition of the apartment surprised the agents; it was filthy and decrepit. If Chaivat had been making a lot of money from child pornography, and it could have been as much as $2,000 a month, he certainly had not been spending it on his living accommodation. The place seemed crowded.

'I couldn't tell who were cops and who weren't,' Martinez observed subsequently.[9] They were greeted by Major Somsak, who explained that he had arrested Chaivat because he had been worried he might give them the slip and run up-country.[10]

At first, they didn't even spot the suspect sitting on the edge of a bed, head in handcuffed hands. As they walked into the bedroom he looked up. The blood drained from his face when he saw O'Malley and Martinez. If they needed proof that Chaivat's real identity was Manit Thamaree, they now found it in the cardboard cartons of letters and photographs. Perhaps things weren't as bad as they seemed; like many child-sex enthusiasts, Chaivat/Thamaree had kept everything.

Many of the letters written to him bore urgent messages: *Please destroy this after you have read it*. Chaivat/Thamaree had even kept all his lottery tickets since 1977. They found four inexpensive cameras – two of them Polaroids – and a spotlight. Some of the soiled linen in the bedroom had the distinctive stripes that Martinez and O'Malley had seen in many of the photographs the suspect had sent them. A hard-bound notebook contained a detailed log of a trip he had made through Europe that had started in the Polish capital of Warsaw. But although it included detailed comments on the accommodation and food at each hotel, it did not pinpoint the year Chaivat/Thamaree had made the tour. However, a set of European and American gay contact directories dated 1978 and early 1979 gave a possible clue.

Then they found the photographs, many of them already familiar. Hundreds of negatives and prints all bore the distinctive style of Caucasian men in sexual acts with Thai or Thai–Chinese girls aged mostly between eight and twelve.

If Chaivat's male models were volunteers, his costs of production and overheads were minimal. He had been making a lot of money by standards in Thailand, where the legal minimum wage of $2.50 a day is close to the real average.

Many of Chaivat's correspondents had sent him stories which graphically documented their fantasies. Some sent photographs and drawings. Included in one file was a set of five sketches made with coloured pencils. They had been sent by Donald Stephenson, known to Chaivat/Thamaree as 'Dan Collins'. O'Malley flipped through the first few.

The top sketch showed a man sitting on an upright chair. He was wearing a Gestapo uniform with swastika armbands, but was naked from the waist down. He was shown impaling a young girl on his erect penis. Apparently aged about eight years old, the girl is crying and blood is coming from her vagina. The second drawing showed a man dressed in Arab clothes. Hanging on hooks on the wall behind him are the bodies of six naked children. Blood runs down the wall. O'Malley replaced the drawings in the file.

A police officer passed another notebook to Tom Winker. It was bound in cheap red material and had the words 'Address Book' embossed on the cover. He flipped it open only to find the first few pages blank. Then he realized that it had been completed from the back in the conventional Thai style. It contained over 150 names and addresses annotated in Thai. The handwriting was neat; the names were in red and the addresses in blue ink. Each entry was numbered. O'Malley's cover-name 'Negus' had the number '125', Martinez (as 'Morgan') was'126'. They noticed that David Techter's name was a later entry at '129'. This explained why they had such problems using *Wonderland* as a reference. At the time they first made contact Chaivat/ Thamaree had not yet heard of Techter and his newsletter. Against each name in the book was the number of the correspondent who had introduced the new contact.[11]

Tuli helped the Americans with the notes in Thai: 'These are the numbers of the contact who introduced this person . . .' The first address was in West Germany, the next in France, the next in the United States. Then Canada, Switzerland, West Germany again, then Italy, Australia, Cyprus, Greece, Holland. There seemed to be no customers in Thailand.

'The small marks here indicate how many orders they placed . . .' Tuli continued. 'The notes include personal details such as age, height, sexual preferences. This says the man is "very sadistic" . . . this one "likes raping" . . . this one "has a big cock" . . .'[12]

The search bore more resemblance to a lucky dip than a thorough scene-of-the-crime investigation. The Thai police indicated that the Americans should help themselves to anything of interest.

After some hours of rummaging through the cartons, an activity which threw no light on Chaivat/Thamaree's financial situation, someone suggested dinner. A policeman mentioned the Sakuntala Restaurant as a local favourite. After loading the evidence into one of the vehicles, they sealed the apartment.

To the amazement of the Americans the meal took precedence over securing the prisoner in a cell for the night. Instead they took Chaivat/Thamaree to the restaurant with them, the Thais reassuring the customs agents that this was simply out of regard for him as a human being.

After months of undercover investigation, O'Malley and Martinez were now expected to dine formally with a twice-indicted purveyor of explicit child-sex material.

In January 1986 while on bail, Manit Thamaree wrote a letter to one of his American correspondents. It read:

> Thank you for you kind letter. I'm sorry to tell you that I am presently out of the photography business so I have no more action pix to sell you. Sorry, Sir. If you can visit Bangkok you will be most welcome here. Please come soonest and meet the YOUNG ONES. I have two new Gs available . . .[13]

Thamaree was tried on 7 April 1986 and pleaded guilty in return for a fixed sentence of one year in gaol with no eligibility for remission or parole. Life in Bangkok's Central Prison had the effect of making him more repentant and he would tell inquiring visitors that all he wanted was 'no more trouble'.[14] On 21 May, 1986 David Techter, the publisher of *Wonderland*, was arrested by detectives of the Chicago Police

Department and charged with child molestation.[15]

The US Customs Service believes that there could be as many as 500,000 paedophiles in America and that they consume some 85 per cent of all the child pornography produced in the world.[16] Thamaree contributed a tiny proportion of this; the big money was being made by magazine publishers in Holland, Denmark, Sweden and West Germany. The former advertising copywriter originating sets of photographs from Bangkok was little more than an irritation compared with these enterprises. Thamaree even had in his address book a list of firms to contact in Europe: Lettrex in Copenhagen; Iverson & Co in Padborg, Denmark; and Exim Trading, also at a Copenhagen address.[17]

# 9

## *Bizarre and Inexplicable Rites: The Law*

In the autumn of 1984, millions of Americans watched an amazing confrontation on a prime-time documentary called *The Silent Shame.*[1] NBC News reporter Mark Nykanen was investigating the European sources of the child pornography being imported into the United States.

'Through contacts in the child pornography underground in Copenhagen,' said Nykanen in the sonorous voice-over, 'we found Blue Movie, an adult bookstore that is really a front for the world's biggest producer and distributor of all kinds of child pornography.' Nykanen walked into the store and was shown some illegal child porn by a woman called Leila Strauss.

The following day she visited Nykanen at his hotel and showed him 'hundreds of samples' of the illicit material she could supply. The correspondent proposed a deal in which he would provide photographs to be used in making new magazines. A further meeting was arranged for the next day which would be attended by Leila's husband, Willy.

The tall Californian loomed over the Strausses as he welcomed them into his room and gestured that they should sit on the sofa. Nykanen explained that he wanted to buy child pornography to sell in the United States. Strauss confirmed that he had come to the right man and enthusiastically described what he had to offer. Throughout the discussion, the Dane failed to notice anything strange about the innocent-looking flight bag positioned on the dressing table opposite the sofa. Strauss said he wanted $10,000 for his magazines and the European rights for Nykanen's new material. The American would have to pay the cost of printing the new magazines from the photographs.

They agreed to meet again and Nykanen showed them down to the lobby. As they reached the door, a film crew ran across the parking lot and Nykanen confronted the Strausses:

'We're from NBC News in America. What do you think happens to the children who are very young – not even in puberty – when they have sex with adults so you can publish the pictures? What do you think that does to them?'

'I don't know,' replied Strauss, the question a little fast for his poor English.

'Do you think it's good for them?' pressed Nykanen.

'No . . . no!'

'But you do that.'

'You say *I* do that?' said Strauss, thinking the American meant he appeared in the photographs.

'But you said you published *Blondie* and *Lolita*.'

'Yeah, but I didn't do it . . .'

Nykanen never did get a coherent answer.

The reporter's approach made good television, but it is not necessary to have contacts in the Copenhagen underground to find Willy Strauss: he is in the telephone book. Vesterbrogade is a long street which starts on the northern side of the Tivoli and runs to the west. It begins moderately up-market (though you would never call it an Oxford Street or Fifth Avenue) and becomes increasingly down at heel until you reach the shop at number 98.

The shop's double frontage is painted bright blue with the words 'Blue Movie' and 'Blue Video' splashed garishly across it in white. Next door, at 102, behind lace-curtained windows, is Willy Strauss's office. When he's not here, he's in the shop or at his latest venture, the Blue Greece restaurant a few blocks back towards the Tivoli.

Most of the limited space in the office is occupied by a huge oval-shaped, marble-topped desk. An ornate *fin de siècle* mirror contrasts with a Korean Airlines map of the world, a high-tech telephone, a Casio miniature TV set, a copier, a stereo system and neat rows of lever-arch files. On a small table by Willy's desk is an expensive electric typewriter – he does much of his own typing. Vintage American sex magazines litter the top of a filing cabinet. Among these accoutrements of routine office life are stained glasses, cans of beer and a near-empty bottle of Scotch – the dregs of another drinking session.

The office is usually crowded by an entourage of Strauss's cronies, few of whom seem to have regular nine-to-five jobs. The style is expensive–casual with white cricket sweaters and plenty of gold in evidence. During one afternoon session, the numbers one to six are scrawled on sheets of typing paper and dice are produced. The bets are made using 100-kroner bills (£10 or $15). You get the same back if your number comes up, twice the stake for a double. The man handling the shaker deftly palms one of the dice each time and adjusts it under the edge of the desk to shift the odds in his favour. 'I look after Willy's black money,' he mutters in an aside. One of the gamblers loses nearly £200 ($300) in less than thirty minutes. Strauss cashes a cheque so he can lose some more.

Although born in wartime Copenhagen, Willy Strauss has inherited the European aristocracy's infamous tradition of preoccupation with the erotic and the unusual. A direct descendant of the twelfth-century Austrian von Strauss family – and with a mother of Polish origin – Willy proudly displays the family coat of arms on his office wall.

After an apprenticeship as a barrack-room 'Mr Fixit' during military service in the Danish army, Strauss started selling porn in 1961, shortly after his release. 'There was plenty of business and I made lots of money because it was illegal until 1969. I started from two angles, a mail order company and a shop.'

Although it helped profits, mere price-boosting illegality was insufficient for Strauss. Even in those days he wanted to take things to extremes. 'Most dealers in Copenhagen showed one kind of pornography,' says Strauss. 'I saw very early that there was only one thing better than normal pornography and that was bizarre pornography, speciality pornography. So in the first years I already had all the different kinds – spanking, bondage, bizarre, rubber, animals (but there was not much material for this). In 1971 I was the first to produce children magazines, at least with pictures.'

Strauss's boast is probably well founded – certainly as far as the modern era of pornography is concerned. His entry into child pornography was perhaps an inevitable consequence of his earlier decision to specialize in the bizarre. But it was also opportunist. 'It all started,' he recalls, 'when an old man – a Danish guy – walked into the shop and said he had these pictures. He was a customer, I recognized him. He called himself "Mr Skol". He gave me the pictures [of a man and a young girl having sex] and asked if I could use them. At first I did nothing with them because I didn't believe in the idea from the beginning – there hadn't been any children pornography made before.'

Strauss took the material anyway and placed it in a drawer of his desk. The opportunity to turn the photoset into a business proposition did not arise until a few weeks later when his printer called him. One of his other customers – a magazine publisher – couldn't pay his bills and, as a result, the printer had a lot of paper in stock which Strauss was offered for a special price. 'So I put the child porn pictures together and said:, "OK, let's make a magazine". We printed the first 10,000 copies. It was the first child-sex magazine in the whole world: *Bambina Sex*. I sold those

10,000 copies on the telephone to other porn dealers in two hours and ordered another printing. By the end of the week, I'd sold 19,000. My costs were 67 øre each one [about 7p or a dime at that time]. I never saw Skol again.'

The £20,000 ($30,000) instant profit from *Bambina Sex No. 1* was a clear indicator of the scale of the market for such material. Strauss immediately planned new issues and new titles. But he needed sources to supply the photographs. 'I got all the pictures from outside, most of them from amateurs. In this business you will find very often people will come to you. For instance, it's very normal here that a widow will come into the shop and say "My husband has died and I found some photographs." She's very embarrassed. "He collected these." For some reason they don't want to throw the photographs out. So either they give them away free or they ask if there's any money in it. As far as I know, if you make some pictures, you enjoy them yourself for a short time, but it's not enough, you want others to see the pictures. So this Mr Skol – or whatever his name was – wanted other people to see his artistic work.'

By that time Strauss was already a ten-year veteran of the trade and had the contacts needed to make an easy sale. Porn dealers throughout Europe already knew him for another notorious magazine: 'The first big mag was *Sadio*. It included the most bizarre things you could print – everything! It was sold everywhere. You'd be surprised, for instance, at the people in Germany. They have a strange mentality; they wanted children, animals and so on, very hard material. In America it's big bosoms and high heels.'[2]

No matter how unusual the material, Willy Strauss never shied away from putting his real name and address into the 'house furniture' of his publications. 'No one had published such things – and it's not the easiest kind of material to put into a magazine,' one of Strauss's associates observed. 'But Strauss put his name and address in these things! So you could imagine after a week or two what sort of result there would be. People sent letters from all over the world and it was always the same thing – new material!'[3]

Strauss confirmed the story: 'I think I made another forty or fifty magazines from the stuff people sent in. It wasn't from professional photographers and I just kept printing it.' *Bambina Sex* and *Lolita Sex* were published as series, but most of the magazines were special issues with titles suggested by the material: 'One day he got some pictures with a girl and a boy and he made a magazine called *Loona and Paul* and another he called *Anna and her Father*. It was a normal kind of business.'[4] Happy to be convinced that if this 'normal kind of business' was legally acceptable, it was also morally acceptable, Willy and his wife Leila became one of the world's biggest sources of commercial child pornography.

Later rather than sooner, the Danes saw the unsavoury side-effects of an across-the-board liberalization of censorship laws: 'Around 1980 they changed the law and it's now strictly forbidden,' says Strauss with a resigned shrug. Copenhagen's retailers themselves were the major cause of the change. 'There were porn shops on Strøget [the pedestrian street] and mothers would walk there with their children and see the magazines in the windows and would make complaints. It was ten years of completely free market before anyone did anything.'

The law might have changed, but Strauss didn't. He had flouted the legislation for most of the 1960s and now it looked as though the 1980s would be just like old times: 'The day after they made it illegal, all the child porn went under the counter and the prices went up ten times. We all started making lots of money again.'[5] But not without the renewed attention of the Copenhagen *politi*: 'When the police first came I put away one magazine of each – I thought that would be nice. But they came again and said this is against the law and they took all the rest of the mags.' Willy Strauss was fined $600 in 1983 after police confiscated more than 10,000 magazines, video tapes and playing cards involving child pornography from his firm. So now Strauss has no child pornography left at all? He grins and waves a hand tattooed with a five-pointed star, then feigns to search the bottom drawer of the big desk. 'Well, maybe I have . . . There will always be a few, people still have them and they buy and sell them. There is still an under-the-counter market here in Copenhagen.'[6]

NBC's *The Silent Shame* was broadcast simultaneously in Denmark and Strauss received another visit from the police. The fact that Nykanen's entrapment appears to be an infringement of Strauss's civil rights did not help the police prosecute the case. But the adverse publicity was enough to encourage Strauss to lie low for a while. Not for very long, however. Ejgl Hall remembers being called to Strauss's office in summer 1986. Spread across the desk was the manuscript in Danish for a story about child sex and a set of ten original drawings showing young girls. They were mostly nude poses, but the most explicit of them showed a pre-pubescent girl sitting on a toilet seat. She is naked, one wrist chained to an ankle as she performs fellatio on a man who is holding her head. Semen is dripping from the penis.

'I said to him, "God in heaven! It is forbidden! No!"' Hall warned him. 'You can write anything you want – but those illustrations . . . I said, "Willy, you'd better call your lawyer before you do it!" A few days later he received a letter from his lawyer saying it's not forbidden! You can do whatever you want in drawings! Yes, it's not forbidden.'[7]

*Lolita Slavinder*,[8] the outcome of that project, soon had its own special window display in Blue Movie and was selling well at Kr58 (around £10 or $15) for the 125-page paperback. Strauss insists he had been confident about the project from the beginning: 'I've been in court twice and I should know the rules . . .' He stimulated the sales drive by telling Denmark's *Ekstra Bladet* tabloid that 'I, Willy Strauss, am the man who has been in court most times for doing pornography with children *and I'm doing it again!* I'll sell a lot – I'll print 10,000, and that's a lot of books in

Denmark. They've tried for twenty-two years to get me, the police. But they can't.'[9]

Hans Christian Andersen would scarcely have approved of Willy Strauss. 'His nice, old mother still likes to believe that he's a nice boy. She comes round with soup and she thinks he does no wrong,' says Ejgl Hall. 'If it were my mother, she would turn in her grave. It really doesn't matter for Willy. I cannot agree all the time that he's doing the right thing. I can say, well, that's fine, that's you, but *I* wouldn't do it.'[10]

Hans Heesters walks across to the 'poison cupboard'. It's the size of a wardrobe and it takes up an entire corner of his office at Overtum 43 in Amsterdam. Heesters is head of Amsterdam City Police's Youth Moral Welfare Bureau. His cupboard contains shelves packed with files. He selects one at random and as he flicks the pages of methodically ordered photo magazines, says with quiet indignation, 'You are looking at pictures which are evidence of a crime being committed.' The magazines he has filed are all child pornography – going back as much as a decade, from Denmark, Holland, Belgium, Italy and France. Some of it depicts heterosexual encounters, some of it is gay male. It is not always possible to tell if the girls in the photographs are fourteen, fifteen, sixteen or eighteen. In the case of the teenage boys it is equally difficult, though some of them are simply portraits, while others show scenes of mutual masturbation. The line between artistic poses and a criminal offence could be difficult to define. Nor is it always possible to identify a printer or publisher.[11]

In late November 1984 hearings of the US Senate Permanent Sub-Committee on Investigations, chaired by Senator Roth, were held in Washington DC on the question of child pornography and paedophilia. Serious allegations were made about Holland. Witnesses testified that it was, with Denmark, the source of 85 per cent of child pornography coming into the United States.

Similar allegations had been rumbling around Capitol Hill since the hearing of evidence a year before, prior to the passage of the Child Protection Act which came into force in April 1984. Indeed, it was in the wake of these earlier allegations that NBC had sent its team out on the trail of Willy Strauss.

At the Roth Sub-Committee hearings on 29 November 1984 Commissioner William von Raab, head of US Customs, described Amsterdam in evidence as 'the 1984 equivalent of Sodom and Gomorrah',[12] a remark which was of course widely picked up in the press. Such a biblical and public dressing-down did not please the Dutch authorities and they decided to look into the US claims.

A Dutch Ministry of Justice working party was set up to investigate the complaints from over the Atlantic. Its brief was to correlate all the information it could find about the import, distribution or export of child pornography centred in the Netherlands and to pinpoint the sources and destinations of any that had been seized. National police, municipal police and detectives collaborated with the public prosecutor's office to produce in August 1986 a report on child pornography which was duly presented to the Minister of Justice.

The working group found that there was no evidence to show that child pornography continued to be produced commercially in Holland, or that there was any organized system of distribution, either domestically or for export. Child pornography may have been readily available up to 1984, but was now to be found only sporadically where a newly adopted Dutch law was not being firmly implemented.

The new law, introduced during 1985, amended the Dutch Criminal Code, making it an offence punishable by a fine or up to three months' imprisonment to publish any form of picture involving sexual acts with anybody under the age of sixteen – the age of sexual consent in Holland.

Most of the child pornography found was of Danish or Dutch origin and an appreciable amount had gone to

Holland from Germany in previous years, though this was now declining. A similar stock was dumped on the Dutch market in the late 1970s by Peter Theander when he decided to stop publishing the material but was unwilling to pulp his remaining inventory.[13] Generally, the report judged, it was 'amateurish material . . . made by child abusers for private purposes [but] which has gradually found its way into the commercial circuit'.[14]

Heesters was a member of the working group. In 1985, during his spell with the group, he was seconded to an FBI course in the United States. At the FBI school in Quantico, Virginia, he heard chief instructor Kenneth Lanning's views on the subject of child abuse, paedophilia and child pornography, a subject he had studied for many years. 'What Lanning told us,' Heesters recalled, 'was extremely interesting and has been very helpful in our work here, particularly his insights into the way child-abusers collect and disseminate child pornography. When we go on house searches now, we know what to look for. But one thing he said took me by surprise: according to him, 70 per cent of the child pornography in the United States originates in the United States with individuals. It gets sent to Europe to be made up into magazines and is recycled back to the States to cover the big demand for the material there. The problem is an American one – it starts there, not with us.'[15]

This revelation placed the dramatic pronouncements of Customs Commissioner von Raab in a somewhat different light. A senior Justice Ministry official put the Dutch approach in an informal perspective: 'The Dutch have always been a trading nation. Whatever commodity can be sold on to the customer the Dutch will trade. That is how we have survived for centuries.'[16]

Seventy per cent of the material seized in Holland came from Denmark, but the working group also redressed the balance sheet a little when it admitted: 'In particular, the *Lolita* series of booklets have given the Netherlands a bad name and still crop up frequently when material is seized, even though they have been out of print for several years. It should be noted that not everything published under the name *Lolita* has been printed in the Netherlands; much of it is of unmistakable foreign origin. In all, the working group came across six [Dutch] firms that were probably concerned in the past with the printing and publication of child pornography booklets. Inquiries revealed that all these firms had ceased their activities, most of them apparently some years ago on commercial grounds.'[17]

Aware of the criticism emanating from Washington, the Dutch authorities had instructed their police as early as June 1984 to visit known pornography outlets. It was a form of pre-emptive strike, anticipating by some months the coming reinforcement of the Dutch law on child pornography, but the police operation seemed to have the desired effect. Renus Rijk, a senior detective inspector in the Dutch State Investigation Service (CRI) at The Hague, says:

> We used all the powers we could at that time to gain some intelligence on this matter. We checked a lot of shops. We pressed, more or less, the people in the shops to stop selling child pornography. We said 'We will arrest you if you continue with it, because it's forbidden and we won't allow you to have it. We will be very strict in future.' And they said 'Well, it's only 1 per cent of our turnover and we don't like to have problems with the police. It's not big business for us, so we will stop it.'
>
> This was just in Amsterdam. We checked again after a few months and there was hardly any child pornography found on the shelves. We checked several times at several places in the Netherlands and hardly any child pornography is to be found at the moment. I realize there will be a couple of books in the porn shops showing child pornography, but it's hidden now.
>
> Now we have a new law and we can act against them. But I think it's not necessary to do that because if we warn people, they will co-operate. Well, there will be some

people who will have stock somewhere and send out child pornography all over the world. But in the meantime, since we started, we have seized three or four big stocks of child pornography. What we seized was very old material. I used to work in the vice squad in Rotterdam nearly twenty years ago and the seizures then, in the 1970s, were the same books, the same pictures, as are being seized now.[18]

Dutch porn distributors were the first to feel the pressure of genuine concern on the part of their politicians and police on the issue of child pornography. It took a little longer before co-ordinated efforts were made to locate and close down some of the identifiable child porn producers operating out of northern Europe. The Americans had already made a declaration of serious intent by setting up an inter-agency task force, in December 1984, to combat child pornography both within the country and abroad. Only a few weeks after it was set up, in mid-January 1985, a high-powered delegation from the US task force visited Europe to urge concerted action against the publishers of child-porn magazines. Representing US Customs on the delegation, which visited Holland, Sweden, and Denmark, were Special Agent Jack O'Malley from Chicago and his colleague John Forbes, at that time attached to the United States Embassy in Bonn, West Germany.

But despite this pooling of international resources, the man notorious for his *Lolita* magazines had already given Dutch police the slip. Based for many years in Dordrecht, outside Rotterdam, Joop Wilhelmus was a child pornographer of international repute. He had founded *Lolita* in the 1970s, using material provided by 'enthusiasts' and had brought out the magazine almost on a monthly basis. Latterly he had bought some of his material from Manit Thamaree in Bangkok. In the face of growing pressure from law enforcement agencies in a number of countries, Wilhelmus had managed nevertheless to keep his business going, soliciting enough of the pictorial material he needed to get as far as issue No. 55 of *Lolita* in 1984. At that point, perhaps because of a trade tip-off or trusting to the natural judgement which had kept him ahead of the law for so long, he crossed the border into Belgium and disappeared from view.

During 1985 the Dutch authorities began to post some successes. But one problem which held them up was the need for specific evidence against Dutch citizens obtained by their US counterparts. Renus Rijk says:

> The Americans blamed us for having sent a lot of pornography to the United States and we asked for evidence. Now and then there are seizures of child pornography in the mail checks at Kennedy Airport and other places. It comes from the Netherlands, that is shown by the postmarks and stamps on the envelopes. But we checked the addresses and so on and the senders were all fake. They gave us a lot of names and addresses and 95 per cent of them were fake.[19]

That was partly explicable, in Rijk's view, by the fact that American visitors to Holland were mailing back child pornography to their home addresses, using false senders' names as cover. But another explanation was disclosed during the Dutch inquiries – the 'post-box route'.

The post-box route out of Holland was discovered after a series of events which began at an apartment on Excelsior Boulevard, East Hopkins, in the Midwest state of Minnesota, USA.[20] At 11 a.m. on 30 January 1985 a small team of US customs and postal inspection officers carried out what is known as a 'controlled delivery' of a package to the address of Jeffrey Michael Abts. The parcel they delivered contained items of child pornography, posted in Holland, which had initially been spotted at the international mail inspection office at Chicago's O'Hare Airport: a copy of *Lolita* No. 50 and an 8 mm film entitled *Incest*. For the offence of receiving Abts would later incur an $800 fine and a suspended prison sentence.

But a search of his home turned up evidence which allowed US investigators to piece together a paper trail leading back to Europe, for Abts had paid by cheque for many of his illegal orders. His bank in nearby St Paul, Minnesota, had, as banks regularly do, returned the cleared cheques stamped with full details of the accounts into which they had been paid. The used cheques led to the account of a firm called BF Verlag (BF Publishing) at a savings bank in the small West German town of Altenkirchen.

The Dutch police, meanwhile, had been making their own inquiries into another address in the notebook of Manit Thamaree: PO Box 1604, Venlo. They discovered that the post office box was registered in the name of a Lothar Gresens, who gave an address in Cologne. Their follow-up query bounced back to the German police. Did they know a Lothar Gresens? In Cologne, the name rang a bell with one of the older detectives – this was a forty-one-year-old West German small-time counterfeiter known locally as 'Lothar die Ratte' – 'the Rat'.

The telephone lines between Cologne and The Hague busied themselves briefly. Before long the local police in the small Dutch town of Venlo on the border with West Germany came up with the answer to a question which had been puzzling their superiors: in a lock-up garage. The garage was rented by Gresens and it contained stocks of child pornography similar to the items seized by US Customs in Minnesota. Gresens was using the Venlo post office box address as a trading 'drop'. Each week he would travel over from Germany to collect orders and payments from it. He packaged the orders up from his stock at the lock-up and posted them in Holland to their various destinations. He took the cheques back with him and paid them into BF Verlag account number 57351030 at the Kreissparkasse bank in Altenkirchen.

'Lothar die Ratte' could not be found at the Cologne address which he had given to the Venlo post office, but he was soon apprehended by German police at his latest address in the town of Mudenbach. Though BF Verlag ceased its operations with his arrest, making specific child-pornography trading-charges stick proved more difficult and when Gresens was eventually remanded in Altenkirchen district court, it was on a specimen charge of possessing counterfeit goods.

The American challenge had been laid down and the Dutch had responded. Honour was to a certain extent satisfied but the European view of the issue may have earned greater currency in America if the Dutch working group's report had been more widely read. Certainly as late as April 1987 – six months after its publication in English – copies had not been passed from US Customs headquarters to the heads of at least two regional task forces concerned with child pornography. And one of these senior officers had been a member of the top US delegation which had done so much to forge close links between investigators on both sides of the Atlantic. In The Hague, Renus Rijk appraised the situation in a characteristically thoughtful way:

> I think in the Netherlands, since the 1970s, the police were not making any investigations of pornography. So, if some countries are blaming you, then you have to investigate, to see what's true, what's really happening. We did, and we found out that it's not a big problem. The thing is, you can only produce child pornography by abusing children. And you have to stop that! And that's our main concern. Not the sending out of books, but production.[21]

Reviewing the results of its researches, the Dutch Working Group on Child Pornography made a revealing point: '[We] increasingly came to suspect that there is a stock of child pornography in the various countries, possibly supplemented by illegal reprints. There is probably no such thing as a "porn mountain"; instead it is more likely that small caches are held here and there, from which material is either released on a small scale by mail order or supplied in larger batches.'[22]

So there is a historical dimension to the present situation, and even a large legitimate producer of mainly mainstream pornography like Rodox in Copenhagen has offered a hostage to fortune by dabbling in an area it could have afforded to ignore commercially. Rupert James admits:

> Yes, we did publish a couple of child porn mags in the mid-1970s. We also did animal sex – mags and films. I suppose we must have started about 1974 or so and it was all over by 1978. One of them was called *Children Love* – I think that was the first – and it went to about thirty issues. The original idea was that everybody else was doing it . . . and in any case, it was supposed to be the softer, affectionate kind of child sex – not rape and brutality and that kind of thing.
>
> Why did we stop? Well, we didn't like the nature of the material which was coming in. Originally we were publishing stuff mostly from the enthusiasts. But, of course, we were publishing it commercially as was everyone else at that time. That encouraged people to actually make the photos and films commercially. That meant we were commercially encouraging the abuse of children. That couldn't go on.
>
> In my opinion we shouldn't have started. That was irresponsible. And we still have problems as a result. For example, the French customs and police always give us a bad time because we are down in their files as child pornographers. They don't listen when we say that all that stopped a long time ago, they don't care.[23]

A company like Rodox could hardly afford to ignore the change in Danish law when the Child Pornography Act came into effect on 1 July 1980. As the Dutch porn distributors were quick to recognize when the official crackdown came in their country a few years later, you do not jeopardize an entire business for the sake of one small sector amounting to perhaps 1 per cent of turnover. Even if Rodox had suffered an attack of moral scruples before mid-1980, it would certainly have been in trouble once the new law came into force if it continued to publish magazines now deemed illegal in Denmark.

There was however a complication, of which Rupert James, who only started his job at Rodox in 1979, could not have been aware. A French employee of the company, Joël Bouillé, appears to have been involved in unsanctioned exchanges of child pornography with an organization called Chick Production Establishment with a business address in Liechtenstein but a contact address in Dordrecht, Holland. Letters written in 1978 and produced in evidence to the Roth Sub-Committee in Washington demonstrated quite clearly that Bouillé had offered to exchange 'our two magazines dedicated to paedophilia' in return for original child-sex photographs.[24]

A Joël Bouillé also features in the address book of Manit Thamaree as contact number 95 with a mailbox number at Vesterbrogade 208 in Copenhagen.[25] Next to his name, Manit had noted at least one sale of pictures of under-age girls. Press photographs taken shortly after Manit's 1985 arrest in Bangkok prove that he had been in possession of copies of the discontinued Rodox publication *Children Love*, suggesting that Bouillé may have offered the Thai pornographer a similar trade to the one he had offered to Chick in Holland in 1978.[26]

The widely respected Danish criminologist Berl Kutchinsky put the case for the defence of his country's reputation in an academic paper published in 1985: 'Even before the final adoption of the Child Pornography Act,' Kutchinsky wrote, 'production had stopped and all child pornography disappeared from the shelves of porno shops. Some under-the-counter sale of old stock occurs in a few places at exorbitant prices ($60 for a magazine which originally cost $6 is not unusual). This prompt and radical reaction can be seen as further evidence that the material is demanded by a small but highly motivated group. No evidence exists of any illegal production of new magazines, nor is such a production likely to occur at least for some years, because there seems to be sufficient material left over from the period before 1980 to supply the small black market. ("Old" paedophiles have obviously accumulated collections of child pornography before it was forbidden.) After the Act went into effect . . . only two cases are known in which persons have been punished with fines for having sold child pornography, while a small number of films and magazines were confiscated.'[27]

But where Rodox and the bigger names have agreed to the legal changes without demur, lone operators like Willy Strauss can be relied on to push the limits as far as possible. He is ready to make a new foray into the US market for child pornography with an English language version of his book *Lolita Slavinder*. But this time it will arrive from an unexpected direction.[28]

Meanwhile, the United States had set up a full-scale commission of inquiry into the entire pornography industry. It was established on 22 February 1985 and, on 20 May that year, Attorney-General Ed Meese announced its membership. After a year's public hearings around the country and some deliberation the Commission duly delivered its conclusions in two massive volumes which are generally known as the Meese Report.[29] In November, only months after the Meese Report came out, the Department of Justice established the National Obscenity Enforcement Unit in Washington DC. The new unit, comprising a law centre and a task force, was headed by Robert Showers, Special Assistant to the Attorney-General. It started work in April 1987. Showers described how his team now has 'a national strategy to go at a $6–8 billion-dollar industry'.[30] Expounding his views on their task, Showers defined what he saw as the problem:

> This industry is responsible for abusing thousands of American women and children every year. Pornography exists because laws at the local, state and federal levels are not being enforced. The NOEU will perform an education function to the American people. It is a parallel with drugs. We have to interdict, but education will deal with consumption. They do not recognize the problem. When people recognize the problem, they will see the ramifications of the industry.

He went on to outline the solutions as he saw them:

> We will be relying on citizen groups who will sponsor briefing sessions throughout the country. RAAP, for example: the Religious Alliance Against Pornography. This is a new non-denominational group which we think will do a good job. We will provide them with the facts. We are going to publish a more digestible version of the Attorney-General's Commission Report. We will put it in more understandable language, in layman's terms. One of our problems was that there was no proper media coverage of the Meese Commission.

Showers's unit intends to gather together specialists from all over the country; attorneys, experts in RICOs (Racketeer-Influenced Criminal Organizations) and in child pornography. It will be involved in operations and intends to start taking the initiative. It will be targeting the *people* who violate the law, not necessarily organized crime figures, but anyone involved in the large-scale distribution of obscene material. Showers continued:

> The President, has elevated obscenity and child pornography to a major issue to be addressed by his administration. The eradication of all child pornography and the removal of hard-core obscenity from the open market are two of our top seven targeted problems. It is our purpose to bring down the organizations who distribute this material.

Showers is certain that they can achieve their ambitious goals without any major changes in US federal law and before the end of the Reagan administration.

The industry is well practised at fighting its battles all the way to the highest court in the United States. This is an expensive and time-consuming business which even one of the main beneficiaries of the process, lawyer John Weston, ridicules: 'Ultimately, the outcome of the conflict cannot be known until at least five of nine justices of the US Supreme Court have agreed on the outcome of a particular case. It is a bizarre and inexplicable rite, and one, given the demonstrated widespread consumer tolerance of and participation in the consumption of "adult" materials, whose justification is frankly unfathomable.'[31]

Untutored in the possible consequences the Washington-sponsored clamp-down might have for him, Roland Scherer in Germany opened his morning mail. He could not believe his luck: any letter postmarked Oak Park, Illinois, had to be from Sheila. Folded inside the letter was an American Airline ticket and a computer-printed itinerary. He looked at the travel directions first: leave Frankfurt airport, 20 January 1987 at 11.05 a.m. on Flight 83, arriving at Chicago O'Hare at 1.35 p.m. the same day. Return about two weeks later on 10 February. Sheila's frequent-traveller ticket was worth $667.10, so she must be eager to meet him, he thought.[32]

The letter was written on the guest stationery of the Sheraton-Stockholm Hotel. Sheila collected hotel letterheads during her travels all over the world and wrote letters to her friends on them. This one was dated 7 January 1987 and confirmed the flight details before asking: 'Can you do me a favour before you leave Germany? Please write letters of introduction to the distributors whose names you gave me and tell them it's OK to do business with me. I'd like to order right away. I'm looking forward to seeing you when you arrive in Chicago. Have a good trip.'

Sheila was the owner of a Chicago porn shop and was

very interested in child pornography. The dealers he had given her were Interlibro in Amsterdam, LHL Ferienhaus in Krusau, Denmark, and both offices of MO Caprice in Rotterdam and Copenhagen. Scherer had started dealing in pornography the year before he began his three years of study at the nearby University of Frankfurt. His first enthusiasms had been writing to pen-pals throughout the world and collecting stamps. This soon graduated to pornography – especially animal and child pornography – and swapping the photographs he took of himself masturbating and having sex with Ute Eckhardt, his girlfriend.[33]

The hobby developed into a business, especially when he found that, as the material was harder to obtain, the prices went up. He could buy child-porn magazines like the *Lolita* series for between $6 and $9 and sell them for twice as much. The 8mm films could be bought for $30 and sold for $50. He would do everything himself, mail out leaflets printed on his Apple II personal computer, process orders and dispatch the goods. Throughout the world he had built up a clientele of about fifty regular customers. It was not big money, but it covered the cost of his personal interest in the material.

Sheila was only one of a dozen American customers for the magazines and films, the best of whom was the notorious child-sex enthusiast Jeannie Alexander (who turned out to be a man). This 'woman' who seemed so willing to offer her young daughters to friends and acquaintances had bought nearly a hundred parcels of material from him. Sheila was not such an avid buyer – after all, she was in the trade herself. In response to her first order in September 1985, he had sent her a copy of *Lolita* No. 55 and then *Children Love* 25, *Nymph Lover* 6 and *Fucking Children* the following month. Scherer sent an 8mm film called *Children's Sex Orgy* as a separate package.

But there was to be a downturn in prospects for the bearded young German. In December 1985 German customs officers turned up at his house in Bensheim-Auerbach with a search warrant and seized his small stock of a hundred items of child pornography, thereby putting him out of business. He was later fined DM10,000 (£3,400).[34] That was the end of Roland Scherer's cottage industry, mail order pornography business. Except for Sheila.

With her there was another dimension: sex. As long ago as January 1986 she had first suggested that he visit her in America. But he had his obligatory military service to fill in the summer and, having paid the fine, money was very short. If he really could help Sheila to find child-porn suppliers, there might be both money and sex as a reward. In October the American woman had written again – this time on the stationery of the Imperial Hotel in Bangkok – begging for information about a supplier in Wiesbaden near where he lived, and suggesting an exchange of photographs.

Scherer replied by return saying that the Wiesbaden wholesaler (Georg Schmitt's ZBF) dealt only in legal material depicting young people: *Teenage Sex, Teenager, Schoolgirls, Sweet Little 16, Fifteen, Teenager in Action, Thai Lolitas* and *Schulmädchen*, none of it of any interest to real child-sex enthusiasts. With the unhelpful letter he enclosed a photocopy of a set of polaroid pictures of himself in various nude and masturbatory poses.[35]

Sheila's reply, on the letterhead of the Royal Holiday Inn in Singapore, included a photograph of herself. She was a stunning blonde wearing a low-cut dress. The letter said she had an airline coupon entitling her to a free round trip anywhere American Airlines fly and she was prepared to let him use it, but it expired in February 1987. 'I am sending you one of my modelling photos which is pretty good,' Sheila's letter continued. 'I hope you enjoy it (and it makes your cock hard). When you visit me I plan to give your cock a good workout. Can you give me the name of the dealer in the Netherlands? I would very much like to have an outlet to purchase the *Lolita* mags because they are in such demand!'

It was an excited Roland Scherer who wrote back the same day agreeing to visit her in January and listing all his Danish and Dutch suppliers. After a long and agonizing wait over Christmas and the New Year her letter arrived with the promised ticket. The 20 January departure was uneventful and the young German enjoyed the attentions of the American Airline stewardesses. It was his first visit to the United States. In his suitcase he had an envelope containing gifts for Sheila. He had bought a dozen sexy pictures of children from Interlibro in Holland and also six photographs of Ute and himself in sexual action. The envelope was small and there would be no problems with customs.

The flight arrived on time and, after the usual delay being 'processed' by the immigration officials, Roland Scherer collected his baggage and, at 2.15 p.m., walked out into the arrivals hall and into the waiting arms of US Customs Special Agent Jack O'Malley and a posse of news and television cameramen.[36]

Scherer's case proved two things. There was still a residual stock of child pornography in the market place with dealers who would supply and distribute. More significantly, it was one more example of the hard-line 'proactive' approach being adopted by agents in the field. That in turn reflected the way child pornography had become a high-profile political issue among competing federal agencies in Washington DC.

In the fifteen years which have elapsed since *Deep Throat* played to packed US audiences from coast to coast, certain other issues have emerged against the broader background of the American pornography business, which have tended to redraw the boundaries within which it functions.

One such instance was the outcry over 'snuff movies'. Producer David Friedman recalls:

> Back in the 1970s, a guy who was the head of Campaign for Decency in Literature (which became the Campaign for

Decency Through the Law – CDL) was making one of his regular speeches on pornography when he suddenly came up with the allegation that the X-rated industry was torturing and killing performers on camera.

The Adult Film Association of America had not heard of such a case and promptly issued a statement disassociating itself and condemning such films. The next week the charge was repeated on a TV show: performers were supposedly being 'snuffed' out and the CDL had evidence to prove it. 'From that point onwards,' according to Friedman, 'these things were called "snuff movies".'[37]

'The AFAA', Friedman continued, 'called on the CDL to hand over the evidence to the authorities so that action could be taken. Nothing happened for a few weeks. I spoke to an FBI contact and asked him if the Bureau had been to see the CDL guy to collect the evidence so they could start a murder investigation. He said they hadn't and shrugged the matter off, saying that the guy at CDL was flakey.'

The matter died down for a while, until a film-maker called Alan Shackleton visited Friedman:

> He wanted to show me a movie. It was called *Snuff*. He had made this thing in response to all the publicity, figuring out that he could make some money out of the deal. He had bought a movie in Argentina and then added some footage to it showing mutilations faked in the same way as I'd done when we made films like *Blood Feast*. The whole thing was pretty awful.
>
> Anyway, I told him I thought the idea was crazy and it was the last thing that the industry needed to be associated with. I begged him not to release it.

There has been a number of unsubstantiated rumours that documentary footage exists showing real brutality and atrocities. It was allegedly shot by military torture teams in Chile, following Pinochet's coup, and also in Argentina during the Videla regime's so-called 'dirty war' against left-wing guerrillas. Other sources such as Honduras, Guatemala and Colombia have been suggested. There are strong grounds for believing that some very brief sequences of this extremely gruesome material were incorporated into a scene in one of the films in the unending *Emmanuelle* series, which are made in Europe. Other examples are said to have made their way to extreme right-wing groups in Italy.

Shackleton got a showing of his fictional 'snuff' film in Hollywood, though it was never shown in any porn theatre. The AFAA picketed the cinema:

> We went down and protested about the showing of the film, which we thought was in bad taste. Some cops from the LAPD's organized crime division came down to the theatre and asked us what we thought we were doing. We told them we didn't think the film should be shown and that it was bad for the X-rated industry.
>
> That brought the whole thing to media attention again, and I offered a reward of $25,000 to anyone who could come up with evidence that the industry had been killing performers on camera. $25,000. It still hasn't been collected and no one has been charged with murder.[38]

Bill Margold corroborates Friedman's version of the genesis of Shackleton's *Snuff*:

> Alan Shackleton imported the Argentinian film into the United States and then added some American footage. If you believe that people have rubber fingers and rubber throats then I guess they really did die. It was just something made to capitalize on a sensational situation. That's all it was. Nobody dies in those movies. They 'die' later on in the American footage and it's American performers. The Argentinian people are the only guerrillaesque-looking types running around.
>
> Some people are fully convinced that we kill our X-rated performers on a regular basis. There are just not enough people to do that. There are mail order films that

are supposedly available in the underground homosexual market that reputedly show some violence. Or murders. The movie *Snuff* which caused great outrage and uproar and recriminations was nothing more than a prefabrication of prosthetics and an Argentinian film all lumped together. It sure as hell caused an uproar because everyone swore that real things were happening.[39]

But the idea had become established in folk mythology that somewhere in the darker depths of the X-rated industry real 'snuff' movies were being made. The fact that some directors exploited this situation in the horror genre with hammy scenes featuring mock amputations and disembowellings did not help to dispel the 'snuff' mythology.

A more recent 'boundary dispute' blew up in April 1986. It centred on the age of a young American woman who began life as Nora Kuzma, passed through the centre pages of *Penthouse* magazine unclothed and began to appear shortly thereafter as Traci Lords, West Coast porn superstar. The only problem for everyone concerned with the making of her films was that she was well under the age of eighteen at the time.

On the face of it, that infringes the US Child Protection Act and constitutes a serious federal offence. The fact that the precocious Ms Lords had misled her various employers by using fake ID in the form of a driver's licence and a passport may not provide an adequate defence for a number of people who have recently been arrested. The irony of all this is that in Europe Traci Lords's films continue to be major revenue earners for the porn barons, since there the legal age of consent is in most cases sixteen. In America the industry is universally angry at what it sees as Traci Lords's money-spinning deception – she was enjoying a $15,000-a-day income.

Another boundary dispute arises as a consequence of the California law on 'pandering' – or procuring for prostitution. Regular attempts have been made down the years to apply pandering laws to the making of sexually explicit films on the grounds that the performers are paid to engage in sexual acts for money. Although this is a state-wide law, its enforcement varies from county to county and the industry there resolves the problem through the simple expediency of travel. What might be out of order in Orange County may be OK in Oakland.

Critic Robert Rimmer maps out the no-go areas for the American pornographer:

> Today, most adult film-makers do not produce films that transgress a 1980 memorandum from the Los Angeles City Attorney's office. The memorandum pinpointed . . . those films and tapes subject to arrest and prosecution. They included scenes of bestiality and masturbation of animals; so-called snuff films . . . and films or tapes showing sex with minors.
>
> The police may also try to censor films on tape that show urination (golden showers), defecation (Marquis de Sade style), or films showing pain or sado-masochistic abuse. However . . . there are many bondage-and-discipline films available on videotape. A few tapes even offer 'fist-fucking', in which an arm, foot or toe is inserted into a vagina; one such sequence appears in the original tapes of *Candystripers*, which were confiscated in a raid by the Los Angeles Police Department in March 1979. If you buy a videotape of *Candystripers* today, that scene has been eliminated.

The well-versed critic goes on to confirm that 'Such [activities] as anal sex, double insertions, orgies and various combinations of group sex are no longer subject to police raids. And, of course, in areas such as Los Angeles . . . as well as San Francisco and New York City, the visual portrayal of "normal" sex, i.e. oral and penile–vaginal sex and masturbation is no longer shocking.'[40]

While Rimmer's recipe for what passes as normal sexual conduct in the big cities might turn off or even disgust 'middle America', it is probably no longer shocking to most Americans to suggest that the Mafia, the Mob, La Cosa Nostra or any other 'organized crime' group has had a long-standing interest in the pornography business. Indeed, the charge that organized crime runs the US pornography industry is a constantly recurring theme in the wider debate on pornography. The assumption being that since the Mob controlled drugs and prostitution, it was only a small step to take over the porn industry which was seen as an offshoot of narcotics and vice.

Always eager to find legitimate and semi-legitimate ways of laundering illicit money, the Mafia families of the United States were quick to spot the high profit potential of the porn trade. Swallowing any initial moral qualms they may have had about the product, they concentrated on areas where they already had a traditional foothold: inter-state distribution and city-centre real estate.

The reluctance of established newspaper and magazine distributors to face the controversy associated with the trade gave figures like Robert 'Debe' DiBernardo the opportunity they were looking for. A leading member of New Jersey's DeCavalcante crime family, DiBernardo bought the New York firm Star Distributors Ltd in the late 1960s. At that time, Star specialized in pin-up magazines, but its new boss soon switched the product-line to hard-core material.

Operating out of a huge warehouse on Lafayette Street on the edge of New York's Little Italy, Star became so successful it was soon able to start a process of 'vertical integration' by buying film-processing laboratories, print shops and publishing firms. Eventually DiBernardo began to move a seemingly endless supply of money into the production of original material.

State and federal authorities believe that DiBernardo also had ultimate control of the $100 million, 200-company porn empire run out of Atlanta, Georgia, by Michael Thevis. During MIPORN, the most concerted federal effort to dent the power of the porn barons, in a telephone conversation monitored by the police, Thevis boasted of owning 90 per cent of the country's peep-show machines. 'Don't forget, Mike,' DiBernardo replied, 'you manage the machines. The family is in charge.'

In a 1978 landmark case in Washington DC, fifty-five-year-old Michael Zaffarano was charged with illegally moving obscene and pornographic materials across a state line. The materials in question were six films with such titles as *Anyone But My Husband* and *Linda Lovelace Meets Miss Jones*, for showing at his DC Playhouse theatre. In spite of the fact that the movies included bestiality and sadism, in addition to more conventional sexual encounters, the Washington jury agreed that two of the films were not obscene and were undecided about the others.

Zaffarano's background was almost as interesting as the case: before moving into the entertainment business, he had been a bodyguard for Godfather Joseph 'Joe Bananas' Bonanno and an associate of Mafia strong man Carmine Galante.

When FBI agents moved against the Mafia porn ring in the famous MIPORN sting in 1981, more than fifty-six men were detained throughout the United States. They included DiBernardo, Zaffarano and the Peraino brothers who had financed *Deep Throat*. It was all too much for Micky Zaffarano, who died of a heart attack within minutes of his arrest.

Cleveland porn baron Reuben Sturman was also targeted in the MIPORN operation but managed to evade federal prosecution until 1985 when a Grand Jury indicted him on tax evasion charges.

It has often been alleged that Sturman is a member of one of the Mafia organized crime families, or that his close association with DiBerdardo in New York confirm him as a 'made' member of the Mob. No evidence has ever been produced to verify this. FBI agents in the MIPORN sting did receive information suggesting that Sturman had paid off large sums to Cleveland organised crime syndicates and there seems little reason to doubt that, like many other US businessmen, he operates with Mafia blessing.

There is certainly ample opportunity for certain kinds of protection racket and laundering operations to move in on the US porn industry. As one observer notes:

> Much has been written, both true and false, about the financial backers and distributors who have made and are making millions in the porno film business. When [pioneer porn film director] Gerard Damiano was asked why he sold his ownership of *Deep Throat* for $25,000, he told reporters he couldn't talk about it. 'Do you want me to get both my legs broken?' he demanded.[41]

Senior members of the American porn scene do not deny long-term Mafia interest in their business, but do deny that it is more extensive today than in other spheres of life in the USA. They cite such other fields as trade unions, sport, gambling, real estate, the construction industry, road haulage and even politics. Producer David Friedman's experiences are typical:

> I represent the Chicago Mob in Los Angeles, according to the FBI. Boy, if that were the case, I'd be living in Bel Air and driving a stretch limousine. For ten years an FBI agent named Finney seemed to do nothing but watch me. I used to take him to lunch. He told me I was on the list of prime targets because I knew two guys who had vowels at the end of their names. Sure, I knew one of them, I used to stop off in his bar from work every night. But that was twenty-five years ago.
>
> I also knew Mike Thevis. After the war when I was Paramount's distributor in Atlanta I used to eat 65-cent 'blue plate specials' in the Ship Ahoy, his father's Greek restaurant. Mike was a bus boy and his sister minded the cash register. Then Mr Thevis put Mike in charge of a news-stand he owned. So that's how Mike Thevis got started.

> Come to that, I've also done business with Reuben Sturman. He is a very well-spoken, very polished gentleman. A very brilliant man.[42]

Bill Margold's reaction to accusations of Mob control is typically blunt and to the point; he retorts:

> There are only a finite number of major companies in the X-rated industry in America. There are lots of little people. But all the little people have sharks looming over them. And all the sharks have whales hanging over them. And all the whales sleep together. They all announce how viciously they hate each other but they all are buddies. So it's all controlled. It's like the juke-box industry in the old days. The distribution is all taken care of. But organization breeds profit.[43]

But Friedman does not take the issue of control so seriously and is dismissive of the idea of a 'grand conspiracy'; he insists:

> The whole idea of this industry being *organized* is so stupid. We are the most competitive people in the world. Naturally, we know one another. Naturally, if it becomes profitable, we will do business with one another. We will trade things off. It is true that we stake out territories, but the [conventional] film industry has done that for years.
>
> The FBI think that the American pornography business is one huge cartel. It's not. This is the last vestige of independent, rugged individualism.[44]

If the authorities are right in equating organized pornography with organized crime, then the corporate body that is the X-rated industry seems unable to shake off some of the parasites it attracts. Bootlegging – illegal copying – has become a major irritant.

Once pornography has become legal, its producers are entitled to the protection of law. Like all publishers and film producers, what concerns them most is the protection of their product through trademark and copyright legislation and international conventions. Their concern is well placed and it would seem that they are more vulnerable to the bootlegging of their material, magazines and videos, than their conventional counterparts.

Modern technology makes illicit copying easier than ever before. Video cassettes can simply be inserted in a VCR for unlawful production to begin. Colour magazines can be disassembled and placed before a process camera or digital scanner in order to make a fresh set of litho printing plates. In some cases the copy will be passed off as being the original, in other cases – including video – the material might be reassembled to form a new product, thus saving the bootlegger some, if not all, of his starting costs.

'Right now there is a lot of bootlegging in South America, especially Argentina and Brazil,' says Kent Wisell. 'And definitely in Italy. That I know for sure. It's awful! They take subscriptions to get a regular copy of the magazines. Then they get the photos out of it and come out with their own copies. Spain is also very bad.'[45] Wisell's remark about Spain was founded on bitter experience. For more than a year, the former sales manager of *Private* had been trying to establish himself as a pornography publisher with the photo-magazine titles *Q* and *Bohème* (see Chapter 4). During a March 1987 business visit to Spain, the burly Swede made a research trip into Las Ramblas, where most of Barcelona's sex shops are to be found. As he browsed the heavily-laden shelves, he was brought up with a start. He recalls:

> There in front of me was the next issue of *Bohème* – No. 2. The girl on the cover was Brigitte (see Chapter 3). He must have photographed the cover from *Q* No. 4 or from *Bohème* 1, because I hadn't published *Bohème* 2 yet. But *Bohème* 2 was going to be exactly that cover. I printed in *Q* 4 and *Bohème* 1 the cover of the next *Bohème* so people could look out for it.

> Even worse, inside is an ad for *Bohème* 3! He just took a picture from his new *Bohème*. The material is fully hard-core stuff bought from France, but with Spanish text. That's completely illegal, to just copy like that. He's using the name *Bohème* which is patented and registered. So it's a copyright infringement and a trademark infringement. Actually, the quality is not bad.
>
> It's good material. It could be worse! But I haven't been paid for it. He has used the name, which I own, the style, the logo, everything is there. He's even got my copyright message on it: 'Copyright Nordic Press. New Swedish Sex Magazine!' It also says 'Made in US', which is stupid. Someone was bootlegging the magazine faster than I could publish it![46]

It is usually difficult if not impossible to identify the source of bootlegged videos and magazines from the material itself, but the angry Wisell was determined to get to the bottom of the matter:

> I checked it with the reproduction company [process house] in Sweden and nothing had been sold, stolen or lost by them. They still had everything and the plates hadn't gone down to Spain yet.[47]

But Wisell speaks Spanish fluently and he interrogated the manager of the sex shop who was selling the illicit copies of *Bohème*. His line of questioning was persuasive:

> The guy who had been ripping off *Bohème* is named José Luis Avillada and his company is Jota Jota Ele in Valencia. Christ! I've met him God knows how many times! I had talked to him about distributing the magazines legitimately. He said that he was going to pay me, but he wasn't at all apologetic. Well, I will resolve the matter in one way or the other, there are lawyers who can take care of it.[48]

At Rodox in Copenhagen, Rupert James maintains two bulky case files on his most serious bootlegging problem.

One of them is stuffed with letters from England. An inch or so from the top is a typical one, neatly typed and with an Otley Road, Leeds, address at the top of the page. It reads:

11 May 1986

Dear Sirs,

I am familiar with your products but am extremely annoyed to find that counterfeit versions are still being sold at high prices in English shops. These are of course sold Cellophane-covered to prevent inspection when purchasing. I enclose part of a copy bought in Bradford. You will note that it is slightly smaller than the original but that a high-quality printing process has been used to copy your material. Inevitably, the contents are a mixture of incoherent rubbish. I hope that you will be able to take some action . . .

I obtained your address from a genuine copy of CC purchased in Amsterdam: the counterfeit magazine does not of course carry your address.

Yours,[49]

Private Lines is one of a national chain of sex shops in England. Its exterior has been fully boarded up to protect it from periodic attack by local feminist groups and there is no external indication of the nature of the business. Hand-drawn signs on the door proclaim a perennial 'Sale'. Strictly, Private Lines is not a licensed sex shop because the local authority denies such licences on the contradictory grounds that the premises are to be used as a sex shop.[50]

In order to avoid problems with the law, the shop stocks a general range of merchandise as a cover for a small range of what purports to be pornographic books and videos. The shop is a single room with separate display sections for magazines and videos. Taped to the front of the cash register was a dog-eared card reading 'All inquiries regarding refunds must be referred to head office. This does not affect your statutory rights.' No sex videos are on display and the sex magazines are hard to find. Visitors seem rare enough to warrant the immediate attention of the callow youth who seemed to be in charge of the shop: 'What can I do for you, squire?' This is all a long way from the comfortable style of Curth Hson-Nilson's Soho in Stockholm.

What appear to be hard-core photo-magazines are displayed in two flimsy cardboard boxes. Every magazine is tightly wrapped in Cellophane, making inspection impossible. Each publication is priced at £12, more than double the price of an equivalent product in the rest of Europe. A selection of 'packs of five mags' is also available for £35. These are machine shrink-wrapped, thus making it impossible to determine what is sandwiched between the two outer magazines.

At first sight it seems that a number of well-known European hard-core magazines are available. These include: Peter Theander's *Color Climax*, *Rodox*, and *Teenage Sex*; Hans Moser's *Foxy Lady* and *Sweet Little 16*; as well as *Ero*, *Busen*, *Fetish* and Berth Milton's *Private*. The shop manager is prepared to bargain over a bulk purchase, but makes some changes to the selection on the grounds that he wants to ensure that the customer has 'the latest of everything'.

Before cashing up the sale the manager produces two video cassettes from under the counter: 'They are very good, very strong. We are now offering *Color Climax* videos.' Both products are in standard black library boxes. The insert cards in the boxes are printed with the *Color Climax* logo, a title and a soft-core photograph. A glance inside one of the boxes reveals a black cassette confirming that it must be bootlegged – all Rodox video cassettes are made from purple plastic. The manager gives a receipt and says to bring it back when trading magazines in for new ones. He would show the customer 'some other, more interesting material'.

The following items were included in a typical purchase (according to the displayed front covers): *Blue Climax* 23, *Color Climax* 120, *Color Climax* 125, *Color Climax* (unnumbered), *Rodox* 22 (all Color Climax, Denmark); *Ero* 22

(Boksenter, Sweden); *Private* 70 (Private, Sweden), *Foxy Lady* Vol 3 No 11 (Verlag Teresa Orlovski, West Germany); and *Fetish* 8 and *Busen* 13 (both of uncertain, West German origin).

A more detailed examination of the magazines revealed the extent of a blatant and widespread fraud. For example, the cover of *Blue Climax* 23 describes it as 'An exclusive magazine from Color Climax Corporation'. The size of the item is a few millimetres smaller than a copy of an original *Blue Climax* 37 supplied by Color Climax (235×160mm instead of 240×170mm). It also has fewer pages (68 instead of 100). The weight of the paper used is much lighter and the print quality very poor.[51]

Page 2 (inside front cover) contains a black-and-white pin-up photograph of a blonde girl wearing leather gear. Page 3 is a full-colour 'contents page' showing one picture from each of four spreads. In the first a girl is apparently licking an erect penis over the caption 'The ultimate in "relaxing" massage'. The point of contact between the tongue and the end of the penis is obscured by a round white sticker 8mm in diameter on which has been handwritten '£12' (the price of the magazine).

Closer inspection shows that the 'sticker' is in fact part of the artwork and has been printed. In the second photograph, a blonde woman is holding a man's erect penis (over the caption 'Sexy tricks in a naughty nightclub'). In the third photograph, a man is performing cunnilingus on a woman balanced on the back of a second woman. This time, the point of contact has been blacked out in the artwork. The caption is 'Fast Eddie tries a call girl for size!'. In the final picture, a white man is apparently engaged in intercourse with a black woman (in the 'doggy position'). This has not been censored, but the sex organs are concealed by the bodies of the performers.

By comparison, pages 2 and 3 of the genuine *Blue Climax* 37 are very different.[52] The inside cover contains an advertisement for models with two photographs. The first shows a woman licking a man's penis (there is semen on her face) and the second a woman having sex with two men, one vaginally the other anally. The rest of the inside cover is taken up by the publisher's 'house furniture' which includes the names of the staff, the company's full name and address and a copyright notice. Page 3 is the contents page with more explicit photographs. None of the photographs is censored in any way.

The rest of this magazine and all the others purchased are after the same style: poor-quality reproductions of the genuine publications which have been censored and arbitrarily reassembled in such a way that they bear no resemblance to the original editions. Rupert James of Color Climax confirms that these counterfeits involve extensive infringement of Rodox Trading's registered trademarks and copyrights. There is one exception. The fake *Color Climax* 120 has a cover photograph which features a black model known as 'Long Dong Silver' who, as his name suggests, has a very long 18¼-inch penis. He is supposedly from Dagenham in Essex.

> Paul Raymond in London owns the rights to that picture set. I bought some of the photographs for one issue of *Color Climax* in November 1982 and paid £1,500 for them. So it is Raymond's copyright that is being ripped off.[53]

On the reverse cover of what pretends to be *Busen* 13 is a copyright notice. In French it reads:

> Tous droits réservés. Réproduction, même partielle, seulement avec l'autorisation de la maison d'édition.

However, the English translation is given with two key deletions as:

> All rights [deletion] on entire contents [deletion] may be reprinted in whole or in part without written permission of the publisher.

The counterfeiter has masked out the words 'reserved' and 'nothing' in order to reverse the meaning and intent of the message.

The bootlegged and censored magazines are also available by mail order direct from the publisher. A typical brochure in the form of a pre-printed letter over the signature of 'Gustav Milton' is posted to prospective customers. Part of the brochure reads:

> As it is an offence to send indecent literature through the post, this leaflet is without illustrations . . . [W]e would warn all potential customers that all the books, magazines and videos we sell contain graphic colour, close-up, photography.[54]

Recipients are invited to send their orders for *Private, Rodox* and *Pussycat* (among others) to Pirate Organization, 34 Upton Lane, Forest Gate, London E7 9LN. This address also appears frequently at the foot of advertisements (listing the Private and Private Line shops as retail outlets) in many British men's magazines.

It is also the address of a company called Conegate Ltd, the directors of which are registered at Companies House as David Sullivan, Cheryl Sullivan and Clive Sullivan. Cheryl and Clive are the wife and brother of David Sullivan, a long-established producer and distributor of low-quality soft-core magazines. His most recent publishing venture was the *Sunday Sport* newspaper, which took over the running of the tabloid *Daily Star* in September 1987.

Rupert James is only one of many European publishers incensed by the situation:

> Sullivan gets more and more impertinent as time goes by. In Europe we have no problems protecting our copyright. But in England we have tremendous problems. In 1980 I commissioned a top firm of English lawyers to look really thoroughly into Sullivan's activities and his business with a view to taking him to court for infringement of copyright. The advice we got from Lord Janner at that time was covered by a simple tenet: he who comes into litigation must come with clean hands. The judge would say

that it was like two burglars arguing over the swag.

In the UK we have a *Catch-22* situation. We decided to answer David Sullivan's advertising by doing some advertising of our own. The magazines [he advertises in] and their lawyers said 'We know Rodox really do sell the real thing and we'd have trouble with the law if we carried your ads – even if they were only saying that Sullivan wasn't selling the genuine magazines. However, we can accept Sullivan's bumf because we know it's not the real thing. Also it will have an enormous effect on our income if we drop his ads.' If you take *Fiesta*, for example, I don't know for certain what their full-colour page rate is, but I think it must be about £15,000. Considering Sullivan is taking twelve full-colour pages and about half a dozen black-and-white pages every year, it represents quite a lot of money.

That's annoying because Sullivan runs banner headlines claiming that he's got 50,000 Color Climax video tapes in stock. We don't produce 50,000 cassettes in a year, so God knows where he's getting them from. This guy has seen how stupid and inadequate the situation is in England and is taking full advantage of it to swindle people.[55]

Similar complaints are made in Sweden by Carl Delvert, sales manager of the real *Private*:

In England this 'Pirate Organization' is duplicating covers and inside it's only trash.

David Sullivan runs that operation. He even calls his shops 'Private'. There was a Royal Air Force officer who wrote to us to complain and I wrote back and said 'We are willing to pay for the bombs if you can bomb the damn place.' He really has the gall to call it a 'Milton Publication' and inside the editor is called 'Gustav Milton' and my boss's name is Berth Milton. This is not the real thing, none of it is.[56]

Understandably, Berth Milton objects to Sullivan's taking his name in vain: 'He is damaging my name and my reputation in England. The *Private* trademark, the logo, everything. These are all legally registered trademarks and copyright – in Sweden and also in Spain, which is an EEC country now. Inside, his magazines are just rubbish. Sullivan even invited me for lunch one day here. He has a flat in Marbella. But I don't meddle with people of his character. He also sends his spies over here to find out how I work. One English guy pretended that he was a photographer and so on. I just asked him some simple questions and it was clear that he was an agent for Mr Sullivan.[57]

Sullivan's company was properly constituted and registered in the UK at Companies House in London. The most recent annual returns for Conegate show a corporation tax payment of £400,000 in 1984. *Catch-22* it may be, but as the wheeler-dealer Milo Minderbinder in Joseph Heller's widely-acclaimed novel constantly declared of his surreal discount business in eggs: '*Everybody* makes a profit . . .' Except the British porn consumer, that is.

# 10

# *The Wide Blue Yonder: Pornography Tomorrow*

In 1987 Spain was still publicly celebrating its new-found freedoms. This was illustrated, in a way that sums up the modern porn scene, by an incident at a bar on the Costa del Sol. A young Spaniard had stopped by for a late-night drink on his way home. The Norwegian barmaid spotted a porn video cassette under his arm. It was called *Amores Profundos*[1] but had been dubbed from American English into Spanish. She asked to see the cassette and then insisted on playing it on the VCR behind the bar for the amusement of the jostling patrons – of both sexes and many nationalities. Only a middle-aged Englishwoman objected, but even she didn't leave.

Although the 'anti-smut' campaigners and the 'radical feminists' may have lost the legal battle against pornography, they are unlikely to give up the fight. But the prognosis for them is poor because the porn barons and the consumers have technology on their side.

Taking the United Kingdom as a case in point, Her Majesty's Customs – in spite of many well-publicized but ill-considered cases – have singularly failed to keep pornography out of the British Isles. Pornography is readily available in the UK to anyone prepared to exert the minimum of effort to find it. The managers of many of David Sullivan's Private Lines chain of sex shops are only too willing to make special arrangements for customers who object to being conned with bootlegged, censored and sloppy reproductions of *Private, Color Climax, Foxy Lady* and their stable-mate video programmes. More than a few managers of neighbourhood video libraries have a special under-the-counter stock for clients they know well enough.

But the major threat to outright prohibition lies not in the hands of junior-league, would-be porn barons, but in the living rooms of the consumers themselves. Such are the characteristics of even the most technologically modest VCR that two such machines in close proximity can form the basis of a start-up business enterprise which can make a small but significant contribution to the proliferation of pornography.

The source material is not difficult to come by. The temporary hiccup in English censorship laws in the early 1980s resulted in the immediate influx of at least 50,000 professionally made video cassettes into the UK from Scandinavia, Germany and the United States. Amateur bootlegging is common and if each of these tapes was duplicated twice (on average) and each of those copies replicated twice more, then at least 350,000 cassettes containing that imported material were in existence at some time or other.

The influx of cassettes did not stop with the change in law. Apart from the occasional tape which might be brought into the country by the many thousands of business travellers shuttling across the Channel and the North Sea, there are the millions of holidaymakers who eagerly depart every year for Spain and other sun-drenched destinations to the south where porn is an unexceptional and inexpensive commodity.

Porn retailers in those countries make a point of ensuring that British tourists are aware of their offerings and many choose the high-quality porn products of Berth Milton,

Peter Theander and Hans Moser in preference to another stuffed donkey, straw sombreros and bullfight posters. As they disembark back in the UK in the small hours of the morning from Thomson Holidays' wide-bodied Boeings they know there is only a slight chance of being stopped as they push their baggage-laden trolleys through the customs green channel. And if an enthusiastic revenue man does find a porn video, the worst that can happen is that he will confiscate it.

The reason why a customs officer will seize a video cassette while allowing quite a large amount of 'personal' porn magazines to go through is that he is well aware of its potential as the seed-corn for perhaps a hundred copies.

Strengthening customs controls will have little effect. Such controls could hardly be tighter than in the Soviet Union, but there is still plenty of pornography to be had in Moscow. For many years regular travellers across the Iron Curtain would risk taking pornographic films and, more recently, video cassettes into the Soviet Union and other Eastern bloc countries. At one time, a major channel was operated by Scandinavian diplomats who echoed the nineteenth-century activities of various British Foreign Office officials who used the diplomatic bag to ship porn from Paris to London.

Along with Western clothes such as tights and denim jeans these proved to be valuable gifts for business contacts with a taste for such things. A British resident of Moscow who regularly travels to the West used to smuggle porn as a matter of routine: 'I always used to try bringing something back in – even if it was soft core. Suddenly it was no longer worth the effort. The interest was still there, but it was being met by a new domestic industry based in the Republic of Georgia. The suppliers in Moscow are called *videonshchiki* – video pushers.'[2] The enterprising Georgians had acquired a Japanese home video camera and were shipping the results north to the more lucrative market of the Russian capital hidden inside trucks carrying fruit and vegetables.

Perhaps the most enthusiastic *videonshchik* was Herman Chernoivanov. After eighteen years of teaching concert piano at Moscow's famous Conservatory Herman developed a new, more profitable interest: pornography. So successful was he that his apartment soon became cluttered with video tape recorders, film projectors, cameras and cassettes. Tapes smuggled into the country by friends and foreigners were dubbed into Russian with the help of his twenty-year-old daughter and then copied for sale on the highly lucrative black market. Customers included shop managers and office clerks, salesmen, doctors, dentists, lawyers, engineers, tailors, restaurant managers, artists and fellow musicians. The cassettes even became a form of currency, good for clothing, car parts and gasoline.

Herman's downfall came in 1986 when he decided to get into the production of original material: an attractive music student he tried to recruit to star in one of his *œuvres* reported him to the authorities. The courts decided that Herman had taken sexual *glasnost* too far and sent him to a labour camp for four years.

Similar interest would seem to exist in the People's Republic of China. The scale may be small: in November 1983 the New China News Agency announced that customs officers had seized 23,000 obscene magazines, 142 video tapes and 15,000 cassettes in the first nine months of that year. But increased vigilance at ports of entry did not help. In June 1985 the Chinese government was forced to set new, increased fines of up to $17,600 for anyone caught smuggling porn into the country.

Even that did not do much good, and two years later an unfortunate Mr Liang Qingxiang, an office worker with the Shanghai Railway Administration, was sentenced to death for showing porn videos.[3] Perhaps even the most determined anti-porn campaigner would draw the line at capital punishment for offenders?

What limits video copying is the current analogue technology of magnetic recording which inevitably entails a loss of quality with each copy made: after five 'generations' (a copy of a copy) the graphic sexual detail resulting from Hans Moser's investment in the latest image-recording techniques becomes lost in a mush of fuzzy heaving and thrusting.

The next generation of video recording will be digital and the loss of quality associated with making copies will become imperceptible. These systems are now becoming prevalent in the professional video world and will be the established norm by the early 1990s. In the world of the domestic consumer, such methods have already been applied to sound with digital audio tape (DAT), a new form of audio cassette which is the subject of much controversy in the musical recording industry. The same advance will soon apply to video.

The physical cassette in which domestic video tapes are packaged is quite bulky. But, just as the music industry is in the throes of migrating from plastic analogue discs to high-quality digital compact discs (CD), video will go in the same direction. Both the West German porn producer Gerd Wasmund (Mike Hunter Video) and the Dutch electronics giant Philips – which pioneered it – would agree that the 'Laser-Vision' video disc system was a false start. Following a long tradition of pornographers being early to exploit new publishing technology, Wasmund was quick to transfer all his topselling sex films on to this *bildplatte* format: *Sex Maniacs, Sensations, Olympic Sex Fever, Las Vegas Maniacs* and three other titles. Only 3,000 of the players were sold in the UK (5,000 in Germany) compared with one million CD players (15 million worldwide) in a much shorter time.

Philips's September 1987 announcement of 'CD-Video' (CDV) confirms the company's commitment to a product design which is bound to succeed in the longer run. CDV discs are able to carry both high-fidelity sound and crisp video images on the same piece of silvered plastic. Each five-inch disc will be able to carry twenty minutes of audio and six minutes of PAL-standard video (five minutes of the American NTSC television standard). Of more interest to the porn industry is the eight-inch disc which will carry twenty minutes of video – the perfect length for one or two segments of old *Swedish Erotica* film-loop material. Twelve-inch discs will be able to carry one-hour programmes – for example the perennial *Deep Throat* cut by only two minutes. The system is likely to be successful, because Philips's £499 Combi player is able to interpret old Laservision discs and CDs as well as the new CDV discs.[4]

Research and development is already well advanced in the design of plastic 'credit cards' on which digital images can be recorded and optically scanned. The advent of such technology makes the policing of borders to weed out all forms of pornography impossible. Combined with digital video recording in the home, this breakthrough will make laws against the popular or commercial replication of pornography totally ineffective.

The phasing-in of high-speed digital telephone lines and computer-controlled exchanges will enable domestic subscribers with appropriate devices to transfer hard-core pornography over the national and international telephone network, should they wish. In case this sounds too far-fetched, there is already debate in the UK about the implication of satellite television broadcasting on censorship.

Some Westminster legislators are concerned that national laws will be ineffective against a broadcasting technology that is no respecter of national boundaries. Their concern could be well founded. Unless European satellite broadcast companies give undertakings to respect the television censorship laws of the British Isles, the 1990s could become the decade of *Porno sans Frontières* or *Porno ohne Grenzen* – 'Porn without Frontiers'. The likelihood of the rest of the continent falling into line with the British is slight – if only because of the constitutional implications for countries like Sweden and Spain.

A few cable television networks in France, Italy, Holland and the United States have already pointed the direction in which programming could go by including at least soft-core material as staple. In the Netherlands, one short-lived pirate television station even specialized in broadcasting non-stop hard-core videos.

It is a sign of the times that the major debate within the pornography industry centres around the issue of quality. Trends in pornography often reflect trends in the media at large.

In the United States, magazine publishing has rarely justified an entry in the annals of porn history. But in Europe the steady improvement in the quality of the visual depiction of sexual activity on paper is self-documenting. Not only has that superior quality been sustained, it has further improved in recent years, predominantly as a result of the concerted efforts of Hans Moser and Teresa Orlovski at VTO in Hanover. Competitors who have rested on their laurels since the early 1970s have already seen the writing on a wall generated by a Quantel graphics computer.

Video recording has brought pornography back in from the cold and dank 'shooting galleries' of America and the 'porn-kinos' of Europe to the warmth of the fireside VCR. But the change in economics that came with the change in technology forced the 'porn mills' of Los Angeles and New York drastically to reduce the quality of their output. It is significant however that in Germany, Mike Hunter's best-sellers are video versions of productions shot on film. Porn critics in America regularly vote the 35mm feature films of the 1970s as the best buy on cassette in preference to the 'shot on video' output of the 1980s. Film-makers like Gerard Damiano, Ron Sullivan (Henri Pachard), Alberto Ferro (Lasse Braun) and Alex deRenzy can still attract the largest fees even when they are recording explicit images directly on to tape.

It would be élitist to suggest that low-cost, low-quality pornography should not be 'shot on video' merely because the critics discern a marked lowering of standards. Commercial pornography should not be confused with erotic art. The up-market porn films of Ferro and Damiano may not yield the quick buck, but their audience stays loyal for much longer than it would for ephemera such as *Don't Get Them Wet!*

Whether consumer driven or demand driven, the market for pornography is growing – but it would be dangerous to make arbitrary extrapolations from the trends. There is a saturation point for the consumption of pornography in society, and it is certainly much less than 100 per cent of the population. Nobody would claim that everyone has a desire to be a regular consumer of pornography.

Indeed, the evidence from all those countries which have legalized pornography in the last twenty years suggests that after a year or two of artificially high sales levels and when transient curiosities have been satisfied, sales then decline and settle at a level which is more indicative of the true market demand. It would seem that for every person who buys or rents porn on a regular basis, there are at least another ten who saw it once and didn't bother again. This puts the lie to the suggestion that porn is in any way 'addictive' for the greater proportion of the human race – even if they could afford it.

So how does the market expand? Informed industry sources contend that the expansion rate is steady and unspectacular. It develops like this because, over the years since the process of legalization started in Scandinavia, new countries have come into the legitimate domain of the porn barons in time to compensate for the post-curiosity decline in markets which decriminalized the commodity some years previously. Once the Spanish, Italian and Greek markets have stabilized, the South American boom will be well under way and providing adequate compensation. When South America has become stable, perhaps Eastern bloc *glasnost* will extend to pornography?

The question of exploitation has come up time and time again in debates about pornography: are customers exploited by unscrupulous dealers and distributors; are performers equally exploited? Few adults involved in the pornography industry complain of being exploited – some do when they leave, but that might be part of a retrospective process of self-justification.

The relative absence of protest about the way the porn industry operates may be a reflection of the income levels and financial returns which can be gained from participation. It is, however, hard to believe that any woman from Sweden (where unemployment benefits can be as high as 75 per cent of previous salary) can be forced into pornography on financial grounds, though some pornographers claim to have noticed an increase in the number of British women doing hard-core modelling work since the surge in UK unemployment during the 1980s.

But there is a form of exploitation that goes beyond consenting adults making pornography for sale to consenting consumers.

Bangkok's night life for tourists is centred on Patpong Road, and is usually just referred to as 'Patpong'. Behind garishly lit façades, bars and night clubs with décor ranging from the tawdry to the high technology of Western discotheques offer the most varied and uninhibited forms of sexual entertainment in the world.

Patpong did not just happen. It has been suggested that Thailand has an unfair share of beautiful women; but it also has an unfair share of poverty. The country has a centuries-old reputation for its liberal attitude to sexual relations. All these conditions made it possible for recent Thai governments consciously to develop and promote sex as the primary tourist attraction.

In the 1960s and 1970s, US soldiers, sailors and airmen seeking 'rest and recreation' provided a substantial local customer base. After the US defeat in Vietnam, it was necessary to look further afield. In a frank address to the provincial governors of Thailand in October 1980, Vice-Premier Rojanasathien warned:

> In the next two years we are going to need money. I therefore ask all provincial governors to transform the interesting sites in their provinces into tourist attractions. Certain forms of relaxation that some of you may consider disgusting and shameful, in as much as they are entertainments of a sexual character, to which tourists are partial, are not to be banned."[5]

Tapping the major asset is not difficult. 'For many people here, the primary motivation is not morality but survival,' one Thai observer remarked.[6] Poor families up-country will sell one of their children in order to feed the others. The prostitutes of Patpong describe their work as 'going with rich men' and most of the hundred thousand or so involved in the capital's sex industry are able to make a substantial contribution to the well-being of their families. But they do that from a relatively small percentage of the total 'take'; the major beneficiaries are the owners of the clubs and massage parlours, the tourist hotels, the tour companies and the airlines who fly in the 85-per-cent-male passenger loads. Lufthansa, West Germany's national airline, has been renamed locally '*Lust*hansa'.

In the noisy bars of Patpong as many as fifty girls – all professing to be eighteen years old – jostle with the clientele. The girls take to the small dance floor in rotation and, for ease of identification, each wears a number-badge. Initial approaches to customers are made by asking for drinks, in return for which the bar pays them a percentage. Sex is available for upwards of US$10.

In the 'upstairs' rooms the girls are naked more often than not. The cabarets take place on stages set behind the bars and the shows include live sex acts, animals, girls bursting balloons with darts fired from tubes held in their vaginas and writing messages using similarly secured felt-tip pens. Much money changes hands and some clubs employ as many as three full-time cashiers. There are no peep-shows or blue-movie theatres: after all, pornography is illegal in Thailand.

Over a beer in a Patpong bar, an experienced and well-connected law enforcement official was asked who owned the clubs. 'Mostly the wives of senior police officers,' he replied. Not organized crime? 'Hmm, what we have here is organized police crime . . .'[7]

An outstanding question in the Thamaree case concerned the source of his 'models'. Obtaining the children was clearly not a problem; the pimps on the streets of Patpong can meet most requirements within the hour. But where did the European men come from? The answer may have been provided by something discovered in Thamaree's files. It was the business card of a London employee of Kuoni Travel Ltd.[8] Kuoni, Swiss-owned and founded in 1909, is one of Europe's largest long-haul tour operators. Thailand features prominently in its sales brochures and one entry in the catalogue for the summer of 1986 reads:

*Night Life Special*

> For those seeking night life in Bangkok we offer the Nana Hotel. The hotel has swimming pool, gardens, coffee shop. Rooms are simply furnished with bath and shower. The hotel is more suitable for single men than families.[9]

Once in Bangkok, some Kuoni representatives have been known to arrange informally for local intermediaries to meet tourists and supply women and young girls or boys to their requirements.[10] It seems certain that Thamaree was involved in this trade. This is illegal under Thai law where the children are under thirteen but, when pressed, the Thai police were unable to supply any information about convictions for engaging children in sex with adults.[11]

Manit Thamaree served time in Bangkok's Central Prison. After the prosecuting attorney asked for a three-year sentence Thamaree successfully plea-bargained for one year without remission or parole. When asked, the Bangkok police were unable to name any other pornography cases where gaol sentences had been handed down. A senior officer who had worked on the Thamaree case expressed surprise that he had gone to prison for as long as twelve months and concluded that American pressure had much to do with the outcome.[12]

Bangkok's leading exporter of child pornography may have been put out of business, but nothing seems to have changed the two conditions which made his business viable; demand from the United States and Europe and the local supply of subjects. The higher ranks of the Thai police would appear to have a vested interest in not making too many waves.

Few participants in the mainstream pornography scene – whether producers, distributors or consumers – dispute the unacceptability of depicting sex involving children. Child pornography is the visual evidence of a criminal act. Although it is clear that this problem has been overstated and misinterpreted, everything that can be done to avoid the physical or mental abuse of a single child should be done. One single case of child abuse is one case too many. But *avoidance* is the key, not merely subsequent detection of the offence, and it is regrettable that the issue has become a political football in the turf wars of Washington DC and on the international diplomatic scene. The positive motives of law enforcement officers engaged in well-intended attempts to stop child abuse are not in question. Unfortunately, the intentions of their political masters sometimes are.

Most men and women – single or married, with or without families – find it hard to understand the motivation of grown men who want to engage in sexual relations with children or pre-pubescent teenagers. Of those who can understand, not many are disposed to consider sympathetically the psychology of such behaviour.

But few honest men would deny finding young women sexually attractive. After all, it is in response to this inclination that there is a market for the 'Traci Lords' of America's X-rated videos, the anonymous ageing youngsters of Peter nder's *Teenage Sex* and Hans Moser's *Sweet Little 16* and even the trail of Samantha Foxes parading across page three of Rupert Murdoch's London *Sun* and most pages of David Sullivan's *Sunday Sport*.

For most men the foremost characteristic of these so-called 'bimbos' is their womanhood: their youth is an important secondary consideration. Yet for some men – and it is almost exclusively men – the ingredient of youth, male or female, is paramount. Their urges may be latent, or acted out in fantasies: they may be substituted in particular ways (sex with women dressed as schoolgirls), or they may be carried out in reality on the unwilling, the immature, the vulnerable, the confused or the precocious.

Paedophilia does not *per se* advocate the molestation of children, though it may be impossible to draw the line between the expression of genuine affection and physical abuse. Societies have tried to prohibit predation on the sexually immature minor by drawing up legislation covering the age of sexual consent, with emphasis on the age of the female. Rules of this nature are generally kept separate from those on violent assault and specifically the crimes of abduction, rape and incest. Cultures have policed and punished transgression according to varying moral codes and climates. In that sense, adult sexual relations with minors and any pornography which depicts it reflect a wider social problem.

There is no evidence to suggest that paedophiles are any more promiscuous than, say, adult-oriented heterosexuals. Given the many pressures on them to resist acting out their fantasies, the majority may well be more self-disciplined than the average heterosexual man or woman. Some experienced police officers on both sides of the Atlantic express the view that in occasional cases, paedophiles can provide young people with the loving and caring relationship they do not have with their parents. Things go seriously wrong when that loving relationship develops into a sexual one.

For dealers and distributors in pornography, such

matters may not always be high on the agenda. They are in a commercial business, and Mark Nykanen of NBC missed the point when he attempted to expose Willy Strauss as a child molester. Pornography depicting children is a product, a commodity which sells, if only to a very restricted market. The fact that it is generally illegal does not make it go away – it merely puts up the price, and therefore the potential profit, to anybody who handles it.

That does not mean that dealers are incapable of making distinctions, or even of drawing the line on what they will or will not stock and distribute. The overwhelming majority of people in the pornography business who have figured in earlier chapters express genuine revulsion at the idea of making child pornography or distributing it in any form. In some cases, their views are even stronger than those campaigning actively against the trade and many freely advocate capital punishment for offenders.

Child pornography forms only a small sector of the overall market – perhaps as little as 1 per cent. It is rarely serviced by professional photographers of the kind who operate in the adult market. It is in many ways a self-servicing market sector, which turns to the established porn trade only when it wants printing or distribution of its enthusiasts' 'collections' – amateur quality photographs or film footage generally recording their own activities which they want to circulate to like-minded individuals as a form of self-justification. Profit is rarely the motive.

But profit *is* the motive of the established mainstream pornographer and the successful ones would consider a marginal venture into such a small and illicit market foolhardy, if not plain stupid. They are now doing so well within the boundaries of the law that handling child pornography would be a reckless step which would threaten their yacht in Marbella, their corporate Cessna, their fleet of Mercedes 500s and their membership of the local golf club. And with little return on capital for all that risk.

There is a common set of questions asked by the curious or the prejudiced whenever the subject of the pornography trade comes up. During the course of a two-year investigation which set out with no preconceived conclusions, and which involved extensive interviews with figures inside the trade in many different countries, some answers began to emerge.

– *Are pornographers all criminals?*

None of the major porn barons has an extensive criminal record. Many are now bona fide, well-established businessmen and women. According to both police and industry sources, there is no 'organized crime' involvement in pornography outside the United States and Japan. Indeed the involvement of the Mob in the US porn scene is more characteristic of American society than of the porn industry itself. 'If the Mafia is supposed to be controlling this business, they are not making a very good job of it,' writer Jared Rutter observed.[13]

Perhaps as a way of dismissing suggestions of any extensive Mafia control, some industry insiders claim that porn in the United States is essentially a Jewish business.[14] Even the 'Debbie' series of porn video titles (e.g. *Debbie Does Dallas*) is considered to be something of an 'in-joke', as producer Dave Friedman explained: '"Debbie" is supposed to be the most popular name for a Jewish-American princess!'[15]

The major porn producers and distributors have almost all had brushes with the law at some time in their careers. But they have not become pornographers because they were criminals, rather they became criminals because they were pornographers at a time when it was against the law.

– *Can pornography be stopped by legislation?*

No. Illegality makes it harder to get, makes it more expensive and attracts criminal interest, but it has never succeeded in making it disappear. Advances in publishing and broadcast technology have already caught the law unawares (as in the UK during the early 1980s) and by the end of the century could well make it an irrelevance.

– *Do pornographers seduce people into appearing in porn productions through the use of drugs, blackmail or physical coercion?*
No. The main source of models for magazines is the advertisements which appear in the magazines themselves: in other words they *volunteer*. Some publishers use agencies or freelance 'scouts' to locate models. Would-be models are well briefed about the nature of the work and few photographers and film directors have the patience to deal with performers who are less than enthusiastic about their commissions.

There is no doubt, however, that there is extensive drug use in the pornography industry throughout the world. This ranges from taking a toke on a marijuana cigarette before going on the set to regularly snorting cocaine. Anything likely to result in the clear physical deterioration of a performer could result in his or her professional downfall: no one finds the track-marks caused by syringe needles attractive, and male actors are useless unless they are able to sustain erections when required. Drugs are also used by people working behind the camera; top director Ron Sullivan (Henri Pachard) admits to being a former cocaine user and now readily condemns the practice.[16] A famous European director is reputed to have blown a $30,000 film advance on the drug.

It has to be said, however, that the problem is most prevalent in California and is probably no worse than the consumption of the drug in conventional Hollywood, the entertainment industry, sports and the higher echelons of corporate management.

– *Are pornographers sex crazy?*
If they are, the evidence is mainly in their work and not in their private lives. But it is undeniable that some photographers and directors exploit any sexual opportunities that might come their way. Magazine editor Bengt Lénberg put it bluntly: 'The guys who take the photographs do so because they want to fuck the women.' And veteran director Alberto

Ferro (Lasse Braun) did not avoid the issue: 'Yes, I used to have relationships with many of the women in my films. "How can I express your sexuality," I would tell them, "unless I have experienced it?" Of course, I don't do this any more.' On the other hand, many of the people featured in this book seem happily married (or remarried), often having children.

– *Isn't pornography a back-street business?*
Not in countries where it is legal. Producers and distributors are listed in the phone book, are easy to find, have comfortable (sometimes lavish) premises and are quite open about and see no reason to apologize for their activities. In Germany Teresa Orlovski often appears on television talk shows and even Al Bloom of Caballero Control Corp travelled to Australia to participate in the recent debate on pornography. On 4 July 1987 the Honourable Ilona Staller became the first hard-core porn star to be elected to public office when she took her seat in the Italian Parliament. 'La Cicciolina' – 'Little Chubby' – guaranteed a good turnout by baring her breasts during campaign rallies.[17]

Quite often, sex shops are to be found in the prime commercial locations in major cities alongside department stores and restaurants with international reputations.

– *Is pornography obtrusive?*
Even where porn is legal, there tend to be restrictions on its distribution and promotion. These restrictions variously limit window displays and advertising, forbid sale to under-eighteens, require retail outlets to be licensed and – in some cases – prohibit direct mail promotion and mail order. Even in countries such as Sweden, Denmark and Holland where there are no laws governing the display of sexually explicit publications, most retailers seem to employ common sense and keep pornography out of reach of young people and those who might be offended.

– *Does pornography cause an increase in sex-crime?*
No evidence of this so far. In Sweden, Denmark and West Germany – all countries where pornography has been legal for over a decade – serious offences such as rape and child molestation have significantly declined according to official statistics. Criminologists, however, are careful to avoid attributing the decline to pornography specifically, but it has now been established that pornography certainly does not seem to cause any increase in sex offences. In Norway, where there has been a strong anti-porn campaign by feminist groups over the last five years, rape appears to be on the increase. The Meese Commission in the United States was unable to get academic researchers (and there are plenty of them) to agree whether pornography causes men to rape or whether many rapists consume pornography. Interestingly enough, rape rarely features in mainstream porn story-lines (much less than it does in conventional movies, TV dramas and books).

– *Is pornography addictive?*
Not so. Recent history has shown that post-legalization sales booms are followed by what people in the trade call 'normalization' (i.e. a flattening off and stabilization of sales). Many people see it out of curiosity but most go back to *Rambo*, gardening and listening to their James Last records. Of course, some people may be obsessed with sexually explicit material but porn does not hold the monopoly as the focus of such obsessions.

– *Is all pornography perverted?*
Sales figures show that well over 90 per cent of pornware depicts what would generally be considered to be in the mainstream of sexual activity. The other 10 per cent does include publications which cater for 'bizarre' sex (such as bestiality, sado-masochism, child sex, saliromania, transsexuality, and even necrophilia). Most forms of 'bizarre sex' are illegal even in countries where mainstream pornography is permitted.

– *Does mainstream adult pornography lead on to harder things?*
No. If this were the case then one would expect to see a steady rise in the proportion of bizarre sexual material to all forms of pornography. Including child pornography, circulation of the 'harder' publications seems to have declined rather than increased over the last ten years.

– *Is pornography consumed only by 'dirty old men'?*
Definitely not. Even those in the pornography business tend to denigrate people who turn to pornography as compensation for their inability to develop relationships with members of the opposite sex. These are often classified as 'the raincoat brigade'. At some point in the recent history of porn, this group may have constituted the majority of consumers. That situation is in reverse; a more liberal sexual climate in most countries provides increasing opportunity for real relationships with real people. Certainly most of the lonely individuals single-handedly feeding small coins into the greedy slot-machines of video booths would readily trade that experience for a chance to develop a relationship with a human being.

If anything, the average consumer of 1980s pornography is a healthy young man. It is no longer unusual for pornography to be bought or rented by couples. A survey by a staid women's magazine in Copenhagen recently revealed that a third of its middle-class, middle-aged readership viewed some porn before retiring to bed with their partners. Figures from the other side of the world support this view: a survey of the Australian mail order market recorded that over 30 per cent of buyers are women. Because of its cost (even in legal markets) pornography tends to be a middle-income hobby. Occasional surveys and regular correspondence from consumers enable publishers to draw very clear pictures of the markets they are reaching.

– *Does pornography degrade women?*
Not according to women in the pornography business. The 'degradation' issue is of course a major plank in the platform

of 'radical' feminists opposed to pornography. Some feminists, however, take the view that those opposed to pornography *per se* are really conservatives because they seek a return to the old censorship laws. Being against the degradation of human beings in pornography or any other sphere of sexual activity is a different matter. Feminists in Scandinavia now tend to concentrate their campaigns against sadistic and masochistic material: they are not against pornography which depicts caring and sensitive relationships.

– *Do pornographers exploit sex for profit?*
Of course they do, but probably no more than hairdressers, makers of perfume and the whole of the advertising industry. In any case, a financial motive does not in itself make the trade fundamentally evil. Furthermore, it would be wrong to assume that the porn barons make extraordinary profits: the bottom lines of the balance sheets are not out of step with those of conventional publishing concerns. Nor is porn gold guaranteed: pornography has its successes and failures, just like any other business.

The exorbitant profits from illegal porn trading tend to be short-lived and have to be offset against possible fines and terms of imprisonment. Not only the barons profit from porn: printing companies, the manufacturers of film and video tapes, shipping firms, telephone companies (from telephone sex), postal services (from mail order operations) and governments (from taxes).

The well-worn cry of moral campaigners against sexually explicit material is that 'nobody wants pornography'. At the same time, they denigrate the industry for the amount of money that lines the wallets of the porn barons.

If the world-wide porn business really does generate annual revenues in excess of $5 billion, it is only because consumers are ready, willing and able to pay over part of their hard-earned income. We found no evidence, nor was any presented to us, that pornography is in any way obligatory. The industry thrives by popular consent. The question is, if so many people exercise that choice by voting with their money, who is to deny them the right? As one industry veteran observed: 'Nobody ever died from an overdose of pornography.'

# *Notes and References*

**Chapter 1:** *The Curious Lech*

1. Reconstructed from contemporary reports which appeared in the *Daily Telegraph*, 1 April 1874, p. 2; the *Morning Advertiser*, 1 April 1874, p. 7; and *The Times*, 20 April 1874, p. 14.
2. *Collins English Dictionary* (1982 edition), Collins, London and Glasgow.
3. Walter Kendrick, *The Secret Museum: Pornography in Modern Culture*, Viking Penguin Inc, New York, 1987.
4. Berl Kutchinsky, 'Obscenity and pornography: behavioural aspects', in Sanford H. Kadish *et al.* (Eds), *Encyclopedia of Crime and Justice*, Free Press, Macmillan, New York, 1983, Vol. 3, pp. 1077–86.
5. Estimate by the authors based on an analysis of company sales and other sources, detailed in subsequent chapters.
6. George Csicsery, *The Sex Industry*, quoted in Robert H. Rimmer, *The X-Rated Videotape Guide*, Harmony Books, New York, 1986.
7. Berl Kutchinsky, op. cit., note 4.
8. Ibid.
9. *Tangerine*, produced by Mark Corby, directed by Robert McCallum, 1978. VCX Select/Essex.
10. William Margold, pornographic scriptwriter, actor and critic. Interviewed by the authors, Los Angeles, California, 8 April 1987.

11. Drs Phyllis and Eberhard Kronhausen, *Erotic Art*, W. H. Allen, London and New York, 1971.
12. Ernest Brenton, 1870, quoted in Walter Kendrick, op. cit., note 3.
13. Walter Kendrick, op. cit., note 3.
14. Drs Phyllis and Eberhard Kronhausen, op. cit., note 11.
15. Ibid.
16. Ibid.
17. Berl Kutchinsky, op. cit., note 4.
18. Samuel Pepys, *The Diary of Samuel Pepys*, quoted in Walter Kendrick, op. cit., note 3.
19. Quoted in Steven Marcus, *The Other Victorians: A Study of Sexuality and Pornography in Mid-Nineteenth-Century England*, Weidenfeld and Nicholson, London, 1966.
20. Quoted in ibid.
21. Quoted in ibid.
22. Walter Kendrick, op. cit., note 3, p. 77.
23. Anon, *Lolita Slavinder*, LAWI ApS, Copenhagen, Denmark, 1986.
24. Sally Beauman, *Destiny*, Bantam Books, London, 1987.
25. Helmut and Alison Gernsheim, *A Concise History of Photography*, Thames and Hudson, London, 1971.
26. Colin Harding, research assistant at British Museum of Photography, Film and Television. Interviewed by the authors, London, 5 August 1987.
27. Robert H. Rimmer, op. cit., note 6.
28. Berl Kutchinsky, op. cit., note 4.
29. Jim Holliday, *Only the Best*, Cal Vista Direct Ltd, Van Nuys, California, 1986.
30. Robert H. Rimmer, op. cit., note 6.
31. *Deep Throat*, produced and directed by Gerard Damiano, 1972. Available on video (with *The Devil in Miss Jones*) from Arrow Films, 85 East Hoffman Avenue, Lyndenhurst, NY 11757.
32. Estimate by the authors. The Theander brothers alone have contributed 90 million of these.
33. 'The Rodox Story 1966–1986', unsigned article in *Color Climax* No. 136, Copenhagen, Denmark, September 1986.
34. Robert H. Rimmer, op. cit., note 6.
35. Paula Meadows. Interviewed by the authors, London, 1 July 1987.

36. Berth Milton, publisher and editor of *Private*. Interviewed by the authors, Costa Mijas, Spain, 13 January 1987.
37. Pisanus Fraxi (Henry Spencer Ashbee), *Catena Librorum Tacendorum*, 1885, p. 345 (reprinted New York, 1962), quoted in Walter Kendrick, op. cit., note 3.
38. *The Woman Who Loved Men*, 1986. Video Teresa Orlovski, Hanover, West Germany.
39. *Love Hotel*, production details unknown. Beate Uhse Video, Flensburg, West Germany.
40. '1987 directory of adult films', *Adam Film World Guide*, Vol. 3, No. 5, p. 22, March 1987, Knight Publishing Corp, Los Angeles, California.
41. William Margold. Interview, ibid., note 10.
42. Bengt Lénberg, editor of *FiB Aktuellt*. Interviewed by the authors, Stockholm, Sweden, 14 April 1986.
43. Ibid.
44. Ibid.
45. Rupert James, English editor for Rodox Trading (Color Climax Corporation). Interviewed by the authors, Copenhagen, Denmark, 17 November 1986.
46. Ibid.
47. Kent Wisell, pornography publisher and former sales manager for *Private*. Interviewed by the authors, Stockholm, Sweden, 6 May 1987.
48. William Margold. Interview, ibid., note 10.

**Chapter 2:** *Real Boom States*

1. Beate Uhse. Interviewed by the authors, Flensburg, West Germany, 3 August 1987.
2. *Hollywood Reporter*, 12 October 1982. Report filed from Munich, West Germany.
3. Berth Milton. Interviewed by the authors, Costa Mijas, Spain, 13 January 1987.
4. Kent Wisell, publisher of *Q* and *Bohème* and former sales manager for *Private*. Interviewed by the authors, London, 9 January 1987.
5. Berth Milton. Interview, ibid., note 3.
6. Ibid.
7. Ibid.
8. Kent Wisell. Interview, ibid., note 4.

9. Berth Milton. Interview, ibid., note 3.
10. Source: former business associates of Berth Milton. Interviewed by the authors.
11. *Private* No. 8, Stockholm, Sweden, 1967. Reproduced in the 20th anniversary issue, No. 75, December 1985, pp. 68–9.
12. Berth Milton. Interview, ibid., note 3.
13. Ibid.
14. Ibid.
15. Ibid.
16. Based on a correlation of information supplied by members of the pornography industry.
17. *Colour Climax* No. 136, Rodox Trading, Copenhagen, Denmark, September 1986.
18. Rupert James, English editor for Rodox Trading. Interviewed by the authors, Copenhagen, Denmark, 17 November 1986.
19. Rupert James, ibid. Interviewed 20 May 1987.
20. Ibid.
21. Martin Tomkinson, *The Pornbrokers*, Virgin Books, London, 1982.
22. Rupert James. Interview, ibid., note 19.
23. *Expo Film Catalogue*, undated but probably 1977, Rodox Trading, Copenhagen, Denmark.
24. Ibid.
25. Rupert James. Interview, ibid., note 19.
26. Ibid.
27. *Color Climax*, ibid., note 17.
28. Rupert James. Interview, ibid., note 19.
29. Ibid.
30. Bengt Lénberg. Interviewed by the authors, Stockholm, Sweden, 14 April 1986.
31. 'We buy porno like never before', by Niels Westberg, *Ekstra Bladet*, Copenhagen, Denmark, 19 November 1986. Note: the authors of *Porn Gold* were required to give no such undertaking.
32. Quoted in ibid.
33. *Color Climax*, ibid., note 17.
34. Ulrich Rotermund, Beate Uhse Video. Interviewed by the authors, Flensburg, West Germany, 3 August 1987.
35. A Cologne-based journalist who formerly worked for a popular German sex-contact magazine. Interviewed by the authors, 25 November 1986.

36. Hans Moser, Verlag Teresa Orlovski. Interviewed by the authors, Hanover, West Germany, 7 August 1987.
37. Peter Schmitt, ZBF Vertriebs GmbH. Interviewed by the authors, Wiesbaden, West Germany, 7 August 1987.
38. 'ZBF – greetings from the giant', *Video Star* No. 5, November–December 1986, pp. 65–8.
39. Peter Schmitt. Interview, ibid., note 37.
40. Ibid.
41. Ibid.
42. 'Organized crime's involvement in the pornography industry', Investigative Services Division, Metropolitan Police Department, Washington DC, November 1978. (Introduced as evidence to the New York Select Committee on Crime, 26 July 1982.)
43. David F. Friedman, president of Entertainment Ventures Inc. Interviewed by the authors, Los Angeles, California, 18 September 1987.
44. 'Organized crime involvement in pornography', US Department of Justice, 8 June 1977.
45. David F. Friedman. Interview, ibid., note 43.
46. Lasse Braun, pornographic film-maker. Interviewed by the authors, Los Angeles, California, 19 September 1987.
47. Quoted in 'The porn peddlers', *San Diego Reader*, Vol. 15, no. 10, 13 March 1986, p. 17.
48. 'The prince of porn', by E. Whalen, *Cleveland Magazine*, August 1985.
49. 'Regarding the extent of organized crime development in pornography', FBI report 6 (1978).
50. 'Organized crime involvement in pornography', op. cit., note 44.
51. Hans Moser. Interview, ibid., note 36.
52. Ibid.
53. Ibid.
54. Ibid.
55. Lasse Braun. Interview, ibid., note 46.
56. 'Erik von Goethe', erotic illustrator. Interviewed by the authors, London, 1 July 1987.
57. Ibid.

**Chapter 3:** *The Monkey Inside Yourself*

1. William Margold and 'Viper'. Interviewed by the authors, Los Angeles, California, 8 April 1987.
2. Ibid.
3. Paula Meadows. Interviewed by the authors, London, 1 July 1987.
4. William Margold and 'Viper'. Interview, ibid., note 1.
5. Brigitte. Interviewed by the authors, Stockholm, Sweden, 8 May 1987.
6. William Margold and 'Viper'. Interview, ibid., note 1.
7. Ibid.
8. *Dogarama*, directed by Lawrence T. Cole, 1969. Not legally available in the USA on video.
9. Paula Meadows. Letter to the authors, 4 July 1987.
10. Torben Dhalvad. Interviewed by the authors, Copenhagen, Denmark, 18 May 1987.
11. Juhani Salomaa. Interviewed by the authors, Tampere, Finland, 11 May 1987.
12. William Margold. Interview, ibid, note 1.
13. 'Viper'. Interview, ibid., note 1.
14. *Pleasure* No. 75, April 1987, Pleasure-Verlag GmbH, Brebra, West Germany.
15. 'We buy porno like never before', by Niels Westberg, *Ekstra Bladet*, Copenhagen, Denmark, 19 November 1986. Translated by the authors.
16. 'Viper'. Interview, ibid., note 1.
17. *Film World Report*, Vol. 5, No. 23, 13 April 1987, Knight Publishing Corp, Los Angeles, California.

**Chapter 4:** *One-Handed Magazines*

1. 'Erik von Goethe', erotic illustrator for *Torrid*, *Foxy Lady* and *De Toren*. Interviewed by the authors, London, 1 July 1987.
2. Kent Wisell, publisher and editor of *Q* and *Bohème*. Interviewed by the authors, London, 9 January 1987.
3. *Private* No. 79, November 1986, Private Super International AB, Stockholm, Sweden.
4. Kent Wisell. Interview, ibid., note 2.
5. Ibid.
6. 'Erik von Goethe'. Interview, ibid., note 1.
7. Ibid.

8. *Video*, Disvisa, Barcelona, Spain.
9. *Film Index '84/85*, Color Climax Corporation (Rodox Trading), Copenhagen, Denmark, 1984.
10. *Film Index '87/88*, ibid., 1987
11. *Hardcore-Programm '86*, Mike Hunter Video GmbH, Cologne, West Germany, 1986.
12. *Video Star* No. 5, November–December 1986, Verlag Teresa Orlovski, Hanover, West Germany.
13. Rupert James, English editor for Rodox Trading. Interviewed by the authors, Copenhagen, Denmark, 20 May 1987.
14. *Teenager* No. 32, November 1985, Silwa Verlag, Essen, West Germany.
15. *Thai Lolitas* No. 13, undated, San Remo Press, Munich, West Germany.
16. *Seventeen* No. 7, 1986, Coer'est – no address, but distributed by Intex, Amsterdam, Holland.
17. Rupert James. Interview, ibid., note 13.
18. Kent Wisell. Interview, ibid., note 2.
19. Hans Moser, Verlag Teresa Orlovski. Interviewed by the authors, Hanover, West Germany, 7 August 1987.
20. Rupert James. Interview, ibid., note 13.
21. *Teenage Sex* No. 7, 1978, Color Climax Corporation (Rodox Trading), Copenhagen, Denmark.
22. *Stimulation* No. 22, June 1986, Color Climax Corporation, ibid.
23. Kent Wisell, publisher and editor of *Q* and *Bohème*. Interviewed by the authors, Stockholm, Sweden, 7 May 1987.
24. Berth Milton, publisher and editor of *Private*. Interviewed by the authors, Costa Mijas, Spain, 14 January 1987.
25. Carl H. Delvert, marketing manager of Private Super International AB. Interviewed by the authors, Stockholm, Sweden, 11 November 1986.
26. Kent Wisell. Interview, ibid., note 23.
27. Berth Milton. Interview, ibid., note 24.
28. Kent Wisell. Interview, ibid., note 2.
29. Rupert James. Interview, ibid., note 13.
30. Kent Wisell. Interview, ibid., note 2.
31. Rupert James. Interview, ibid., note 13.
32. Analysis based on research by the authors and interviews with businessmen in the pornography industry.
33. Dave Patrick, editor and chief photographer of *Spectator*.

Interviewed by the authors, Oakland, California, 10 April 1987
34. Ibid.
35. Carl H. Delvert. Interview, ibid., note 25.
36. Ibid.
37. Kent Wisell. Interview, ibid., note 2.
38. Carl H. Delvert. Interview, ibid., note 25.
39. Rupert James, English editor for Rodox Trading. Interviewed by the authors, Copenhagen, Denmark, 17 November 1986.
40. Kent Wisell. Interview, ibid., note 23.
41. *Aktuell Rapport* No. 15, 10 April 1986, Tre Mag AB, Stockholm, Sweden.
42. Viggo Berggren, general manager of LH Postorder AB. Interviewed by the authors, Solna, Sweden, 15 April 1986.
43. Rupert James. Interview, ibid., note 39.
44. Peter Schmitt, deputy director of ZBF Vertriebs GmbH. Interviewed by the authors, Wiesbaden, West Germany, 7 August 1987.
45. Uli Rotermund, deputy chairman of Beate Uhse AG. Interviewed by the authors, Flensburg, West Germany, 3 August 1987.
46. Kent Wisell. Interview, ibid., note 23.
47. Ibid.
48. Ibid.
49. Carl H. Delvert. Interview, ibid., note 25.
50. 'Italy warms to its sorpasso sunrise', by William Scobie, London *Observer*, 21 June 1987, p. 15.
51. John Lark, Mature Media Group, Canberra, Australia. Interviewed by the authors, Frankfurt, West Germany, 1 April 1987.
52. Carl H. Delvert. Interview, ibid., note 25.
53. Berth Milton, publisher and editor of *Private*. Interviewed by the authors, Costa Mijas, Spain, 13 January 1987.
54. Torben Dhalvad, publishing consultant and former editor-in-chief of *Rapport*. Interviewed by the authors, Copenhagen, Denmark, 18 May 1987.
55. Carl H. Delvert. Interview, ibid., note 25.
56. Bengt Lénberg, editor of *FiB Aktuellt*. Interviewed by the authors, Stockholm, Sweden, 14 April 1986.
57. Berth Milton. Interview, ibid., note 53.
58. Viggo Berggren. Interview, ibid., note 42.
59. Berth Milton. Interview, ibid., note 24.
60. 'Erik von Goethe'. Interview, ibid., note 1.
61. Kent Wisell. Interview, ibid., note 23.

**Chapter 5:** *The Secret Pages*

1. Torben Dhalvad. Interviewed by the authors, Copenhagen, Denmark, 17 November 1986.
2. *Bel Ami* is now distributed on video by Video-X-Pix of New York. The original production date is uncertain, but probably 1975 or 1976. This is reputed to be the last film Harry Reems appeared in. It was shot in Stockholm, and has been rated by one American critic as a 'classic'.
3. Bengt Lénberg. Interviewed by the authors, Stockholm, Sweden, 14 April 1986 and 7 May 1987.
4. Torben Dhalvad. Interviews, ibid. note 1, and 18 May 1987.
5. Ibid.
6. Arja Utriainen. Interviewed by the authors, Tampere, Finland, 11 May 1987.
7. Jan Sjölin. Interviewed by the authors, Stockholm, Sweden, 7 May 1987.
8. Juhani Salomaa. Interviewed by the authors, Tampere, Finland, 11 May 1987.
9. Bengt Lénberg. Interviews, ibid., note 3.
10. Kent Wisell. Interviewed by the authors, London, 9 January 1987 and Stockholm, Sweden, 7 May 1987.
11. Torben Dhalvad. Interviewed by the authors, Copenhagen, Denmark, 18 May 1987.
12. Dhalvad was wrong: the magazine closed down in summer 1987.
13. Torben Dhalvad. Interview, ibid., note 11.
14. Bengt Lénberg. Interview, 7 May 1987, ibid., note 3.

**Chapter 6:** *Out of the Porn Ghetto*

1. David F. Friedman, president of Entertainment Ventures Inc, producer and distributor of pornographic feature films. Interviewed by the authors, Los Angeles, California, 7 April 1987.
2. Ibid.
3. Kenneth Anger, *Hollywood Babylon II*, Arrow Books, London, 1986.
4. David F. Friedman, ibid., note 1. Interviewed 18 September 1987.
5. *Deep Throat*, produced and directed by Gerard Damiano, 1972. Available on video (with *The Devil in Miss Jones*) from Arrow Films, 85 East Hoffman Avenue, Lyndenhurst, NY 11757.

6. Jim Holliday, *Only the Best*, Cal Vista Direct Ltd, Van Nuys, California, 1986.
7. Ibid.
8. Ibid.
9. David F. Friedman. Interview, ibid., note 4.
10. Ibid.
11. *The Devil in Miss Jones*, produced and directed by Gerard Damiano, 1972 (see note 5).
12. Jim Holliday, op. cit., note 6.
13. Robert H. Rimmer, *The X-Rated Videotape Guide*, Harmony Books, New York, 1986.
14. Jim Holliday, op. cit., note 6.
15. *Hustler* magazine, October 1984.
16. *The Opening of Misty Beethoven*, produced by L. Sultana, directed by Henry Paris (Radley Metzger), 1976. Video-X-Pix, 430 West 54th Street, New York, NY 10019.
17. Jim Holliday, op. cit., note 6.
18. *Take Off*, produced and directed by Armand Weston, 1978. Video-X-Pix, 430 West 54th Street, New York, NY 10019.
19. Robert H. Rimmer, op. cit., note 13.
20. *Born Erect*, produced and directed by Jon Sanderson, date unknown. Now available through Caballero Control Corp, 21540 Blythe Street, Canoga Park, CA 91304.
21. *Bordello*, produced and directed by Lee Hassel, 1974. Arrow Films, 85 East Hoffman Avenue, Lyndenhurst, NY 11757.
22. *Diversions*, produced by Valerie Ford, written and directed by Derek Ford, 1976. Home Entertainment Club of America (Video Audio Electronics), 153 West 4th Street, Arcade Building, Williamsport, PA 17701.
23. *Hardcore-Programm '86*, Mike Hunter Video GmbH, Hohe Pforte 4–6, 5000 Cologne 1, West Germany.
24. Alberto Ferro (Lasse Braun), pornographic film-maker, *Berliner Zeitung*, 26 November 1975.
25. Alberto Ferro. Interviewed by the authors, Los Angeles, California, 19 September 1987.
26. Alberto Ferro, ibid., note 24.
27. Alberto Ferro, remark in unpublished biographical manuscript, 1987.
28. Alberto Ferro. Interview, ibid., note 25.
29. Ibid.

30. Ibid.
31. Ibid.
32. Alberto Ferro, comment in unpublished ms, ibid., note 27.
33. Alberto Ferro. Interview, ibid., note 25.
34. Ibid.
35. 'Erik von Goethe', erotic illustrator. Interviewed by the authors, London, 1 July 1987.
36. Tuppy Owens, publisher. Interviewed by the authors, London, 8 June 1987.
37. 'Erik von Goethe'. Interview, ibid., note 35.
38. Alberto Ferro. Interview, ibid., note 25.
39. Ibid.
40. Falcon Stuart. Interviewed by the authors, London, 28 September 1987.
41. Alberto Ferro, unpublished portion of letter to *Libération* newspaper, Paris, 2 April 1987.
42. *Lasse Braun's Liebesgeflüster, French Blue*, directed by Lasse Braun. Mike Hunter Video GmbH, Hohe Pforte 4–6, 5000 Cologne 1, West Germany.
43. Alberto Ferro (Lasse Braun), pornographic film-maker. Interviewed by the authors, Los Angeles, California, 21 September 1987.
44. David F. Friedman. Interview, ibid., note 4.
45. Alberto Ferro. Interview, ibid., note 43.
46. *Sensations*, directed by Lasse Braun, 1975. Mike Hunter Video GmbH, Hohe Pforte 4–6, 5000 Cologne 1, West Germany and Caballero Control Corp, 21540 Blythe Street, Canoga Park, CA 91304.
47. Alberto Ferro. Interview, ibid., note 43.
48. Tuppy Owens. Interview, ibid., note 36. (Confirmed by another source.)
49. Ibid.
50. Alberto Ferro. Interview, ibid., note 43.
51. Falcon Stuart. Interview, ibid., note 40.
52. 'Erik von Goethe'. Interview, ibid., note 35.
53. Alberto Ferro, ibid., note 24.
54. Alberto Ferro, op. cit., note 41.
55. Jim Holliday, op. cit., note 6.
56. Falcon Stuart. Interview, ibid., note 40.
57. Alberto Ferro, ibid., note 24.

58. David F. Friedman, Interview, ibid., note 4.
59. Alberto Ferro. Interview, ibid., note 43.
60. Gerd Wasmund (Mike Hunter), president of Mike Hunter Video GmbH. Interviewed by the authors, Cologne, West Germany, 26 November 1986.
61. *Sex Maniacs*, produced by Gerd Wasmund, directed by Lasse Braun. Mike Hunter Video GmbH, Hohe Pforte 4–6, 5000 Cologne 1, West Germany.
62. *Sin Dreamer*, produced by Gerd Wasmund, directed by Lasse Braun. Mike Hunter Video GmbH, Hohe Pforte 4–6, 5000 Cologne 1, West Germany.
63. *Express*, West Germany, 13 September 1978.
64. Hans Moser, photographer and publisher of pornographic magazines and videos. Interviewed by the authors, Hanover, West Germany, 7 August 1987.
65. Mike Freeman, pornographic film-maker. Interviewed by the authors, London, 7 September 1987.
66. Ibid.
67. Hans Moser. Interview, ibid., note 64.
68. Ibid.
69. *Die Abenteuer der Josefine Mutzenbacher*, Herzog Films. No further details are available on the original, and it does not appear in any current German video/film catalogue. However, it did give rise to a number of imitators, loosely derivative of the original. These are still available: cf. *Die Beichte der Josefine Mutzenbacher* (*The Confessions of Josephine Mutzenbacher*), Tabu Video, Bochum, West Germany.
70. West German magazine writer and editor. Interviewed by the authors, Cologne, West Germany, 24 November 1986.
71. Gerd Wasmund. Interview, ibid., note 60.
72. *Las Vegas Maniacs*, produced and directed by Mike Hunter, 1983. Mike Hunter Video GmbH, Hohe Pforte 4–6, 5000 Cologne 1, West Germany.
73. *Sex Loose* (*Las Vegas Maniacs*), ibid. Video Company of America, 9333 Osso Avenue, Chatsworth, CA 01311.
74. William Margold, pornographic scriptwriter, actor and critic. Interviewed by the authors, Los Angeles, California, 8 April 1987.
75. Gerd Wasmund. Interview, ibid., note 60.
76. Ibid.
77. Martin Tomkinson, *The Pornbrokers*, Virgin Books, London, 1982.
78. 'With your little basket in your hand – new to the Federal

Republic, Pamkino – how to get round a law', by Petra Meister, *Die Zeit*, 11 April 1975.
79. Ibid.
80. *Memories within Miss Aggie*, produced and directed by Gerard Damiano, 1974. Arrow Films, 85 East Hoffman Avenue, Lyndenhurst, NY 11757.
81. 'Federal judges have decided: all porn cinemas to close', by Bernd Bader and Rolf Thissen, Cologne *Stadt-Anzeiger*, 17 February 1977.
82. David F. Friedman, president of Entertainment Ventures Inc. Telephone conversation with the authors, 27 August 1987.
83. West German magazine writer and editor. Interview, ibid., note 70.
84. Uli Rotermund, vice-president of Beate Uhse AG. Interviewed by the authors, Flensburg, West Germany, 3 August 1987.
85. David F. Friedman. Interview, ibid., note 1.
86. Ibid.
87. *AFAA Bulletin*, November 1982, Los Angeles, California.
88. Ibid, August 1983.
89. William Margold. Interview, ibid., note 74.
90. Jim Holliday, op. cit., note 6.
91. Robert H. Rimmer, op. cit., note 13.
92. Quoted in ibid.
93. Ibid.
94. Ibid.
95. William Margold. Interview, ibid., note 74.

**Chapter 7:** *Hooks to Hang Dreams On*

1. John Weston, lawyer and counsel to the Adult Film and Video Association of America. Interviewed by the authors, Los Angeles, California, 6 April 1987.
2. David F. Friedman, president of Entertainment Ventures Inc, chairman of the AFVAA. Interviewed by the authors, Los Angeles, California, 18 September 1987.
3. Quoted in Robert H. Rimmer, *The X-Rated Videotape Guide*, Harmony Books, New York, 1986.
4. Robert H. Rimmer, ibid.
5. 'Sex shows feel the pinch', by Christopher Reed, *Guardian*, 1 June 1987. David F. Friedman. Interview, ibid., note 2.

6. *Wall Street Journal*, 15 December 1979.
7. 'VCRs: coming on strong', *Time*, 24 December 1984.
8. 'Video's Big Macs set to clean up', by Peter Dean, *Guardian*, 1 June 1987.
9. David F. Friedman. Interview, ibid., note 2.
10. Christopher Reed, op cit., note 5.
11. Robert H. Rimmer, op cit., note 3.
12. Alberto Ferro (Lasse Braun), pornographic film-maker. Interviewed by the authors, Los Angeles, California, 19 September 1987.
13. David F. Friedman. Interview, ibid., note 2.
14. Uli Rotermund, vice-president of Beate Uhse AG. Interviewed by the authors, Flensburg, West Germany, 3 August 1987.
15. 'Erik von Goethe', erotic illustrator. Interviewed by the authors, London, 1 July 1987.
16. Paula Meadows, porn actress and erotic artiste. Interviewed by the authors, London, 1 July 1987.
17. Mike Freeman, pornographic film-maker. Interviewed by the authors, London, 27 July 1987.
18. Frank Russell, writer. Interviewed by the authors, London, 1 July 1987.
19. Paula Meadows. Interview, ibid., note 16.
20. Ibid.
21. Ibid.
22. Mike Freeman, pornographic film-maker. Interviewed by the authors, London, 7 September 1987.
23. Rupert James, English editor of Rodox Trading (Color Climax Corporation), Copenhagen, Denmark. Telephone conversation with the authors, 9 July 1987.
24. 'Erik von Geothe'. Interview, ibid., note 15.
25. Mike Freeman. Interview, ibid., note 22.
26. Paula Meadows. Interview, ibid., note 16.
27. Mike Freeman. Interview, ibid., note 22.
28. Paula Meadows. Interview, ibid., note 16.
29. *Don't Get Them Wet!*, 1987, Vidco, 1207 Vose Street, North Hollywood, CA 91605.
30. Ron Sullivan (Henri Pachard), producer and director of pornographic films and videos. Interviewed by the authors, Los Angeles, California, 22 September 1987.
31. William Margold, pornographic scriptwriter, actor and critic.

Interviewed by the authors, Los Angeles, California, 19 September 1987.

32. Gerd Wasmund (Mike Hunter), president of Mike Hunter Video GmbH. Interviewed by the authors, Cologne, West Germany, 26 November 1986.

33. *Olympic Fever*, produced and directed by Phillip Marshak, 1979. Arrow Films, 85 East Hoffman Avenue, Lyndenhurst, NY 11757. Released in Europe as *Olympic Sex Fever*, Mike Hunter Video GmbH. Hohe Pforte 4–6, 5000 Cologne 1, West Germany.

34. William Margold, pornographic scriptwriter, actor and critic. Interviewed by the authors, Los Angeles, California, 8 April 1987.

35. 'Confessions of a cooze-spot man', by Bob Alieu, *Erotic X-Film Guide*, Vol. 5, No. 11, November 1987, Los Angeles.

36. William Margold. Interview, ibid., note 31.

37. Ron Sullivan. Interview, ibid., note 30.

38. William Margold. Interview, ibid., note 34.

39. Ron Sullivan. Interview, ibid., note 30.

40. William Margold. Interview, ibid., note 31.

41. *American Desire*, produced, written and directed by Lasse Braun. Released on video in 1981 by Caballero Control Corp, 21540 Blythe Street, Canoga Park, CA 91304.

42. Alberto Ferro (Lasse Braun), pornographic film-maker. Interviewed by the authors, Los Angeles, California, 21 September 1987.

43. William Margold. Interview, ibid., note 31.

44. Uli Gross, writer. Interviewed by the authors, Cologne, West Germany, 24 November 1986.

45. Gerd Wasmund. Interview, ibid., note 32.

46. Ruper James, English editor for Rodox Trading (Color Climax Corporation). Interviewed by the authors, Copenhagen, Denmark, 20 May 1987.

47. John Lark, Mature Media Group, Canberra, Australia. Interviewed by the authors, Frankfurt, West Germany, 1 April 1987.

48. Rupert James. Interview, ibid., note 46.

49. *Film World Report*, edited by Jared Rutter, Knight Publishing Corp, 8060 Melrose Avenue, Los Angeles, CA 90046.

50. Jared Rutter, editor of *Film World Report*. Interviewed by the authors, Los Angeles, California, 22 September 1987.

51. *Film World Report*, ibid., note 49, Vol. 5, No. 23, 13 April 1987.

52. Uli Rotermund. Interview, ibid., note 14.

53. Rupert James. Interview, ibid., note 46.

54. Jim Holliday, *Only the Best*, Cal Vista Direct Ltd, Van Nuys, California, 1986.
55. Rupert James. Interview, ibid., note 46.
56. Ibid.
57. Gerd Wasmund (Mike Hunter), president of Mike Hunter Video GmbH. Letter to the authors, 3 December 1986
58. *Hardcore-Programm '86*, Mike Hunter Video GmbH, Cologne, West Germany, 1986.
59. Kent Wisell, pornographic publisher. Interviewed by the authors, Stockholm, Sweden, 7 May 1987.
60. William Margold. Interview, ibid., note 34.
61. Jared Rutter. Interview, ibid., note 50.
62. Uli Rotermund. Interview, ibid., note 14.
63. Ibid.
64. Rupert James. Interview, ibid., note 46.
65. Jared Rutter. Interview, ibid., note 50.
66. 'The video revolution', *Newsweek*, 6 August 1984.
67. *Time*, op. cit., note 7.
68. David F. Friedman. Interview, ibid., note 2.
69. Robert H. Rimmer, op. cit., note 3.
70. Ibid.
71. Ibid.

**Chapter 8:** *The Collectors*

1. Business card in the authors' possession.
2. Reconstructed from interviews with; Thomas E. Winker, Customs Attaché, and Rungroeng Tulalamba, Customs Investigator, US Customs Service, Thailand – Bangkok, 14–15 May 1986; Special Agent Jack O'Malley, US Customs Service, Chicago – Chicago, 5–6 June 1986; Special Agent Ramon Martinez, US Customs Service, Child Pornography and Protection Unit, Washington DC – Washington DC, 10 July 1986.
3. Photocopies of all the letters in the authors' possession.
4. Copy of indictment No. 81-80494, US District Court, Eastern District of Michigan, in the authors' possession.
5. Copies of *Wonderland* in the authors' possession.
6. *USA* v. *Donald Stephenson and Manit Thamaree*, US District Court for the Central District of California, June 1985. Grand Jury indictment in the authors' possession.

7. Reconstructed from interviews, ibid., note 2.
8. Ibid.
9. Special Agent Ramon Martinez. Interview, ibid.
10. Major R. Somsak, Bangkok Metropolitan Police. Interviewed by the authors, Bangkok, Thailand, 15 May 1986.
11. Photocopy of Manit Thamaree's address book in the authors' possession.
12. Customs Investigator Rungroeng Tulalamba. Interview, ibid., note 2, 15 May 1986.
13. Text supplied to the authors by a law enforcement official.
14. Manit Thamaree, convicted child pornographer. Interviewed by the authors, Central Prison, Bangkok, Thailand, 15 May 1986.
15. Special Agent Jack O'Malley. Interview, ibid., note 2, 5 June 1986.
16. Senior Special Agent John J. Sullivan, US Customs Service, Child Pornography and Protection Service. Interviewed by the authors, Washington DC, 10 July 1986.
17. Photocopy of Manit Thamaree's address book in the authors' possession.

**Chapter 9:** *Bizarre and Inexplicable Rites*

1. *The Silent Shame*, NBC Television, network broadcast, 22 November 1984. Correspondent, Mark Nykanen.
2. Willy Strauss, pornography publisher and distributor. Interviewed by authors, Copenhagen, Denmark, 18 November 1986.
3. Ejgl Hall, writer and associate of Willy Strauss. Interviewed by the authors, Copenhagen, Denmark, 18 November 1986.
4. Ibid.
5. Willy Strauss. Interview, ibid., note 2.
6. Ibid.
7. Ejgl Hall. Interview, ibid., note 3.
8. *Lolita Slavinder* (Lolita Slaves) – subtitled *En bog om seksuel brug og misbrug* (*A book about sexual use and abuse*), LAWI ApS, Copenhagen, 1986.
9. Willy Strauss. Interview, ibid., note 2.
10. Ejgl Hall. Interview, ibid., note 3.
11. Hoofdinspecteur J. M. C. M. Heesters, Gemeentepolitie Amsterdam, Chef van Jeugd en Zedenpolitie. Interviewed by the authors, Amsterdam, Holland, 29 May 1986.
12. 'Child pornography and paedophilia', report of hearings

before the Permanent Sub-Committee on Investigations of the Committee on Governmental Affairs, US Senate, 98th Congress, Second Session, Part 1, US Government Printing Office, Washington DC, 1985, p. 10.
13. Rupert James, English editor for Rodox Trading (Color Climax Corporation), Copenhagen, Denmark. Telephone conversation with the authors, 14 August 1987.
14. Verslag van de Werkgroep Kinderpornographie (Report of the Working Group on Child Pornography), Stafbureau Voorlichting van het Ministerie van Justitie, s'Gravenhage (The Hague), Holland, August 1986, pp. 26–7.
15. Hoofdinspecteur J. M. C. M. Heesters. Interview, ibid., note 11.
16. Senior official at the Netherlands Ministry of Justice. Interviewed by the authors, Amsterdam, Holland, 28 May 1986.
17. Report of the Working Group, op. cit., note 14, pp. 10–11.
18. Inspecteur M. J. M. 'Renus' Rijk, Centrale Recherche Informatiedienst. Interviewed by the authors, The Hague, Holland, 19 March 1987.
19. Ibid.
20. The following sequences are based on a number of interviews by the authors with officials in the United States, West Germany and Holland.
21. Inspecteur M. J. M. Rijk. Interview, ibid., note 18.
22. Report of the Working Group, op. cit., note 14, p.6.
23. Rupert James, English editor for Rodox Trading (Color Climax Corporation). Interviewed by the authors, Copenhagen, Denmark, 20 May 1987.
24. 'Child pornography and paedophilia', op. cit., note 12, p. 32.
25. Photocopy of Manit Thamaree's address book in the authors' possession.
26. Photograph in the authors' possession.
27. 'Pornography and its effects in Denmark and the United States: a rejoinder and beyond', by Berl Kutchinsky, *Comparative Social Research*, Vol. 8 (1985), pp. 301–30, JAI Press, Greenwich, Connecticut.
28. Willy Strauss, pornography publisher and distributor. Interviewed by the authors, Copenhagen, Denmark, 21 May 1987.
29. Final Report of the Attorney-General's Commission on Pornography, Vols. I and II (1,960 pages), US Department of Justice, Washington DC, July 1986.

30. H. Robert Showers, Special Assistant to the Attorney-General, US Department of Justice. Interviewed by the authors, Washington DC, 15 April 1987.
31. John H. Weston, written submission on behalf of the Adult Film Association of America to the Attorney-General's Commission on Pornography, Los Angeles, California, 16 October 1985.
32. Documents in the authors' possession.
33. Ibid.
34. Ibid.
35. Ibid.
36. Ibid.
37. David F. Friedman, president of Entertainment Ventures Inc. Interviewed by the authors, Los Angeles, California, 18 September 1987.
38. Ibid.
39. William Margold, pornographic scriptwriter, actor and critic. Interviewed by the authors, Los Angeles, California, 8 April 1987.
40. Robert H. Rimmer, *The X-Rated Videotape Guide*, Harmony Books, New York, 1986, pp. 11 *et seq*.
41. Ibid.
42. David F. Friedman. Interview, ibid., note 37.
43. William Margold. Interview, ibid., note 39.
44. David F. Friedman. Interview, ibid., note 37.
45. Kent Wisell, publisher and editor of *Q* and *Bohème*. Interviewed by the authors, Stockholm, Sweden, 7 May 1987.
46. Ibid.
47. Ibid.
48. Ibid.
49. Photocopy of the letter in the authors' possession.
50. Visit made by the authors, 1 June 1987.
51. Counterfeit copy of *Blue Climax* No. 37, purchased by the authors at a Private Lines shop and in their possession.
52. *Blue Climax* No. 37. Color Climax Corporation, Copenhagen, Denmark, 1985.
53. Rupert James, English editor for Rodox Trading (Color Climax Corporation), Copenhagen, Denmark. Telephone conversation with the authors, 8 October 1987.
54. Brochure in the authors' possession, published by Pirate Organization, 34 Upton Lane, Forest Gate, London E7 9LN.
55. Rupert James, English editor for Rodox Trading (Color Climax

Corporation). Interviewed by the authors, Copenhagen, Denmark, 17 November 1986.
56. Carl H. Delvert, marketing manager of Private Super International AB. Interviewed by the authors, Stockholm, Sweden, 11 November 1986.
57. Berth Milton, publisher and editor of *Private*. Interviewed by the authors, Costa Mijas, Spain, 13 January 1987.

**Chapter 10:** *The Wide Blue Yonder*

1. *Amores Profundos* (*Deep Love*), *Primero Parte de 'Porno Girls'*, directed by George Lewis. Video-System SA, Barcelona, Spain.
2. British resident of Moscow. Interviewed by the authors, Moscow, 1987.
3. 'Death sentence', Associated Press report, the *Guardian*, 24 August 1987.
4. 'Date set for Philips CD video player', by Nick Radlo, *Broadcast* weekly trade paper, London, 11 September 1987.
5. Quoted in 'Sex tours in south-east Asia', by Elsa Ramos, *World View 1984*, Pluto Press, London, 1984, p. 97.
6. Resident of Bangkok. Interviewed by the authors, Bangkok, Thailand, May 1986.
7. Ibid.
8. Special Agent Ramon Martinez, US Customs Service. Interviewed by the authors, Washington DC, 10 July 1986.
9. Kuoni Travel Ltd, Summer Long-Haul Brochure, 1986.
10. Mark Nykanen, NBC Television, Chicago. Interviewed by the authors, Chicago, 6 June 1986.
11. A senior officer in the Bangkok Metropolitan Police. Interviewed by the authors, Bangkok, Thailand, May 1986.
12. Ibid.
13. Jared Rutter, editor of *Film World Report*. Interviewed by the authors, Los Angeles, California, 22 September 1987.
14. Ron Sullivan (Henri Pachard), pornographic film and video director. Interviewed by the authors, Los Angeles, California, 21 September 1987.
15. David F. Friedman, president Entertainment Ventures Inc. Interviewed by authors, Los Angeles, California, 18 September 1987.
16. Ron Sullivan. Interview, ibid., note 14.
17. 'Italy warms to its sorpasso sunrise', by William Scobie, London *Observer*, 21 June 1987, p. 15.

# *Index*


A & L International, 167, 168–70
AB BETA, 200–2
Abts, Jeffrey Michael, 326–7
actors, 83–118, 369
Adult Film Association of America (AFAA), 221–3, 246, 337, 338
AIDS, 114–17
*Aktuell Rapport*, 146, 166–7, 168, 177–9, 182
*Album International*, 170
Alexander, Jeannie, 334
anal sex, 98–9, 133
*Anal Sex*, 133, 139
Arrow Films, 231, 257
Ashbee, Henry Spencer, 16, 25
Avillada, José Luis, 346

Baldwin, Peter, 125, 126–8
Baltic Press, 177, 179, 181
*Bambina Sex*, 317–19
Bardot, Brigitte, 191
Barrett, Rohna, 106–7
Bartkowski, Walter ('Charlie Brown'), 212–14, 234
Bartylla, Siegfried, 218
Bauer-Film, 218
*BéDé Adult*, 127
Bell, Alan, 207
Benn, Art, 236
Berggren, Viggo, 146
BF Verlag, 327–8
Blood, Charlie, 187
Bloom, Al, 143, 231–2, 256, 370
Bloom, Noel, 227, 230
*Blue Climax*, 120, 131, 139, 348, 349–50
Blue Movie, 314–16, 320
Boccaccio, 100, 230
*Bohème*, 124, 135–6, 138, 145, 345–6
Boksenter, 138, 145
bondage, 8, 16, 133–4
Bonnier, 165
bootlegging, 344–53, 355
Bouill, Jol, 330
Bourdon, Sylvia, 204, 206
Braun, Lasse (Alberto Ferro), 24, 73, 98, 202–4, 208, 209, 214, 223, 229, 230, 236, 240, 253, 256, 360, 370
Brewer, Albert, 220
Brigitte, 88, 91, 92, 93, 97, 98–9, 100–1, 103, 105, 110–11, 114, 345

'Brown, Charlie' (Walter Bartkowski), 212–14, 234
*Busen*, 348, 349, 350
Butler, Jerry, 94, 97, 237

Caballero Control Corporation, 68, 74–5, 77, 143, 191, 203, 227, 230, 231, 232, 247, 250, 253, 256–7, 260, 262, 253, 370
cable television, 359–60
Calvista International, 138, 150
Campaign for Decency Through the Law (CDL), 336–7
Candy Film, 57, 62
Cannes International Film Festival, 204, 207–8
Carrera, Monique, 255–6
Catalina Video, 117
*Cats*, 179
Chaivat (Manit Thamaree), 267, 268–313, 325, 327, 330, 364–5
Chambers, Marilyn, 112, 196
Chernoivanov, Herman, 357
Chick Production Establishment, 330
child pornography, 16, 133, 265–313, 314–36, 364–7
China, 11
Los Christianos, 156–7
cinema *see* films
Cole, Lawrence T., 254
Color Climax Corporation, 348–9, 350, 352
*Color Climax*, 47, 53, 55–7, 59–60, 63–4, 73, 130–1, 139, 140, 157, 160, 348, 350, 355
Conegate Ltd, 351–2
Consumer Electronics Show (CES), 252
Cooke, Ivor, 213
Coppola, Francis Ford, 109, 190
copyright, 344–53
La Cosa Nostra, 3, 75, 341
*Cover Girls*, 133
'cum shots', 7, 31

Damiano, Gerard, 19, 192, 194–6, 216, 219, 223, 225, 231, 343, 360–1
Dark brothers, 243
*Deep Throat*, 19, 109, 191, 192–4, 195, 196, 204, 223, 224, 225, 231, 336, 342, 343, 359
del Rio, Vanessa, 89, 112
Delta Boek, 274, 276, 287
Delvert, Carl, 136, 142–3, 144, 145, 149, 151, 153, 352
Department of Trade and Industry, 235
deRenzy, Alex, 195, 196, 208, 360
*The Devil in Miss Jones*, 194–5
Dhalvad, Torben, 114, 161–2, 167–71, 152–3, 172, 181–2, 184–5
DiBernardo, Robert 'Debe', 341–2
*Don't Get Them Wet!*, 27, 236–8, 239, 241, 242–3, 245, 246, 258, 361
Dorfman, Ron, 236
drugs, 103–4, 369
Dutch Working Group on Child Pornography, 328–9

Edwards, Eric, 89, 196
Entertainment Ventures Inc., 188
*Ero*, 120, 135, 139, 160, 348
*The Erotic Adventures of Candy*, 223
*Esquire*, 161
Essex, 231, 250, 257, 262
Evans, Candy, 111–12
*Exciting*, 131, 139
*Express*, 169–70, 171
*Extra*, 169
Exxon Cinema Club, 217

FBI, 75, 76, 323, 337, 342–3
feminism, 373
Fernandez, Joao, 109
Ferro, Alberto (Lasse Braun), 197–212, 213, 214–15, 229, 234, 236, 243–5, 360–1, 369–70
fetishism, 8
*FiB Aktuellt*, 162, 163–7, 173–4, 177, 178, 181, 185–6, 187

15, 133
*Film World Report*, 247–52
films, 57–9, 62, 188–226; decline of cinema audiences, 227–9; economics, 223–6; history of, 18–21; loops, 20–1, 62, 74, 191, 203–4, 259; 'snuff movies', 336–9
Fine, Jeanna, 112
Flynt, Larry, 142, 180–1
Forbes, John, 325
Fox, Samantha, 366
*Foxy Lady*, 53, 81, 120, 126, 132, 139, 157, 159, 160, 348, 349, 355
Freeman, Mike, 86–7, 213, 232–6
*French Blue*, 204–5, 209
Friedman, David, 19, 72, 73, 188–90, 193–4, 196, 208, 213, 219–23, 225, 227–8, 230, 263, 336–7, 343–4, 368

Geerts, Charlie, 73, 77, 146, 150, 253
Gillis, Jamie, 89, 196, 255
Gold Star, 125–6, 158
Goldstein, Al, 142, 222
Gresens, Lothar, 327–8

Hagen, Leif, 77, 146–7, 155–6, 166, 179
Hagen Import, 145, 146
Hall, Ejgl, 320, 321
Hampshire, Russell, 231–2
*Happy Birthday*, 87, 233–4
Harding, Colin, 17–18
Hartley, Nina, 129, 255
*Hausfrauenpornos*, 21–2, 130
Hawse, Roger, 125, 126–8, 160
Hayler, Henry, 4–6, 17–18, 82
Heesters, Hans, 321, 323
Hefner, Hugh, 46, 197
Hel-Print, 177
Henderson, Mike, 192
Herzog Films, 214
Hessel, Lee, 196
Hinduism, 10–11
Holliday, Jim, 18–19, 195, 196, 223
Holmes, John, 89, 97, 192, 196
homosexuality, 174–5
Horner, Mike, 236, 255
Hson-Nilson, Curth, 43, 120, 154, 156, 348
Hunt, Nelson Bunker, 59
Hunter, Mike, 22, 68, 128, 215, 245, 255–7, 260–1, 358, 360
*Hustler*, 8, 73, 142, 158, 180–1, 195, 260

Intex, 68, 73, 77, 138, 146, 150, 257

*Jallu*, 172–3, 175
James, Rupert, 29–30, 56–7, 130–2, 133–5, 136–7, 140, 144–5, 234, 254, 255, 261–2, 329–30, 346–7, 350, 351–2
Jeremy, Ron, 101, 255
Jews, 368
Johnson, Jimmy, 216

*Kalle*, 114–15, 172–6
Keeler, Christine, 213
Kendrick, Walter, 6, 10, 16
Kin, Anne-Elise, 212
Kodak, 199
Krüger, Hans, 211, 216
Kuoni Travel Ltd, 364
Kutchinsky, Berl, 7–8, 12, 13, 330–1

'La Cicciolina', 150, 370
*Lady Domina*, 81, 134, 159
Lanning, Kenneth, 323
Lark, John, 150–1, 247
*Las Vegas Maniacs*, 215–16, 224, 231, 358
Lehtimielmet, 172–7
*Lektyr*, 162, 163–6, 178, 181–4, 186–7
Lénberg, Bengt, 27–9, 61, 162–8, 170, 172, 177–81, 182–4, 185–7, 369
Leonard, Gloria, 94

*Lesbian Love*, 133, 139
lesbianism, 7, 99, 133
Leslie, John, 67, 89, 112, 196, 254
Lewis, Herschel Gordon, 190
Liang Qingxiang, 357
*Life* magazine, 163, 177
Lindsey, John, 57, 217
*Lolita*, 284, 323–4, 325–6, 334
*Lolita Sex*, 319
*Lolita Slavinder*, 16, 320, 331
loops, 20–1, 62, 74, 191, 203–4, 259
Lords, Traci, 67, 169, 255, 339, 365
*Love Inferno*, 208–9, 214
Lovelace, Linda, 19, 92–3, 192, 193, 254
Lynn, Amber, 107, 255
Lynn, Ginger, 255, 256
Lynn, Maria, 165

McCallum, Robert, 195, 225
McGee, Bill, 279, 281, 282
MacLaine, Shirley, 102–3, 108
Madsen, Keld, 62, 116–17
Mafia, 2–3, 33, 76, 216, 219, 341–4, 368
magazines, 20, 44–57, 119–60; distribution, 141–57; economics, 140–1; formulas, 27–9; illicit copying, 345–53; names, 135–6; print runs, 52–3, 139–40; printing, 137–8; Scandinavian, 161–87; size, 136; strip cartoons, 124–8; video reviews, 128–30
Maier, Brigitte, 204, 205, 207
Malcolm, Derek, 235
*Man and Wife*, 192–3
Margold, Bill, 27, 30–1, 83–91, 93–8, 100, 103–5, 106–9, 111–15, 195, 215, 216, 222–3, 225–6, 236, 238, 239–42, 250, 338–9, 344
Martinez, Ray (Roy Morgan), 270–86, 289–312
Meadows, Paula, 24, 86–7, 89, 90–1, 94–5, 98, 102, 105–6, 107–8, 109–10, 232–4, 235, 236, 244
Meese Commission, 331, 332, 371
Meister, Petra, 218–19
Metz, Manfred, 208–9, 214
Metzger, Radley, 195, 196, 223
Meyer, Russ, 19, 190, 224
Milton, Berth, 20, 24–5, 42–53, 82, 120–3, 130, 136, 137–8, 139, 150, 155, 157, 158, 180, 189, 197, 348, 352–3, 355–6
MIPCOM, 234, 252
MIPORN, 341–3
Miranda, Vince, 216
models, 83–118, 369
Monroe, Marilyn, 197
Moore, Roger, 207
Moser, Hans, 26, 77–82, 126, 128–9, 132, 133, 134, 137, 139, 159, 203, 212, 213, 231–2, 246, 248, 348, 356, 358, 360, 366
Murdoch, Rupert, 366

National Obscenity Enforcement Unit (USA), 331–3
NBC, 314–15, 320, 322, 367
*New Cunts*, 133
*Newsweek*, 262–3
Nicholas, Paul, 211
Niekerk, Sidney, 232
Nielsen, Sven, 78, 79
Nykanen, Mark, 314–15, 320, 367

Obscene Publications Squad, Scotland Yard, 235
*Olympic Fever*, 240, 246, 358
O'Malley, Jack (Jack Negus), 267–70, 282–312, 325, 326
*The Opening of Misty Beethoven*, 195, 223
Orlovski, Teresa, 26, 77, 78, 80–2, 128–9, 132, 158, 257, 360, 370
Owens, Tuppy, 105, 125, 158, 206, 235

Pachard, Henri, 102, 195, 236, 250, 360, 369

Padet, Lieutenant Colonel, 266, 296–8, 301
paedophilia *see* child pornography
Palmer, Gail, 223
PAM (Porno American Movies), 217
Pamkino, 217–19
Patrick, Dave, 142
peep-shows, 20–1, 22–3, 74, 191, 203–4, 259–60
*Penthouse*, 73, 136, 158, 170, 204, 339
Pepys, Samuel, 12–13
Peraino brothers, 194, 231, 342
Peter, Horst, 77, 132, 209, 210, 253, 261
Philips, 358–9
Phillips, Evans ('Big Jeff'), 199, 213
photography, 17–18
Pinochet, 337
*Pirate*, 50, 180
Pirate Organization, 351–2
*Playboy*, 8, 46, 72, 73, 136, 149, 158, 161–2, 170
*Pleasure*, 115–16, 120, 136, 139, 153, 160
plots, 23–7
Pompeii, 9–10
porn barons, 32, 33–82
Presam, 145, 154, 180
Pretty Girl International, 239
*Private*, 30, 44–53, 73, 120–3, 131, 136, 137, 138, 139, 141, 142–4, 148–9, 150–1, 153, 157, 158, 160, 180, 345, 348, 349, 351, 352–3, 355
Private Lines, 347–50, 355
PS, 168–9
*Pussy Galore*, 220–1
Pussycat cinemas, 216–17, 223, 228–9, 230

*Q*, 124, 135–6, 138, 158, 345

Rahm, Rolf, 77, 82, 133, 135, 145
Rakoff, Ian L., 207
rape, 27, 371
*Rapport*, 114, 152–3, 167–8, 170–1, 184, 185
*Ratto*, 172, 173, 175
Raymond, Paul, 350
RCT Video, 60, 246, 247
Reagan, Ronald, 332–3
Reems, Harry, 19, 89, 108, 165, 192, 193, 194–5, 196, 206
Rijk, Renus, 324–5, 326, 328
Rimmer, Robert, 7, 18, 22, 224, 263–4, 340–1
*Rodox*, 348, 351
*Rodox Special*, 131–2, 139
Rodox Trading, 53–64, 68, 116, 128, 130–2, 133–5, 137, 139–41, 144–5, 147, 150, 191, 230, 234, 247, 254–5, 257, 260, 261–2, 329–30, 346–7, 350, 351–2
Rojanasathien, Vice-Premier, 362–3
Roos, Gerd Joachim, 219
Rotermund, Uli, 37, 39, 40, 68, 219, 232, 261
Roth Sub-Committee, 321–2, 330
Russell, Frank, 86–7, 102–3, 232–3, 236
Rutter, Jared, 248, 250, 368

sadism and masochism (S & M), 8, 16, 133–4, 371, 373
St Claire, Sheri, 113, 117
Sakuntala Restaurant, Bangkok, 265–7, 312
saliromania, 50, 371
Salomaa, Juhani, 114–15, 174–6
Sanderson, Jon, 196
satellite television, 359
Savage, Herschel, 89, 255
Saxon's, 184
Scherer, Roland, 333–6
Schmitt, Georg, 69–70, 73, 81, 82, 129, 133, 147, 335
Schmitt, Peter, 69–70, 82, 129, 147
Schubert, Karin, 129

Scott, James A., 273, 275, 278, 280
*Screw*, 8, 73, 142, 222
*Se*, 162, 163, 166
Seka, 86, 89, 92, 108, 112
*Sensations*, 205–8, 209, 223, 231, 245, 256, 358
*Seventeen*, 133
*Sex Bizarre*, 133–4, 139
*Sex Maniacs*, 253, 256, 358
*Sexy Girls*, 133
Shackleton, Alan, 337–8
Sheila, 333–6
Showers, Robert, 331–3
*The Silent Shame*, 314–15, 320
Silvera, Joey, 89, 95–6
Sin, Bob, 204
*Sin Dreamer*, 240, 256
Sinclair, Peter, 209
Sjölin, Jan, 88, 173–4
*Snuff*, 337, 338–9
'snuff movies', 336–9
Soho Sex Shop, Stockholm, 154–5, 156
Somsak, Major, 301, 309
Sony, 130
*Spectator*, 142
Spelvin, Georgina, 89, 102–3, 108, 192, 194–5, 196
Spinelli, Anthony, 195, 196, 223
Springer Verlag, 185
Staller, Ilona ('La Cicciolina'), 150, 370
Star Distributors Ltd, 76, 341
Steinman, Joe, 232
Stephenson, Donald, 290–1, 311
Stevens, Carter, 225
*Stimulation*, 135, 140–1
Stoeckli, Eduardo, 40
*Stopp*, 166, 167, 177, 179, 181
Strauss, Leila, 314–15, 319
Strauss, Willy, 314–21, 322, 331, 367
strip cartoons, 124–8
Stuart, Falcon, 204–5, 207, 208, 209
Sturman, Reuben, 70–6, 203–4, 205, 207, 243, 260, 342–3, 344
Sullivan, Cheryl, 351
Sullivan, Clive, 351
Sullivan, David, 351–3, 355, 366
Sullivan, Ron, 102, 236, 239, 240, 242, 250, 360, 369
Sumner, Bob, 225
*Sun*, 366
*Sunday Sport*, 351, 366
Suomen Miestenlehdet Oy, 172–7
*Swedish Erotica*, 230, 232
*Sweet Little 16*, 81, 132, 133, 159, 348, 366

Taboo cinemas, 217
Tabu Films, 214
*Take Off*, 196, 223, 225, 231
technological advances, 358–60
Techter, David, 275–7, 278–80, 281–2, 286–8, 290, 291–2, 311, 312–13
*Teenage Schoolgirls*, 131, 132, 139
*Teenage Sex*, 131, 132, 135, 139–40, 157, 348, 366
*Teenager*, 132
telephone sex, 164–6, 170–1, 176
television, cable, 359–60
*Thai Lolitas*, 133
Thamaree, Manit (Chaivat), 267, 268–313, 325, 327, 330, 364–5
Thawee, Police Colonel, 265–6, 302, 306–7, 309
Theander, Jens, 20, 21, 39, 47, 54–63, 80, 134, 159, 202, 230
Theander, Peter, 20, 21, 39, 47, 54–64, 80, 82, 116, 130, 132, 134, 137, 147, 159, 202, 204, 230, 231–2, 234, 246, 247, 253–4, 323, 348, 356, 365–6
Thevis, Michael, 341–2, 343
Thomas, Paul, 89, 196, 255
Tinsley, Duane, 180
*Toren*, 126–7
*Torrid*, 125–6, 158
tourism, 362–4

Tove, 135
transsexuals, 134, 371
Tre Mag, 179–81
*Truth or Dare*, 86–7, 233, 234, 236
Tuli, 298, 299, 301–3, 306–8, 311–12
Turner, Tina, 170
TVX, 230

Uhse, Beate, 33–41, 69, 82, 148, 214, 219–20, 256, 257, 260, 261
US Customs Service, 141, 313, 322, 325–8
US Department of Justice, 73, 75, 295, 331
US Internal Revenue Service, 76, 113
Utriainen, Arja, 172–3, 175–7

Van Dam, Albert, 206
Van der Heeul, Ari, 150
VCA, 231, 250
Videla, General, 337–8
Video General, 241
Video Kongress, 252
video review magazines, 128–30
*Video Star*, 128–30, 248
Videorama, 150, 253
videos, 60, 159, 184–5, 227–64; casting, 238–9; customs controls, 355; decline of cinema, 227–9; distribution, 253–8; economics, 186, 245, 257, 258–64; editing and duplication, 245–7; *Hausfrauenpornos*, 21–2, 130, illicit copying, 345, 348, 355–8; locations, 239–40; promotion, 247–53; quality, 360–1; scripts, 236–8; technicians, 241–2; technological improvements, 358–9; video booths, 22–3, 259–60
Videx, 233–4
Villroy, Jean, 206
Vincent, Chuck, 195, 196, 208
Viper, 27, 84, 87–8, 90, 91–2, 95, 99–100, 101–2, 103, 104, 107, 115, 117, 236
'Von Goethe, Erik', 119, 125–8, 158, 234, 235
Von Raab, William, 322, 323
VTO (Verlag Teresa Orlovski), 68, 77–82, 128, 132, 246, 260, 349, 360
Vydra, Alan, 40

Wallace, George, 220
Wallach, Joachim 'Jo', 46
Wasmund, Gerd, 209–12, 214–16, 224, 239–40, 245, 255–7, 358
Waterfield, David, 217
Weston, Armand, 196
Weston, John, 227, 333
Wilhelmus, Joop, 284, 325–6
Winker, Tom, 265–7, 296–309, 311
Wissell, Kent, 30, 45, 99, 120, 123–4, 134, 135–6, 137–8, 139, 143–4, 145, 148–9, 158–9, 160, 180, 345–6
Wolff, Uschi, 207
*Wonderland*, 274–5, 276, 279–80, 289, 291, 311, 312

X-Rated Critics Organization (XRCO), 195–6, 245, 246
*XL*, 181

Zaffarano, Michael, 342
ZBF Vertrieb, 64–70, 73, 77, 81, 129, 133, 138, 141, 147–8, 335
Ziehm, Howard, 195, 196